Julius Caesar's Civil War

Julius Caesar's Civil War

Tactics, Strategies and Logistics

Julian Romane

Pen & Sword
MILITARY

First published in Great Britain in 2023 by
Pen & Sword Military
An imprint of
Pen & Sword Books Ltd
Yorkshire – Philadelphia

Copyright © Julian Romane 2023

ISBN 978 1 39908 942 5

The right of Julian Romane to be identified as Author of this work has been asserted by him in accordance with the Copyright, Designs and Patents Act 1988.

A CIP catalogue record for this book is
available from the British Library.

All rights reserved. No part of this book may be reproduced or transmitted in any form or by any means, electronic or mechanical including photocopying, recording or by any information storage and retrieval system, without permission from the Publisher in writing.

Typeset by Mac Style
Printed in the UK by CPI Group (UK) Ltd, Croydon, CR0 4YY.

Pen & Sword Books Limited incorporates the imprints of Atlas, Archaeology, Aviation, Discovery, Family History, Fiction, History, Maritime, Military, Military Classics, Politics, Select, Transport, True Crime, Air World, Frontline Publishing, Leo Cooper, Remember When, Seaforth Publishing, The Praetorian Press, Wharncliffe Local History, Wharncliffe Transport, Wharncliffe True Crime, White Owl and After the Battle.

For a complete list of Pen & Sword titles please contact

PEN & SWORD BOOKS LIMITED
47 Church Street, Barnsley, South Yorkshire, S70 2AS, England
E-mail: enquiries@pen-and-sword.co.uk
Website: www.pen-and-sword.co.uk

Or

PEN AND SWORD BOOKS
1950 Lawrence Rd, Havertown, PA 19083, USA
E-mail: Uspen-and-sword@casematepublishers.com
Website: www.penandswordbooks.com

Contents

Acknowledgments — vii
Maps — viii
Introduction: Julius Caesar and his Civil War — xiv

Section I: Italy — 1

Chapter 1 Civil War Erupts — 3

Chapter 2 The Struggle in Italy — 16

Section II: War in Spain — 27

Chapter 3 Rome, and the March to Spain — 29

Chapter 4 War in Spain — 37

Chapter 5 The War in Spain Conclusion — 46

Chapter 6 Massilia — 54

Chapter 7 Curio in Africa — 63

Section III: War Against Pompey — 73

Chapter 8 Caesar Faces Pompey — 75

Chapter 9 Pompey Reconsiders his Strategy — 84

Chapter 10 The Struggles in the Lines — 94

Chapter 11 The Battle Front Shifts — 103

Chapter 12 Pharsalus — 112

Section IV: War in the East — 121

Chapter 13 Caesar in Egypt — 123

Chapter 14 The Battle of Alexandria — 131

| Chapter 15 | Victory Fades Away | 143 |
| Chapter 16 | Veni, Vidi, Vici | 153 |

Section VI: War in Africa — 163

Chapter 17	The African War Begins	165
Chapter 18	Caesar Builds a Strong Base in Africa	174
Chapter 19	Difficulties in Africa	184
Chapter 20	Decision at Thapsus	194

Section VII: The Second Spanish War — 203

Chapter 21	Caesar Returns to Rome	205
Chapter 22	Caesar's Second Spanish War	213
Chapter 23	The Struggle Ends	222
Chapter 24	The Civil Wars End	230

Appendix I: Caesar's Siege of Massilia and Vitruvius' On Architecture — 236
Appendix II: Queen Cleopatra and Julius Caesar — 237
Appendix III: The Museum and Library at Alexandria — 241
Appendix IV: Caesar and his Army — 247
Appendix V: Warships in Caesar's Time — 257
Appendix VI: Projector Machines in the Late Republic — 263
Appendix VII: A Short History of the Roman Republic to Caesar's Civil War — 266
Appendix VIII: The Economy of the Classical World — 278
Appendix IX: Caesar's Commentaries: Sources, Purpose, Composition, and History — 286
Bibliographies — 297
Index — 307

Acknowledgments

Thanks to Philip Sidnell for his encouragement and patience. I appreciate Irene Moore's sensitive editing. Matt Jones did a superlative job of guiding my manuscript through the labyrinth of turning a raw narrative into a published book. Special thanks to the proofreader, Tony Williams, who made critical corrections to my manuscript. My wife, Judy, helped me with her support and patience.

Cæsar's Provinces.

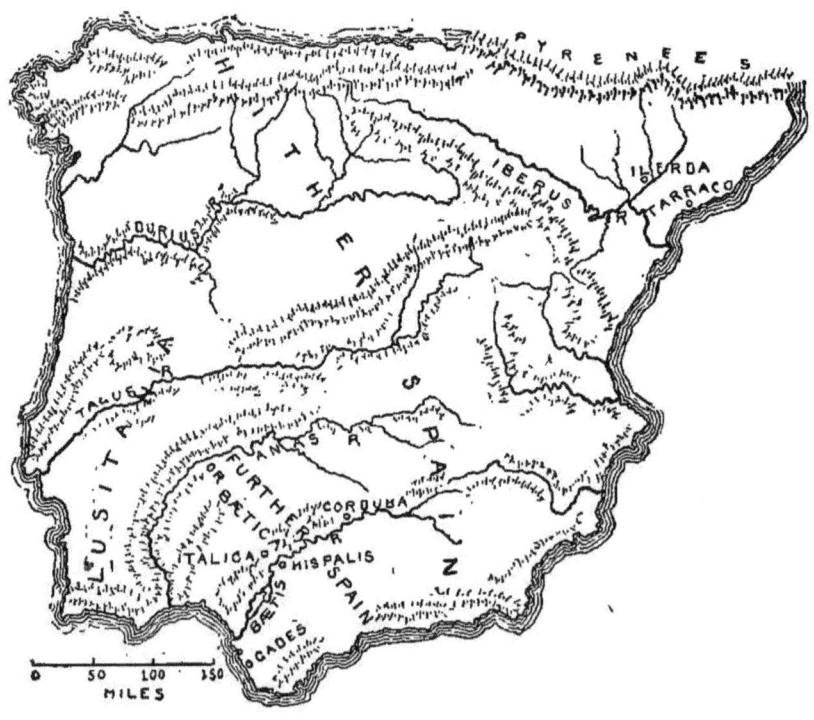

Farther Spain.

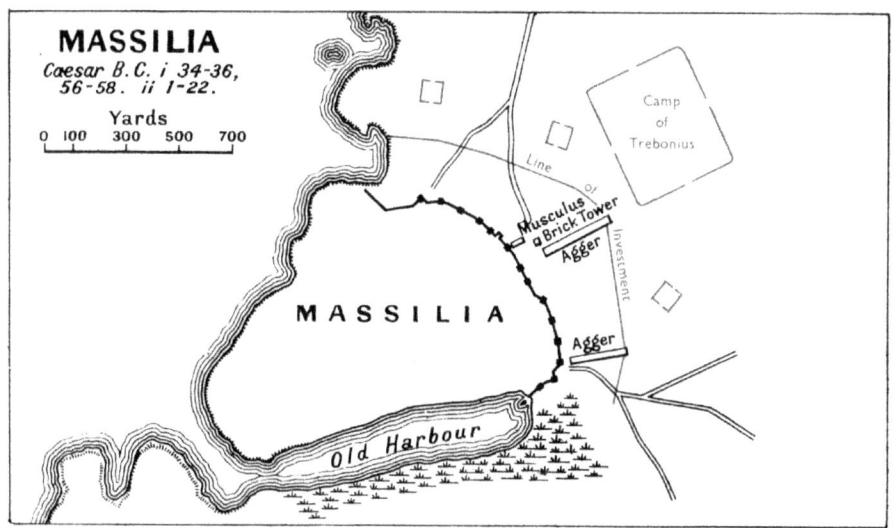

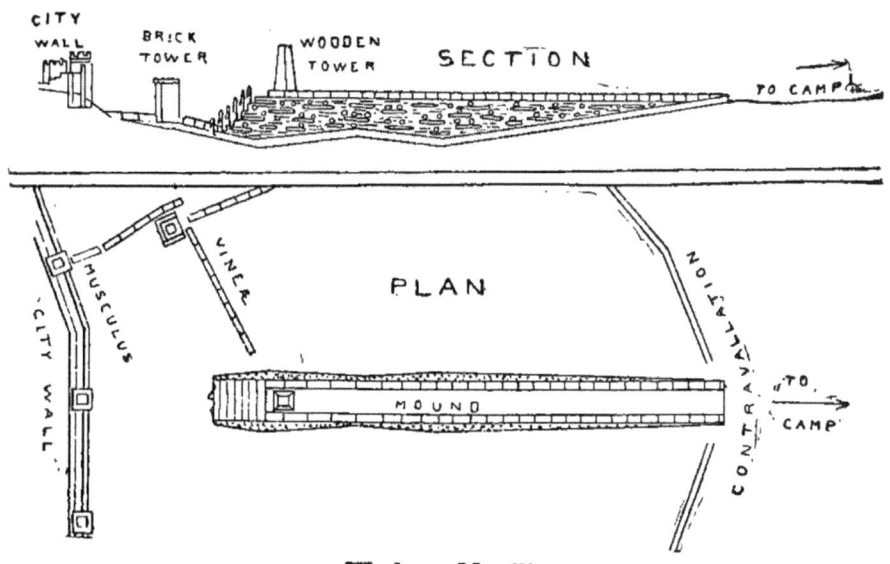

Works at Massilia.

Epirus and Macedonia.

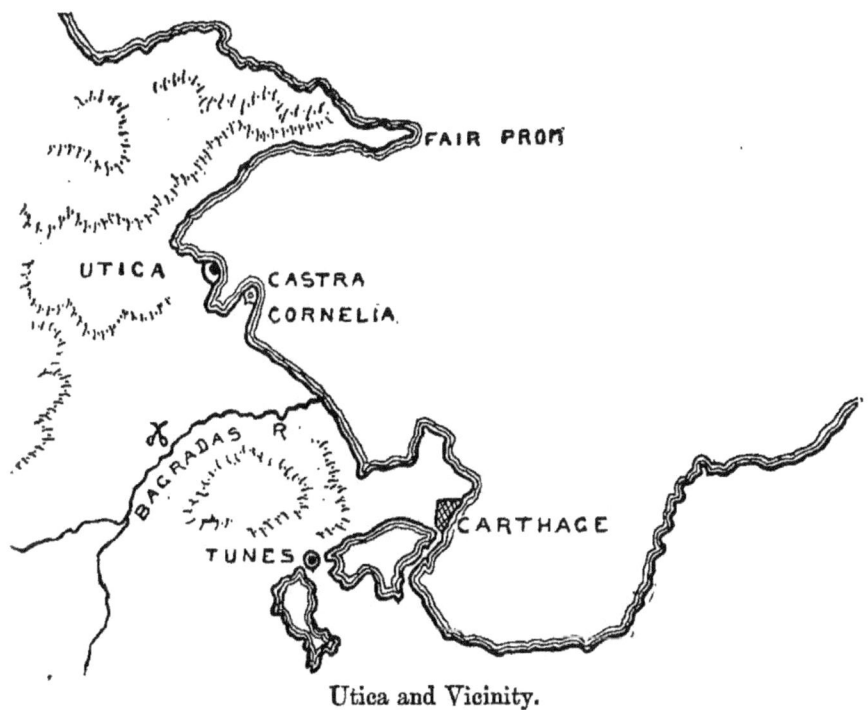

Utica and Vicinity.

Alexandria.

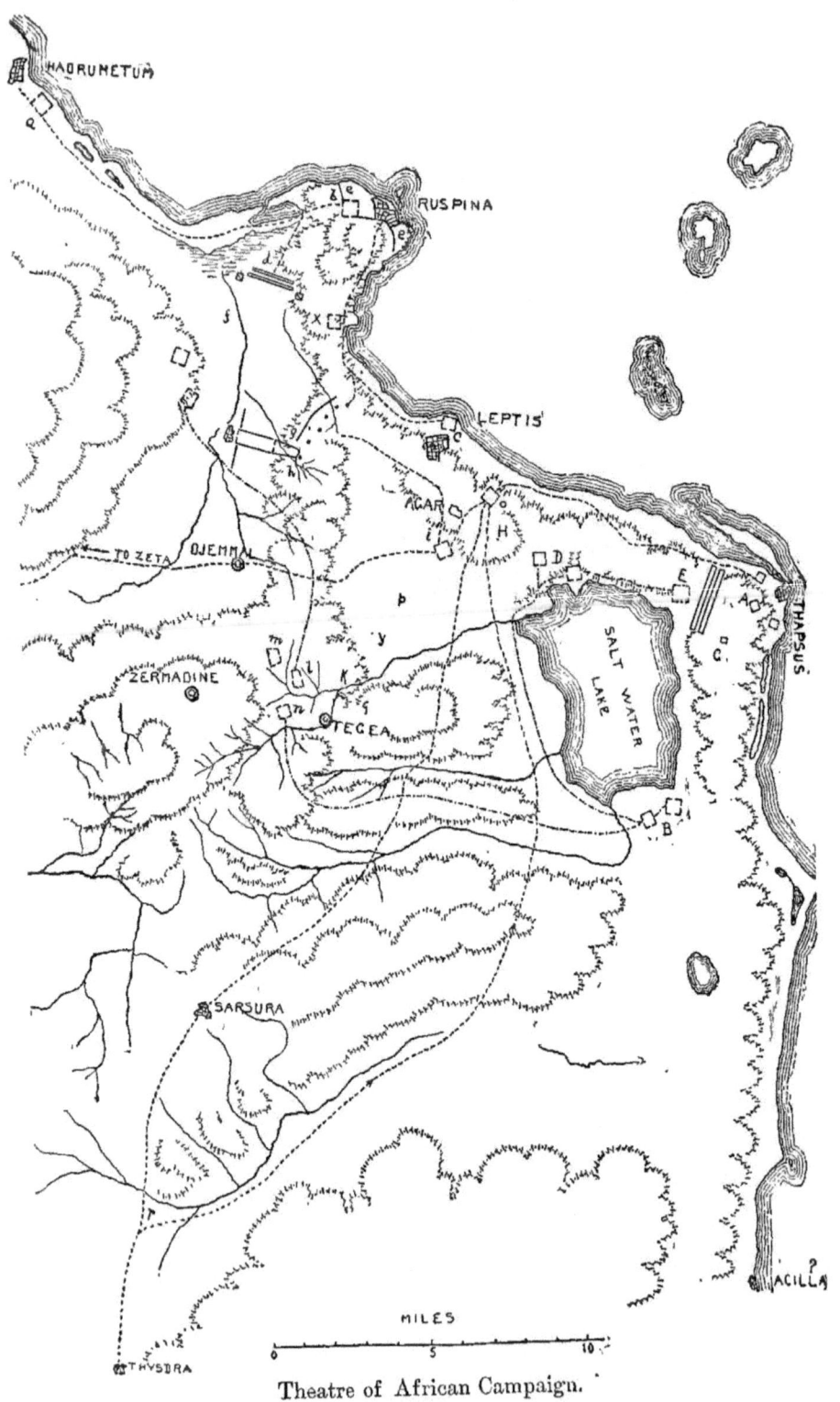

Theatre of African Campaign.

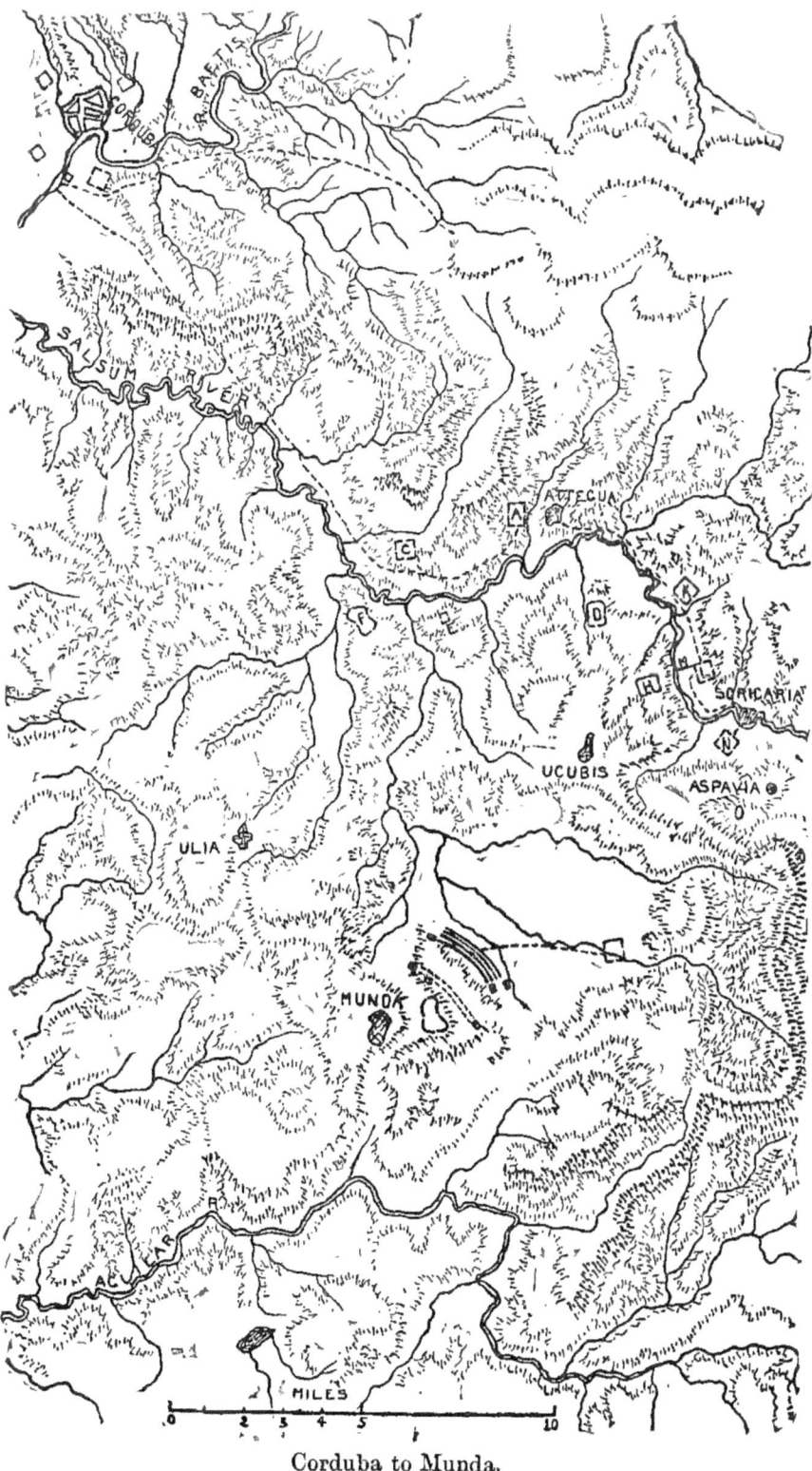

Corduba to Munda.

Introduction:
Julius Caesar and his Civil War

Julius Caesar won nearly every battle; even in defeat, he managed to turn the tables on his enemies and emerge victorious. His military powers were extraordinary for his time and remain so through history. Today, some two thousand years since a crowd of Roman senators stabbed him to death, Caesar's shadow falls across the modern world, an image of bloody conquest and authoritarian answers to messy deliberative government. In his lifetime, Caesar won some sixty battles; in his civil wars he fought against the best his fellow Romans could bring against him and their efforts all failed. Caesar built the Imperial Roman Empire on the shattered remains of the Roman Republic; reverberating still today, this event shaped the course of human history. Instead of a loosely held group of lands surrounding the Mediterranean Sea, the centralized and efficient administration of Rome drew the ramshackle provinces of the Republic together into a unitary state stretching from the Atlantic Ocean to the Syrian deserts, and from the depths of the Sahara to the German forests.

At the time and ever after, people sought answers to the question, how did he achieve his victories? Julius Caesar knew the question would be asked and, from the beginning of his military career, decided to provide his own answers. Caesar left notes describing his campaigns, published as Caesar's Commentaries. Here are the commander's own thoughts and understandings of his wars. This collection of campaign narratives is one of the great works of world military literature.

In this book, I write of Caesar's wars with his fellow Romans. Here, his art of war is illustrated in manoeuvres to trap his enemies, forcing them to fight his legions in bloody battles in which he destroyed them. Behind the curtain of swords and shields, Caesar tells of the movement of his supplies and the cutting off of his enemies' supplies. Without food and water, the war is lost.

There are many accounts of Caesar and his wars. What makes this account worthy of your attention are the descriptions of Caesar's actions integrated with the analysis of his purposes for the action, combined with an understanding of his logistics. Here, I depict not only Caesar's manoeuvres but also demonstrate how these actions resulted in his success. Caesar's objective in his civil wars was not simply winning the war. He strove to subdue the Mediterranean world to his personal will. Further, his methods belie modern concepts of military operations: his strategy was to simply rely on his tactics. His main question was not, how many? But rather, where were they? He marched against his enemies and attacked. Whatever trouble he found himself in, he depended on the sharp swords of his men to cut down the forces which he faced. Courage, persistence, relentless combat, not brilliance nor ingenious manoeuvres, brought victory.

Caesar won these wars, destroying or cowering his enemies and so changed the world. Because he prevailed, his name became the title of power and authority. Caesar followed Caesar as lords and masters of vast numbers of people. As Kaiser or Tzar, Caesars remained in power for millennia; the title imperator, bestowed on Caesar as his personal name by the senate, became emperor; his legal power, imperium, became empire. This accomplishment was not cheap. Caesar's campaigns took years and cost many hundreds of thousands lives.

Many modern commentators are sceptical about claims regarding results accomplished through a person's long-term planning. Rather, they view human affairs as the end product of opportunities and happenstance. They say Caesar simply fell into the roles he had by taking one step at a time without regard for any long-term plan; if it was not Julius Caesar who became ruler of the Roman Empire, someone else would have done the same thing. Caesar fought the civil wars to survive and in order that he would survive, he fought until he was the only one left. It was the configuration of social-economic developments which generated the momentum forcing centralization of the Republic's administration and Caesar simply fell into this pattern. That may well be, but that is not what I think the evidence shows.

Ever since Caesar served in Spain as a subordinate official, he looked at the Republic and saw what he needed to become supreme: political connections, a loyal and well-trained army and the wherewithal to support the structures needed to manage the above. With a unitary command and personal freedom of action, he would then eliminate his enemies' force one by one – which he did. This is not an opinion based on hindsight; I see this as the result of day-by-day planning, long term ambition, and insight into the strengths and weaknesses of those who would stop him. This is very clear in his accounts of the civil wars.

This account of Caesar's Civil Wars

In this narrative of Caesar's campaigns in his civil wars, I describe his manoeuvres, tactics, and means of supplying his forces in as much detail as possible. Because it is in the many details that victory is found, to comprehend how Caesar won, we need to follow his actions as closely as possible. My account is based in good part on Caesar's own writings; but there are also other important sources which have come down to us, providing useful materials, and all the sources need careful consideration because nothing is ever simple and direct.

My account begins with the start of the Civil Wars. Section one covers Caesar's invasion of Italy; section two, is about his stay in Rome, consolidating his power and recounts the march to Spain and his battles there; in section three, we look at the battles on Caesar's strategic flanks, the siege of Massilia and Curio's attempt to seize Africa; section four is the war against Pompey in the Balkans ending with the Battle of Pharsalus. After Caesar's victory over Pompey, section five follows Caesar east, to Alexandria and Pontus; section six covers the war in Africa, ending with the death of Cato; and in section seven, Caesar finally defeats the last of his enemies in the Second Spanish War.

I include nine appendices which explain important points regarding the Civil Wars. The first appendix looks at the question of whether the siege described in Vitruvius is the same as Caesar's siege of Massilia; the second, looks at the relationship between Cleopatra and Caesar; third, is the question of the burning of the Library at Alexandria; and fourth looks at the structure and personnel of Caesar's army. Appendices five and six look at the warships, their capacities and fighting methods and then the design of the torsion projector engines. Appendix six is a short history of the Roman Republic from the Gracchi to Caesar's invasion of Italy; and seven is a discussion of the Roman economy. The last appendix is an extended discussion of Caesar's commentaries, their composition and purpose and how the text travelled through time. There is a general bibliography as usual, but also there are specific annotated bibliographies which cover specific topics.

Caesar's narrative of his war is one of the basic military texts which include the Persian War, the Peloponnesian War, Alexander's campaigns, and the Punic Wars. Since the Renaissance, these texts are basic to the study of war. The Civil Wars are unique in that they describe a wide-ranging series of campaigns against similarly equipped and trained forces. They are a head-to-head contest like no other.

'*The powerful do as they are able and the weak must accept it.*'

Thucydides 5, 89

Section I

Italy

Chapter 1

Civil War Erupts

The City of Rome, Autumn 50 BC

It is the autumn of the year, 50 BC by our reckoning, by the Roman calendar, the Year of Consuls Paullus and Marcellus. In Italy, the lovely landscape grew abundant crops, livestock, and grapes; the management of the land was handled by an assortment of families, villages, and towns. From each village and town, all roads ran to Rome. Here was the great city. Masses of people and vast quantities of goods collected at this nexus of power and corruption. The crowded buildings rose high in the air. Rome's seven hills had deep scarps that were more precipitous than they are now. In the scarps, cave-houses extended downward improved by dried mud bricks and roofing of reed, willow, and timber. The hill slopes, winding defiles and deep valleys supported the stacked cellular structures that rose high into the air. The Romans called these tall buildings, *insulae*. Legislation, demanding separate free-standing structures, gave architectural form in order to generate legal definition. Pliny described Rome as a *urbs pensilis*, a suspended city. (HN xvi 36)

The urban sprawl spread far beyond the ancient walls; an imposing mass of brown speckled with green, sometimes so ugly as to be picturesque. The city magistrates managed hundreds of labourers directly or by contract to fight the never-ending battles against the filth which collected everywhere, bringing in water to clean and flush the winding streets and closely packed tenements. The great monuments to the divine were not so as to impress visitors from the eastern Mediterranean. Smallish brick and terracotta buildings of awkward design held life-sized images of fairly grotesque deities. Only the temple to Jupiter, the Best and Greatest, on the Capitol Hill offered any competition to the eastern buildings. Recently built by Greek architects with columns taken from the unfinished Athenian Temple of Zeus, the temple housed the cult statue of Jupiter, only slightly larger than a life-sized man and of traditional Etruscan style. No one ever commented on the building's beauty.

The living heart of the city was spread through her streets and neighbourhoods. The ever-present transactions between seller and buyer, often for a pittance but also large sums and everything in between, gave life to the populace and city. This was the world of the *taberna*, the shop. Not the booths of Classical Greece but permanent rectangular buildings, often with living quarters on an upper floor, or a rectangular space on the ground floor of an *insula*, where the *tabernarius* lived their private lives, making a living in the city. During the Second Punic War, almost a century and a half before, with the introduction of the *denarius* coinage, the numbers of shops began increasing. After Hannibal ceased being a concern, the retail economy took off. *Taberna* were of many kinds: luxury shops with exotic perfumes and art works; craft shops with cloth and leather goods; and, of course, food of all kinds. There were luxury eating establishments and fast-food vendors; furniture, bedding, building materials, and charms were readily available, at a price.

Beyond the shops and craftsman, lived the Roman elite. In favoured spots, either hilltops or near important state structures, instead of tall *insulae*, there spread low, one- and two-storey buildings, surrounded by walls over which vegetation hung. Within, there were spacious quarters, decorated in magnificent style, holding works of art and carefully crafted furnishings. Within these walls, squads of well-trained slaves served the princesses and princes, the noble Romans, the beloved of the gods, the masters of the world. Different from those born of the muddy earth, the noble Romans descended from gods. The divine spark that inhabited the human bodies of Roman aristocrats came through families and clans interconnected by Roman marriages as they travelled through generation after generation.

In each family, a *pater familias* oversaw investments of property and influence. As the foundation of their wealth, the noble Romans owned farms and villas, large and small, spread across Italy and into the more settled provinces. Some grew exotic fruits and vegetables along with prize horses, pigs, fowl, and fish for the owners' display and consumption. Others grew cash crops for markets. In times of trouble, the villas provided safety and security. Wealth, however, was to be used. Slaves made a fine investment, particularly in the city: skilled craftsmen, able negotiators, fine teachers, all made good money; and, at the end of their successful career, the slave bought his freedom and became a client of the noble family and clan.

Business led to more investment, city real-estate being profitable. Blocks of apartment *insulae*, with stores on the ground floor made money along with the necessary construction and maintenance crews to keep them going. Slaves made the best managers; they would hire the unskilled citizens as day labour. The economy revolved around skilled slaves and unskilled freemen.

Below the noble Romans, there were large groups of plebeian magnates, not noble but equestrian. Rich families, many involved in contract business with the Roman State, these people managed the day-to-day running of the city: the armies and the provinces. Intermarried with many noble families, the upper circles of equestrian society directed the actual work required by the Senate and people. Below the magnates, there existed tens of thousands of established citizen families involved in the myriad activities which made up the business of Rome. Merchants, builders, manufacturers, handling raw materials, making finished products, importing, and exporting goods, constant buying and selling: the core of Rome was busy people making money in a money economy with loans, mortgages, banks, and taxes. Many plebeians were freedmen, successful slaves who received their liberty and so became Roman citizens because his or her work was more profitable for less trouble than being a slave. They married and had children who were now full Roman citizens.

At the bottom of Roman society were those citizens who had neither skills nor education, who lived in a world distant from the tranquillity of orderly life. The recipients of the Roman dole, mob and muscle for hire, these people provided the force needed by different political factions, the lawless agents who stole and killed, and the security guards to maintain law and order.

Rome was the economic and political centre of Italy, the pleasant, fruitful land, settled and rich. Constellations of towns and villages spread over the countryside, housing a prosperous elite served and fed by troupes of clients and slaves. Beyond Italy were the fruits of the Roman imperium, sophisticated cities and rude tribes, rich mines, and extensive agrarian estates, all organized to send riches to Rome and her favoured masters.

The Republic

Rome was ruled by the Senate and People. No man was king. The Roman People ruled themselves, handling their public matters through deliberations and elections. In many ways, this was an exercise in chaos, but a group of understandings and a list of rules provided a basis of order: this was the Republic. Starting in 60 BC, an alliance formed of three powerful political leaders: the first, the military commander, Pompey the Great, as he had himself called; the second, Crassus, the richest Roman, with extensive properties and financial resources, and third, the subtle crafty Julius Caesar as a balance to the other two; Pompey married Caesar's daughter, Julia, so strengthening his hand. The three men held most of the instruments of power, distributing offices, provinces, and rewards as they wished. Contemporaries who were not pleased with the arrangement called the alliance, 'The Three-Headed Monster'. It could not last; Marcus Crassus thought if he could make conquests as important as Pompey's, he would lead the alliance. His Parthian campaign ended in disaster with the loss his army and life in 53 BC. Caesar's daughter Julia had died in 54; Pompey no longer needed Caesar and Caesar, in the midst of his Gallic conquest, no longer needed Pompey.

Caesar's civil war broke out suddenly in the first month of 49 BC. Caesar sought to strengthen the Republic by reordering and reforming how the administration functioned; Pompey sought to strengthen the Republic by supporting the aristocratic senate's domination of the administration. The senators supporting Pompey thought they had caught Caesar in a trap from which he could not escape. Caesar offered a compromise in a letter he sent to the senate. The consuls, Marcellus and Lentulus decided to withhold the text from the senators, believing Caesar's offer would only confuse their plans. They wanted the senate to decree Caesar an outlaw and remove him from power. They believed their plot was certain to bring Caesar down. Caesar proved them wrong. Here is how he explained his solution:

Caesar's Account

The presiding consuls in the Senate of Rome, C. Marcellus, and L. Lentulus, acknowledged their receipt of Caesar's message. They faced a group of tribunes who were demanding to hear Caesar's words. After a bitter and lengthy argument, the House relented about reading the message to the assembled senators but refused to allow any motions regarding it. After the Tribune Mark Antony read Caesar's letter, the consuls presented a motion regarding the state of public affairs. Consul Lentulus pledged he would support the Republic if the senators expressed themselves boldly. On the other hand, he continued, if the senators attempt to win Caesar's favour just as they had many times, then he will look to his interests, 'He as well as they had that line of retreat open. The favour of Caesar was open to all.' So Scipio Nasica, Pompey's father-in-law, spoke clearly: Pompey would support the Republic if the Senate did, but, if the Senate chose to equivocate, then Pompey would go his own way, without fail. The Senators took Scipio's words as direct quotes from Pompey. While the Senate was meeting within the old walls of Rome, Pompey and his two legions were not far beyond the walls.

Some other members had advanced more proper motions. Marcus Marcellus pointed out that they should wait until the levy was complete, and the Senate would have armed forces at their disposal, then they could deal with the problem. Under Marcellus' standing, Marcus Calidius proposed that Pompey should leave Italy and go to his provinces, the two Spains. That way, the two legions, taken from Caesar in the first place, would go west with Pompey and not threaten Caesar. Marcus Rufus repeated Calidius' motion, changing some words to better suit the situation.

To these motions, presiding consul Lentulus responded with loud and biting sarcasm. The consul refused to put forth Calidius' motion, at which point, Marcellus, fearing public condemnation, withdrew his standing. The consul's demands, the threat of Pompey's legions, and threats from Pompey's allies in the Senate pushed the House to approve Scipio's motion. Even though the majority did not agree with it, the resolution stipulated that Caesar would disband his army before a fixed date or be guilty of open treason. Two tribunes, Mark Antony and Quintus Crassius rose to veto the resolution. But the presiding consul challenged the legality of the action because proceedings involving the appointment to consular provinces were exempt from veto.

The House erupted in uproar as members exchanged different opinions. The enemies of Caesar applauded each speech as they became more nasty and bitter. As evening came on, the Senate dispersed. Pompey invited all the senators to come to his residence that night, outside of the old walls, so he could reinforce their actions against Caesar and stiffen support for Caesar's enemies. Veterans across Italy had flocked to Rome in hopes of finding a high position in the new army along with opportunities of plunder and wealth. The next morning, Pompey called on the veterans to attend a rally in Rome. Also, he invited many of the soldiers of the two legions formerly commanded by Caesar. The centre of the city, especially the *Comitium*, was crowded with military commanders and officers. After the rally, the Senate convened with an overflowing house, Pompey's partisans and Caesar's enemies joined together. This crowd forcibly voiced their demands against Caesar, threatening those who disagreed, warning those who waived and making sure they made the right choice. In fairness to Caesar, before the House issued a decision, one of the censors, Lucius Piso, and a praetor, Lucius Roscius, offered to take the resolution to Caesar for his response within six days; others suggested a larger delegation.

All efforts to bring a measure of moderation failed in the face of forceful speeches by the consul Scipio and Marcus Cato. Consul Lentulus had enormous debts which he could only settle by gaining a lucrative command in the provinces; he even bragged to his friends that he, too, would reach supreme power like Sulla. Scipio had similar ambitions, but, as Pompey's relative, he saw his future as a leader of Pompey's organization. Marcus Cato had a long-standing hatred of Caesar and opposed him whenever he could. As for Pompey, flattery from Caesar's enemies and his inability to accept any rival for power drove him to ignore their former friendship and become Caesar's enemy. Among other actions, he had demanded Caesar's two legions be sent east, but when they came to Rome, he took them over. The only way he saw to resolve his rivalry with Caesar was by the sword.

Now, Caesar's enemies rushed procedures forward, disregarding standard practice. The House refused any effort to contact Caesar regarding the charges. The House refused to accept the tribunes' constitutional right of veto or even secure their safety. The reason for haste in the House was the presentation of the Final Decree, which was passed only through division. In all previous times, a unanimous House stood together. This decree, issued only when the country was in danger of destruction, directed the consuls, praetors, tribunes, and proconsuls to take all measures for the safety of the City and Republic.

The year had begun on 1 January. Consul Lentulus entered his office and called the Senate together by 3 January. By 7 January, the House had set out on the road to civil war. The tribunes fled to Caesar, who was at Ravenna, awaiting to negotiate a fair solution to the impasse between him and Pompey. During the next few days, Pompey continued to pressure the Senate to move against Caesar. The Senate continued meeting outside the city boundaries; there, Pompey came and directly addressed the senators. He told the members of the House how brave they were to face down Caesar, followed by an account of the military forces under his command. Ten legions, ready for war, waited for his orders.

Further, Pompey proceeded to relate the information he had secretly received from agents he had placed in Caesar's army. The men were not loyal. They distrusted Caesar, and when the crisis came, they would not fight for him. After some debate, many of Pompey's requests passed. The House ordered new troops enrolled and money released to Pompey as he organized his forces for war.

The Senate also saw fit to distribute provinces to men who did not hold office: Syria went to Scipio, Gaul to Lucius Domitius, others gained as much as they had supported Pompey. These appointees, without confirmation from the people, offered proper vows and hurried off to their provinces. Both consuls left the city, which had never happened before and was never supposed to. Lictors remained on duty for men who were no longer in office, something never seen before. Agents of Pompey and the consuls spread throughout Italy, raising troops, collecting money, seizing valuables from

Civil War Erupts 9

towns and temples. Commandeered property and plundered wealth flowed into Caesar's enemies' hands. Lost were distinctions between the divine and the human. Chaos ensued.

Then Caesar appealed to his troops on hand, the XIII Legion. He talked about how he was suffering at the hands of his political rivals and charged Pompey with actions not based on law and the Republic but because of petty jealousies about Caesar's success. The very fact that Pompey's action resulted in the expulsion of the people's tribune demonstrated his disregard for the legal process. And the passage of the decree which calls the Roman People to arms in defence of the Republic, without any clear and immediate threat, compounded an assault against Caesar's very person. Now, if they valued their supreme commander under whom they had achieved great success, they must protect him. The soldiers readily responded with cheers and acclamations. They stood ready to defend their commander and the rights of the people's tribunes.

Caesar sent a number of military tribunes ahead with some of his boldest soldiers, dressed as civilians, to enter the town of Ariminum and take control of it. That evening, Caesar left dinner early, saying he felt ill, and took a two-horse carriage to Ariminum. His cavalry escorted him. In his account, Caesar says simply he passed into Italy; other accounts make a point of marking the crossing of the Rubicon as a major decision. Appian comments that Caesar's resolve wavered, saying if he failed to cross, the misfortune was his but if he crossed the river, the misfortune was for all mankind. Then, a comment repeated by many authors, he quoted the proverb, 'the die is cast'. Once past the Rubicon, Caesar took Ariminum at dawn and continued his offensive, taking important positions, capturing all before him by bribes or terror. Panic swept across the countryside, as refugees fled, spreading news of Caesar's vast forces marching across the land. Supported by his troops, defiant of his enemies, Caesar advanced to Rimini, thus marching armed soldiers out of his assigned province into Italy, across the Rubicon. So said Caesar in his version of events.

The View of those who Opposed Caesar

For many Senators and their Equestrian allies, the problem was simple: if Caesar returned to Rome with his armies intact, still holding office, and able to draw on state credit, he would control the Republic. As Cicero said, Caesar was too big for the constitution (Ad Att. 7.9). Caesar's ascendancy was clear since Crassus's death in his disastrous attempt to conquer the Parthians. Pompey was a pleasant, cheerful man who enjoyed power and life. Now Pompey was pushing sixty years of age. He had put on weight and was not healthy. Caesar was only a few years younger than Pompey, but his ambition burned with a bright flame; always active, never at rest, Caesar's dynamic style impressed everyone who saw him. The suspicion, shared by friend and foe alike, was that Caesar planned to erect a monarchy to replace the Republic.

Those who wanted to preserve the free Republic understood that they had to weaken Caesar significantly if the Republic was going to survive. Only by bringing up his many indiscretions, assumptions of unauthorized power, and violations of law could his opponents hope to break his hold on his armies, clients, and provinces. In the autumn of 50 BC the crises arrived, and some conflict appeared inevitable. Cicero was wrapping up his administration of Cilicia and waiting for transport to Rome in Ephesus. When he heard the news, he included it in his ongoing correspondence with his friend Atticus. He had said in his letter of October 1, *'Terrible news, Caesar will refuse to dismiss his army.'* He adds, *'Spero falsa sed certe horribilia!'* (I hope this is wrong, but it is undoubtedly horrible! *Ad Atticus* 6.8).

Near the end of the third week of December, Cicero was staying at Formiae. He was pondering the future and explaining his thoughts to Atticus.

> *'I will support the "right party or the right enough party"* and adds, *'stupid us, we should have opposed Caesar when he was weak. Now he has eleven legions, as much cavalry as he wants, the northern tribes across the Po, the city mob, the people's tribunes, the callow youth. He is a leader of authority and boldness. They say, 'Fight or become slaves!' If we win, prosecutions will come, and if we lose, slavery anyway. My lamp just went out, or I would write more.'* (*Ad Atticus* 7.7).

Cicero talked with Pompey on 25 December, running into him on the road to Formiae. They spoke from the eighth hour until vespers. Said Pompey, in many words and acute observations: he did not want peace. Cicero went on,

> *'Pompey thinks even if Caesar is elected consul without recourse to military force, he will still abolish the Republic. And, when Caesar hears of the actions of the Senate, he will give up the idea of a consulship this coming year and will stay with his army in his provinces. But, if Caesar is foolish enough to bring military pressure, Pompey expressed supreme contempt for him because of the strength he had on hand and that of the Republic.'* Cicero asks Atticus, *'What do you think. It does occur to me, "Mars acts as he pleases." Yet, speaking with a man of war whose abilities by many successful*

operations about the risks of a hollow peace, I'm satisfied with his course of action. Pompey not only is not seeking peace, he fears it.' (*Ad Atticus* 7.8)

Cicero sums up his thought in a long letter in the next day or so. His comments on the Senate's strategy are pertinent because he had a strong sense of how to fight wars and knew all of the people in the Senate's leadership. He said, *'Many different possibilities occur, but if Caesar attacks, we must decide whether to hold the city or abandon it; the key being how to cut Caesar off from food and supplies.'* And adds, *'if we must fight, the time depends on chance, the plan of campaign on circumstances.'* (*Ad Atticus* 7.9)

The Issues at Hand

Caesar had seen conflict coming for some years. In many ways, his operations in Gaul were preparations for the coming collision of social-economic factors and political institutions. The Republic's structural inefficiencies had grown worse as years passed. Demands for liberty led to corruption; demands for reforms produced chaos. Laws had become so entangled that those guilty of the worse crimes slithered out of trouble. Significant efforts at reforming the administration were proposed and tried but never quite got the job done. Caesar had the answer, so he believed. He did not want to become a king like some eastern Greek monarch or Parthian Shah: they were as entrapped in institutional nonsense as bad as the Republic. No, Caesar would become a director of the organization, a first citizen of good administration. He would rectify the calendars, the courts, the laws, and the state to provide honest and efficient government.

Caesar did not have any master scheme or intellectual blueprint for reforming the Republic. Instead, what he offered was – himself. He would be the moderator who would make the necessary decisions to improve the Republic's efficiency. He would make objective decisions based on the facts of the matter for the benefit of everyone. His ambition was not to dispossess any group or class of what they had but rather let each do what he could with what he had without taking undue advantage of others. And his soldiers would keep the peace. All his supporters had to do was allow Caesar to accomplish this task.

Caesar's enemies, on the other hand, had many agendas. Many feared for the Republic, a free government of free men; they did not want to become Caesar's slaves. Some feared for their livelihood. What if Caesar did end corruption, where would they go. All feared civil upheaval: riots, looting, murder, mass confiscations, mass executions, these had often accompanied the best of intentions. Each had their friends and their friends' friends. But all they had in common was their enemy, Caesar.

Pompey and the Senate represented many different interests and areas. Caesar described himself: his strategic task was to keep his enemies separated so he could defeat them, one by one. This was the bottom line for Caesar; he had prepared for this day. In the beginning, Caesar had ten legions at hand, his army of Gaul. These were numbered from VI to XIIII, and also the Alaudae (Larks) V raised from Transalpine Gaul. Since the Alaudae was not composed of Roman citizens, Rome did not recognize it. His legions were battle-hardened, experienced killers who knew the trade and the tricks of hand-to-hand combat. All his centurions were skilled and practised in years of experience. For ten years, these men marched and counter-marched in summer and winter through Gaul, fighting fierce opponents in wars of no quarter. These were brutal, dangerous men. Caesar's supplies came from his four relatively poor provinces: Cisalpine and Transalpine Gaul, Narbonese, and Illyricum. He had no fleet nor any access to the more prosperous provinces. When the Senate passed the Ultimate Decree, Caesar's legions were spread across Gaul; four were among the Belgae, four among the Aedui all in winter quarters, and two at Narbo protecting Caesar's rear in case Pompey's legions advanced from Spain. Caesar had strong forces at hand, but his position had no depth; all he had was four poor provinces, a mighty army but no significant recruiting ground, and plenty of money on hand, but money quickly evaporates.

Pompey held ten legions under his command. Two, he had received from Caesar in the previous year for a war against Parthia that never happened; these he numbered I and III. There were seven legions in Spain under his lieutenants and another one under the proconsul Domitius Ahenobarbus in Italy. As the prominent commander of the Senate's forces, Pompey represented the Republic, its authority, and resources. All the provinces along Mediterranean shores were at his command, and his career had taken him throughout Rome's empire except Gaul. In Italy, Pompey had Caesar's former legions based at Luceria, the proconsuls in the northwest, and several new legions in the process of formation.

The strategic problem was stark. If Pompey thrust his legions in Italy in front of Caesar's advances, it would be like sending a flock of sheep to stop a pack of wolves. Caesar was strong now but was limited in the amount of long-term resources. Pompey's forces in Italy were weak, but he had immense resources if he could organize them into a practical instrument.

Caesar had sat at Ravenna while the Senate prepared the Ultimate Decree. When he looked beyond the borders of his provinces there were two roads to

Rome: one from Bononia across the Apennines to Arretium; the other down the Adriatic coast to Fanum and the southwest. By initially avoiding central Italy, Caesar would seemingly allow Pompey an advantage. But, occupying the coast towns, Caesar would secure his supply lines and open many paths to central Italy. His course was obvious.

The Campaign Begins

The tribunes, Antony, and Cassius, along with Curio and others, fled Rome, reaching Ariminum on 11 January. Caesar left Ravenna on the same day and arrived at Ariminum the next day, joining his supporters. Caesar stayed at Ariminum with two cohorts, raising troops. He needed his legions in Gaul for the war and had ordered them to come, but a fortnight would pass before they would arrive. He needed to keep the routes open for them to approach and to expand his holdings in Italy to collect and hold supplies. Pompey, for all his bluster, hoped Caesar would not march but enter into extended negotiations. Pompey knew he did not have the strength to defend Italy. His seven legions were in Spain, and the two in Italy were formally Caesar's and so not trustworthy. He ordered the raising of troops, but that was only useful if he could stall Caesar for a significant time. The consuls divided Italy into districts, each under a prominent Senator. The senators raised troops and began training. The truth was Pompey had no forces to back up the Senate's position.

By 14 January the news that Caesar was not waiting for negotiations but was advancing into Italy reached Rome along with waves of refugees fleeing from Caesar's soldiers. His soldiers were dependable, and he did not intend to spend much time negotiating. Many Senators were disappointed that loyal legions did not just appear and blamed Pompey. Cato suggested Pompey became supreme commander of Roman forces, but many Senators feared putting such powers in a single pair of hands. Influential Senators recommended sending envoys to Caesar to make peace, but the consuls refused.

Caesar ordered Mark Antony with five cohorts to occupy Arretium while he remained at Rimini with two cohorts, raising troops. Also, Caesar sent the remaining three cohorts of XIII to the coast towns of Pisaurum, Fanum, and Ancona. During these few days, word reached him that Praetor Thermus was at Iguvium with five cohorts, making the town ready for defence. Iguvium near the Flaminian Way could block the routes from Gaul needed for reinforcements and supplies. Caesar also heard from his supporters among the town-people of their great loyalty to him. Confident in his hold on Pisaurum and Rimini, Caesar ordered Curio to march the three cohorts occupying those towns toward Iguvium. Aware that Caesar's troops were coming, Thermus did not trust the townspeople's loyalty. He pulled his troops out of Iguvium and marched away, but his troops deserted and went home. Curio received an enthusiastic welcome from Iguvium's citizens on 20 January and Caesar's position was secured.

The Senate sent Roscius and L. Caesar (no relation to Julius) to open negotiations with Caesar. Pompey told them in private to appeal to Caesar as a fellow Roman and essential official. Included in their documents was a letter from Pompey to Caesar expressing Pompey's high regard for Caesar and suggesting they find a peaceful way to resolve the current problems. Caesar returned a cordial response, reminding Pompey that the Senate had withdrawn the Law of the Ten Tribunes. So, he lost six month's tenure in office, and this seriously weakened his chances of gaining another consulship. Still, Caesar was willing to make significant concessions to keep the peace: Pompey should go to Spain after disbanding his forces in Italy; Caesar would release his army and handover his provinces to his successor; then, after guaranteeing a free election, the Senate and people would administer the Republic. Caesar continued: he and Pompey needed to meet to iron out the details of such an agreement. But, while Caesar was considering Pompey's message, he continued to improve his position, taking Iguvium and concentrating some cohorts at Ancona.

As more refugees flooded into Rome, Pompey decided the time had come to pull out; he had no intention of trying to defend the city. On 17 January he issued a directive to the consuls and the senators to follow him south. Anyone who did not leave was a supporter of Caesar. Pompey left the city on 18 January; the next day, rumours swept through Rome that Caesar's cavalry was at the gates, and Caesar himself was just behind them. Consul Lentulus, opening the treasury to take moneys for Pompey, became so frightened he took what he wanted and left the city in such a hurry that he forgot to lock the Sacred Treasury of Special Need. Consul Marcellus and most of the other magistrates immediately followed with large trains of wagons carrying their wives and households.

In the middle of all this, Cicero commented: *'Our Gnaeus* (Pompey), *with what strategy he planned or is going to develop, I don't know. He sticks his troops in towns, immobile. If he takes stand in Italy, we will all fight with him, but if he withdraws, then we will all disagree. To this, it is certain: either I'm nuts, or all this is stupid and brainless.'* (*Ad Atticus* 7.10)

L. Caesar arrived at the Senate's base near Capua, on 23 January. Here were collected Pompey, Labienus, the consuls, and leading senators. They now heard Caesar's answer and agreed to accept the terms, provided Caesar withdrew his garrisons from the towns he occupied. Pompey ordered a response written out, including a statement assuring Caesar that because he served the Republic, his election as consul was confirmed, and he could celebrate a triumph. Two days later, in Capua, the consuls and leading senators met to ratify the terms drawn up under Pompey's direction. All agreed, although they distrusted Caesar, they would take him at his word. Even Cato agreed. They dispatched the document on that same day and then waited, balancing between hope and fear.

Cicero did not trust Caesar.

'I ask you, what is all this… This man, out of his mind, ever miserable! He does all this for nothing but the greatest good! For where is there dignity without respectability? How is it responsible to command an army without legal authority, to occupy towns bringing about a revolutionary change to your government and many other crimes to "win God's greatest gift, a crown"… Well, let him have his wish! I, for my part, wish but to enjoy the fantastic gift of the sunshine on me rather than win any sort of kingdom.' (Ad Atticus 7.11) 'The extreme peril to which my safety and that of all loyal citizens, and indeed that of the whole body politic is exposed, you may infer from our having abandoned our homes and our very country to either rapine or conflagration… And thus, when Caesar, going mad, obliterating his name and honour, occupied Ariminum, Pisaurum, Ancona, and now, Arretium, we abandoned Rome; whether wise or bold, is beyond dispute.' (Ad Atticus 7.12)

Caesar waited for Pompey's response. On 29 January, Roseicus and L. Caesar delivered Pompey's answer. Caesar found it wanting. (Why take half of a prize when with a push the real award is yours?) On the same day, Caesar marched eleven miles to Auximum.

Chapter 2

The Struggle in Italy

Caesar's Offensive

Caesar's legions were coming from Gaul, battle-ready just like the troops of the XIII Legion. These soldiers were different from the local legions, the city watches or even Pompey's forces in Spain. For ten years, they had fought a bloody aggressive war in Gaul. Caesar's war in Gaul was not for some fine ideas or sacred causes; the war was strictly a violent struggle for wealth and power. The Gauls had known the Romans for centuries and they disliked them intensely. The Romans had fought the Gauls repeatedly and they understood the Gauls' strengths and weaknesses.

Subtlety and adroit manoeuvres did not win these battles; rather victory came from hard hand-to-hand fighting and face-to-face struggles, in which the strongest, toughest soldiers survived. And Caesar made sure the victors were the Roman soldiers. Training, discipline, food, and hygiene along with plunder and rapine made Caesar's soldiers the toughest in the Mediterranean world. He demanded strict discipline in the field and camp, but off duty he allowed the boys to have their fun. When Caesar marched his troops into Italy, he was bringing a force of skilled killers and ruthless rapists who had little regard for their enemies, civilian as well as military. The soldiers looked and smelt different, animal skins and tartans covered their well-worn armour. Peasants and aristocrats feared them and avoided their paths. When Caesar's cohorts marched into a town, his enemies left as fast as they could. While we don't hear directly in the sources about the fate of Caesar's enemies captured by his soldiers, Caesar's noted clemency for a few tells us there was a different result for many. Those who survived joined Caesar. Once his soldiers occupied a town, this ensured its loyalty even after the soldiers left.

When Caesar saw he was well received in the coastal towns of Pisaurum, Fanum, and Ancona, he withdrew his garrisons from them, trusting to their citizens' loyalty. He marched his troops toward Auximum. Here, Caesar's enemy Attius Varus, with a number of cohorts, was using the town as a base from which to send senators throughout Picenum, raising soldiers. The councillors of Auximum went to Varus and told him that the town's loyalty was to Caesar and they would allow him entrance. Varus saw danger ahead if he remained in Auximum so he withdrew his cohorts and marched away. But some soldiers of Caesar's First Century followed and brought Varus to battle. Varus' men did not stand; many fled to their homes, and some joined Caesar. Caesar welcomed the support of Auximum and the newly joined soldiers.

Pompey had moved his operations south while Caesar advanced along the eastern coast. He ordered the two legions he had taken from Caesar to come from Apulia and camp south of Capua. These were excellent soldiers but where their loyalties lay was doubtful. Here, the senators came, setting up a sort of administration in exile. Many senators went out to promising locations, raising troops from settled veterans and raw recruits. They inducted some 300 gladiators from the large training schools in Capua, granting them freedom and forming cavalry formations.

Cicero has left us a vivid image of the commotions that erupted because of the exit from Rome, ignited by the passionate fear of Caesar. In his *Letters to Atticus*, Cicero expressed astonishment at the lack of forethought and confusion which arose from the impulsive decision to go to war with Caesar compounded by Caesar's quick military response. Of course, rational politician as he was, Cicero thought an understanding with Caesar, something always fluid and manageable, was better than war. On 5 February Cicero wrote:

> *'I have abandoned hope of peace: but our party takes no steps for war... Caesar is said to be tearing along, and is nearly on us, not to join battle – there is no one to join it with – but to cut us off from flight. Now, if that is to be in Italy, I am ready to die with her – and on that I need not ask your advice: but if the struggle is beyond her borders, what am I to do?'*

(He continues, remarking that hardships, the incompetence of the Senate leadership, and Pompey's dithering, pushes him to stay and deal with Caesar, but his friendship with Pompey, the justice of the cause of the Senate, and the disgrace of dealing with a tyrant pushes him to leave.) (*Ad Atticus* 7.20)

On 8 February Cicero continues,

> *'The discovery I made at Capua was that no reliance is to be placed on the consuls and that no levy is being made anywhere. Recruiting officers do not dare to show their faces when Caesar is at hand and our leader is nowhere to be found and takes no action. No one signs up. The lack is not desire but hope. Our Gnaeus* (Pompey), *o miserable and unbelievable affair, he does nothing! He has no spirit, no plans, no substance, no involvement.'* (*Ad Atticus* 7.21)

> Even worse, that night, Cicero wrote, *'I see there is not a foot of ground in Italy which is not in Caesar's power. I have no news of Pompey and I imagine he will be captured unless he has taken to the sea. What incredible speed! While our side... What can I do? To what land or sea can I go, to follow a man when I don't know where he is.'* (*Ad Atticus* 7.22)

Caesar's driving actions contrasted with the Senate's confusion and dithering. Settling Auximum, he travelled through Picenum, Pompey's homeland, receiving welcome and supplies from local officials. Even the town of Cingulum, sponsored by Caesar's former lieutenant, Labienus, offered to follow Caesar's command. Veterans and new recruits came to join his forces and now the XII Legion arrived. With the main bodies of both XII and XIII, Caesar approached Asculum, the main town of Picenum. Cornelius Lentulus, a former consul, and at one time an ally of Caesar commanded the garrison of ten cohorts at Picenum for Pompey. Lentulus had taken the nickname Spinther, because he looked like a famous actor of that name. When Caesar with his two legions approached, Lentulus Spinther pulled out, marching his cohorts to reinforce Pompey. On the march, many soldiers left Lentulus' command to join Caesar.

Some distance from Asculum, Lentulus met Pompey's lieutenant, Vibullius Rufus, hurrying toward Asculum with newly raised troops to take command and strengthen the garrison. Hearing of Caesar's approach with two legions of the Gallic army, Vibullius removed Lentulus from command and took over his remaining troops. Soon meeting with the withdrawing garrison of Camerinum, consisting of six cohorts, Vibullius marched a total of thirteen cohorts to Corfinium, where sat Caesar's senatorial successor to the administration of Gaul, proconsul Domitius Ahenobarbus with some twenty cohorts. As proconsul he was not under Pompey's command but as an independent commander, he needed to coordinate his actions with Pompey. Domitius found the news of Caesar's march exhilarating. Corfinium was an important point in the Apennine mountains; forty years ago, the town was the capital of United Italy in the Social War. From Corfinium, straight west of Rome, a strong force could block the east coast roads or threaten the city itself, to the west. Certainly, Caesar could not simply by-pass the town on his march south. Domitius wanted Caesar to besiege Corfinium so he could impale Caesar's forces on his fortification until Pompey could come and decisively defeat Caesar.

At Asculum, Caesar planned his next steps. He had sent out scouts to round up Lentulus' deserted soldiers, placing them into his units; then he spent a day organizing food supplies. Once he put his formations and trains in order, Caesar marched toward Corfinium. Three miles from the town, his scouts located the bridge that led to Corfinium. Domitius had assigned five cohorts to guard the crossing. Caesar's leading cohorts deployed and Domitius' men, rather than get tangled with the Gallic veterans, pulled back toward Corfinium. Caesar brought his formations forward and camped near Corfinium, settling in for a siege. Agents came to him, reporting strong support for him in the town of Sulmo, just about seven miles from his camp. However, Senator Quintus Lucretius and five cohorts occupied the town. Caesar sent Mark Antony with five cohorts of the arriving VIII Legion. When the townsmen saw the cohorts' standards, they opened the gates, welcoming Antony and his soldiers. Lucretius and his lieutenant escaped by jumping over the wall, but Antony's men captured the lieutenant. On the same day, Antony returned to Caesar with his prisoner and five additional cohorts. Caesar accepted the senate's soldier into his forces and released the lieutenant.

As Caesar's army deployed into their camps around Corfinium, Domitius saw his ambition realized. Caesar was going to besiege him in this fastness and as long as he could hold out, Caesar's offensive had stopped. Domitius ordered Corfinium's walls repaired, mounted projector machines on the towers, and offered his own lands to the soldiers, four acres per man and more for veterans and officers. Money was no object because many refugees had fled to Corfinium, businessmen, senators, and landowners and they all feared Caesar. Domitius sent a message to Pompey in Apulia. He described Caesar's deployment around Corfinium and explained how they could trap Caesar in the narrow country and cut him off from supplies and reinforcements if Pompey immediately marched a strong army to Corfinium. On the other hand, if Pompey did not defeat Caesar quickly, Caesar threatened to do serious harm to the Senate and Pompey.

Cicero, Pompey, and Caesar

All of Italy, peasants through to aristocrats, followed the moves of Caesar and Pompey. Whoever won would make a great deal of difference, even for many slaves. Rumours and speculations spread from kitchen servants to senators, from cleaning women to matriarchs. All that was said is lost except for some letters from Cicero.

> 'On the evening of 9 February, I got a letter from Philotimus declaring that Domitius has a reliable force, the cohorts from Picenum under the command of Lentulus and Thermus have joined his army. They can cut Caesar off and he knows it. And more at Rome, the Loyalists' hopes are restored, and Caesar's people are dashed. I am afraid this is a dream.' (*Ad Atticus* 7.23)

Cicero saw things looking up because he hoped the disturbances were about to end. The leading senators and their supporters believed Caesar faced defeat. None of them considered Pompey. The old commander had fought many campaigns, age and good living had made him cautious, but ambition still burned brightly. He knew better than to engage Caesar in open battle: one won or lost a battle; Pompey had no intention of losing to Caesar, rather he would slowly strangle him by avoiding a set battle and letting Caesar waste away. He had mentioned to Cicero if war came, he would abandon Rome and even Italy.

Proconsul Domitius seems to have known Proconsul Pompey's strategy and did not agree with it. He thought he could impose battle on him. Pompey was unaware of Domitius' plans as his letter to Cicero says, '*L. Domitius with twelve cohorts and fourteen cohorts brought by Vibullius is on the march toward me. He intends to leave Corfinium on 9 February, and behind, C. Hirrus with five cohorts follows.*' (*Ad Atticus* 8.11a) Just a few days later, when the thirty-some cohorts did not arrive, Pompey realized Domitius was ignoring his plans. He immediately sent a letter to Domitius, expressing his displeasure:

'*I am really amazed that you do not write to me, and I had to find out from others rather than you about the situation. We cannot face our enemy with divided forces. I hope by concentrating our forces we will receive praise from the Republic and the people. Even more, you ordered, as Vibullius wrote to me on 9 February, the army was to start on the march, coming to me. What reason was there that made you change the plan? Now, that reason, which Vibullius wrote to me, is silly, that you stopped your move because you heard Caesar left Firmum and came to Truentinum. Really! The nearer the enemy comes, the quicker you need to join with me, so Caesar cannot block your march or cut you off from me. ... Again, and again, I ask you and I beg you, as I did in my original letter, come to me at Luceria on the first day possible, before those forces, which Caesar has started to gather, join together in a strategic spot and separate you from us. But, if there are those who hold you back to safeguard their villas, it is necessary for me to order you to send to me the cohorts which have come from Picenum and Camerinum abandoning their fortunes.*' (*Ad Atticus* 12b)

Rumours of the rift between Domitius and Pompey flew through senatorial circles, encouraging some and disheartening others. Cicero wavered between hope and fear; one day,

> *'O'miserable affair! Pompey always succeeded in bad causes; in good, he failed. He understands the former because it is not hard, not the latter. For it is a difficult art to manage public affairs well. (Ad Atticus 7.25)* Then, a few days later, *'Things have become more cheerful in the last two days. I have given up my preparations for flight. ... I know whom I have to fear and why. But if the war I foresee comes, I shall not fail to play my part. ... For, if war comes, I am determined to be with Pompey.' (Ad Atticus 7.26)*

Pompey was having nothing to do with this effort to make him change his plans. He again wrote to Domitius:

> *'It is necessary to have a strong army which we know is able to thrust through the enemy's lines or is able to occupy an area and repel all of the enemy's attacks. We do not have such a force at this time because Caesar holds most of Italy and we do not have an army with sufficient fighting power or large enough to face his soldiers. And thus, it is necessary we have the greatest regard for the danger facing our Republic.'*

Next, Pompey wrote to the consuls, telling them what he needed to have done.

> *'I, considering the dispersal of our troops no help for the Republic nor a means of protection for ourselves, sent to L. Domitius a message: first order of business, come to us with all forces possible. If he was uncertain about his situation, he needs to send to us the nineteen cohorts that he has, which were marching to me from Picenum. The fact is, my fear is real; as Domitius is cornered and does not have the forces to defend his position because he has doled out my nineteen and his twelve cohorts to three towns, some occupying Alba, some Sulmo, so that even if he wanted, he cannot march.... Now, I need to tell you, this is a very troubling event. I want to free the many fine soldiers from the dangers of a siege, yet I am not able to go because I don't think I can trust the two legions to march to that place. I have also not been able to pull together more than fourteen cohorts because two went to Brundisium and I did not think I could let Canusium be left without a garrison.' (Ad Atticus 8.12a)*

Pompey had developed a plan to collect his forces at Brundisium and ship them to Dyrrachium.

Many of Caesar's opponents were dismayed when they found out there was no decision at Corfinium. The result they saw: a long and drawn-out struggle, expensive and bloody. Cicero, who feared Caesar, hoped for a negotiated settlement, as probably did most of the senators. He wrote,

> '*is not this departure from the city, this flight, a sign of fear and confusion? What conditions were so unacceptable that abandoning our homes was better? I understand the terms were bad but were they worse than this? So, Pompey will restore the Republic? When? And more, how is this hope going to be done? Are not the Picenum lands lost? Is the way to Rome open? Is not all moneys, both public and private in the hands of the adversary? Finally, there is not policy, nor forces, no bases where those who want to defend the Republic may concentrate. ...* (A message came just as Cicero was writing this letter so Cicero added the following) *Caesar has reached Corfinium and Domitius is there and will fight. Pompey cannot abandon him, but he sent Scipio ahead to Brundisium with two cohorts and told the consuls he wants one of them to tail the legion raised for Faustus to Sicily.*' (*Ad Atticus* 8.2)

Despite Cicero's hopes, Pompey could and did march away, leaving Domitius to Caesar's benevolences.

Caesar's Offensive Continues

Hopes of a settlement also attracted Caesar. His forces had the initiative and should the Senate's representatives come to him, he had the upper hand. By pinning Domitius and his forces in Corfinium, he sought to force Pompey into an engagement. Just three years before, Caesar had decisively defeated the Celtic confederation in a similar engagement at Alesia. His reinforcements kept marching towards him; his men were enthusiastic and close proximity to Pompey's army could only weaken their resolve. But Pompey also foresaw this result, as he told the Senate at the beginning of this dispute, once committed, he would not falter. He would destroy Caesar. He marched his forces toward Brundisium.

Caesar's tactics included speed, the faster he moved, the more he outmanoeuvred his enemies. Within three days of arriving at Corfinium, his men had constructed a strong camp and stockpiled supplies of corn from the neighbourhood. The rest of VIII Legion arrived along with twenty-two cohorts of new levies from Gaul and some 300 horsemen sent by the king of Noricum. Caesar placed these men in a new camp on the other side of Corfinium. He constructed lines that enclosed the people of Corfinium within their walls. While Caesar's men dug trenches and erected palisades,

Pompey's message reached Domitius inside Corfinium. Domitius found himself not only abandoned, but held at fault for being trapped. Feeling that such news would hurt morale and if he could hold out long enough, Pompey would still come, Domitius told his military tribunes and centurions that Pompey was coming, and they needed to wait patiently.

The contents of Pompey's letter became known to Caesar. Whether the information leaked to Domitius' officers through Caesar's agents or out of Domitius' headquarters, the defenders quickly found out that Pompey was not coming; they wanted to join Pompey if they could leave Corfinium. Caesar waited for Domitius' forces to react, allowing his men to continue building siege works but not preparing for a direct assault. Officers and men inside the town discussed their situation together, while some wanted to surrender, others were for holding out. In their meetings, they did come to blows but the situation in which they were stuck together demanded a single, unified answer and fights could not achieve that end. The military tribunes and prime centurions blamed the whole mess on Domitius, accusing him of secretly planning to flee with just a few companions. These officers then sent a message to Caesar at night, telling him that they wanted to surrender and had seized Domitius.

When he received this message in the night, Caesar stayed his hand, choosing caution over immediate action. There were many important Romans in the town, senators, local magnates, and their families. If the transfer of power got out of hand, both defending and attacking soldiers could run rampant, looting and killing. Caesar knew that small events often upset major actions. The important people in Corfinium were not all his enemies, some probably supported him, but fear of the advancing Gallic troops sent them scurrying. Many others really did not care who ruled in Rome as long as their estates and towns remained as they were. Those who supported Pompey might even change their minds when Pompey pulled out of Italy. By releasing all these people, unharmed and in possession of their goods, Caesar would lessen the fear his advance caused among those not deeply involved in politics.

At dawn on 21 February Caesar marched a force of elite soldiers to Corfinium's gates. He ordered all the Roman refugees to assemble before him and ordered the soldiers to treat them with respect. Soon, here stood senators and businessmen with their families. Caesar sent them with their property on their way. This even included Domitius, imprisoned by Corfinium's magistrates, sent on his way with sixty *sestertii* he had deposited in the public treasury.

Then, he assembled the defending soldiers with their commanders and ordered them to take an oath to himself and joined them to his forces. By mid-morning all was set and Caesar marched toward Apulia. He had stayed at Corfinium only seven days.

Pompey and Caesar at Brundisium

While marching his formations from Luceria through Canusium toward Brundisium, word came to Pompey that Caesar had taken Corfinium. Pompey added urgency to his order for all his forces to make for Brundisium; unsurprisingly, many cohorts of veterans abandoned their commanders and joined Caesar. Brundisium was the centre of Pompey's operation. He ordered all shipping on the coast collected in the harbour to transport troops and supplies across the Adriatic to Dyrrachium. By the time Caesar left Corfinium, both consuls and a large force of troops had sailed to Dyrrachium, and Pompey remained at Brundisium with twenty cohorts. By holding both Brundisium and Dyrrachium, Pompey commanded the Adriatic Sea and the sea approaches to south Italy from both east and west.

Caesar marched with his main body of six legions, four veteran and two of new levies being whipped into shape. Not trusting Domitius' cohorts, Caesar sent them to Sicily. His agents told him Pompey remained in Brundisium and perhaps there remained a chance of coming to an agreement with him. Caesar sent a high-ranking prisoner to Pompey with an offer for a personal meeting. As long as Pompey stayed in Brundisium, Caesar's purpose was achieved because if Pompey refused to negotiate, he planned to trap the proconsul and his troops. Once he reached Brundisium, Caesar began building the trap. As usual in Caesar's narratives, he gives a technical description of his construction operation.

Brundisium harbour consisted of an inner and outer bay, the inner being two wings surrounding the town and connecting through a narrow channel to the broad outer harbour. It was at the narrows connecting the inner and outer harbour that Caesar intended to set the trap for Pompey and his forces. First, he set his forces to construct an earthen-based wooden palisade cutting off the town from the land side. Then he directed his best construction crews, using impressed labour, at the narrows connecting the inner with the outer harbour to build his trap for Pompey and his forces. On either side of the narrows, Caesar had moles pushed out in the shallows, reinforced with rubble aggregate. Where the water became deeper, he directed the construction of two heavy square rafts, some 30 Roman feet (marginally less than an English foot) a side, anchored to the bottom on each corner.

Placing the two rafts at the edge of each mole, Caesar ordered more rafts constructed making a connected chain of rafts from one side to the other. The rafts, connected together, formed a roadbed once the soldiers placed soil on top, so making a raised causeway allowing soldiers to have ready access from either side of the channel. To protect men on the roadway, craftsmen installed wood parapets on both sides of the roads. On every fourth raft, the artificers built two-storey wooden turrets with protected battlements to defend the roadway from attacking ships.

Once Caesar's construction plan became clear, Pompey seized large cargo ships in the harbour and fitted them out for battle. These were *Onerarias*, capable of transporting three thousand amphorae. Pompey's craftsmen constructed turrets of three storeys, higher than the turrets on the rafts, and reinforced the bows. His soldiers placed projector machines and incendiaries in the turrets and along the sides. As Caesar's project progressed, Pompey's ships rowed up to the works, shooting missiles and flaming projectiles to stop the construction while from Caesar's turrets and parapets missiles and arrows flew toward the ships. Even as battles continued day after day, Caesar believed that peace was still possible and sent envoys to put proposals to Pompey, but the only response from Pompey was that there could be no negotiations because the legal authorities, the consuls, were absent.

Pompey's attacks on Caesar's works continued for nine days. Still, Caesar's project was done and threatened to block any escape by Pompey and his men. Then the fleet that had transported the consuls and Pompey's army to Dyrrachium returned. Caesar's water fortifications faced attacks on both sides, the oared warships carrying turrets in the outer harbour and turreted cargo ships in the inner, battered at Caesar's works, but Pompey saw that holding Brundisium overall was impossible. Determined to maintain order and keep his forces safe from a sudden assault, he ordered the town's gates sealed, the streets barricaded, and hidden pitfalls constructed to hinder Caesar's advance into the town. Once ready at nightfall, Pompey sent his archers and slingers to man the walls and pulled his heavy troopers back silently. After loading his ships with men and supplies, he gave the signal and the light troopers left their positions, embarking on small boats. Caesar, informed by townspeople of Pompey's plans, prepared scaling ladders and positioned his soldiers to assault the town walls when he gave the command. As soon as Pompey's light troops left their posts, Caesar gave the order for the assault. His troops went over the wall easily, but townsfolk told them about the traps and covered pits. Caesar's soldiers moved through the town with caution by circuitous paths, only reaching the docks after Pompey's ships had left, but collecting many small boats many troopers pursued Pompey's ships.

As Pompey's troops embarked his sappers, guarded by veteran soldiers, disembarked from boats onto Caesar's barricaded bridge. They cut the cables of the anchors which held the structures in place. Some of Pompey's oared warships grappled some rafts and pulled them out of place allowing an opening through Caesar's construction. Pompey's ships, towed by oared boats, passed through the opening, although two of the ships fell foul of the works. Caesar's pursuing soldiers with the help of the garrison on the works captured the two ships and the men they carried. It was 17 March.

Caesar immediately wanted to follow Pompey's army, but the proconsul had collected all the ships along the Adriatic coast and sent them to Epirus. It would take months before a suitable number of ships could arrive. Nevertheless, Caesar had captured Italy in only two months.

Section II

War in Spain

Chapter 3

Rome, and the March to Spain

Caesar in Rome

Caesar held Italy but Pompey's escape meant the war was far from over. The first task facing Caesar was calming the disruptions taking hold in Italy. As news spread that Pompey and his senatorial supporters with their dependants had left Brundisium, panic struck their clients, creditors, and related businesses in Rome and Italy. In the last major violent upheaval some thirty years before, when the different sides won and lost, the fighting factions destroyed whole families with their networks of estates and business. Vast amounts of wealth changed hands quickly but not securely. Survivors remembered the fear; they told their sons and daughters, who told their children. Now, fear was everywhere and devastation was coming. Caesar found himself balanced between two different problems: his Gallic army and new recruits, especially the veterans, were looking for wealth and land while at the same time the populace and remaining senators wanted stability and security for themselves and their property.

When Caesar's soldiers had marched south, markets collapsed. Real estate prices fell because the political tumult menaced their titles. Creditors demanded payment but refused to lend. Cicero complained about '*nummorum caritas*' (high coast of coin) as he juggled the finances of his brother Quintus and his own. Added to the financial crisis was the fact there were more than sixty thousand armed, dangerous men looking for wealth and fun along with military officers requisitioning goods at will. Moreover, the grain shipments stopped and famine struck Rome. If Caesar could not calm the situation Italy would descend into anarchy. Only one thing would allow Caesar to control circumstances: he needed money, a lot of money.

His legions, brutal and hard, were Caesar's first concern. After Pompey and his forces sailed to Epirus, Caesar reorganized his forces, inducting new men into veteran cohorts, granting promotions and rewards. He assigned strong garrisons to strategic towns: one, at Brundisium, another at Hydruntum (Otranto), and a third at Tarantum, so his forces dominated the Italian coast opposite Epirus, keeping Pompey at bay. For the moment, Caesar allowed his soldiers to reside in the nearest towns for rest and relaxation while he solved his money problem. The solution was in Rome.

Caesar left Brundisium on 25 March, saw Cicero on the 28th, and arrived in Rome on 31 March. Mark Antony along with an advance party had come to Rome several days ahead of Caesar. They organized a proper reception for Caesar, noting his friends and those not so friendly. Popular feelings leaned toward Pompey more than toward Caesar, but Caesar was the power in Italy and Pompey was far away. Antony convened the Senate outside the walls so Caesar could preside over the meeting. He spoke at some length about the reasons for the war, explaining his position as reasonable and those of his opposition as perverted by hate. But Pompey, he continued, was a reasonable man and they should send a messenger to him to negotiate a peace.

Caesar requested the Senate allow him access to the treasury. This, the Senate granted, but Tribune Lucius Metellus vetoed the permission. Caesar ignored him, questioning his legal competence to act as a tribune, but Metellus went to the treasury and stood guard until Caesar's soldiers arrived. He told them they had no legal permission to open the locked treasury. Curio told Cicero that Caesar's immediate thought was to have Metellus killed but that would ignite a massacre. Caesar needed to keep Rome's good will so he ordered his soldiers to ignore Metellus with the result that several soldiers picked him up and moved him out of their way. They then broke the bars blocking the entrance and pulled out the silver bullion. Caesar took the coin and bullion not only from the public treasury but also all the bullion from the sacred reserve, instituted centuries ago for an emergency defence fund to protect Rome from the Gauls. When some officials questioned the legality of Caesar's withdrawal, he responded that since he had conquered the Gauls, there was no longer any reason for the separate treasury.

Sending a large amount of silver to the mint, Caesar ordered the striking of a new issue of *denarii*, which became one of the largest issues of the Republic. On the obverse, there is an elephant stamping on a snake and on the reverse there are priestly instruments. The meaning of these symbols is clear: Caesar is the elephant, Pompey the serpent, and the coin is struck under the auspices of the High Priest of Rome. Caesar's writings and expressions are always simple and direct, he never beats around the bush or gets over-involved with minutiae. Thus Caesar solved his money problem.

Rome's populace remained suspicious of Caesar: his soldiers took what they wished and threaten to take more, indeed, Caesar seemed to be in the same place as Marius and Sulla, being generous in need but once in power, then what? Caesar understood he needed to approach his enemies in a way quite different from Marius and Sulla. He made it clear that if someone did not threaten violence against him or his followers, he did not consider them enemies, just fellow citizens who disagreed with him. He respected property, only sequestering the holdings of those in arms against him and they were far away in Epirus. He expected to minimize discontent in the city and Italy by providing efficient administration so he put Aemilius Lepidus in charge of Rome, Mark Antony in charge of Italy, Gaius Antonius in Illyria, and Licinius Crassus in Cisalpine Gaul.

Caesar had asked the Senate to appoint envoys to negotiate with Pompey. The Senate had approved the motion but did not find anyone willing to go. For three days, the Senate discussed different ways to send the envoys but accomplished nothing. Tribune L. Metellus, supported by Caesar's enemies obstructed all Caesar's efforts and many days were wasted. Rather than waste more time, he left Rome on 6 April and went further into Gaul to organize his expedition to Spain.

From the time he saw Pompey's ships leaving Brundisium, Caesar had considered his next offensives. He wanted to finish business with Pompey, but Pompey had collected or destroyed all the ships along the Adriatic coast. To bring ships in from the west coast and Sicily in the middle of winter would take months. Caesar's question was whether he could defeat Pompey in the east before Pompey's Spanish legions marched north into Gaul and then invaded Italy while Caesar was occupied with Pompey in the east.

Nothing was final until Caesar had solved his money problem but now, he had to make his decision either to attack east and face Pompey or attack west and remove the Spanish threat first. Pompey would only become stronger the longer Caesar left him to his own devices, but he would never make his eastern forces tougher than Caesar's troops. The Spanish legions were a hard fight, but the rewards were great. Huge silver and gold mines produced most of Rome's bullion; by taking Spain, Caesar would ensure a massive, steady money supply, and cut off one of Pompey's main resources. Caesar decided he would march to Spain but before he marched north, he needed to secure Italy. Pompey's forces held Africa, Sardinia, and Sicily; Caesar needed to push those forces out or cut their supply lines.

The Problems of Africa, Sicily, and Sardinia

Africa was important to Italy, but if the grain shipments came, Caesar could ignore who administered their provinces. The Senate appointed Tubero to govern Africa. But, when Tubero finally sailed there, he found Attius Varus in command. This Varus had commanded at Auximum when Caesar began his offensive. He quickly lost his cohorts and fled to Africa. He had been propraetor in Africa only a few years before. Finding the land in chaos when he landed, Varus quickly assumed command and local authorities readily followed him. He raised a levy, organizing two legions. While he supported the Senate's cause, he and his supporters thought they could manage the African provinces better than some appointee no one knew or knew too well. Varus' fleet met Tubero's ships as they approached Utica and refused to allow them to land. Tubero tried to talk his way to shore, begging to land because of a sick son, but still permission was not granted. Varus remained in command of Africa, solidifying his position by supporting the interests of the great planters who grew the grain that went to Rome and the large shipping concerns that transported it. They were happy as long as they received payment.

After Caesar settled matters in Rome, he sent instructions and money to the coastal towns in the west of Italy to collect all their serviceable ships. He assigned ships to his legate Valerius and to his propraetor Curio. Valerius sailed with one legion to Sardinia. The island was in the hands of M. Cotta when Valerius was fitting out his transport fleet. In the capital of Sardinia, Caralis, a popular rising expelled Cotta from the town. Fearing the whole island was against him, Cotta fled from Sardinia, travelling to Africa. Valerius occupied Caralis on 20 May and Sardinia was Caesar's.

Propraetor Curio with two legions sailed to Sicily. M. Cato governed the island for the Senate, overseeing the repair of old warships and building new ones, while his agents recruited fresh troops in southern Italy and Sicily. Hearing about Curio's approach, Cato complained bitterly that Pompey had led him and the Senate into an untenable spot by entering an unnecessary war without any preparation. Curio sent his legate, Asinius Pollio, to Messina. Cato arrived and asked Pollio if he had a senatorial order to take over the administration of Sicily. Pollio replied, 'The ruler of Italy has sent me to conduct his matters', and told Cato that Curio was bringing the main force. Cato responded that to spare lives he would leave without resistance and he fled Sicily on 23 April.

The Battle for Spain Begins

Pompey and his staff in Dyrrachium considered their withdrawal from Italy a strategic retreat. Their concern was how to defeat Caesar and restore the Republic. Caesar's main strength was his army of Gaul and although he now controlled Italy, there were enough people there who did not support him to allow a successful counter-attack when the time came. Pompey's strength rested in sea power which he understood and had directed successful naval operations. Caesar knew about sea power but his experience in Gaul was, for the most part, on land. Should Caesar cross over the Adriatic, Pompey could cut his communications with Italy. Pompey saw Massilia as the key to the Western Mediterranean and by holding Massilia, he forced Caesar to go overland if he wished to attack Spain. Pompey had seen to this before he left Italy and arranged the pressures and inducements to accomplish this objective. His agents throughout the Roman lands spread rumours: Pompey was in Africa, he was going to march along the seashore to the south of Spain to attack north into Gaul; Pompey was leading his army north, through Illyricum into Gaul.

Pompey sent Vibullius Rufus to Spain with directives for his Spanish forces. Second only to Caesar's Gallic veteran army, Pompey's Spanish army was the strongest military force in the Mediterranean. He had three loyal and experienced commanders in Spain: Afranius in Nearer Spain with three legions; Petreius in Further Spain from the pass of Castillo to Anas with two legions; and Varro with two legions in the lands of the Vettones running from the Anas through Lusitania. Lucius Afranius, Pompey's personal friend and Consul for 60 BC, was the acknowledged leader in Spain.

Vibullius conferred with Pompey's Spanish commanders. They would defend the Spanish provinces by concentrating forces in the northeast of Spain. Either Caesar would come by the coast road, where he could easily find supplies but face the series of fortresses guarding the route or he could come through the mountains, where both sides would have supply difficulties, but he might think he could do better with a smaller but well-organised army. Initially Petreius would march from Lusitania through the lands of the Vettones with all the forces he could muster, while Varro would stay and defend Further Spain with his two legions. The legates raised tribal troops from their subjects. Once organized, Petreius marched his troops to the northeast joining with Afranius's troops there. The force collected to face Caesar: Afranius' three legions, Petreius' two legions together with some eighty cohorts of well-disciplined tribal troops, some armed as legion infantry, the rest as light infantry and about ten thousand tribal cavalry. These commanders posted small detachments on the frontiers of their provinces and at the heads of passes to warn of Caesar's approach.

While the Spanish armies mobilized, Caesar ordered three veteran legions camped at Brundisium to march north toward Massilia and he soon followed through Nearer Gaul toward Massilia. His agents in Pompey's camp confirmed Pompey's interests in that town. The coming Spanish campaign was not an easy prospect as Caesar saw that forces from Massilia could block his supply routes. He either had to control Massilia or mask the town with a strong blockade. Soon, he heard news that the people of Massilia supported Pompey and the Republic. They closed their gates, refurbished their walls, and received assistance from the nearby Albici People who long had recognized Massilia suzerainty. The townsmen stockpiled grain and materials to make weapons and set up workshops for manufacturing arms and armour.

When he approached Massilia, Caesar summoned fifteen important men of the town. He declared to them that it was unwise to resist the legitimate requests of Italian authority. He would take the town if necessary. After returning to Massilia, the men report Caesar's message to the town council and people. They send back their answer: *'Understanding the Roman People are now divided into two factions, one led by Gn. Pompey and the other by G. Caesar, we cannot make the decision which is right. We have received great benefit from both men. Therefore, we are neutral in this matter and will not support either man.'*

While Caesar continued negotiating with the leaders at Massilia, Domitius the defender of Corfinium, arrived at Massilia with a fleet. The town welcomed him as a legitimate representative of Rome. Domitius had seized seven large merchant ships in Italian ports and he staffed these with his own slaves, freedmen, and tenants. He had made common cause with a group of important young men of Massilia, representatives of families that had long received Pompey's patronage. The young men were returning to Massilia after leaving Rome when Caesar had taken over. Embarking the young men on his ships, Domitius' fleet had sailed to Massilia.

Appointed as commander of military forces at Massilia, Domitius ordered the Massilian fleet to sail out into the western Mediterranean, seize all the merchant ships they could find and bring them back to Massilia. Their craftsmen converted the captured ships into instruments of war, cannibalizing some ships to provide for the rest. The town authorities increased stockpiles of food and stored the other goods, preparing for a blockade. Caesar was ready for this contingency. He ordered Arelate to build twelve warships, finishing them in only a month and send them to Massilia. Also, the three veteran legions coming from Brundisium were about to arrive. Caesar organized a strong blockade of Massilia. He placed the sea forces under D. Brutus and appointed G. Trebonius supreme commander in the area.

While Caesar planned the siege of Massilia, he sent his legate, G. Fabius, into Spain leading three legions which had wintered around Narbo. He had carefully considered which route to take. The main military road ran along the coast down to the mouth of the Ebro and Caesar's informants told him that Afranius and Petreius expected that he would come that way. Instead,

Caesar decided to order his army to march through the Pyrenees to the upper reaches of the Sicoris River and then move south to Ilerda. His objectives were the Pyrenees passes now garrisoned by Afranius' detachments. Once Fabius seized the passes, Afranius knew that Caesar's army was coming this way. Afranius marched strong forces to hold Ilerda. In support of Fabius' campaign, Caesar had ordered the rest of his Gallic field army to follow which consisted of six legions with five thousand auxiliary infantry. He also sent his three thousand cavalry personal guard and another three thousand cavalry recruited from the Gallic nobles who supported him. And, as a final preparation to bind his forces together, Caesar borrowed money from his tribunes and centurions, at interest, and awarded the moneys to his soldiers. He did this to ensure his officers were invested in his campaigns and to gain the goodwill of the soldiers.

Fabius marched with his three legions out of the mountains toward Ilerda along paths which followed the river Sicoris. As the legions marched south, Fabius sent agents to local tribes and communities, giving them presents and letters granting rewards for supporting Caesar. The legions built two bridges over the winding Sicoris four miles apart and set up a camp near Ilerda. The Pompeians had foraged the lands near the river, removing all useful materials so Fabius had to send out long-distance foraging parties. When Afranius and Petreius, in command of Ilerda, saw Fabius's forces arrive they dispatched strong cavalry patrols to harass his foragers. Fabius's cavalry took up Afranius' challenge and on-going skirmishes rumbled across the landscape.

Rather than have his cavalry withstand the worst of Afranius' attacks, Fabius sent two legions across the nearest bridge to protect a large group of foragers with their pack train and provide cover for the cavalry force. Suddenly, a severe rain and windstorm struck the area, unexpected in its power. Evidently the storm had drenched mountains to the north for some time. The river Sicoris swelled and swept Fabius' nearest bridge away, trapping both legions, the foragers, their pack animals, and cavalry on the wrong side of the river. The flood carried the bridge wreckage, loose fascines and fixtures, past Ilerda. When Afranius and Petreius saw the wreckage, they supposed that the storm had destroyed Fabius' bridge and his foragers were in trouble. Afranius ordered four legions and all his cavalry across Ilerda's stone bridge. Assuming battle formation, the four legions advanced against Fabius' two.

These two legions were commanded by the veteran L. Plancus who ordered them to retreat to higher ground. There, Plancus ordered the legions into a back-to-back formation, protecting their rear. The four Pompeian legions and cavalry attacked Plancus' two, but the higher ground and all-around defence allowed the two legions to repel the Pompeian forces. The two cavalry forces then engaged, swirling around each other. Soon, each side saw an approaching mass marching under the standards of two legions. Fabius, once he heard about the ruined bridge, assumed that the Pompeians would attack his foragers and their support. He sent two legions at double time across the furthest bridge and when these formations approached the battlefield, the Pompeians broke off the fight and returned to their camp. Fabius' foragers, cavalry and four legions marched across the further bridge and returned to their camp. Fabius had established the Caesarians' hold in the north of Spain but how long he could keep his position in front of the Pompeians' growing power remained a question.

Chapter 4

War in Spain

Caesar Arrives

Just two days after Fabius' victory, on 23 June Caesar arrived with his personal guard of 900 elite cavalry. The damaged bridge was undergoing repair and Caesar ordered it finished even if the craftsmen had to work through the night. After studying the lay of the land, he drew his large baggage train into Fabius' camp and chose six cohorts to guard the camp and bridge. The next day, Caesar marched the rest of his forces out of the camp and advanced in the three-ranked battle formation to Ilerda. This formation stopped near Afranius's camp and stood to arms, offering battle. Afranius marched his army out of his camp and formed up in line of battle, stationing his men on the steep slope just below the fortified stockade of his camp. Afranius refused to advance but would receive Caesar's attack. Caesar saw that advancing up the slope was no way to fight even for his excellent soldiers.

Rather than make a bloody assault, Caesar decided to build a camp about a thousand feet from the foot of the slope leading to Afranius' camp and close to Ilerda. If Afranius' centurions saw workers constructing a camp behind Caesar's soldiers, they would surely assault Caesar's line. Rather than having his working troops panicked by a sudden attack, Caesar ordered the work to progress without constructing a palisade on top, invisible to Afranius. The work proceeded with a fifteen-foot-wide trench facing the Pompeian forces which was masked by Caesar's troops. His first and second lines remained under arms facing Afranius' pressure while his third line secretly dug the camp's trenches. Toward sunset, Caesar stood down his first and second lines and withdrew the soldiers to the trench where they settled for the night.

The next day he stationed his main force behind the trenches. He ordered the transport of rocks and wood from some distance to build a strong rampart around the expanded campsite. Caesar instructed three legions to dig trenches and erect ramparts, each on its side of the square, enclosing the camp. The remaining legions he placed between the Pompeians and his new camp. They stood in open order, armed with missiles and supported by archers, so should Afranius decide to attack, the lightly armed troops could hold them off until the other legions could get into battle order.

Afranius and Petreius saw what Caesar was accomplishing. They sent several cohorts down the hillside to threaten Caesar's troops, but rather than sound the general alarm, Caesar trusted the three legions he posted in front of the construction work would hold off any spoiling attack. The Pompeians decided not to take the risk of a full-scale assault but withdrew into their camp. On the third day, after Caesar's men finished their camp, he brought in the rest of his cohorts with his baggage and abandoned Fabius' old camp.

Between the town of Ilerda and the Pompeian camp stretched a plain of about a thousand feet in the middle of which rose an isolated prominence. Caesar thought by occupying the hill he could cut off the Pompeian's forces from the supplies in Ilerda. Out of his camp, he marched three legions in battle order toward the hill. Once they reached within striking distance of the slope, Caesar ordered a select unit of the advanced guard to charge the hill. When they started running, Afranius' cohorts stationed in front of his camp also started running toward the hill, and they were closer than Caesar's soldiers. Afranius' men reached the hill before Caesar's men and the sides clashed in battle with Caesar's men having to retreat. Caesar sent in another group of men, but they also had to retreat behind his deployed three legions.

The tactics used by Pompey's Spanish legions surprised Caesar's soldiers. After years of fighting Spanish tribes, the soldiers had adopted the Spanish tribes' methods of attack, which proved effective against Caesar's Gallic-trained troops. Cohorts charged their opponents not as close-ranked armoured infantry but open-order light troops, with spears, arrows and slings, striking at the enemy then swiftly running off to a distance. Well trained and practised, the Spanish soldiers threw Caesar's attack formations into confusion because by striking here, retreating there, they appeared to be everywhere. Caesar had taken great pains to train his men to keep ranks, stay with their standards, and stand their ground. When the Pompeian cohorts struck Caesar's troops, confusion took hold of both centurions and soldiers. Not being able to devise a practical course of action, the formations fled in confusion, pulling the Pompeian troops with them. Retreating past the exposed wing of Caesar's three legions, the panicked troops dragged the exposed wing with them.

The collapse of his legions surprised Caesar. He called on his men to stand firm, ordered his attendant centurions to bring up the IX Legion, which soon came to him, then personally led the IX toward the walls of Ilerda. The threat of the IX reaching Ilerda frightened the Pompeian commanders because Caesar's soldiers might sweep over the wall and plunder their stocks.

They withdrew the attacking Pompeian soldiers, ordering them to rush to Ilerda's wall to defend them. Unfortunately, three cohorts of the IX pushing up the hill on which Ilerda sat entered rough ground facing a steep rocky escarpment. They found themselves trapped in ground dominated by nearby heights. When they tried to withdraw, arrows and rocks rained down on them, causing many serious injuries. The three cohorts found themselves trapped in a closed space, blocked on both sides by precipitous descents, and faced a steep ascent. If they pulled back, the enemies' missiles would cause severe casualties while help was cut off from both sides.

In front of the IX's three cohorts, the ground rose slightly toward Ilerda's walls for about 1,200 feet. Here, the cohorts stood, facing their enemies. The enemy troops above rained missiles from the heights on three sides. The Pompeian commanders sent fresh cohorts to relieve those who had fought a long time, making certain their men did not become fatigued. Caesar sent fresh cohorts through the missile storm to reinforce the three-cohort front, allowing battered worn-out cohorts to withdraw. After five hours, Caesar's forces had defied the Pompeians' efforts to crush them despite high casualties. The men dressed their ranks and, swords in hand, charged up the hill toward Ilerda's wall. They cut down the first enemies they met and the rest fled. The IX cohorts reached the town wall and began to climb over. While the wall remained well defended, the Pompeians stopped their missile attack and opened a route for the cohorts to withdraw which they did. As the three cohorts carefully retired down, away from Ilerda, Caesar's cavalry rode up through the broken ground to interpose themselves between the IX infantry and the Pompeians, allowing the infantry to leave the field without fear of surprise attack.

The engagement was costly to both sides. In the first attack on the hill, Caesar's force lost about seventy men dead, including the First Centurion of the XIV Legion and some 600 wounded. Pompey's side lost five centurions and more than 200 men. Both sides claimed they did better than their opponents, given the situation. The result, however, was that the Pompeians not only held the hill in question but fortified it.

Supply Problems

Even though his effort to seize the strategic height near Ilerda failed, Caesar maintained forceful pressure on the Pompeians. Reinforcements and supplies were coming over the mountains; with these, he would push the Pompeians even harder, forcing them to see the errors of their ways and join Caesar. In Rome, his supporters looked forward to his continuing victories, and in

Spain his army was confident in his leadership. By the end of June (solar calendar, early May), Caesar's continued success for six months had brought many supporters to his party and disheartened many in Pompey's senatorial party.

Then, misfortune struck. Two days after the battle in the hills, on 29 June a wild storm blew down from the mountains and across the plains near Ilerda. The river Sicoris overflowed its banks, carrying away both bridges Fabius had built. To the west, the river Cinga also flooded, leaving Caesar's camp and army isolated. Tribes friendly to Caesar to the north and west could not deliver supplies; enemies cut off his foraging parties and blocked the large supply trains coming from Gaul and Italy. Caesar depended on those supply trains to reprovision his camp as food stocks and fodder were low. Afranius's camp, on the other hand, was well-provisioned. Using the stone bridge across the Sicoris River the Pompeians kept supplies and fodder coming.

The Sicoris remained flooded for a week. Caesar's men had to wait until the damaging floods subsided before they could cross the river, but the current remained swift, and the Pompeians kept men well-armed with missiles posted opposite crossing sites. Caesar's caravans of supplies and reinforcements had to camp to the north behind the flooded rivers. His stalled caravans included official legations from Rome and allied states, the sons of important people coming to join him, sutlers, representatives of different interests along with suppliers in a wagon train of some six thousand people including wives, children, and slaves. Behind the first caravan, there was another long train with Ruteni archers and Gallic cavalry. The Pompeian agents brought word to Afranius about the backed-up caravans. He marched out of Ilerda at night across the stone bridge with three legions and all his cavalry.

Afranius marched his force toward the massive collection of soldiers, wagons, goods, families, and slaves. Out of the dawn, his cavalry attacked along a widespread front. The Gallic cavalry quickly organized and assailed the Pompeians. Afranius' cavalry could not break this smaller force. When the Gallic defenders, who lost only a few men, saw the standards of Afranius' legions coming in the distance, they turned and withdrew to nearby hills. Still, the battle with the Gallic cavalry lasted long enough for the caravan masters to organize their charges, move to high ground, and construct an impromptu camp. In the battles that day, the Caesarians lost about 200 archers, a few cavalrymen, and some camp followers and livestock. Afranius' legions and cavalry camped, waiting to overwhelm Caesar's trains the next morning.

The stoppage of his reinforcements and caravans left Caesar's camp in great need. The price of corn went up and up, not only because of actual dearth, but because many now feared Caesar's cause was lost. Caesar did what he could, seizing and buying cattle to supplement the food supplies and putting a good face on a dire situation, but all he really could do for the moment was wait. Afranius and Petreius were overjoyed to see Caesar's troubles and out of what they saw, they made more. The Pompeians sent letters to Rome, saying how the war was over and they would soon capture Caesar's supplies and repulse his reinforcements and that Caesar was at the end of his career. Pompey's followers in Rome celebrated their coming victory by leaving Italy to join Pompey's camp in Epirus, some so they could be among the first to bring news of victory to Pompey, others so they would not be last to join the victor.

But Caesar had other ideas. He ordered his craftsmen to construct light boats, such as he had used in Britannia some years before. Built upon keels made from bound branches, with frontal framing ribs securely attached, the craftsmen fabricated hulls of twisted wattling in a hide covering. The boats they manufactured were about twelve feet long and five feet wide. The design of these boats allowed two wagons coupled together to carry one boat and easily transported them for long distances. Once the night darkened, Caesar accompanied the boat-wagon train, defended by a legion, while they marched twenty-two miles to a river site, out of view of the Pompeian scouts.

As dawn broke on 12 July, Caesar's men launched the boats, transporting an advance guard across the river. While the boats continually crossed to the far side, bringing more men, those already there began digging in, fortifying the crossing site with a deep trench in front of a rampart. Caesar sent an entire legion to the far side and had his engineers begin constructing a stout bridge. Just as he bridged the Rhine with a sturdy bridge built on piles, so in just two days, working from both banks of the river, Caesar's men completed the bridge. Caesar had sent messengers to the supply caravan camps and his foraging parties. Soon the supply trains, envoys, auxiliary forces with their families crossed the bridge and travelled toward Caesar's camp.

He stopped the trains crossing the bridge for a brief time while sending the greater part of his cavalry across to the far side. Moving out in a large, organized formation, the horsemen swept across the plains and hills. They came upon parties of Pompeian foragers and supply dumps, cut down the men, and gathered up the goods. As they advanced, the cavalry isolated large groups of Pompeians with their livestock. Afranius sent out light cohorts to rescue the men and recover the livestock. Caesar's cavalry peeled off a strong force to guard the booty and direct the goods toward the bridge, allowing the rest to engage the light cohorts advancing on them. One cohort advanced toward the cavalry and the horsemen surrounded the cohort and killed them all. The cavalry returned and crossed the bridge without loss and much booty. When Caesar returned to his camp, news came of his victorious naval battle at Massilia.

Caesar Seizes the Initiative

Unexpected storms upset Caesar's schedule of operations, but his most remarkable military talent was his ability to respond to adversity with imagination and insight. Once he restored his communications, he knew that his massive reinforcement so overwhelmed the Pompeians that there was little they could do to either defeat or, indeed, to withstand his forces. Immediately, he pushed his troops across the bridge. The cavalry reinforcements added to those already with Caesar made his covering force formidable; the Pompeian cavalry avoided engagement with Caesar's horse; more, they ceased foraging anywhere near Caesar's forces. They fled whenever his forces came near, stayed in camp during the day and only went out foraging at night. What succeeded on the field echoed throughout the land. When Fabius had initially arrived, he contacted local Celtic settlements, looking to gain their support. Later, Caesar had continued to contact the Celtic groups. When the issue was in doubt, the Celts stayed in nominal allegiance to Pompey. After Caesar forced his way through the Pompeian forces to receive his reinforcements and supplies, he began looking like a better investment than Pompey. The rumours about Pompey's approach through Mauritania proved false, and the news of Caesar's victory over Pompey's fleet appeared accurate. Soon, five major Celtic settlements, one on the river Iberus (River Ebro), pledged allegiance to Caesar who requested his new allies to send corn. Long trains of pack animals came to the camp while distant states also abandoned the Pompeians and joined Caesar. The Iberus settlement had allowed the Pompeians to recruit a cohort of their men as part of their army, but the men abandoned them and joined Caesar's army instead.

Once he secured his communications and made important alliances with Celtic powers, Caesar knew that he needed to construct a nearer path across the Sicoris River to increase pressure on the Pompeians. The bridge he had built was strong but was forty miles to the north. His engineers identified a stretch of rapids about three miles from their camp and Ilerda where, with a little work, they could fabricate a manageable ford across the River Sicoris. Caesar was always at his best when he could call on his engineers who were able to construct works that changed battlefield conditions to a degree unimagined by Caesar's opponents. His engineers designed a network of canals to divide the river into several channels, each thirty feet wide, allowing workers to construct a path that forded the river. From the top of Ilerda's fortress, Afranius and Petreius saw Caesar's labourers digging channels. They conferred with their staff, looking at alternative actions. Once Caesar had reopened his communications, his strength could only increase while Afranius and Petreius could not build up a much larger force than those at hand. If they pulled a significant force north to Ilerda, their supply lines were more vulnerable than ever. On the other hand, if they pulled their forces south to the Hiberus, they would secure their supplies and face Caesar. They decided to move their operations about thirty miles to Octogesa.

Near the Iberus, Octogesa was well fortified and stood on a strong site. The Pompeian commanders ordered the erection of a bridge of boats over the Iberus, planning to make Octogesa a centrally located base from which they could thwart Caesar. Loyal settlements up and down the Iberus had sent supplies, cavalry and auxiliary troops, to Octogesa. Afranius and Petreius hoped to spend the winter there but first they had to get there. The Pompeians marched two legions out of Ilerda, across the Sicoris on their stone bridge, ready to march toward Octogesa. Scouts brought news of the Pompeians' movements to Caesar while he oversaw the canal digging. He understood he needed to act for should the Pompeians make their way to Octogesa and access their bridge of boats, he would lose all his hard-won advantages because the Pompeians would gain access to plentiful supplies and all the reinforcements they could wish for. Further, with the loss of his advantage, Caesar's allies would look to their own advantage. Despite his excavations requiring more time, Caesar sent his force of cavalry.

When Afranius and Petreius saw Caesar's cavalry fording the Sicoris, they hastened their move out of Ilerda. Leaving two Spanish cohorts in the town, they pulled out in the night of 24-25 July, crossed the Sicoris, and marched to the two legions who had left the day before. The force carried twenty-two days' worth of corn for the legions, but the auxiliary troops had to find their supplies. Caesar sent his cavalry to harass the Pompeians' march while directing his supply trains north, over the bridge he had constructed after the flood. After midnight the Pompeians abandoned their camp, seeking to steal a march on Caesar's cavalry. Soon, however, his cavalry created consternation in the Pompeian rear and along their flanks.

Standing on the heights above their camp near Ilerda, Caesar's soldiers watched their cavalry fight with the Pompeian infantry. At times, the cavalry cut off parts of their enemy's column. The Pompeians formed up in a mass of cohorts and charged the cavalry, scattering it here and there, and then the Pompeians resumed their march and the cavalry formed up again. Caesar's men talked together, upset because they saw the war continuing needlessly. They discussed their concerns with their centurions and military tribune commanders and while they proclaimed their willingness to battle against the enemy and the elements, they begged Caesar to lead them to the fight. They were willing to cross the river in the same way as the cavalry.

Caesar was a superb and subtle leader of men who always avoided the charge of being a commander who built his success on the corpses of his men. Still, soldiers had to fight to win. If Caesar ordered his legions to cross a deep and swift river and the flood swept many away, then obviously, Caesar did not care about his men, only about his reputation. On the other hand, should the men demand to cross the river, why then, Caesar was propelled forward by his brave men who loved him, and great was the success of his men who cared not about their own lives so Caesar might prevail. A nod here, the unspoken word there, a few small bags of *denarii* passing around, and suddenly men were clamouring for Caesar to lead them across the river.

Moved by the enthusiasm of his men, Caesar prepared the river crossing. First, he instructed each centurion to pull out from the ranks any man who did not have the stamina or desire to withstand the river crossing. Caesar left these men with his weakest legion to hold his camp. Then he ordered his legions to strip down their equipment to cross, bearing a minimum of weight. Those in charge of supplies led trains of packhorses across the river, some above the crossing spot, to break the current and some below. The men marched through the water between the trains. A few men were swept off their feet and carried away by the current, but the men holding the lower pack train caught them all. Caesar did not lose a single man.

Once across, his army put on their trappings, took up their shields, and formed up in triple line battle array. The soldiers moved forward in double-time and by afternoon, they had caught up with Pompey's troops, who had started from Ilerda just after midnight. A lookout on a high prominence reported to Afranius that Caesar's troops were approaching. After Afranius saw the lines of soldiers spread out in the distance, he directed his troops to higher ground, where he formed them in battle order. Caesar saw this manoeuvre and put his men at rest to save them from exhaustion. Then Afranius ordered his men into marching order and began heading for the cover of rough ground, which was only about five miles away. Caesar brought his legions to march order and they moved quickly to head off the

Pompeians. When Afranius saw Caesar's men were ahead of him, he halted his march. Although it was just mid-afternoon, the Pompeians made camp.

Afranius' salvation was close. If he could reach those hills and defiles, he easily could delay Caesar's advance with small detachments blocking all the routes. That way, he could march most of his men to and over the Iberus and he had a chance of defeating Caesar – so said Caesar in his commentary. No matter what it took, that is what Afranius should have done, but, instead, he took account of his men's fatigue and rather than marching, they camped and decided to start again in the morning.

Caesar advanced to the nearest hill and camped. He had cavalry pickets out, keeping eyes on the Pompeians. Near midnight, at a creek where Pompeian water carriers went, the horsemen grabbed a Pompeian soldier who told them that Afranius was in the process of silently pulling out of the camp to get to the rough ground. Caesar immediately ordered the horns to blow and the drums to beat the signal to break camp. The Pompeians, as Caesar intended, heard the noise of Romans breaking camp. Sudden fear took hold of officers and men: fear of being caught by Caesar's fast-moving legions while they were out of formation, over-loaded with baggage, and forced to fight in the dark. The Pompeians returned to their camp.

The next day, scouts from both camps spent the morning looking at the landscape to see the different ways an army might march. Each side discovered the same thing: the troops were sitting in a flat plain. About five miles away, along one side, there was rough and rocky ground that could provide excellent defensive positions so that an army, defending paths and heights with a few men, could reach Octogesa and the Iberus – but the Pompeians might gain this advantage only if they got to the hills first.

Chapter 5

The War in Spain Conclusion

Afranius Attempts to Escape

The Pompeian commanders met in council. Afranius and Petreius asked whether they should evacuate their camp in the coming night or wait until dawn. Some suggested they go at night, taking care to ensure secrecy. Reaching the rough country was easy, provided that Caesar did not know they were leaving. Others pointed out that Caesar kept a close watch and would know as soon as they started to pull out. More importantly, if they had to fight in the dark, order and discipline were lost, but in the light of day, officers saw their men and the men knew they were in the view of others. After discussion, they agreed that they would leave the following day.

But they did not leave the camp in the morning. As the light sprang up on the eastern horizon, Caesar led his troops out from his camp, marching away. When the Pompeian men saw Caesar marching away, they assumed he was returning to Ilerda and they ran out of their camp, congratulating each other that Caesar had run out of supplies and had to retreat. The officers basked in their praise; their strategy was successful. However, their problem was their inability to comprehend Caesar's determination or his subtelty in manoeuvre. His march took a path away from both camps, then, out of sight of the Pompeians, turned in a half-circle toward the rough lands.

The Pompeians kept watch on Caesar's departing soldiers and scouts followed at a distance. After some time, they saw the columns swinging to the right; then, the lead elements marched beyond the line of their camp. Suddenly, the situation became clear: Caesar had outflanked them. Running back to their camp, they told the officers about Caesar's manoeuvre. The cry, 'To arms!' rang out. The Pompeians' whole force fell in, appointed a few cohorts to guard the camp and baggage, and doubled-marched towards the Iberus.

As the two armies raced for the hills, Caesar's soldiers cut across the country against the landscape's grain while the Pompeians had to turn every so often to repel Caesar's cavalry. For Caesar, no matter what happened, the result was clear: he had the Pompeians pinned. Even if they reached the hills first, they had lost their baggage and cohorts left in their camp.

Caesar's men cut across rocky heights and descended into the plain in front of the advancing Pompeians. The appearance of Caesar's army in front and his cavalry behind shocked the Pompeian commanders. They ordered the legions to pivot and occupy a nearby hill, taking a defensive stance. Afranius selected four cohorts of light troops and directed them to run to a high ridge and establish a fortified camp. Once they had gained a foothold on the ridge, Afranius planned to march the whole Pompeian force there, fighting off Caesar's soldiers, as necessary. From the top of the spine, they would march along the line of the heights to Octogesa.

As the light cohorts rushed across the plain, Caesar's cavalry saw them. The cavalry commanders ordered attack formation and charged the light troops. Swerving around the infantry, the horsemen repeatedly struck at the lightly armoured men from all sides. With their small shields, the cohorts could not avoid the spears and arrows of the horsemen. In the sight of both armies, Caesar's cavalry slaughtered the Pompeian cohorts.

Caesar, surrounded by his staff and main centurions, saw the Pompeians huddled together on the top of their hill. All their standards stood together with the men crowded around. No one made a move to help the light troops while Caesar's cavalry slaughtered them. Their soldiers did not form ranks and files but massed in groups. Staff members and lead centurions spoke out: now is the time to attack and finish this fight! Cohorts sent messengers saying they were ready to attack! But Mighty Caesar forebears: our opponents are fellow citizens of Rome; we need to convince them to surrender and avoid pointless bloodshed. (At least, this is what Caesar wrote in his account of this campaign.)

Caesar pulled back rather than threatening attack, opening a path for the Pompeians to withdraw off the hill and return to their camp. Simultaneously, he posted guard units at the defiles leading into the mountains so the Pompeians could not escape easily. After the Pompeians settled in their camp, Caesar camped his army nearby.

The following day, the Pompeian officers conferred together and took stock of their position. They could not reach the Iberus; the only alternatives were to march to Tarraco (Tarraco in Tarragona) or return to Ilerda. They were not going to receive supplies; water was available, but Caesar's cavalry threatened the carriers. Without water, they were lost. Distributing cavalry squads, bands of auxiliary troops, and regular cohorts along the water path, Afranius and Petreius began constructing a fortified passageway from their camp to the water, the officers working alongside the men.

While the officers and troops were working on the water path, those left in the camp walked to Caesar's camp ramparts. Calling out, they asked about friends and relatives in Caesar's legions. The Pompeians talked with the Caesarians about the position in which they all found themselves. Finding Caesar more trustworthy than their commanders, they tried to negotiate a surrender. Their only demand was that neither Afranius nor Petreius be killed. While these talks continued, many soldiers, centurions and military tribunes came to see Caesar and some of his officers went to the Pompeian camp. Caesar pledged leniency, and his previous actions showed this was trustworthy. The soldiers and officers congratulated themselves that the war was over for them.

Defeat Comes to Afranius

News of fraternization between the soldiers came to the officers and men constructing the water path. Afranius immediately returned, not particularly upset with the turn of events. Petreius, on the other hand, was not about to give up. He armed his retainers, called up his staff, and surrounded himself with his barbarian horse guards. He charged up to his camp's rampart, scattering the soldiers who were talking together. His soldiers, he sent back into his camp, but Caesar's soldiers, he had cut down. His soldiers, fearing the worst, wrapped their cloaks around their left hands, drew their swords, and backed toward the guards defending the gate. Petreius entered the camp and calmed the upheaval.

Going around his camp, Petreius restored discipline and order. He called the soldiers to an assembly in front of the praetorium and demanded they take an oath to uphold Pompey and the Senate. He took the pledge himself, gave it to Afranius, followed by the military tribunes, centurions, and soldiers, administered century by century. He had the camp searched for any Caesarian soldiers. Petreius ordered immediate execution for all of Caesar's soldiers found within his camp in front of the assembly. The state of war between the camps had returned. (28 July)

The conspicuous ferment in the Pompeian camp broke the calm in Caesar's camp. Escaping Caesarean soldiers brought tales of slaughter and threats. Caesar made it clear that Pompeian soldiers in his camp should return to their camp. Many military tribunes and centurions, however, requested he allow them to join his forces. They, no doubt, were clear about who commanded the winning side. Caesar accepted them and maintained their rank and pay schedules.

The Pompeians were in trouble and the whole army knew it. They could not batter their way through Caesar's legions; their basic ration of corn to make porridge was secure, but there was no foraging, and getting water was a problem. However, while the legionaries were fed adequately, the auxiliary troops had no supplies other than what they could scrounge. Many auxiliary troopers left Africanus' camp and joined Caesar every day because they received food. Meanwhile in their camp the Pompeian commanders planned their next move. Tarraco would solve all their problems, but it was too far away so they decided to return to Ilerda, where they still had stores of supplies. They pulled out and started their march to return to where they started.

Caesar sent his cavalry to harass the Pompeian rear and he then followed with his legions. This time, the Pompeians were ready for him. Officers and men devised new tactics to continue marching despite the efforts of Caesar's cavalry. A select group of cohorts held the rear of the marching column; they faced the approaching cavalry, repelling them with missiles while shielding themselves. While the first group met the cavalry, a second moved swiftly down the road to take a stand, and the first group withdrew past them.

If the army's route ascended, the natural protection offered by the terrain helped them repel any danger easily because the men marching in front could use their higher position to protect their comrades who were climbing up behind them. Still, when they had to cross a valley or declining slope, those who were ahead could not help those coming later because Caesar's cavalry kept throwing missiles from their higher positions against opponents who had their backs turned. In these situations, the Pompeians' answer was to turn the legions about and charge the cavalry. Once they pushed them back, the legions turned and ran down to the level plains, where the cohorts resumed their tactics. And so, the Pompeians marched across heights and valleys, one after another. Their cavalry was useless and needed protection from Caesar's cavalry within formations of the marching legions.

Proceeding this way, the Pompeians marched about four miles, advancing, halting, and fighting. The army reached a steep hill, climbed the slope and made camp. They dug a trench and built a rampart facing one side, one with an easy ascent. They did not unload their baggage animals, indicating they were not going to stay long. Caesar soon came with his legions and seeing the Pompeians settled, he ordered the legions to camp and set up their tents while sending the cavalry out to forage. At about noon, seeing Caesar's men well occupied in camp routines, the Pompeians suddenly set themselves in motion, descending the hill and marching away. Caesar saw this, ordered the legions to pack up, and left a few cohorts to guard the baggage. He marched after the Pompeians, recalled his cavalry, and ordered the foragers to follow with the baggage in the evening.

Caesar's cavalry quickly caught up with the Pompeians and launched into harassing their rearguard again. This time the cavalry was prepared for the Pompeians' tactics: fighting was fierce and many soldiers and even centurions fell. After days of trying to evade Caesar, the soldiers were tired and dispirited, they understood that Caesar's cavalry was dangerous, and his legions were deadly. Caesar had trapped the Pompeians and now, he threatened their destruction. The Pompeian officers decided to camp where they were because they could no longer face Caesar's soldiers. While trying to escape from Caesar, the Pompeians had pushed deeper into the wild country. There was no water where they camped, they were running short on supplies, had no fodder and little water. But Caesar's forces no longer threatened attack.

Rather than attack and kill many Roman citizens, even though they opposed him in arms, Caesar intended that they should voluntarily surrender because of the lack of water. He did not attend camp but allowed his soldiers to rest so they could swiftly follow the Pompeians if they tried to escape again. In their camp, fortified with trenches and ramparts, the Pompeians searched for water by digging deep holes, but they found nothing. They moved their search area in the night by extending their trench-rampart lines to enclose a new space where they dug seep holes during the day. The next day they repeated the operation. The results were that they exhausted themselves and still found no water.

Meanwhile, Caesar had his men build trenches enclosing the Pompeian camps. In one last effort to solve their predicament, the Pompeians sent out many men to search for a water source somewhere nearby. They found that they were near the River Sicoris, so, if they could get to the river, they could solve their water problem, but right now, without fodder or water, their animals were getting weaker and began dying. The Pompeians killed many of their pack animals so they would have more food and blood to drink.

Since the Pompeians halted, three days had passed. Caesar's men had started to construct a trenched blockade of the enemy camp, but it was not completed. The Pompeians were at the end of their strength but decided to disrupt Caesar's trench work. They put their army into battle formation and marched out of camp in the mid-afternoon, drawing up their battle lines. Caesar immediately had the alert sounded and ordered his force to deploy. He had no intention of launching an attack because, while his forces would undoubtedly prevail, the Pompeians would quickly withdraw into their camp. Further, the camps were only 2,000 paces apart, and the two deployed armies together occupied two-thirds of this space, so only less than 700 paces separated the two battle formations.

The five Pompeian legions formed two lines with a third line consisting of their auxiliary cohorts. Caesar's five legions formed three lines: the first line consisted of four cohorts from each of the five legions, so twenty cohorts formed the first line. Three reserve cohorts from each legion stood in the second line, and the third line also included included three cohorts from each legion. So, Caesar's legions lined up in a vertical formation, legion next to the legion. Archers and slingers stood in the enclosed open spaces, with the cavalry forming wings on each flank. Both armies stood looking at each other across the area between them. Afranius had accomplished his purpose; he had stopped Caesar's fortification work. He suspected Caesar was not about to attack because he thought Caesar wanted a surrender rather than a slaughter. He was right. At sunset, both sides withdrew to their camps.

The following day, Caesar ordered his soldiers to complete the fortification works. Afranius spent the morning talking with scouts, searching for a ford in the River Sicoris just beyond the campsites. Caesar's scouts reported to him that the Pompeians were looking for crossing places in the river. Caesar sent German light troops and some cavalry units to occupy the crossing sites. Afranius saw he had no recourse but fight to the death or surrender. His men, thirsty, hungry, and exhausted, could not win so he sent agents to Caesar to initiate negotiations.

Afranius asked that the talks should be between themselves so that Caesar could hammer out difficulties, but this Caesar refused although he agreed to negotiations. He required discussions in the open, in a space visible to all in both armies and within the hearing of many. Afranius' son went to Caesar's headquarters as a sign of good faith, and both commanders met surrounded by the officers and men of both armies. Afranius started the discussion by observing that while he and his men fought for Pompey as was their sworn duty, they could no longer resist and so have come to depend on Caesar's rightful mercy.

Caesar responded with a tirade against the proud ambition and illegal actions of Pompey and his followers. Further, Afranius' army was not only created to beat Caesar, but unjustly murdered some of Caesar's men when all admitted they had a truce. The soldiers did their duty and should have no punishment: the commanders did wicked things to avoid doing just what they now had to do. However, Caesar is merciful. Let them immediately disband their army, and all could return home in peace.

With that announcement, all of Afranius' men raised their hands in assent and their voices in agreement. The soldiers made it clear that they wanted immediate discharge, not some promise to be deferred if inconvenient. And so, it was agreed. Caesar provided food and allowed the surrendered soldiers to collect water. He guaranteed the soldiers that they would receive their release as citizens with full pay. Those who lived in Spain could leave immediately; the rest would travel under supervision to the boundary between Gaul and Italy as citizens and then go as they chose.

Caesar Takes Spain

Before Caesar crossed the Rubicon, Marcus Terentius Varro held command for Pompey in Further Spain. When word came that Caesar marched into Italy, he announced his respect for Caesar while affirming his loyalty to Pompey. He repeated his remarks many times, establishing his neutrality. It was then, as information began to come that Caesar was delayed at Massilia, that Petreius joined with Afranius with large forces, and that Nearer Spain was united in support for Pompey, while Varro declared Caesar was the enemy of the Republic. He received many letters from Afranius telling him about their successes in holding back Caesar. Varro held a levy through his province, organizing two legions and some thirty auxiliary cohorts. He collected a large quantity of wheat, sending some to Massilia and some to Afranius.

Varro saw the need for a navy and ordered the authorities in Gades to build ten large warships and contracted for the authorities at Harpalis to build many small support boats. He appointed Gaius Gallonius, an equestrian and friend of Domitius, as military commander at Gades and sent six cohorts for garrison duty. To pay for the increased expenditure, Varro granted the income and treasury of the temple of Hercules to Gades. Also, he announced that he had information from dependable people that Caesar was losing battles and his soldiers were deserting him. To keep the administration and military forces functioning, he required the province to raise 18,000,000 *sesterces*, 20,000 pounds of silver, and 120,000 measures of wheat. The threat of the civil war coming to their communities frightened the Roman inhabitants, and they had little choice but to agree to the demands. Varro compelled the whole of his province to pledge loyalty to Pompey; those whom he thought supported Caesar had to bear heavy impositions, support garrisons in their communities, and suffer severe punishments when they openly backed Caesar. When he found out about Caesar's victory at Ilerda he prepared for war. He would base his forces at Gades, defending the town and its island just off the coast with two full legions and the warships he had built, protecting the massive supply of wheat he had collected. He thought he could keep the war going using the supplies on the island, no matter what Caesar did in the rest of the province.

Once he had defeated Afranius and the Pompeians in Nearer Spain, Caesar was hard-pressed with many vital problems requiring his attention at Massilia, in Italy, and most significantly in Rome. Still, he decided that he could not leave Spain until he held the whole land. He needed to protect his supporters in Further Spain and crush any possibility of a Pompeian revival. After he sent two legions into Further Spain, Caesar went ahead with his personal guard of 600 horsemen, sending before him a messenger with his order for all the magistrates and influential men in the province to meet him at Corduba (Córdoba) on 24 August. After the authorities at Corduba passed Caesar's edict on to all the communities in Further Spain, each community sent representatives of their councils to Corduba, and every important Roman citizen planned to attend Caesar there. Once the town council of Corduba was sure that Caesar was coming, they shut their gates against Varro, organized a town defence force to man the town walls, towers, and outposts, and took two cohorts in the neighbourhood under orders. At the same time, Carmona, the strongest town in Further Spain, expelled the three cohorts left by Varro as a garrison, proclaiming the town for Caesar.

After reports of these events came to Varro, he pushed harder to reach Gades. He feared the rising tide of support for Caesar might encourage some to block his way. This issue resolved itself when he received an official notice from Gades' town council: their gates were closed to him, and they had expelled his associate, Gallonius. The story spread; the chief men of the town convinced the garrison cohorts to support Caesar as both the winner in the war and as a more generous commander. The influential men then told Gallonius he could leave Gades and go about his way or face imprisonment. The story spread through Varro's troops and Gallonius quickly left Gades. While Varro was in his camp, within his sight, the men of the Local Legion, as it was called, pulled up their standards, declared for Caesar, and marched to Harpalis, setting up camp in the town's forum without troubling anyone. The town's people welcomed the men. Varro, left with just one legion and their loyalty not secure, decided to march to Italica but friends came to him and told him the gates of Italica were closed to him.

Varro knew he was defeated. He sent a message to Caesar that he was defeated and surrendered his legion. Caesar sent Sextus Caesar to receive the legion and ordered Varro to go to Caesar at Corduba. Once there, Varro gave Caesar an account of revenue and expenses, delivered the chests of money on hand, and informed Caesar of the whereabouts of ships and wheat supplies. The war in Spain was over.

Chapter 6

Massilia

The Siege of Massilia Starts

When Caesar knew the Pompeians had taken hold of Massilia, he sent for his legate Trebonius, who commanded some of Caesar's legions in the lands of the Aedui. Trebonius received Caesar's order on 26 April to march three legions to Massilia. He arrived on 16 May and constructed his main camp overlooking Massilia. Once the legions settled, Caesar, Trebonius, and their engineering staff examined Massilia's walls, drawing up plans to place their siege lines. Caesar remained at Massilia for about a month, organizing finances, supplies, and reinforcements. While there, Caesar conferred with Trebonius and the engineers as construction started on the siege works.

Massilia was an old and prosperous seaport; the town formed a triangle, two sides facing the Mediterranean Sea and extending inland. The walls were old, well made, and recently repaired. Once the Pompeians took over the town, they strengthened and reinforced the walls facing the land side. Caesar's engineers designed a ditch and earthen rampart extending across Massilia's landside, blocking the town from the land across. Of course, the seaway was open, but Caesar had twelve ships constructed and ordered ships sent from Italy. Massilia had regularly stocked military supplies, food, and a plentiful water supply. The town leaders appointed Apollonides as commander who intended to ensure the siege would be long and hard.

Trebonius sent out agents to collect many pack animals for transporting lumber, bales of brush, and fill back to the siege lines along with many labourers to construct the siege works. There were brick manufacturing plants near Massilia which held large stocks of brick and remained in operation so the besiegers would have an unlimited supply of masonry materials. The blockading ditch and rampart structure, extending from sea to sea, had a height of eighty feet from the ditch bottom to the rampart's top. The engineers selected two sites for the assault works: one near where the town wall came to the harbour and another facing the central town gate. The assault design followed accepted practice; Caesar's men would build a long ramp leading up to the base of the town walls. On top of the ramp, they would construct a reinforced trellis with a strong roof protecting workers bringing material to extend the ramp. A tall, fortified tower rose back where the ramp emerged out of the blockade ditch. The ramp near the harbour had a level path, but the other had to pass over a deep depression, now the valley of St Martin, some eighty feet deep. When completed, using a system of rollers, pulleys, cables and teams of animals, the workmen would pull the tower up the ramp to rise over the town walls and allow archers and projector machines to clear the walls.

Caesar's works were obvious to the defenders of Massilia. They prepared to meet the threat, strengthening their walls and building wooden platforms on top of towers to hold large projector engines and platforms for archers' teams. Caesar left Massilia on 13 June with his cavalry escort. Trebonius continued the siege works as the ramps extended toward Massilia's walls. The trellises' roofs consisted of foot square timbers bolted together, sheltering the workmen carrying earth to extend the ramp. In the front of the trellises, covering the whole face of the construction, stood an armoured front sixty feet tall, made of heavy timbers and covered with flame-resistant materials.

As the fronts of the two ramps drew toward the wall, the Massilians prepared to stop them. The defending engineers directed the catapulting of poles twelve feet long and a foot in diameter with spiked heads from the tops of the town walls' towers. These missiles were strong enough to break through the four layers of roofing covering the trellises and penetrated the armoured fronts. After the large projector engines broke sections of the siege constructions apart, smaller projectors and archers shot flaming arrows and combustible materials at the siege works. The number of Massilian projectors and archers shooting at the works often overwhelmed the workmen and slowed progress considerably. To keep annoying the besiegers, groups of defenders, particularly members of the Albici warriors, raided the works, throwing firebrands and killing workers. Sometimes the soldiers caught and slaughtered the raiders, but they returned.

War at Sea

After he suffered defeat as commander at Corfinium, Domitius rode across Italy, passed through his estates, and enrolled his retainers as troops. He and his small army stole ships from Western Italian ports and made for Massilia. Domitius' arrival had tipped the scales in the city to Pompey. With his fleet of seventeen ships added to the ships in Massilia's harbour, the Pompeians had a sizable fleet but few warships.

Seapower suddenly became important in the western Mediterranean. The few warships that remained around were old but sound. Most Roman warships at this time were about the same length, the differences in types were reflected by width. Most of these ships were quadriremes, 'fours' and wider quinqueremes, 'fives'. The training of their crews, however, was only in basic manoeuvres. Caesar appointed Decimus Brutus commander of his fleet, including the twelve warships he had ordered built at Arelate and others commandeered from various ports. Brutus anchored his ships at an island near Massilia.

On 5 July, the Massilians rowed their fleet out of the harbour to engage Caesar's fleet. Domitius commanded his fleet of seventeen ships, eleven of them with protected decks. Domitius rode with the protected ships, crewed by his peasants and herders. The other six ships with open decks carried archers and Albiei warriors. Along with the warships, a swarm of open boats sailed out with the fleet. The whole fleet advanced with trumpets blaring and standards to the fore.

Decimus Brutus' fleet had far fewer ships than the Massilians. Moreover, Caesar's twelve ships at Arelate were made from unseasoned lumber and were too broad; they did not manoeuvre well. For the rest, Brutus had only merchant ships crewed by commanders and crews who did not even know the names of warship vocabulary. But Caesar had allowed his bravest men, shock troops and centurions, to volunteer for duty on his fleet. Brutus equipped the ships with large grappling hooks, strong cables, and a full supply of pilums, spears, and specialty missiles. Caesar's agents in Massilia had reported to Brutus that the Pompeian fleet was getting ready to depart. Brutus' fleet made ready and rowed out to meet Domitius' fleet.

Trusting to his ship's speed, Domitius rowed to gain sea room and avoid Brutus' ships. Advancing in line ahead, they rowed around Caesar's fleet. As they passed, Domitius directed his protected ships to break out of line and attack isolated ships, two to one, or at least smashing their oars. Brutus' ships were heavier than the Massilians; he kept pushing ahead in a group, throwing 'claws' and grappling the protected ships. Then fierce fights broke out between valiant soldiers and tough mountaineers. All the while, storms of missiles from both sides rained down. Brutus' ships advanced. They readily allowed two Massilian ships to attack one of theirs, grabbing both and fighting on opposite sides of their ships; the highly trained soldiers boarded both enemy ships, killing the herdsmen and mountaineers in large numbers. Caesar's soldiers sank some of Domitius' ships and captured more. Domitius had to retreat and retired back to port in Massilia. He had lost nine ships, some sunk, the rest captive.

Trebonius' siege works at Massilia slowly advanced: fire and missiles flew back and forth; labourers carried earth, clay, and stone to the ramp face, extending the structure closer and closer to Massilia's walls. Week after week, the work continued. Fighting as hard as they could, the people and leaders of Massilia saw the handwriting on their walls. Months it may take, but after the news came that Caesar had prevailed at Ilerda, they were sure their city would fall. Messengers from Massilia travelled to Pompey's headquarters, begging for assistance. Pompey ordered Quintus Lucius Nasidius to organize a fleet and sail to Massilia. After acquiring sixteen manned warships, including some with bronze rams, Nasidius sailed from the Adriatic to the Sicilian straits. Passing between Sicily and Italy, Nasidius with his fleet landed at Messana. The city officials and senators fled while the Pompeians looted supplies and seized a warship sitting in the harbour

Nasidius and his fleet sailed toward Massilia. When he left Messana, he had sent ahead a swift boat to Massilia, telling Domitius that he was on his way and that the Massilians should prepare their ships for another naval battle. After their loss in the first sea battle, the Massilians had restored their fleets' strength by taking out of the docks an equal number of merchant ships and converting them into warships. There were large numbers of sailors, ships' craftsmen, and pilots in the besieged town, so manpower was no problem. Moreover, they took fishing boats, covered their decks to provide shelter for rowers, and installed projector engines on them.

With the fleet fitted out, the townspeople assembled to see their young men sail out of the harbour. Older men, matrons, and young women offered prayers as they begged with tears that their young men save Massilia. With banners waving, drums beating, and horns sounding, the fleet sailed off to meet Nasidius at Taurois. The Massilian youth were ready to die to save their town; their rowers and crews knew their business and they all believed victory was theirs. Once the fleets joined, they formed into battle formation. The Massilians were on the right-wing and Nasidius, the left.

Decimus Brutus had information about Nasidius' arrival. Another sea battle was coming and his fleet was stronger than in the previous battle as he had the six warships captured in battle repaired and strengthened. The men were in good spirits; they considered their opponents easily defeated men. Later in August, the Massilian and Nasidius' fleet rowed toward Brutus' fleet. Brutus' ships took up a tight formation and as the Massilians approached, Brutus loosened formation with the pilot of each ship heading toward an enemy ship. Coming near the Massilian craft, Brutus' crews threw grappling hooks and closed with the enemy. When the Massilians saw one of their ships grappled, they closed in to defend the stricken ship. This was just what Brutus' commanders wanted: the closer together the Massilian ships came, the easier they were to attack. The Albiei fought with courage equal to the Roman soldiers but without Roman training. The small boats with projectors and archers also closed in, throwing missile storms against Brutus' men. The fighting was fierce and bloody.

Decimus Brutus sailed in his flagship bearing standards and flags, directing his fleet, and encouraging his men. Two triremes prepared to attack his flagship. Coming from the two different sides, the triremes manoeuvred to ram. Brutus, very aware of the threat, ordered the timing drum beat quickened, so the rowers launched his ship forward. The two triremes, moving swiftly to ram, missed the flagship and ended up ramming each other. The collision damaged both, and one floundered because its ram was ripped off. Seeing the two triremes damaged, two of Brutus's ships attacked and sank them. The battle turned against the Massilians. Brutus's forces captured four of their ships and sank five with no loss. Nasidius saw the defeat and decided to leave the area. Adding one of the Massilians' ships to his fleet, he sailed off to Hither Spain.

The Siege Continues at Massilia

A small, fast ship was the first of Domitius' beaten fleet to enter Massilia's port. Crowds waited to learn the results of the battle. Told of defeat, a great cry erupted from the mass of people that quickly spread through the town. It seemed as if Massilia had already fallen! However, after the remainder of the fleet docked, calmer emotions prevailed and determination and perseverance took hold: they would defend the town and beat Caesar's army. The projector engineers and archers continued their bombardment of the siege works. At the same time, bold units suddenly emerged from the gates and hidden doors in the walls and attacked the craftsmen and labourers constructing the siege works. Because of the missiles, the fire descending from the walls and the damage done by the raiders from within the town, Trebonius' works ground to a halt.

To intercept the raiders, Caesar's troopers had constructed small shelters near the exits out of which they had come. Engineers came to the shelter near the city gate where construction of the right-side siege ramp had stalled. The engineers decided they could build a tower to overlook the city walls, and then they could bring up machinery to under-cut the fortifications. After setting up shelter sheds, the engineers ordered a covered way dug from the end of the siege ramp to the tower site. Labourers could now safely move materials up the incomplete siege ramp to the tower construction site.

Workers dug foundation trenches for the tower down to solid and constructed foundations under cover of strong sheds. Then, they began building a stout, solidly built tower.

Thirty feet square with five feet thick walls, the builders faced the exterior with Roman brick; the wall's core was *opus incertum* (stone, brick, mortar, rubbish all together). The interior walls were *opus mixtum* (rock and brick fragments mortared into a smooth surface). The workers laid the masonry under a strong wooden roof shelter, constructed of thick beams supporting heavy roof rafters, following the dimensions of the masonry structure, with a raised centre which came to a conical point. The rafters extended over the line of the masonry walls, and hanging down from the rafters were sheets of heavy material that provided protection from the missiles that continued to rain down. Further, thick interwoven cables hung further down from the beams another four feet, covering the working space of the tower exposed to missiles from Massilia's walls.

When the wall height reached the level for a second floor, the builders installed timbers embedded in the wall masonry to carry the second floor. They continued to raise the masonry wall but only as far as the wooden shelter allowed. Then, the builders jacked up the whole roof support, raising the protecting roof to reach another story. They removed the covering sheds and continued building the tower for six storeys. On the seventh floor that was the top of the ceiling of the sixth floor, the builders raised their protective roof almost another storey, constructing a firm platform for many projector engines. The besiegers dominated the wall and gate below with openings in the walls sited to target essential points on the defending wall and the top platform.

Sure that the men in the tower would dominate the top of Massilia's walls and towers, the engineers oversaw the fabrication of a covered shed some sixty feet long and about eight feet wide. First, they laid two large laminated and spliced beams in parallel lines four feet apart. Connectors held these beams in place, the whole structure made of two-foot by two-foot members. The builders raised posts to carry a sloped roof structure of stout members that covered the sixty-foot gallery. The roof rafters extended almost to the ground, protecting the interior space. The workers covered the roof edge with three-inch square tiles to support the roofing of terracotta tiles. Over the tiles, they placed treated hides covered with non-combustibles to deflect flaming oil and the like.

The gallery's head was level with the tower, some sixty feet from Massilia's walls. Using levers, pulleys and rollers, the workers pushed the structure up against the town walls, flat against the masonry. The town defenders understood that the well-constructed shed would allow the besiegers to undermine the wall. Fear spread throughout Massilia. The defenders brought cranes to the wall facing the siege shed, brought up massive boulders, and pushed them over to fall on top of the shed. But the massive timbers and interlocking structure held: the boulders rolled off without damaging the shed. Then the defenders filled large amphorae with pine resin and pitch. After igniting the materials, they threw them down on the shed. The amphorae broke, spreading fire, but the material rolled off the steep roof, and the flames could not start a fire on the non-combustible roofing. Soldiers in the gallery used poles and long-handled pitchforks to push the flaming rubbish away from the shed. All the time the Massilians tried to damage the shed, the soldiers in the tower rained missiles and arrows down on them, causing many casualties and disrupting their efforts.

Inside the end of the siege shed lodged against the town wall's masonry, soldiers shattered the joints of the wall's bottom courses. Once they levered the massive foundation stones out, they could burrow through the rubble core of the town wall, digging into the neighbouring tower. Undermining the tower's foundations, they shored it up with wood, packed combustibles around the wood, fired the mass and withdrew back into the shed. The tower suddenly settled; the front-facing fell forward and threatened the whole tower with collapse. To the citizens of Massilia the reality was apparent: if the tower gave way and Caesar's army entered the town, thousands of armed men would flood the streets, loot, rape, murder, and set fires. Further, not only would the riff-raft riot, but all sorts of people would take advantage of lawless opportunities. Rather than fighting to the end, the city senate and important citizens opened the gates and walked out without arms, but with fillets on their heads, reaching out their hands as supplicants.

The opening of the town gates and the appearance of the Massilian delegation immediately drew the attention of the besieging army. All the officers, soldiers, and labourers who witnessed the procession stopped what they were doing and turned to see and hear what was going on. The commanding officers drew together some distance down the road from the gates. The Massilians, with raised hands, came toward the commanders; when they stood before them, as one, all prostrated themselves. Their spokesmen begged the officers to desist from further action with great emotion until Caesar came. Significant injury would occur if the tower should fall and opened Massilia to the besieging army. They recognized their defeat and would open the town to Caesar without question. Trebonius and his staff agreed; they decided their job was done. There was no longer a reason for the struggle to continue. They appointed sentries to guard the siege works and allowed the men to return to camp.

Trebonius was ready to agree with the Massilians because Caesar had urged him to preserve the town from assault. Massilia was an essential part of the Roman community in the western Mediterranean and its destruction would damage many interests. But even more, Caesar was right: the soldiers were looking forward to sacking the town and collecting loot besides other imagined pleasures. They blamed Trebonius for their loss and were not pleased with the result of the siege. In Massilia, the Pompeians continued to plot ways to hold the town.

Several days later, at noon and with a strong wind blowing, Caesar's dispirited soldiers found diversion away from the siege works. The few who remained were relaxed or asleep near the equipment with their weapons stacked, when suddenly, a strong contingent of fighting men burst out of the town gates. They carried touches and flammable materials for the siege machines leading to the town gates. They ignited fires in all the devices they could reach. The flames took hold in the high wind and then spread. The alarm raised, soldiers rushed out of the camps, swords in hand, to run down the raiders who pulled back under the town wall. There, they found protection from Caesar's men when a rain of arrows and missiles from the walls above repulsed the soldiers. Under the walls, the raiders set fire to the siege shed and masonry tower, and the flames consumed all the siege works. The labour of months disappeared in a day.

The next day, the raiders again advanced out of Massilia with torches, going toward the siege ramp and tower near the harbour. Now, however, Caesar's men were at the ready. They charged the Massilians, slaying many and driving the rest back into the town. Trebonius and his staff looked at the wreckage and discussed ways to repair the damage. There was no more timber material available in the neighbourhood. One siege ramp and tower were still in place; the second was destroyed, including the masonry tower and the siege shed, which undermined the town's tower. The engineers presented a new plan: rebuild the siege ramp destroyed by the flames and move the remaining tower to the reconstructed ramp.

The engineers told Trebonius that they had devised a new method of constructing a ramp. They could use the existing tower near the harbour once they transferred it to their reconstructed ramp and accomplish this quickly. They built two masonry walls, six feet thick, brick exteriors holding a rubble core, the space between the two walls as wide as the damaged ramp. They roofed this space over with matrixes of cross members supporting clay roofing. There was insufficient support in the underlying broken ramp but the workers bridged this space with reinforced trussing. With the masonry walls giving protection on the sides, the front of the ongoing work protected by a substantial screen, and the clay roofing covering the top, the work moved along swiftly. Moreover, openings in the walls allowed guards to repel any attack coming out of Massilia.

When the new ramp reached near the town wall, and the siege tower moved to the lower part of the ramp, the engineers installed tackles and pulleys. Using the wall tops as rails, drawing against pulleys firmly set near Massilia's walls, teams of oxen and men tugged on massive cables which pulled the tower up the ramp in a matter of hours. Suddenly, what looked like a failed siege became even more threatening than previously. The tower was so close and high that any effort to batter at it with projector engines proved fatal to the operators. The peace party gained the upper hand in the town. Their envoys begged for a restoration of the original terms. Since his equipment gave him the advantage over Massilia, Trebonius granted the terms: they would wait for Caesar.

Chapter 7

Curio in Africa

The Expedition Lands

Once Caesar had defeated Afranius and set out for Corduba, G. Scribonius Curio who had taken Sicily for Caesar, organized an expedition to conquer Africa. Holding Sicily with four legions that had defended Corfinium, he so despised Attius Varus that he decided to take only two legions and 500 cavalry for the campaign because supplies might be short, and he did not think he needed more. Varus, as recounted above, had taken Africa almost by default. He supported the senatorial faction but ran Africa as an almost independent entity, continuing to supply grain to Rome, keeping the local magnates happy. Curio set out from Lilybaeum on Sicily's coast on 8 August and after spending two days and three nights on the voyage, landed at Anquillaria, near Mercury point.

The landing was well protected from summer storms. The town of Clupea sat on the other side of the Mercury Point peninsula, about twenty-two miles straight across the promontory but a long way around by sea. L. Caesar, supporting Varus, commanded a fleet of ten warships stationed at Clupea. The ships were veterans of the pirate wars of Pompey. Varus had them taken out of storage and launched to protect his African lands from any threats. When young L. Caesar heard about the many enemy warships descending upon Africa, he feared defeat and capture. He ordered his flagship, a decked trireme, beached on the nearest shore and took his staff by land off to Hadrumetum, a garrison town protected by a legion commanded by Varus' lieutenant Longus. The rest of his fleet sailed to Hadrumetum without a problem.

Curio's naval commander, the *quaestor* Rufus, sailed around Mercury Point with his twelve warships and found the abandoned trireme sitting on the beach. Rufus had his men attach ropes to the ship and pulled it out to sea and sailed back to Curio with his fleet and prize. Curio sent Rufus and his fleet to Utica and set out to follow with his two legions. After a two-day march the legions arrived at the River Bagrada. Curio left his legions under the command of the legate Rebilus and rode out with his cavalry to reconnoitre the way to Utica. He was particularly interested to find out if

Varus had occupied the old camp set up by Scipio during the Third Punic War. From his campsite on the Bagrada to Utica was merely three miles but between the camp and the town ran an imposing ridge, with a steep scape toward Utica and a milder incline facing away. At the sea end of this ridge sat the site of the old Roman camp. Having to march around the rough country, passing a wide marsh, was more than six miles.

Curio found Varus had neglected to take advantage of that strategic site. Looking down toward Utica he saw Varus' camp situated up against Utica's wall, near the Gate of Baal on one side and the foundations of the theatre on the other. So placed, Varus's camp was in a well-protected place. Further, Varus saw masses of people carrying goods and carts loaded with materials entering the town. He immediately detached a strong cavalry force to appropriate as much of that property as possible.

In Utica, Varus' scouts had kept him informed about Curio's mission and numbers. His lookouts saw Curio's cavalry riding toward the lines of peoples and goods. This was expected because when Varus had taken Africa, he made an alliance with King Juba of Numidia. Pompey had saved Juba's throne and in a trial in Rome, Caesar had pulled Juba's beard to make a point; further, Curio had proposed a law that would have confiscated Numidia from Juba. Juba gave support to Varus because he hated Caesar and Caesar's men. Juba had assigned six hundred cavalry and four hundred foot to Utica and Varus sent them out to oppose Curio's cavalry. The two forces collided and the Romans proved much stronger than the light Numidians. After a hundred and twenty Numidians fell, they retreated back into Utica. As Curio's fleet approached the landing at Scipio's camp Curio issued a notification to the merchant ships in the harbour near Utica: either they sailed to Scipio's landing, or his fleet would treat them as an enemy. As soon as they heard about the notice the merchant ship commanders sailed to meet Curio's fleet.

Curio returned to his camp on the Bagrada. Plenty of supplies poured into the camp and the troops were pleased with their victory, and acclaimed Curio Imperator. The next day, Curio marched his two legions to Utica and began building a camp near the town. Before the troops completed the trench and ramparts, scouts came to Curio with news that Numidian cavalry and infantry were marching against them, which explained the large dust cloud on the horizon. This was a surprise. Curio sent his cavalry to slow the enemy and ordered the scattered soldiers who were building the entrenchment to quickly take up battle formation. But, before the troops had accomplished their evolutions, the Roman cavalry hit the Numidians. The Roman horse, well armoured, struck the enemy light horse and scattered them. The Numidians had marched in a mass without formation and their cavalry bolted, leaving the light infantry unprotected. Roman horsemen slaughtered many of the foot soldiers as they tried to hurry into Utica's gates.

The Struggle Continues

Curio's men completed their camp and settled down for a comfortable siege, but all was not well with his two legions. Domitius had recruited both when he was organizing Pompey's defence against Caesar; for the most part, the men came from two peoples in central Italy: the Marsi and the Paeligni. Both were part of the garrison defending Corfinium and had surrendered to Caesar after Domitius had fled the town. Caesar inducted all of Corfinium's defenders into his forces without a change in their command structure, but he sent them out of Italy to keep them from the temptations of changing allegiance. From Sicily, the two legions had come to Africa. Just what the soldiers thought about all this was of no concern to their commanders who would have no problem executing anyone they thought disloyal.

Some of Curio's troops preferred to fight for Pompey. Two Marsi centurions with their staffs of twenty-two men defected to Varus the next night. They told Varus and his officers that many of Curio's troops were eager to join him and they urged him to come face to face with the troops and offer to open negotiations. Varus thought this was worth a try so the next morning, he marched his army out of Utica and drew them up in battle formation. Curio, hoping for a victory, marched his two legions out and drew up his men in battle order. Both forces faced each other across a narrow ravine with steep slopes.

Varus had a surprise for Curio. In his camp was a distant relative and supporter of Pompey, Quintilius Varus. This Varus had been *quaestor* in Corfinium and popular with Domitius' soldiers. Caesar had dismissed him from his service, and he came to Africa. Quintilius Varus knew who in Curio's legions were open to a change of allegiance. So, while the armies faced each other, he came forth and exhorted his former companions in arms to return to their oaths, not to forsake the cause for which they had joined Domitius' army and fought against Caesar. Further, he spoke of rewards for joining again with those fighting for the Republic. The troops stood mute and both sides withdrew into their camps.

Once settled back in their camp, Curio's soldiers and officers became agitated: who might desert? Should they join with Varus? Would some wait until the battle to leave the rest in the lurch? Curio called a council of his commanders and centurions to thrash out the matter. He requested suggestions and his officers offered two different courses of actions: either attack Varus' forces as soon as possible and try to use the pressure of combat to hold the men together, or pull back to Scipio's old camp, refortify it, collect supplies from the fleet and if things get worse, withdraw completely.

Curio rejected both suggestions. One showed no spirit; the other showed far too much. One group wanted to flee without honour; the other wanted to fight on the unfavourable ground. Rather, he pointed out that they should just wait and look for better options. After he dismissed his council, he called an assembly of all the soldiers and addressed them in a spirited and forthright matter. He reminded them about the battles they had won and that rather than throw all this away, they should be a part of Caesar's victory. The troops received Curio's speech with enthusiasm and repudiated any disloyalty. In the end, Curio welcomed their unanimous agreement to march to battle as soon as practicable.

The next day, Curio deployed his two legions along the same ravine as before. To strengthen his soldier's confidence, he led from the front. Varus' troops marched out of the camp to meet Curio's advance and the two armies faced each other across the ravine. Both sides waited to see who was going to attempt to descend and cross the gulley and so be at a disadvantage. Soon to their left, Curio and his men saw Varus's whole cavalry force descending into the valley, accompanied by many light foot intermixed among the horse. Curio ordered his cavalry, reinforced with two cohorts of select foot, to intercept the enemy force. Seeing Curio's cavalry charging toward them, Varus' horse bolted and fled the field, leaving the foot to face Curio's horse. The foot tried to escape but Curio's force surrounded and cut them down.

Varus's men stood thunderstruck at the sight of their routed cavalry and slain comrades. Curio and his staff agreed, now was the time. Calling to his legions to advance, Curio jumped into the ravine and began to climb the other side. The sides were too steep for someone simply to scramble up alone; comrades had to support comrades. Amidst this tumult Varus' men wavered, fearing Curio's cavalry was coming behind them. Before Curio's men actually crawled up the far side, Varus' lines broke and ran, pell-mell, to their camp. The number of soldiers trying to force their way through the camp gate caused a scrambling mass.

All the soldiers, Varus' and Curio's, dressed more or less alike so a number of Curio's men intermixed with Varus' troops. A soldier of Curio, Fabius from the lowest order of Romans, was the first to mix with Varus' troops in the scramble at the gate. He was seeking Quintilius Varus, in order to kill him. He called out Quintilius' name, acting as if he was one of his men with important information. Quintilius turned to see what the matter was and

Fabius struck at him with his sword, but Quintilius, aware of the danger, parried the sword with the top of his shield. Quintilius' bodyguard quickly cut Fabius down.

As this tumult continued, the press at the camp gate increased. More soldiers died in the crush than were slain in the fight. When Curio's soldiers approached Varus' men who still had not entered the camp, they broke off and fled into the town. Curio and his staff surveyed the camp: the defenders had set their ramparts and defenders were ready for battle. Curio's men had neither the equipment at hand nor supplies in ready reach to start a siege. They all marched back to their camp. In the end, the only soldier who died was Fabius whereas Varus' lost about 600 killed and 1,000 wounded. Further, many of Varus' men made their way into the protection of the fortified town. Late in the night, Varus withdrew the remainder of his soldiers back into the town, leaving only a trumpeter and some tents.

King Juba Intervenes

The next morning, Curio ordered his men to collect their siege materials. He marched them out and set up a blockade around Utica complete with trenches enclosing the town. The inhabitants of Utica included many supporters of Caesar, Roman businessmen, along with local tradesmen and artisans. All these people and their households were fearful of the ongoing battles. Among the inhabitants, the question of how to surrender was foremost. Groups of citizens met with Atticus Varus, requesting him to avoid actions that would destroy their town. However, messengers of King Juba arrived, saying the king was close with strong forces and they should stand firm.

The same information quickly passed to Curio, but he didn't believe it. News had come regarding Caesar's success in Spain; Curio thought King Juba would eventually support Caesar and would avoid battle with Caesar's agent. Trusted scouts brought word that Juba and a strong army were only twenty-four miles away. The Kingdom of Numidia was a minor Hellenistic state under a strong monarch who provided a balance between the competitive societies that made up his state. The largest part of King Juba's army was a mass of tribal light troops. There were many infantry armed with nothing more than a few spears, bows, and light shields backed up by light horsemen, riding small horses without saddles or bridles, but controlled with a baton; their weapons were spears. The numbers were large, but they had little staying power. Juba used these troops to attack disorganized enemies and reconnaissance. The king's main units were mercenary Spanish and Gallic cavalry, mercenary heavy infantry, and a strong formation of elephants.

Curio's staff made clear the reality of Juba's military forces; if his forces were caught between Varus's legions in Utica and Juba's mercenaries, the result would be swift destruction. Curio pulled his troops out of the siege works and marched to the old camp of Scipio. He had the camp refortified, stockpiled food, and collected lumber; he also sent to Sicily, ordering his other two legions and the rest of his cavalry to come to Africa. The refurbished camp provided ample space for the troops and supplies along with ready access to the sea allowing for an unbreakable communication route with Sicily. Curio had his men settle in for a lengthy struggle.

But after he had decided on one strategic plan, a man who claimed to be a deserter from Utica, came to Curio with the tale that King Juba was delayed because of a rebellion at Leptis and had sent only the lord Saburra with a few reinforcements to Varus. Curio immediately changed his mind. Rather than staying in camp, he would march out, destroy Saburra's forces and take Utica. At nightfall, Curio sent his whole cavalry force to find Saburra and see just what forces he had. It was still dark when the cavalry found Saburra's camp on the River Bagrada. The cavalry attacked, catching the Numidians asleep. After killing many and capturing some, the cavalry returned to Curio in the morning.

Curio, anxious to learn the result of the cavalry raid, had left his camp before sun-up and met his returning horsemen some six miles out. He had with him his two legions, leaving only five cohorts as a camp garrison. The cavalry commander told Curio how well their raid had succeeded and paraded his prisoners. Curio asked an important prisoner who commanded the Numidian camp at the Bagrada. The prisoner replied that was Saburra. Curio was overjoyed, and saw easy pickings. King Juba, being occupied with a revolt, had his best troops far away. Saburra was obviously bluffing. He showed off the prisoners, horses, and plunder to the troops, suggesting that easy victory was just down the road. Curio hastened forward, ordering the cavalry and legions to march as fast as possible to face Saburra but his men were less enthusiastic.

In actual fact, King Juba and his crack troops were waiting for Curio's army just six miles from Saburra's camp on the River Bagrada. The whole setup, the story about the revolt, the lax discipline in Saburra's camp, was all part of a trap Juba devised for Curio. After Curio's cavalry withdrew from their raid, Saburra sent word to King Juba that Curio was on his way. Juba dispatched his two thousand Spanish and Gallic cavalry and his heavy infantry to Saburra while he followed with more troops and sixty elephants. Saburra deployed his light cavalry and infantry in front of his camp but told them after the initial contact to show fear and then withdraw. At a given point, he would give the signal to turn and attack.

Curio, believing that he was chasing a defeated enemy, hurried his troops down from higher ground into the plain. He had to halt because both the cavalry and infantry were fatigued. Saburra, keeping a close watch on Curio, was ready for him and signalled his troops to form a line of battle. Saburra rode up and down the line, exhorting his men to be brave, all in sight of Curio. Then, Saburra launched his foot and horse against Curio's troops. But Curio's forces were not as strong as Curio imagined: many had fallen out on the march; others did not have the will or loyalty to fight. Only a little better than 200 cavalry and a few cohorts followed Curio's lead. His troop charged the Numidians, who gave way, but the cavalry could not pursue far because their horses were blown. Soon, more Numidian cavalry appeared on their flanks and rear. When a cohort would charge out of formation to disperse their tormentors, the Numidians side-stepped their advance and reformed, attempting to cut them off from the rest of Curio's forces.

King Juba saw that Curio's men had become confused, not doing very well either keeping their ground or counter-attacking. This was just the time, Juba saw, to feed more reinforcements into the mix, so while his Numidians became stronger, Curio's men became weaker. Surrounded by their enemies, Curio's troops huddled together; there was no place for the wounded except next to the unwounded; they were threatened from all sides and in despair. Curio found his orders and pleadings falling flat. He rallied his men with the cry that they should find safety on a nearby ridge. As a body, the soldiers pushed forward, carrying their standards and wounded.

Saburra saw the manoeuvre and sent his cavalry to intercept. They reached the hill before Curio's men and this was the end for Curio's forces; panic set in, some running away wildly and were quickly cut down by Saburra's cavalry; others simply falling to the ground unhurt but giving up anyway. Curio's cavalry commander, Gaius Domitius, told Curio to take heart, surrounded by his mounted bodyguard, they would return to the camp and safety. Instead, Curio fought on to his death. A few cavalrymen escaped the slaughter, along with those who had fallen out of the march but the infantry with Curio all died.

The fleeing soldiers streamed back to the camp. Marcus Rufus was in command of the camp and received the fleeing men, but panic spread from the frightened men to the five-cohort garrison. All the soldiers gathered together, demanding Rufus withdraw back to Sicily; stories of King Juba's power, the quality and quantity of troops, his many elephants were astonishing and frightening. Rumours spread from Utica to the fleet.

Men cried out that Juba's fleet was on the way to destroy the Caesarean fleet. When Rufus requested the ships come near to his camp where he had landing sites constructed, sailors told him they could see the dust of Juba's advancing army and believed his ships were just over the horizon. The fleet commander, Flamma, ordered his ships to raise anchor and sail away. The merchant ships heard the same stories but Asinius Pollio, who had managed to escape the lost battle, took a small boat out to the merchant ships and begged their commanders to pick up soldiers. Most sailed away, not waiting to see if the stories were true. Only a few boats came to transport the army off the beach. The whole garrison and support troops crowded the shore, imploring rescue. However, the mass of men mobbed the few boats, overturning some, sinking others. Many of those who gained the merchant ships were robbed and thrown overboard. Only a few escaped to Sicily.

The rest had to return to camp. That night, they sent centurions to Varus in Utica, offering to surrender. In the morning, King Juba saw the cohorts in front of Utica. He declared them his property. The king ordered most of the soldiers executed and sent a few skilled or important men back to his kingdom. Then he rode into Utica with his personal guard and escort of Roman Senators, arranged matters to his satisfaction, brushed off Varus's complaints about the way he was going to deal with the prisoners, and returned to his kingdom. Pompey and the senators in Macedonia awarded honours to King Juba but those in Rome proclaimed Juba an enemy of Rome and recognized Bochum and Bogud as rightful rulers of Numidia.

Caesar Settles Affairs in the West

In Corduba, Caesar called an assembly of representatives of the towns and important people of Further Spain. He thanked all those who helped him, Roman citizens who held their towns for Caesar, the local magistrates for expelling Pompey's garrisons, the people of Gades who took possession of their town, and the army officers who came to the province as garrisons, then protected them by their valour. Caesar remitted the special taxes Varro had imposed, forgave the fines Varro levied against his supporters, and rewarded communities for their loyalty. Two days later, Caesar travelled to Gades and restored the treasures and income to the temple of Hercules and appointed Q. Cassius to manage the province with four legions. Then, on 11 September, Caesar set sail in the ships Varro had built. He arrived at Tarraco in a few days and when he landed, he met with representatives from the most important communities of Nearer Spain, giving out honours to towns and individuals after which he took the road to Narbo and then on to Massilia.

At Massilia, the townspeople were in a bad way. Pestilence had struck, the food supply, old stock of millet and stale barley, was spoiled and outside their walls, many thousands of hardened soldiers were looking forward to profiting and fun at their expense. The people of Massilia hoped Caesar could control them when they surrendered. A few days before Caesar arrived, Domitius and his closest followers took three warships and rowed out into the stormy seas. Brutus' blockade ships saw the three ships leaving the harbour, pulled up their anchors, giving chase. Demetrius' ship drove into the storm, a dangerous action but no more threatening than being caught by Caesar. The other two ships, not wanting to face the storm or Brutus' ships, sailed back into the harbour and surrendered. Now, Caesar was ready to accept Massilia's surrender.

Caesar received the leaders of the town and told them the terms. They brought out and piled up their weapons and projector machines; handed over their warships and delivered all the money in their treasury. Beyond that, Caesar left two legions as a garrison and let the town council sort out their own problems. After dealing with the Massilians, Caesar received messages from Rome. They formally informed Caesar that the praetor Lepidus had nominated Caesar as dictator and that passed. The new dictator sent his army to Italy and set out for Rome.

Mutiny of IX Legion

With Spain in his control and Massilia occupied, Caesar faced east; there he saw his objective, Pompey, who waited for him in the Balkans and Greece. From Spain came silver in large amounts, enough silver to pay for Caesar's path to victory without extracting it from allies and subjects. Pompey, Caesar knew from his agents, was plundering the east of money and strengthening his legions for the coming battles. This had been Pompey's plan from the start: he abandoned Italy to Caesar, hoping that Caesar would find himself entangled between dissatisfaction in Rome, the Republican forces in the west, and his forces in the east. The best outcome for Pompey was that Caesar would impale himself on the western armies, but this did not happen, so Pompey's next step was to strengthen his eastern forces and let Caesar come east.

While his objective was clear, Caesar knew many difficulties remained ahead in his path. His hard-fighting legions could quickly destroy their opponents, but victory in battle did not ensure support among those whose ambitions and desires mattered in the scheme of things. Rich money lenders, powerful local political operatives, influential speakers, and popular military leaders, officers, and enlisted soldiers, all needed Caesar's careful consideration. That Caesar's power was brittle, that he faced threats from many quarters was made clear when news came to Massilia about the mutiny of the IX Legion in Placentia. Caesar immediately set out toward Placentia, arriving before word of his coming. He suddenly assembled the legion after hearing from the legion's officers what had upset the men.

The clamorous soldiers repeated their complaints: the officers and those in charge were prolonging the war, and they had not received the two years' pay of 500 *denarii* promised them back in the late winter when the war began. Caesar told the men that he would have none of this disobedience. They all swore an oath of loyalty to him, and now, faced with an implacable enemy threatening Italy, they wanted to quit. No! He would dismiss the legion from service after he decimated it (executing every tenth man chosen at random). There would be no pay, nor could any of them ever join a Roman army. This response shocked the men and they begged forgiveness. After an extended back and forth, Caesar agreed to keep the legion in service but a list of 120 men, drawn up by the officers of those who caused the most trouble, would receive punishment. Twelve of the 120 men were marked for execution, but only eleven were killed, one man proving he was not guilty. Instead, the centurion who marked him down suffered execution. Caesar went straight to Rome after he settled the mutiny.

Section III

War Against Pompey

Chapter 8

Caesar Faces Pompey

Caesar Arrives in Rome

When Caesar was travelling to Rome after pacifying Spain, Marcus Lepidus, praetor, had overseen an assembly of the people to determine if they were going to elect a dictator. After the motion passed, Lepidus immediately nominated Caesar, contrary to usage. As expected, the assembly voted Caesar as dictator and when Caesar entered Rome, he accepted the office. He understood this position required great tact but did not want to appear as arbitrary or vindictive. He needed to restore some sense of normality to the city and lower tensions.

When Pompey had controlled Rome after the war began but before he evacuated from Brundisium, he kept a detachment of his personal guard to maintain order in the city. Under Pompey's direction, many of Caesar's supporters found themselves indicted under Pompey's bribery law and convicted by a special court. The conviction forced them into exile. Rather than restore all these people by fiat, Caesar brought the matter before the popular assembly which legislated their recall. Following Caesar's will, the assembly granted a return to all exiles except Milo.

Famine had struck Rome; the price of grain was high, and starvation was killing people. Caesar underwrote the cost of shipping wheat from Africa. People also requested that he decree all debts abolished because the upheaval undermined business, resulting in property and goods losing value. Caesar refused and instead, he imposed an economic reform to restore confidence in the lending business and the money supply. With his shipments of silver coming from Spain, Caesar had secured the money supply; now, he had to ensure confidence to lenders and creditors. Lenders had recalled their loans on many properties because of the falling values; because when values fell, property owners were unable to raise cash or collect rents. Tribunes had stopped lenders from raising their interest rates but either a lot of property would change hands at great loss or Caesar would have to find a solution that satisfied both lenders and creditors.

Caesar decreed that arbitrators would appraise properties based on their values before the current troubles started. These arbitrators presented their appraisals to the borrowers who could use them as collateral for pre-existing loans. However, Caesar understood that while cash supplies were large, circulation remained tight. To solve this difficulty, he assumed that many people were hoarding coins. He decreed that he would enforce an old law that no one should hold more than 15,000 *denarii* in silver or gold. The idea behind this enactment was to get money flowing again, to encourage those who had the wherewithal to pay their lenders and the lenders to make new loans. His objective was to direct investments from cash into business ventures. Since he had contracted with many producers to supply his armies, money was coming into the system and by expediting the circulation of cash, he created a business boom. Further, Caesar was not interested in using his economic policies in a punitive manner: he refused to allow slave informers to tell how their masters were gaming the system. As long as money moved, Caesar didn't care.

Caesar held the Latin Festival, symbolizing the unity of the People of Rome, then he held elections for all offices for the new year. The People elected Caesar and Publius Servilius as consuls and filled the offices of praetors and the rest. The effect of these new officials was a major step toward calming things down. So many elected officials had fled Rome that tribunes had taken over offices of the aediles to manage Rome city services; Caesar also appointed priests to fulfill all important religious duties. Now the city would begin to return to normal. Caesar appointed new governors, Marcus Lepidus to Spain, Aulus Albinus to Sicily, Sextus Peducaeus to Sardinia, and Decimus Brutus to Gaul. He awarded citizenship to Cisalpine Gaul. Caesar issued these decrees and then resigned his dictatorship. All of these enactments were done after only eleven days in office. His dictatorship did not violate the constitution and accomplished many desirable results. In reality, of course, he remained in power. But, alongside his military might, he had at least plausible legal authority granted by the Senate.

Just after the winter solstice, Caesar set out to confront Pompey. He had crushed the senatorial faction in the west and now, his back secured, he needed to tackle his enemies in the east as soon as possible. He took all the silver and gold offerings from the Capitolium and other temples to cover expenses and marched to Brundisium, even before he entered his consulship. He had ordered twelve legions and all his cavalry to concentrate there. He wanted to sail across the Adriatic and face Pompey as soon as possible. But, after the year of upheaval and battle, the legions had lost many men and were significantly under strength; even worse, Pompey's people had taken almost all of the shipping away. At best, Caesar could ship only 15,000 legion foot and 500 horse to Epirus. Agents brought information describing Pompey's preparations. During the year Caesar fought in the west, Pompey had set about collecting and organizing a force powerful enough to overwhelm Caesar.

Significant difficulties faced Caesar in his efforts to gain a foothold in Epirus. While he was in the west, Caesar had instructed his lieutenants to see about setting up a base in Epirus from which he could challenge Pompey. He had sent Publius Cornelius Dolabella to prepare a base but Marcus Octavius and Lucius Scribonius Libo, commanders of Pompey's fleet drove him out. Then they trapped Gaius Antonius, Mark's brother, on a small island and captured most of his men. Having repulsed Caesar's forces, Octavius decided to eliminate Caesar's supporters on the Dalmatian coast.

Octavius sailed his fleet along the coast. He caused trouble for most of Caesar's supporters there, stirring up the tribes. The town of Issa turned from Caesar to Pompey but when Octavius approached Salonae, with promises of benefits for supporting Pompey along with threats of destruction should they refuse, he found the Roman citizens of Salonae committed to Caesar. Octavius prepared to besiege the town. Salonae sat on top of a hill; the Roman citizens quickly built wooden towers to reinforce their fortifications. Still, compared to Octavius' troops, they were very few. Not deterred, they liberated and armed their slaves and had their wives, daughters, and servants cut off their hair to construct projector machines.

Seeing the activity in Salonae, Octavius began setting up five siege camps, isolating the town. The main difficulty facing Salonae was the lack of a large supply of wheat so they sent envoys to Caesar to request help. Enough was found that the siege dragged on. Eventually, Octavius' garrison grew tired; at noon, the Salonaens placed their women and boys on their walls, so the besiegers would not notice any unusual activity. All the men of Salonae, property owners, former slaves, and the rest, stormed out of Salonae's gates and quickly overwhelmed the garrison of one camp, then pushed on until they repelled and dispersed the besiegers of all five of Octavius camps. His soldiers fled to their ships and Octavius had to follow. Since winter approached, Octavius withdrew to Dyrrachium

Pompey in the East

Caesar was attempting to overthrow Rome's established order, no matter what he said or did. He had to look for support from many different interests and worked diligently not to unnecessarily make enemies other than those hard-core supporters of Rome's oligarchs. Pompey, on the other hand, had the full support of the main Roman senators, priests, and property owners.

With typical Roman arrogance, he intended to draw the men, money, and goods he wanted from the eastern lands no matter what the cost to Rome's subjects. Pompey ordered his men to get what was needed and they saw to it, adding something to make their efforts rewarding. Pompey needed money, soldiers, ships, and food.

He demanded large sums of money from the provinces of Asia, Syria, and from all the client kings and rulers. Even more, Pompey required the tax-collecting companies to pay into his treasury years' worth of taxes which they could collect in the future. Of course, in order to raise the necessary funds, the tax companies forced the taxpayers to produce the funds to satisfy Pompey and include a nice profit besides. To secure their status, the two hundred or so senators who supported Pompey assembled in Thessalonica. They dedicated open space for the auguries as assumed in the role of the Roman People. While they could not elect new officials, they propogated the existing officers.

Nine legions of Roman citizens formed the core of Pompey's army. Five came from Italy, one, formed of two understrength formations in Cilicia which Pompey called the Gemini; settled veterans in Crete and Macedonia formed another; Lentulus raised two more in Asia. To these Roman legions, Pompey recruited auxiliary soldiers to serve with his Romans from Greece. He expected to receive the two-legion garrison of Syria under Scipio. Added to the regular foot, Pompey brought 3,000 archers, 1,200 slingers, and 7,000 cavalry, made up of Gauls, Persians, and others. Pompey's eldest son, Gnaeus, brought 500 troops of Gabinius' garrison from Alexandria. Pompey brought 800 of his own slaves and freedmen and hired select, well-trained mercenaries.

Pompey collected a large fleet of warships and transports to defend the east and attack Caesar. They came from Corcyra, Athens, the Cyclades, Pontus, Bithynia, Asia, Cilicia, Syria, Phoenicia, and Egypt; further, he contracted with all the major shipbuilders for new ships. Gnaeus Pompey commanded the Egyptian fleet; D. Laelius and G. Triarius commanded the Fleet of Asia; C. Cassius, the Syrian Fleet; G. Marcellus, the Rodians; Scribonius Libo and M. Octavius, the Liburnian and Achaean fleet. Overall command rested in the hands of M. Bibulus.

He needed large amounts of food, particularly wheat, and had his agents collect the goods from Thessaly, Crete, Cyrene, Egypt, and Asia. The massive army and fleet he had collected were unprecedented. The amount of food taken for Pompey's forces meant that people in the eastern provinces were going to starve. This was just the fortunes of war as far as Pompey was concerned. He set up base camps at Apollonia and Dyrrachium and occupied all the towns along the Adriatic coast with small garrisons. His fleet guarded the coast, keeping an eye on Caesar's forces near Brundisium.

Pompey spent his time drilling troops, taking part in the exercises himself, foremost among his men despite his age. He gained the trust and love of his soldiers and people came from everywhere to see the spectacle. Pompey addressed the assembled senators, business magnates, along with the officers and men of his army. The speech, essentially a recapitulation of what had happened and condemnation of Caesar, was well received. All pledged their undying support for their cause. The winter was coming, and Pompey thought the weather was too bad for Caesar to attempt a crossing of the Adriatic. Furthermore, his agents in Rome would keep Caesar busy. He ordered his fleet to patrol the seaways and sent his army into winter quarters in Macedonia and Thessaly.

Caesar had captured L. Vibullius Rufus, Pompey's main engineer, twice, once at Corfinium and another time in Spain. Both Caesar and Pompey had great respect for Vibullius, for his technical skills and his integrity. While Caesar was marching to Rome, he entrusted Vibullius with his peace offer to Pompey. The offer included the following: both sides have suffered serious losses; both sides are powerful. Now was the time for Caesar and Pompey to submit their dispute to the Senate and People of Rome. Equally strong, both leaders should disband their military forces. Caesar added as an enticement, that he would disband all his land forces.

Vibullius landed on Corcyra. While he believed Caesar's offer was a serious effort to end the war, he knew that more important were the facts of Caesar's build-up of men and ships ready to land on the coast of Epirus. He hurried on to Pompey, changing horses at every town to bring news of Caesar's actions to Pompey. At that time, Pompey was in winter quarters at Candavia on the Via Egnatia. When Vibullius met him, Pompey saw that danger was facing him right now and he immediately started long marches in order to reach the Adriatic coast before Caesar landed. He wanted to reach Apollonia before Caesar captured the town.

Caesar Lands in Illyricum

Caesar's agents informed him that Pompey was staying in winter quarters and his commanders were more concerned with improving their camps than worrying about a possible attack. Caesar decided that he would test the fortunes of war and launch an expedition to the opposite shore. After he set up camp in Brundisium he called his legions together and held an assembly. He told them the end of their trials was near, one more campaign and final victory was at hand. He ordered them to find a place for their slaves and baggage in Italy and prepare to march light. The soldiers cheered him and affirmed they were at his command.

Stepping down from the speaker's platform, Caesar led the way to the cargo ships at the docks. His few warships guarded the seas off Sardinia and Sicily, so he had only armed merchant ships. He oversaw the loading of five legions of foot and 600 select horse onto the ships, but storms arose which kept the ships in harbour and the soldiers and Caesar waited out the tempest. As the force waited, two more legions arrived and these too, Caesar loaded on cargo ships.

On the fourth day of the new year the storms abated, and the fleet sailed toward Epirus. The next morning, Caesar directed his ships to the south of Apollonia along the rocky Ceraunian shore where they landed on a small sandy beach. The troops disembarked near a small place called Palaeste. Each ship manoeuvred in good order, unloading men and supplies, and returning to station making way for the next. Not a ship was damaged in difficult circumstances on a dangerous coast. Once the fleet was unloaded, Caesar sent it back to Brundisium. That night, he led the troops, divided into small units to traverse the landscape, over a rough and narrow path to the town of Oricum. At first light, Caesar deployed his troops in front of the town. Pompey's commander at Oricum was L. Torquatus who occupied the town with a unit of Parthians. He ordered the gates closed and prepared to defend the walls, but when he ordered the local Greek soldiers to arm and mount the wall, they refused, and the townspeople demonstrated their support for Caesar. Torquatus saw that his situation was untenable and surrendered the town. Once he controlled Oricum, Caesar marched on Apollonia. There, L. Staberius commanded and he ordered the reservoir in the citadel filled and the fortifications refurbished. He demanded the townspeople give hostages, but they didn't surrender anyone and refused to close the gates against Caesar. Staberius left Apollonia without telling anyone. The townspeople sent word to Caesar inviting him to take possession of the town and soon, the local communities and then the whole of Epirus recognized Caesar's authority.

While Caesar was taking Oricum, Lucretius and Minucius, with eighteen warships on the seaside of Oricum, led a convoy of cargo ships carrying wheat for Pompey's forces. Fearing Caesar might suddenly attack them, they sank the cargo ships and fled to Dyrrachium. Caesar assembled his army and congratulated them on their achievements in mid-winter: crossing the sea without warships, taking Oricum and Apollonia without a fight, and capturing Pompey's supplies without his knowing it. Now he and his army marched day and night toward Dyrrachium.

Pompey Marches West

Pompey, notified by agents before Caesar landed, mobilized his soldiers, and marched from Macedonia toward Epirus as fast as possible. Hearing about Caesar's occupation of Apollonia, he feared for Dyrrachium. He ordered his army to march day and night, double-time, to reach Dyrrachium as soon as possible. Many soldiers fell out of the line of march unable to keep up the pace and fear of running into Caesar's forces.

But Pompey reached Dyrrachium with a core force before Caesar's men and he ordered his men to begin setting up a military camp. As the rest of his troops trickled in, his officers made a show of unity. Labienus, Caesar's former second in command, pledged loyalty and obedience to Pompey, followed by the army commanders, officers and centurions. When Pompey's arrival became evident to Caesar, he decided to set up camp on the River Apsus, at the border of Apollonian territory, and go into winter quarters. Pompey, likewise, pitched a camp on the other side of the Apsus.

Pompey had stationed strong naval forces in the Adriatic to forestall just such a move as that made by Caesar. Laelius oversaw the command of eighteen Asiatic ships blockading Oricum and Caesar's old enemy, Bibulus commanded one hundred and ten ships on Corcyra. Word came to both commanders that Caesar was sailing, but agents reported that Caesar's fleet included twelve strong warships centred on a squadron of four protected ships. Laelius' lieutenants did not think their ships were up to a fight with Caesar's war fleet so they stayed in port. Bibulus, caught off guard with his ships laid up and crews dispersed, could do nothing immediately. Early the next morning, Bibulus put his ships in order and sailed out but he was too late to intercept Caesar's loaded fleet. However, under the command of Fabius Calenus, Caesar's fleet sailed too late to pick up the evening winds and found itself becalmed. Bibulus came across about thirty empty transports, he attacked, setting them all on fire and killing the crewmen.

When Caesar marched out of Oricum toward Apollonia, Bibulus' fleet began blockading all the landing places on the Adriatic coast from Corcyra to Dyrrachium. Because Caesar managed to out-manoeuvre Bibulus, as he had often done, Bibulus was angry at being made the fool again. Bibulus kept his fleet at sea ready to intercept any reinforcements that might come for Caesar. All this was obvious to Caesar. At Brundisium his lieutenant, Calenus, had boarded the rest of his legions and the cavalry on their fleet along with supplies. The fleet set sail and began proceeding toward Epirus when Caesar's messenger reached him, telling Calenus that Pompey's fleet had blocked all the ports and shores. Caesar's dispatch ordered Calenus to return to Brundisium. A civilian supply ship failed to follow the return signals and sailed on and reached Oricum where Bibulus attacked and took it. He ordered all the crew, slaves, even the ship's boys killed.

Bibulus' blockade was successful but in retaliation, Caesar sent armed units to all beaches and landing places, so Bibulus' fleet was unable to get water and wood or put ashore at all. Roman warships did not have the capacity to stay at sea longer than a few days. The blockade required Bibulus to keep his fleet at sea and with nowhere to land, the men in the fleet suffered. Bibulus ordered merchant ships from Corcyra to bring water and wood and transfer them to his warships. The date of the blockade was about a week after the solstice and storms were frequent; the sea was often rough, and Bibulus' men had to use sails to catch rainwater.

Libo joined Bibulus and they took their warships near Oricum's walls. Calling out, they gained the attention of the commander of the walls, M. Acilius, and garrison commander Statius Marcus. Libo and Bibulus told them they wished to secure terms of settlement from Caesar. While a courier carrying a letter that itemized the issues they wanted to discuss with Caesar, they requested a truce, which, incidentally, would allow them to land for supplies and rest. Caesar's officers were aware that he was seeking peace terms and had heard of Vibullius's mission to Pompey and agreed to recommend the truce to Caesar.

At that time, Caesar was with a legion collecting supplies from Buthrotum over against Corcyra. After the courier gave him the letter, he left the legion and hurried to Oricum. When he arrived, Caesar, Acilius, and Marcus invited Bibulus and Libo to a conference. Libo came and made excuses for Bibulus not coming because of his personal antipathy to Caesar. Libo affirmed he was interested in finding an end to the current unpleasantness but unfortunately, he went on, Pompey made all decisions. So, if Caesar would be good enough to send his demands to Pompey, then they could negotiate together and, of course, the truce would continue.

Caesar told Libo to grant his agents safe passage to Pompey or bring Pompey's agents here. Regarding a truce, since the fleet blocked his reinforcements and supplies, he was keeping the fleet from gathering supplies from the lands under his control. If Libo wanted a concession, that was fine, as long as he offered one in return. Still, Caesar went on, they could plan for negotiations without any concessions. Libo decided he could not receive Caesar's agents nor agree to issue safe conduct, but said he needed to submit the whole question to Pompey. As a sign of good faith, he went on, Caesar should allow the ships to land. However, Caesar saw that Libo's approach was only an effort to fool him into granting a truce and he refused. Indeed, conditions in the fleet were bad; Bibulus did not accompany Libo because he was ill. Cold and physical hardship brought on a severe sickness that killed him. The fleet command fragmented after Bibulus died, and each group of ships began independent operations.

After the upset caused by Caesar's landing and Pompey's occupation of Dyrrachium calmed down, Vibullius joined with his friends, Libo, L. Lucceius, and Theophanes, all of whom were close to Pompey. They presented Caesar's offer to Pompey, hoping to end the civil war. Pompey refused to hear them. He did not see how any agreement would not be a victory for Caesar. He refused any discussion of terms other than Caesar's surrender. Vibullius made sure Caesar heard what Pompey had decided.

Chapter 9

Pompey Reconsiders his Strategy

Pompey at Bay

When Pompey evacuated Italy, he believed he had trapped Caesar in a vice between his Spanish armies and the Republican troops in the east. He intended Caesar's cause to suffer from the lack of money to pay soldiers and to buy supplies; Caesar would have to confiscate property and requisition goods and that would lead to great unpopularity. A year later, Pompey's Spanish armies were gone, Caesar had the silver of Spain and was sitting, albeit with a weak force, facing Pompey in Epirus. Pompey needed a new strategy. Always practical if not very imaginative, he assumed victory would come with more money and men, than Caesar. Money was the first consideration because it bought men, supplies, and allies but in the Classical World money meant hard cash. Military powers needed coinage in silver or silver and gold bullion. Pompey could tap into eastern coinages and mint silver from the Macedonian mines. Caesar's money was in Italy and Caesar was in Epirus. No doubt he brought some strongboxes of coinage with him but that would last only so long. Pompey ordered his commanders to keep Caesar's reinforcements from coming and above all, keep his strongboxes of coinage in Italy. That would weaken him. To strengthen his forces, Pompey ordered the Republican governors and magistrates to collect as many men and as much money as possible.

Quintus Caecilius Metellus Pius Scipio Nasica was typical of the senatorial nobility who supported Pompey. Rich, corrupt, debauched, and deceitful, the great nobles of Republican Rome believed the Republic existed for their benefit alone. Other people were of small worth, except as tools or foils. Scipio Nasica had attached himself to Pompey after Caesar's daughter Julia died. Scipio offered his daughter, the gentle Cornelia, widow of the younger Crassus who was lost with his father in the Parthian debacle, as a wife for Pompey. He had pushed Pompey into the politics of upheaval and helped make him Caesar's enemy. He was a prime mover behind the ultimatum which brought about the final break between Caesar and Pompey in January 49. Scipio Nasica became proconsul of Syria at that time including the whole of the Levant from the frontiers of Egypt to the borders of Cilicia. When he arrived, he rounded up Caesar's supporters and killed many of them. After leading an expedition against some mountain tribes on the Cilician border, his soldiers proclaimed Scipio as Imperator.

Scipio oversaw the rich cities of Antioch, Damascus, Jerusalem, and many prosperous towns. When Pompey needed money, Scipio Nasica was the man to collect it. He demanded advance payment for two years of regular taxes and imposed all sorts of new taxes, on slaves, columns on buildings, and many other incidentals. Roman citizens had to loan money to his administration while tax companies had to produce the two years of taxes immediately. What had been a prosperous economy fell into a deep depression. Further, Scipio pulled all the troops out of Syria, even though the Parthians were energized after they defeated and killed Crassus and his legions. As the summer waned, Scipio marched his army north to winter in Pergamum, treating Asia Minor as he treated Syria.

As winter came, Scipio and several senators went to Ephesus because they heard the Temple of Diana held large money deposits which the priests were not surrendering. An important dispatch from Pompey reached him as he approached Ephesus. Caesar had landed! Scipio quickly turned about to prepare his soldiers to march to Macedonia.

Pompey Faces Caesar

As soon as he secured Dyrrachium, Pompey marched south toward Apollonia intending to defeat Caesar before Antony came with reinforcements. Caesar quickly organized a striking force to engage and defeat Pompey, but when he reached the River Apsus, he found Pompey's troops numbered far more than his own. He halted at the river, built a camp, and sent a peace proposal to Pompey in order to mask the fact that he was hesitant to fight at this time. Pompey, fully aware of Caesar's weakness, rushed his engineers to bridge the river, but when the advanced guard charged across the structure, it collapsed, isolating Pompey's spearhead. Caesar's troops cut them down. The morale of Pompey's troops was not good. Made up of different units having no connection to each other, for the most part, garrison troops with limited training, the soldiers had little confidence in themselves facing Caesar's experienced and trained killers. Pompey decided to wait to engage Caesar on better terms.

Each side remained in their well-fortified camp and could look across the few hundred feet that separated them from their enemy-fellow soldiers. By common agreement, neither side shot projectiles or arrows at the other. Often, soldiers or officers called across the stream, talking to relatives or friends. Sometimes they discussed the issues that separated them. Soon, Caesar sent a spokesman, P. Vatinius, to make the argument for compromise and peace. He addressed Pompey's side, 'Should not citizens be permitted to send envoys in safety to fellow citizens about peace?', he queried. And so, he continued for some time. Both sides listened quietly.

Officers on the Pompeian side responded that Aulus Varro would come the next day and discuss arrangements for spokesmen to come and explore these issues. Both sides set a specific time for this meeting. The next day, many soldiers from both sides came, all hoping for an end to the conflict. Titus Labienus spoke for Pompey. He began to dispute issues with Vitinius when suddenly a storm of missiles from Pompey's side broke off the discussion. Vatinius was well protected by his guards' shields, but many were hit, including high-ranking officers, centurions, and soldiers. Labienus exclaimed, 'No more talk! There will be no peace until Caesar's head is brought in!'

Trouble in Rome

At the time that Caesar and Pompey and their forces were looking at each other across the River Apsus, the praetor M. Caelius Rufus started his term of office announcing that debtors needed his assistance. He called for the option for citizens to appeal the rulings of Caesar's arbitrators regarding valuation and payments. Caelius was a notorious firebrand, agitator, and supporter of Pompey. He set his tribunal near the chair of the city praetor, Caesar's man, G. Trebonius in an obvious attempt to upset Caesar's settlements. But Trebonius understood the ins and outs of the financial difficulties facing Rome during the crisis. Most of the decisions were more mediations rather than imposed arbitrations. Further, Trebonius and Caesar's supporters needed to make Caesar's settlement work: anyone who really wanted to cause trouble about the arrangements faced threats, not only to their property, but their lives. No one took up Caelius' offer of help.

Caelius, finding his efforts to cause trouble for Caesar unsuccessful, brought before the popular assembly a law ruling that payment of owed money need not be made for six years from the day the law was passed and more, the debtor would pay no interest in that amount of time. Essentially, this law would undermine not only Caesar's efforts at economic stabilization but would also cause the whole credit-financial structure to collapse. Caelius appealed to the radical segment of the crowd. Consul Servilius and the magistrates of the city opposed Caelius' law. While a large group supported passing the law, a greater number opposed it. Caelius withdrew his law and substituted two other laws: one allowed renters to live for a year rent-free and the other allowed the cancellation of debt. The large mob who supported Caelius charged the tribunal. In the confusion, Caelius forced Trebonius off the stand.

These disturbances upset the senate. Consul Servilius brought a motion before the fathers condemning Caelius' unprincipled actions. The senators decreed that Caelius be removed from office and excluded from the senate. Caelius responded by calling a public meeting but Trebonius' soldiers pushed him and his supporters off the platform. Caelius claimed he was following Caesar's lead in his actions and announced he was going to him to straighten out these misunderstandings. Instead, Caelius secretly sent a message to Milo, offering an alliance to further both of their interests.

Milo had fought on the streets of Rome during the disturbances in the fifties. He supported Pompey, participating in the killing of Clodius in 52 and was permanently exiled. Caelius offered his help if Milo returned with his band of gladiators and, together, they could build their own regime in the south of Italy and then offer their services to whoever came out on top in the civil war. Milo went to the area of Thurii with his gladiators, planning to raise the local population in conjunction with Caelius' planned uprising. The area around Naples was critical to his plot: with his headquarters at Casilinum, Caelius intended to seize Capua and then take Naples. But the Roman citizens at Capua knew all about Caelius and the radical programme he represented; they closed their gates to him and spread the word that he was a public enemy. When his scheme failed, he disappeared.

Different, and more subtle than Caelius, Milo sent dispatches to the local communities in Lucani, informing them that he was acting by the order and authority of Pompey, given to him through Vibullius. He attempted to incite those with considerable debts to take matters into their own hands, but few paid him any attention. So, instead of dealing with the debtor problem, he freed many slaves from the subterranean prisons in which they languished and mobilized them as a force to seize power. With these men, he put the town of Cosa under siege. By the time he organized the operation, the praetor Q. Pedius had marched a legion to the area and trapped Milo's forces between his legion and Cosa's walls. In the action, a rock thrown from the walls struck and killed Milo. At the time Milo was before Cosa, Caelius surfaced in Thurii, where he tried to gain power through the agency of certain townsmen and bribing Caesar's Gallic and Spanish horsemen stationed as the town garrison. Caesar's soldiers were much too well informed about corrupt Roman ways to fall for Caelius' promises. They simply killed him and so, Italy was at peace and remained under Caesar's power.

Antony Defends Brundisium

Mark Antony was in command at Brundisium. After Pompey's navy destroyed Calenus' ships returning from Caesar's first landing, Antony followed Caesar's orders to keep his troops stationed around Brundisium and his ships in the harbour. As weeks passed Caesar wanted more troops but what he needed even more were strongboxes filled with coins. He needed to pay troops for their continued service, pay the suppliers of goods, particularly for food, and the ever necessary 'gratuities' for favours. In midwinter, Caesar attempted to cross to Brundisium in a small boat only to have the rough seas force him back.

Pompey and his advisors knew that Caesar's money and reinforcements were still in Italy. They wanted to pin them there. Libo commanded a fleet of fifty warships that were blockading Oricum and Pompey ordered him to attack Brundisium. Swiftly approaching the port, Libo's ships encountered a flotilla of cargo ships which he attacked and burned except for a grain ship which he captured. The sight of the burning ships alerted Brundisium's defenders to the danger facing them. Later at night, Libo landed soldiers supported by archers on an island just beyond Brundisium's outer harbour, easily expelling the small garrison there. So satisfied was Libo with his success that he sent back most of his fleet so they could land, repair, and refit. He sent a message to Pompey, saying that with the forces at hand, five protected quadriremes and their support boats, he could stop any reinforcements leaving Brundisium.

Mark Antony was an experienced, bold commander; his soldiers loved him and his loyalty to Caesar was unquestioned. When Libo and his fleet appeared in front of his harbour, Antony began planning ways to defeat him. He ordered all the pinnacles from the fleet to be collected and brought to the inner harbour. There were about sixty boats and Antony had them reinforced with bulwarks and roofing and manned with select soldiers, each one a fierce fighter. He sent the armoured pinnacles to different places along the coast, each one stationed by itself.

Never one to sit without doing, Antony had the Brundisium yards build two triremes. He picked select crews of experienced rowers who were told to act as if they were new to the sea. The two ships, rowed in a very clumsy manner, had almost reached the mouth of the outer harbour. When Libo saw those struggling ships, he thought they would become important prizes of war so he sent out his five quadriremes to collect them. As Libo's warships approached the triremes, they somehow picked up speed and moved into the harbour. The commanders of the quadriremes ordered more speed, thinking their prizes were just beyond reach. Just as the quadriremes reached the triremes, a signal rang out and the pinnacles emerged from out of nowhere, or so it seemed to the quadriremes' crews. The pinnacles attacked from all sides and quickly captured one quadrireme and repelled the others.

When Antony had prepared for this attack, he also sent strong cavalry squads to areas of the coast where ships might put in for water. While Libo occupied an advantageous position on his island, there was no water there. Now, he could get none along the coast nor did he have the facility for long-range shipments. He had to abandon the island and return to Epirus. He had failed.

Antony Brings Reinforcements

From the middle of January, (mid-November, solar time) through mid-March (mid-December, solar time) Caesar and Pompey had camped on either side of the River Apsus. Caesar thought Antony had missed several opportunities for sailing when the storms had stopped, and the winds blew right. Caesar wrote strong words to Antony and his officers, telling them to lose no time sending the troops and money. He instructed them to sail toward Apollonia's coast, to the south of Dyrrachium, or toward the Labeates, to the north. Both landing areas were far from the bases of Pompey's fleets, based on Corcyra and Dyrrachium. At the same time, Pompey sent instructions to his fleet, demanding that they keep watching for the movements of Caesar's fleet, to keep Caesar's force from landing. They had already failed once; they had better not fail again.

At Brundisium, Antony, the commander-in-chief, and Calenus, commander of the fleet, understood Caesar's anxieties but knew they would rather take care not to endanger the fleet loaded with elite troops and horses. An inopportune moment and if things went wrong as was very possible, they could lose the whole fleet, men, and money. If that happened, Caesar's chance of victory would almost disappear. Still, rough seas and bad weather were risked, and the fleet did set out for the Epirus coast. On the second day, the fleet sailed past Apollonia. Pompey's scouts brought word to Dyrrachium. There sat the Rhodian fleet under Coponius; he put forth in a failing wind, eager to catch Caesar's fleet, but the south wind grew stronger, pushing Caesar's fleet before Pompey's. Still, Coponius persisted in his pursuit. Caesar's fleet sailed past Dyrrachium with Pompey's fleet following. If the wind fell, Coponius would have Caesar's overloaded ships at his advantage. Three miles beyond Lassus sat the harbour of Nymphaeum, which gave protection from the southwest winds but not from the south winds. Calenus ordered the fleet to enter the harbour, seeing the weather as less a threat than Coponius. Almost marvellously, just after the fleet entered that harbour, the wind shifted from the south, where it had blown for two days, to blowing from the southwest. While Caesar's fleet safely sat in harbour, the southwest wind grew into gale force, driving Pompey's fleet, sixteen large, protected warships, onto rocks. All the ships were lost, killing most of their crews and fighting men. Caesar's men rescued many survivors and sent them home.

When the sun was setting, two straggling transport ships were separated from Caesar's fleet and anchored opposite Lissus. Pompey's commander, Otacilius Crassus, sent out some pinnacles to capture the two ships. Crassus opened negotiations with the two ships, promising fair treatment if they surrendered. One of the ships carried 220 new recruits and the other ship had less than 200 veterans on board. The new recruits, suffering from rough water and seasickness, fearing the number of the enemies, accepted the promises of good treatment and surrendered.

The ship with veterans, equally suffering from the high seas and sickness, had no intention of surrendering, but rather than put up a fight and lose, their spokesman indicated they wanted to surrender but needed to nail down conditions. As the talks proceeded, soldiers forced the ship's helmsman to steer the ship onto the shore. After the ship grounded, the veterans set up a temporary camp in the night. The next morning, a cavalry unit of some 400 riders, supported by a gang of locals attacked them. Well trained, experienced, and used to working together, Caesar's veterans repulsed the attack. The small unit then counter-attacked, breaking through Pompey's force and gaining Antony's lines without casualties. Crassus' men marched the recruits who had surrendered, before him. Crassus ordered them all killed.

Following the escape of Caesar's veterans, the Roman citizens of Lissus, who Caesar had established in the town previously, opened the gates for Antony and his forces. Otacilius Crassus and his small garrison fled the town and headed toward Pompey. Antony put his newly landed forces together, three veteran legions and one raw legion with 800 cavalry. He sent the transport fleet back to Brundisium for another shipment of men and provisions, but kept a collection of Gallic longboats at Lissus so if Pompey sent an invasion force to Italy, Caesar could send a pursuing force. Antony sent to Caesar the information about how many men he brought and where they were.

Both Caesar and Pompey learned of Antony's sailing at the same time because Antony's ships passed Apollonia and Dyrrachium. Both sent scouts to see where Antony landed but they found nothing for a few days.

Otacilius Crassus reached Pompey and Antony's messenger found Caesar simultaneously. Pompey marched out of his camp on the Apsus that night and the next morning Caesar marched out of his camp on the other side of the Apsus. Pompey had a clear route toward Lissus, but Caesar had to make a long detour to arrive at a ford to cross the river. Using forced marches, Pompey attempted to secretly approach Antony, forbidding fires at camps so as to remain unobserved. Antony, a shrewd soldier, had scouts out and knew Pompey's location. He kept his men in camp for a day and sent scouts to contact Caesar and his forces. The next day, Caesar joined Antony. Pompey, not wanting to face two armies, withdrew to a new camp near Asparagium, a town dependent on Dyrrachium.

Caesar sends Troops into Greece

After Caesar had joined forces with Antony, he recalled the legion he had stationed protecting the seacoast near Oricum and concentrated some of his forces to initiate an offensive into the interior of Greece and Macedonia. He wanted to secure more supplies and gain manoeuvring room. Caesar had the advantage of his supply of coins and Spanish silver, he did not need to plunder, rather he could pay for what he needed. Spokesmen had arrived from Thessaly and Aetolia requesting that Caesar send garrisons to protect their lands from Pompey's collectors and pledging to obey his instructions. Caesar sent to Thessaly, Cassius Longinus with XXVII Legion of recruits, and 200 horse; to Aetolia, he sent Calvisius Sabine's with five cohorts and a squad of cavalry; both teams were to buy supplies and send them to Caesar. Into Macedonia Caesar ordered Domitius Calvisius with two legions, XI, and XII, and 500 horsemen and to free Macedonia, he allowed Menedemus, exiled by Pompey, to return to an enthusiastic reception.

Caesar's forces accomplished their objectives and supplies came. The Aetolians allowed Calvisius to remove Pompey's garrisons from Calydon and Naupactus and so Caesar held Aetolia. In Thessaly, Cassius and his legion found the land split between a Pompeian faction and Caesar's supporters. An older leader, Hegesaretos, supported Pompey and a young aristocrat, Petraeus strongly backed Caesar with his men and wealth. Domitius marched into Macedonia and met with many envoys from the towns. They begged for protection from Pompey's forces and told him that Scipio with the eastern legions was coming. This news caused rumours and panic to spread quickly: Scipio and his legions were here. It was true, Scipio was marching against Domitius but about twenty miles from his camp, he changed route and headed toward Thessaly, to confront Cassius Longinus.

The change in direction and speed of march meant that Scipio's arrival was simultaneous with the news of his advances. Indeed, to move faster, Scipio left M. Favonius with the legions' baggage at the River Aliacmon, on the border of Macedonia and Thessaly along with eight cohorts for protection.

The cavalry of King Cotys of Thrace, a supporter of Pompey, was raiding those they believed were Caesar's partisans on the border of Macedonia and Thessaly. Hearing of Scipio's offensive, they rode toward Cassius' camp. Cassius, knowing that Scipio was marching toward him, thought the approaching dust clouds raised by the cavalry were Scipio's advanced guard coming through the mountains into Thessaly's plains. He mobilized his legion and withdrew toward Ambracia. Scipio was pursuing Cassius when a courier came to him with a letter from Favonius: Domitius was advancing against the baggage train and the eight cohorts could not defend against those forces. Scipio, understanding his soldiers' possessions were in the train, immediately ordered his army to turn about and march back to his base camp. They marched day and night; the vanguard of Scipio's army arrived at Favonius's camp while Domitius' army was evident only by a dust cloud on the horizon. Domitius' efforts saved Cassius while Scipio's speed rescued Favonius.

Scipio stayed in camp by the River Aliacmon for two days allowing his men to rest and resupply. Domitius had constructed camp just across the river. On the third day, early dawn, Scipio advanced across the Aliacmon and quickly built a new camp. The next morning, he drew up his army before his camp, challenging Domitius. Understanding that if he did not respond, he would look weak and ineffectual, Domitius drew his army out in battle order and marched out into the plain between the two camps. He pushed his battle line toward Scipio's line but had to halt because Scipio did not move from under his camp's rampart nor across the ditch in his front. Domitius had to restrain his troops but was not going to accept fighting at a disadvantage by having to cross the ditch. His bluff called, Scipio withdrew his troops back across the river and marched up an elevation to construct a new camp.

After Scipio had settled into this new camp, taking a few days for resupply, he set up an ambush to catch Domitius' foragers while they collected fodder for their horses. Demetrius' Prefect of Horse, Q. Varus lead a small cavalry contingent into the ambush area; suddenly, Scipio's men attacked. Varus' cavalry quickly reformed ranks, withstood the assault and counter-attacked. They killed almost eighty of Scipio's soldiers for the loss of two of their own. Now, seeing how Scipio planned to proceed, Domitius plotted his revenge. Pretending low provisions, he struck camp as if to march some considerable distance to find better foraging country. He marched only about three miles but hid his army in ravines and hills. Scipio, thinking here were easy pickings, sent his cavalry to track Domitius so his soldiers could attack while Domitius was on the march. When, however, Scipio's horse reached Domitius' trap, the neighing of horses created suspicions that all was not right, Scipio's advance guard turned about and retired on their main body. Judging the trap sprung, Domitius' cavalry charged Scipio's units, cutting off two squadrons, killing or capturing all their men including Scipio's prefect of cavalry.

Chapter 10

The Struggles in the Lines

Formation of the Lines

Once Antony landed, Caesar withdrew his garrisons stationed along the coast near Oricum but left five cohorts to guard the town. Antony left many warships at anchor near Oricum in order to provide a naval force on the coast of Epirus. Caesar's commander Acilius Caninus ordered the ships drawn into the inner harbour behind the town and moored them to the shore. Then he had a merchant ship sunk, blocking the port entrance. He had another ship attached to the hulk to protect it and had a tower built on the guard ship. Soldiers manned the ship ready to defend the harbour opening.

Young Gnaeus Pompey, commander of the Egyptian fleet, sailed to Oricum and prepared to attack the harbour. His engineers set up tackle and windlass on a barge to pull the sunken ship out of the harbour mouth. To protect the engineering work, the young Pompey screened their barge with several warships each one bearing a tower of a height equal to that of the defending warship. As the windlass pulled the hulk away from the harbour entrance, the archers and projector machines in Pompey's towers overwhelmed the defenders in their tower. Pompey's ships forced their way into the outer harbour. Some landed soldiers with ladders to assault the town walls while the rest of the ships kept up an arrow storm against the walls. The defending fighting men on the ship swiftly abandoned their posts and fled by boats.

Young Pompey's soldiers seized the defending ship and advanced across the breakwater which joined the town at the shore. His engineers drew four biremes across the breakwater on rollers using push bars and so, his forces attacked Caesar's beached warships from both sides. Young Pompey's ships drew off four of Caesar's ships and burned the rest. Leaving his naval commander, Laelius, to blockade the port of Oricum, young Pompey sailed north to Lissus. There, he attacked and burned thirty merchant ships left in the port by Antony. His soldiers assaulted Lissus, but Caesar's soldiers successfully defended Lissus' walls. After three days and the loss of a few men, the young Pompey withdrew.

The destruction of his fleet left Caesar without communications with Italy for either supplies or more reinforcements. He needed to bring the war to an end because the longer it dragged on, the more the issue was in doubt. Word came to Caesar that Pompey had arrived at Asparagium with a strong force. Caesar wanted to bring Pompey to battle and marched his army toward Pompey's camp, taking Parthini on the march from Pompey's garrison, and camped opposite Asparagium on the third day. The next morning, Caesar deployed his army in battle array, challenging Pompey to fight but Pompey refused to leave camp, rejecting Caesar's challenge so Caesar returned his army to camp. He needed another approach. The following day, he marched out of camp and headed east into rough country. He could not cross the river because the operation would separate his forces into two groups, allowing Pompey a significant advantage, so he advanced on Dyrrachium by a roundabout route. He hoped Pompey would withdraw to Dyrrachium, where he kept all his supplies and equipment. When informed that Caesar had marched out of camp toward the east, Pompey assumed Caesar was pressured by a scarcity of food, but soon scouts brought the news that Caesar turned north. Now, Pompey understood Caesar was marching on Dyrrachium and quickly ordered his army to march north.

He knew that Pompey's army of recruits never marched fast and told his soldiers that he needed them to march as fast as possible so he could steal a march on Pompey. With only a short stop at night, Caesar reached Dyrrachium in the morning. In the distance, he could see Pompey's army marching toward him. Caesar immediately ordered his men to make camp. Pompey found himself cut off from his base in Dyrrachium. Rather than fight his way through Caesar's forces, Pompey marched west, to the sea at a place called Petra, sitting on a bay that served as an acceptable port. Sending instructions to his fleet, Pompey ordered them to bring supplies from the Adriatic and Asia.

Now, Caesar saw there was no quick end to the war and supplies were getting shorter. He sent officers with a foraging party deep into Epirus' rough country. The local villages were connected in a food distribution network and Caesar thought he might collect more food than near areas. But Pompey's men had already ransacked all the villages in the whole area, going as far as digging for hidden food. Pompey had stockpiled his supplies at his base, Petra. The failure of his own foraging efforts suggested to Caesar that Pompey had backed himself in a corner. He had collected all the local supplies and his own forces in a narrow strip of coast surrounded by rough country. By blocking him in position, Caesar could render Pompey's strong cavalry useless and make him look weak to his allies to the east.

Pompey's scouts quickly reported that Caesar sent his soldiers to occupy hilltops and build fortifications. While Caesar's camp separated Pompey from Dyrrachium, the seas were open between the town and Pompey's base at Petra. Since most of Pompey's equipment and supplies, including food and fodder were in Dyrrachium, he could not march off and leave the town for Caesar to pick up. Nor could he attack Caesar in a pitched battle because Caesar's troops were tougher than his. Pompey's recourse was to push at Caesar's lines, forcing his troops as far away from Pompey's lines as possible. Pompey's men built twenty-four fortified bases in a connected circuit of fifteen miles. Within the perimeter, Pompey's men sowed crops for fodder. Caesar's lines were more extensive than Pompey's because, while Pompey would not engage in a direct assault to remove one of Caesar's bases, still, he sent archers and slingers to harass his troops. Caesar's men fabricated leather and cloth coverings to ward off the missiles but many were killed and wounded.

The struggles became intense. The IX Legion seized a hilltop and began building fortifications; Pompey's men took a nearby hilltop and shot missiles at the men of IX. While on one side, a cliff isolated the hilltop, on the other, an easy ascent led up to IX's position. Pompey's men assailed the height and archers and slingers were backed up by a mass of light troops and projector operators. The soldiers of the IX were hard-pressed. Caesar, seeing his men's plight, ordered them to retire from the hilltop. When the force pulled back down the slope, Pompey's men fought all the harder, believing Caesar's elite force was retreating in fear. The IX pulled up, forming a defensive stance.

While they struggled, Caesar organized a counter-attack. He ordered a team of elite troops to advance toward IX Legion, setting up a line of mobile bulwarks and digging a trench across the slope, and placing units of archers and slingers in places to strike at the Pompeian missile throwers. Once the relief force was in place, Caesar ordered IX Legion to withdraw. As they began to move, the Pompeian forces formed up to block their path and force the bulwarks. Caesar, fearing the withdrawal would end up in a rout, had Antony use his very loud voice to call orders to the IX. The trumpets sounded and Antony ordered the legion to charge. Dressing ranks, the legion's front ranks hurled their pilums in unison at the Pompeians on higher ground and charged at a run up the hill, smashing the Pompeian line. The Pompeians fled, falling over the overturned bulwarks and ditch. The men of IX felt they had completed their task killing many of the Pompeians and losing only five of their fellows. They marched a short space away and finished building this part of the fortified line.

Caesar observed that he was engaged in a new style of warfare, unprecedented in history. Here was a large army, supported with supplies delivered across the waters, being barricaded by a smaller force holding long lines of fortifications with few supplies at hand. Pompey feared to fight Caesar's soldiers who, in turn, wanted nothing better than to force a fight and defeat the Pompeian army. Caesar's men were suffering from food shortages. All the wheat was gone and now the soldiers accepted barley, even legumes and greens. Meat from Epirus was readily available, so the army was not going to starve. The army maintained high morale because they had gone through this before: the war in Spain a year before, while they experienced difficulties at times, turned out well, and the wars in Gaul involving great difficulties were victorious. Pompey's soldiers, finding their opponents eating root vegetables made into a kind of bread, made loaves of the same plant and hurled them over their walls.

Soon, the wheat crop was starting to ripen and plenty was in sight. Caesar's soldiers were in fine spirits, healthy with abundant water. Deserters from Pompey's forces, however, told a different story. Caesar had his men dam and divert all the streams that ran into the area occupied by the Pompeians, so while food and supplies came by sea, they were short of water. By extraordinary efforts, the Pompeians preserved their cavalry horses, but they had to slaughter all their other animals. Many of the troops were in a bad way; not being inured to the hardships of war, they suffered from the constant toils required to keep the fortifications and camp functioning. Their latrine systems were defective, and sickness had come. Morale was sinking.

The Day of Six Battles

While Caesar and Pompey were facing each other in Epirus, their men, their supporters, and the Mediterranean world recognized that this struggle was existential for the Roman Republic and its dominions. One man would win, the other would lose; the loser would die and his followers would lose property, and many of them, their lives. The winner would remake the Mediterranean world to suit his interests. When the struggle began more than a year ago, Pompey's side saw victory was soon going to be theirs, but Caesar foiled their expectations. Now, he was in Epirus, holding Spain and Italy. Even worse, Caesar had them trapped in a small area. The men of Pompey's forces knew they must win. They redoubled their efforts to destroy Caesar's hardened soldiers. First, Pompey had to conserve his strength: his cavalry horses would perish if they did not get more water and fodder, so Pompey ordered all the remaining horses loaded on his ships and transferred to Dyrrachium, where pastures and water were abundant. And second, Pompey began to plan for Caesar's downfall. He sent some messages to Caesar, carried by his own agents saying they represented dissatisfied members of Dyrrachium's garrison. If Caesar came in person, they would surrender the town.

Caesar was looking for ways to weaken Pompey's forces; he knew morale was low because they feared Caesar's veterans. He decided that the most damaging thing he could do was to take Dyrrachium. The word that Pompey's garrison at Dyrrachium would join his side if he came to them in person was very tempting. Yes, it might be a trap but if it were true, Caesar could remove Dyrrachium from Pompey's control and Pompey would have to move his forces to keep them supplied. At night, Caesar set out with a small but strong formation, hoping for a welcome at Dyrrachium. In the dark, Caesar marched his force toward an unobserved way between the sea and the marshes that protected the town walls. Advancing deep on the narrow path between marsh and sea, he waited for someone to come from the town. Suddenly, strong forces attacked him in front and back. The Pompeians had transported their men by sea and laid ambushes into which Caesar fell. He lost many fine men and nearly perished himself.

Pompey was pleased; his projected coordinated attack against Caesar was beginning well. Observing Caesar's soldiers near his base camp, Pompey's commanders noted a cohort on guard duty collected in groups near their earthworks at night and left their fires burning. Organizing strike teams of archers, the Pompeians picked their way through the darkness, placed themselves in good shooting positions, and let loose volleys of arrows. Once done, they threaded a path back to their lines. Caesar's soldiers learned to light fires and then stay away from them. On this night, the raid became a full-scale attack.

When Caesar had left his camp for the attempt on Dyrrachium, he had put P. Sulla in charge of the camp. Sulla sent out two veteran legions to support the cohort defending the attacked section. The legions initially hit their enemies hard, repulsing their front line and the rest fled. Rather than allow the two legions to follow up their initial strike, Sulla recalled them and settled them back in his camp as a defence force. Many officers and men complained, saying now was the time for a major push but Caesar had instructed Sulla to be careful and not to get drawn into a full engagement. Pompey withdrew his force to a distant hill from which they could keep watch on Caesar's lines nearby.

In total on this day, six battles engulfed Caesar's forces: three against Caesar near Dyrrachium and three Pompey launched against Caesar's lines, scattering his attacks so he could stop forces in one section from reinforcing other sections. In one battle, a centurion commanding three of Caesar's cohorts fought off a full legion and repulsed it from their position. In another battle, a formation of German auxiliaries advanced beyond Caesar's lines, slaughtered many of Pompey's soldiers, and returned without any casualties. In all, the fighting did not go well for Pompey that day; he lost about 2,000 men, many officers, and six military standards. Caesar's side had only twenty men killed (except for those killed in Caesar's attack on Dyrrachium) but in the area where Pompey's archers attacked the redoubt, every soldier there was wounded, including four centurions of one cohort, each one of whom lost an eye. The men collected some 30,000 arrows that the Pompeians had shot at the fortification and the centurion Scaeva had 120 holes in his shield. Caesar, impressed with Scaeva's service in holding the redoubt, granted him 200,000 *sesterces* and promoted him from the eighth cohort to the first centurion of the first cohort. Then he presented the eighth cohort with double pay, more food and decorations.

Pompey took stock of his forces, finding some of his commanders were competent and brave but many of them were weak and cowardly. He ordered his soldiers to strengthen his defensive works facing Caesar, posted units to guard the most vulnerable point, and marched his best troops back to his base camp. Caesar marched his field army toward Pompey's base camp and after entrenching a position, paraded his army in front of Pompey's camp, challenging battle. The front line of Caesar's legions stood just beyond the range of projector machines. Pompey saw that if he did accept the challenge, his supporters would think he was not going to win the war but if he fought with Caesar's soldiers, he would probably face defeat. Pompey's solution to this conundrum was a half measure: he led his army out of camp and paraded in front of his ramparts. His third line rested on the camp rampart and remained in the throwing range of troops in the camp. Caesar had no intention of attacking at such a great disadvantage. If his soldiers prevailed, Pompey could easily withdraw into his fortification leaving the battle inconclusive.

The Lines Stabilize

Caesar had recovered Aetolia, Acarnania, and Amplhilochi through the efforts of Cassius Longinus and Calvisius Sabinus. He thought Pompey's hold on Greece was weakened and he sent Q. Calenus along with some cohorts to seize Achaea. Pompey's commander in Achaea, Rutiliius Lupus, blocked the Isthmus of Corinth, but Calenus convinced the governing powers of Delphi, Thebes, and Orchomenus to join Caesar and took the few holdouts in the area by assault. When Caesar found out about Scipio's arrival in Macedonia, he began planning to approach him with the intention of ending the war. Caesar's friend, A. Clodius, was also a close friend of Scipio. Giving Clodius letters by his own hand and developing an approach to convince Scipio to push Pompey toward making peace, when Clodius arrived at Scipio's headquarters, he was well received. At first, he talked at length with Scipio but soon, he could only meet Scipio in the company of others. After the war was over, Caesar found out Scipio decided to ignore his offers because he and Pompey had decided on Caesar's destruction. His mission had failed, Clodius returned to Caesar.

Caesar and Pompey had fought for many months without decisive results: sometimes one side gained an advantage and then the other side. The logistics of the two sides were complementary; Pompey had food shipped in and a strong base in Dyrrachium, but he needed water and fodder, while Caesar controlled the water supplies and plenty of lands from which his men collected fodder, but food had to come from a long distance and was sparse. Like two skilled and powerful wrestlers, Caesar and Pompey tussled in Epirus, each trying to grasp an edge, in order to leverage a flip of their opponent's power. Pompey had gained an advantage when he moved his cavalry horses to Dyrrachium and from there to pasture.

Pompey thought to bring more horses to Dyrrachium and gather a strong cavalry force there, which was a threat to Caesar's supply lines. The way from Dyrrachium to the pastures passed along two different roads each one of which passed through narrows. Caesar sent teams of soldiers to each pathway and dug earthworks to provide cover for archers who would slaughter every horse they saw. When Pompey heard of Caesar's barricade of the pastures, he ordered the horses to embark on transports and returned to his entrenchments. He had fodder shipped in from Corcyra and Acarnania, but the transports could not supply a sufficient amount for the number of horses. Soon, many of the horses would become useless. The only answer, it appeared to Pompey, was an attack on Caesar's lines.

The Affair of the Allobrogian Brothers

In the midst of all the details of these complex operations, Caesar found out he needed to hear a serious complaint delivered by a large contingent of Allobrogian officers and men. Always personable, understanding the current situation was not easy, Caesar needed to take care not to have lingering antagonisms fester. The gracious aristocrat paid close attention to his soldiers' complaints and was surprised by what he heard. Through their spokesman, backed up by the assent of a crowd of soldiers, Caesar heard that the Allobrogians' commanders, the brothers Egus and Raucillus, were taking a cut of all of their pay; they had appropriated the rightful plunder of the soldiers and sent that plunder home to their own properties. Further, they informed Caesar that the brothers had submitted inflated returns of the numbers of men in each unit, in order to collect more money for themselves.

In many ways, this problem was a crisis for Caesar and his army. He needed the loyalty of his fighting men and nothing eroded loyalty more than corruption, particularly from the perspective of those who saw themselves being cheated. The adherents of the Allobroges had long been a symbol of Caesar's support for those who supported him. This Gallic tribe had dealt with Romans and the Roman Republic for generations. Settled south of Lake Constance and west of the Rhône, the name means 'foreigner' or something similar. Polybius tells us that Hannibal ran into the Allobroges on his march to Italy. They appear as a confederation of warriors who had recently arrived. Hannibal negotiated and fought his way through the tribal lands. By 120 BC, the Allobroges had become a settled people, still with warrior ambitions but not seizing the lands of others. The Romans defeated the Allobroges in battle and incorporated them into their new province, Gallia Transalpina, 117 BC. Within the province, the Allobroges kept their lands and maintained autonomy.

In the following decades, Allobroges leaders played Roman political games with skill and success. They sued governors for corruption; they developed political interests in Rome, working with the Senate and with those opposed to the Senate; they even became involved in Catiline's conspiracy, coming out on top because of a clever double game. They rebelled in 62 BC, fighting successfully but surrendering to Roman might; still, they maintained their warrior reputations. Caesar had known Allobrogians since his youth. When he was ready to make war in Gaul, Caesar had made some sort of agreement with Adbucillus, a prominent member of the Allobroges elite. Throughout his campaigns in Gaul, Caesar found the Allobroges' support important. Adbucillus had two sons, Egus and Raucillus. They accompanied Caesar's armies throughout the Gallic Wars. Honouring their father through his awards to the two sons, Caesar granted them lands and the command of the allied Allobrogian horse. They were a critical part of Caesar's forces. These were the men accused of corruption by their own subordinates.

Caesar was deep into games of intrigue. To suspect everyone of being an enemy only led to making that a fact; not to be aware of the fact, however, that anyone might switch sides for a variety of reasons was naïve and Caesar wasn't naïve. Whether Caesar had suspicions about the brothers or was really surprised is beyond our knowledge, but their brazen collecting funds showed they were getting ready for something. Rather than create an open confrontation, in which all manner of traps might spring, Caesar tells us that it was not time for punishment, that in consideration of their bravery, he could forgive a lot of their percolation and postpone the whole matter. Indeed, Caesar said he spoke to them in private, telling them that they could expect all from him, but they should not steal from the men. Now, of course, the brothers were on the spot and had to quickly decide what they were going to do. Their own men had conspired against them; Caesar had an eye on them, and whatever secret plans they had made either had to be done or forgotten.

The decision was clear: first, pretend nothing happened except silly mistakes; second, defect to Pompey with as many men and as much money as possible. Followed by influential clients, possessing many fine horses, the brothers plotted their exit from Caesar's side. After an unsuccessful attempt on the life of prefect of the horse, Volusenus, as a distraction, the brothers passed over the lines to Pompey's side and were taken directly to the commander's headquarters. Since almost all defections from one side to the other went from the senate's side to Caesar's, Pompey was pleased that two such well-known leaders and their entourage had come to him. He paraded them around his lines, showing them off to his officers and troops. And they were valuable because both brothers were deeply involved in the management of Caesar's lines and forces. Pompey looked forward to the coming battles for which he was preparing.

Chapter 11

The Battle Front Shifts

The Lines Break

A number of officers and scouts followed the Allobrogian brothers to Pompey's camp having carefully examined Caesar's lines for strengths and weaknesses. Pompey, who had already determined to attack Caesar's lines, was pleased. Going over all the information collected together, Pompey's commanders presented him with a battle plan to break Caesar's lines. For seventeen miles, these lines contained Pompey's forces. From the sea in the north, near Dyrrachium, to the sea in the south, an inner and outer fortification met any would-be intruder. The point chosen for the attack, the greatest weakness in Caesar's lines, was at the extreme southern end. Here, where the lines met the Adriatic, there was an opening.

On the far southern extremity of Caesar's fortifications, the lines ended on the seashore. There, Caesar had ordered a fifteen-foot-wide ditch dug as the main defence against Pompey's army, backed up by an earth rampart ten feet high and wide. Some 600 feet back from the ditch and rampart, he ordered another fortified line, facing outward. This consisted of a more modest rampart topped with a stockade. But, while these earthworks were done, the soldiers had not built cross stockades facing the sea or blocked access down the way between the two fortified lines. The brothers told Pompey about this flaw in Caesar's fortification and here, Pompey decided to attack.

Pompey's commanders organized a strong strike force, requiring each man to carry a bundle of willow branches along with equipment to construct earthworks. Added to these heavy infantry troops, Pompey assigned units of light foot and archers. To transport this force, Pompey collected a large number of skiffs backed up by cargo ships. The strike force embarked at night and silently waited off the coast without lights, covered by warships from Dyrrachium. That night, Pompey collected sixty cohorts near the southern extremity of Caesar's lines.

This stretch of the lines was under the protection of IX Legion, commanded by Lentulus Marcellinus. But Marcellinus was ill and so Caesar appointed Fulvius Postumus as assistant commander The commanders had assigned two cohorts guarding the line's extremity. Just before dawn, a formation of spearmen and archers disembarked from the ships and attacked the south stockade with arrows and javelins. Caesar's soldiers defended themselves by throwing well-aimed stones, but the willow branches tied around the attackers' upper bodies deflected the stones. On the other side of the lines, Pompey's cohorts began to fill the ditches on the front which faced his south. Soon, Pompey's soldiers attacked using ladders to scale the ramparts. As they assaulted the ramparts, Pompey's projector engines launched masses of missiles and his teams of archers released an arrow storm, adding to the surprise and confusion. Caesar's men began digging a small but strong fort facing their threatened north rampart. But, once IX Legion's two cohorts were fully engaged defending their position, the heavy infantry of the strike force landed in between the inner and outer works of Caesar's lines. They hit the IX's cohorts on the flank, and with no blocking position behind which to defend, the two cohorts disintegrated and fled, down the alley between the lines.

Runners quickly reached Marcellinus in his camp. He gathered some cohorts and sent them, double-time, to support the defenders. The panic-driven troops, fleeing the Pompeian attack, ran head-on into the advancing reinforcements. Panic is contagious. The fleeing troops overwhelmed the reinforcements followed by the Pompeian shock troops. Marcellinus sent more reinforcements who were also swept up in the collapse. Courageous action by an eagle-bearer saved an eagle, but the result remained a debacle. The only centurion of the first cohort who survived the fight was the senior centurion of the second maniple.

Pompey's cohorts continued advancing along the alley. Backed up by strong reinforcements, their movement toward Marcellinus' camp struck terror into the defenders. Word passed to the next garrison camp up the line, commanded by Mark Antony. He quickly organized twelve cohorts and marched them to face Pompey's advancing soldiers. The forces clashed: Pompey's men fought hard but had to assume a defensive posture. Caesar's men rallied and positions stabilized as Caesar, using his signalling system from station to station, brought more troops to the threatened area. He came to the southern part of his lines and saw what Pompey had accomplished: he had breached Caesar's lines near the sea and established a strong camp ensuring his troops' access through the lines. Pompey was no longer besieged and Caesar's strategy had failed. He needed to rethink his next moves. To temporarily hold Pompey in check, Caesar ordered a fortified base built near Pompey's newly built camp.

Later that day, Caesar's scouts noticed a legion-sized formation of Pompey's soldiers marching near the seashore, screened by trees. They were making for the earthworks initially constructed by IX Legion when Pompey had attacked the north rampart. Caesar had occupied the fort but then abandoned it because he thought a large camp would be a more effective check on Pompey than dividing his forces. Now, however, Pompey put men in the fort, having them build a much larger camp, leaving the smaller earthworks as a citadel; then Pompey's men dug an entrenchment from the camp to the Genusus River, about 400 paces north beyond the camp. But, once his legions had built the camp, Pompey withdrew them to his main camp nearby, leaving only a single legion in the citadel.

Caesar had his scouts view this camp from different vantage points. They assured him that the camp was occupied by just one legion. Since the camp was about five hundred paces from Pompey's main camp, Caesar planned to attack the smaller camp, rush the one legion garrison, and then defend the camp from Pompey's counter-attack. Leaving two cohorts in his base camp doing the normal everyday work, Caesar led thirty-three cohorts in a double line against the single legion in the fortified camp. Among his force were the men of the IX Legion, sadly depleted of centurions and fighting men.

Leading the right-wing, Caesar and his men charged the camp's rampart before Pompey in his base camp knew anything about the attack. Driving the Pompeians from their rampart with missiles, Caesar's soldiers began breaking down the iron spike studded gate. Pompey's commander, Titus Pulio who had trapped and captured G. Antonius, led his brave soldiers defending the camp but was overwhelmed by Caesar's numbers. Bursting into the larger camp, Caesar's men scattered many of the defenders. The rest retreated into the citadel. Regrouping, Caesar's men carried the citadel, killing the few men who still tried to defend the fort. An easy victory or so, it seemed but things went wrong.

Caesar's right-wing mistook the entrenchment running from the camp to the river as part of the camp. They spread out, looking for the gate, which wasn't there. Soon, they found out this was just a single line without defenders, they broke through it and advanced forward. The whole cavalry followed right behind. The operation took some time and word of the attack reached Pompey. He immediately withdrew five legions from their work and led them to the battlefield, the ranks of marching men visible to Caesar's soldiers in the newly won camp. Pompey's cavalry rode across the plain in ranks, impressive in their order. His scattered soldiers fleeing defeat rallied and turned, falling into formation and again faced Caesar's forces. Now the balance of combat was reversed.

Pompey's fresh troops brought the hope of victory while Caesar's troops felt the fear of defeat. Pompey's troops who remained inside the camp Caesar's men had just taken, occupied the main gate facing Pompey's forces, holding it to allow the relief forces entry. Pompey's cavalry surged ahead, making for the path over the river entrenchment made by Caesar's right-wing. Caesar's cavalry, seeing that they were badly positioned, turned and drove pell-mell, back over the opening in the entrenchment, riding down anyone in their way. The right-wing infantry began to flee back to the opening only to find the crush of men and horses blocking their way. Many soldiers jumped down into the ten-foot-deep ditch, only to be crushed by others jumping on top of them, so the path was finally opened on top of the dead and dying soldiers who filed into the ditch. The soldiers of the left-wing in the camp saw the panic on the right and quickly withdrew from the camp and away from the battlefield. Panic was everywhere. Caesar tried to halt the confusion and fear, but the soldiers let go of their standards when Caesar grabbed them and kept on running. No-one turned to rally; everyone ran past Caesar. His army was out of control.

Caesar was shocked. In his account of the civil war, written in the third person, he shifts to first-person here, saying, *'credo'* (I believe) that Pompey was so surprised with the sudden collapse of Caesar's army, he feared the retreat was an attempt to trap him. Caesar then observed that the entrenchment from the camp to the river, which had hindered his army's advance, also blocked Pompey's pursuit. In these two battles in one day, Caesar lost 960 men, including thirty-two military tribunes and centurions. The majority of deaths happened in the ditch and rampart, men who died without wounds made by weapons. Thirty-two unit standards remained on the field.

Pompey's men rejoiced in their victory. They proclaimed Pompey as Imperator, a title Pompey maintained but without display. Not quite sure what to do with his captives, Pompey handed them over to Labienus, Caesar's former second in command. He paraded the prisoners, called them fellow soldiers and asked if veterans like them practised running away – then he ordered them all killed.

The victory seemed secure: now Pompey and his supporters had won the war. They had defeated the mighty Caesar and now had only to collect the spoils. All they needed to do was to finish their enemies off. However, Caesar saw the situation in a different way. Bad luck and faulty reconnaissance had foiled his plans. The time had come to change his operational strategies.

New Battle Plans

Caesar ordered all his garrisons in the lines to pull out and join his troops in his new camp south of the lines. Marching to a site where all assembled, he mounted a tribunal and spoke to his army. He praised them for all the successes that had been accomplished: the capture of Italy, the winning of Spain, and crossing the Adriatic to trap Pompey's army here. His plans were good, but misfortune, misadventure, and mistakes happen. When things go wrong, they must assist fortune by their own efforts. They all must work harder now to repair by bravery the damage foisted on them. At the end of his speech, he made examples of some who failed to do their job. A number of standard-bearers felt his wrath, held up to public ridicule, and demoted to the lowest rank. The soldiers and officers discussed their options. Many wanted to march against Pompey and defeat him in battle, but Caesar remained unsure about the temperament of the majority of the army after the debacle.

He understood the abandonment of the lines threatened his food supplies because much of the wheat was stockpiled across a wide area; nevertheless, following his new plans, he moved boldly forward. First, he saw to the care of his sick and injured soldiers; then at nightfall, having ordered all his readily available supplies and impedimenta collected in the southern camp, he sent them east along the River Genusus to a crossing, then south to Apollonia. Caesar instructed the baggage-train people to move as quietly as possible and not stop for any reason until the baggage reached Apollonia. He sent a legion as a guard. Once the baggage train was well on its way, Caesar ordered his army, except two legions, to leave the camp by all of the gates so the press of men would be far less than if they all left by one exit. Once out, they followed the baggage train. At sunrise, Caesar followed the rear guard, leaving a small staff to maintain the signals and daily routine to hide from Pompey's forces the fact that they were abandoning the camp.

In the early morning, Pompey became aware that Caesar had abandoned his fortifications and was marching away. He ordered his army to follow Caesar, sending his cavalry to harass Caesar's soldiers. At the crossing of the River Genusus, Caesar's troops became congested because of the difficulties of descending and climbing up the river's steep banks. Pompey's cavalry threatened to attack the rear guard. They formed up to meet the attacking horse. Caesar sent his cavalry, reinforced with 400 light infantry, to defend his troops from Pompey's attack. Caesar's men repelled Pompey's force, killing a few and routing the rest. By mid-morning, Caesar and his troops reached the spot he expected, his old camp at Asparagium, where he had confronted Pompey earlier in the year. Caesar kept his troops in the camp and drew in all his cavalry.

Pompey, following with his whole force, occupied his old camp near Asparagium. Many of his men, with nothing to do, because the camp was already built, stacked their weapons in their tents and went out to forage. Other soldiers, mindful that in their rush to catch Caesar, they had left many wagons and personal baggage behind, returned to their former camp to retrieve their goods. Caesar was aware of this fact. About noon, he gave the signal to march. The formed-up force marched out of the camp, foot and horse. Pompey could not pursue it because much of his army was dispersed. Caesar managed to march eight miles beyond Pompey's force before he camped. That night after twilight, Caesar collected the supplies and tools his troops carried as part of their kit in a baggage train and sent it on his march route. Just before dawn, he led out his troops, now in light marching order. They were ready to quickly meet any challenge in case Pompey's force appeared unexpectedly. His army crossed deep rivers and traversed difficult paths without loss. Pompey, disappointed that Caesar had stolen a march on him, ordered forced marches to catch Caesar but was unable to do so. Pompey abandoned his pursuit and began exploring other options.

Caesar reached Apollonia and allowed his soldiers to rest while he prepared for further operations. He placed his wounded in care, paid his soldiers in full, rewarded his allies, and garrisoned the towns he held. He developed a new campaign plan: if Pompey marched east to combine with Scipio in Macedonia and attack Caesar's forces under Domitius Calvinus, Caesar would pursue, blocking Pompey's route to Dyrrachium, and force Pompey to battle; if however, Pompey launched an invasion of Italy, Caesar would order Domitius to join him and so united, his army would march north through Illyricum to confront Pompey. Or again, should Pompey bring Apollonia and Oricum under siege, excluding Caesar from the coast, then he would quickly march east to blockade and threaten Scipio and so draw Pompey into Macedonia. With these plans in mind, Caesar wrote instructions to Domitius, telling him what he wanted to be done, and began a march east toward Domitius, after ensuring his wounded were left at various places. He installed four cohorts at Apollonia, one at Lissus, and three at Oricum.

At the same time, Pompey faced the problem of figuring out what Caesar was going to do. To Pompey, the problem was simple: if Caesar was marching against Scipio, Pompey needed to march to his relief; on the other hand, if Caesar intended to stay on the coast, in order to receive reinforcements from Italy, then Pompey would march east and attack Domitius. Either way,

Pompey decided to move east. The result was that both Caesar and Pompey decided to move east in order to bring relief to their allies and defeat the other. But Caesar wanted to secure both his bases: Domitius' position in Macedonia and Apollonia on the Adriatic. Pompey had a simpler solution by marching east and so moved faster than Caesar. Marching light, he intended to reach Candavia near the Macedonian frontier.

While Caesar and Pompey duelled for advantage, Domitius knew nothing of the crisis exploding on the coast. He had to move his camp away from Scipio in order to gather supplies and settled into a new camp at Heraclia, on the road from Candavia and so was in the path of Pompey. Nor did Caesar have any recent information about Domitius. As soon as Pompey saw Caesar withdrawing from his lines, he sent letters to all towns and provinces announcing Caesar's great defeat. Many who had supported Caesar now began thinking of a future dominated by Pompey. Messages sent from Caesar and from Domitius failed to arrive. Fortunately for Caesar what had looked like a failing became an advantage.

The Aollobroges, followers of the brothers who defected to Pompey, served as scouts for Pompey's advancing army. A squad of them came upon some of their fellow tribesmen who served with Domitius; they could not stop bragging about Caesar's great defeat, telling how Caesar was on the move and Pompey was coming ahead of him. In a mere four hours, Domitius received the news that he was in danger and Caesar needed support. Anticipating Caesar's route, Domitius broke camp and joined up with Caesar near Thessaly's border at Aeginium. The united army marched toward Gomphi, the first town on the route from Epirus.

The leaders of Gomphi had sent envoys to Caesar when he began his campaign in Epirus, pledging their support; but now Pompey's announcements of victory unsettled them. Androsthenes, master of Thessaly, thinking Pompey was going to win, convinced the leaders of Gomphi to collect all the local crops and goods into the town and hold Caesar off. He also sent messages to both Scipio, based in Larisa, and Pompey, on the road to Macedonia, requesting relief from Caesar's attack. He made clear the fact that Gomphi was a strong and well-provisioned town and so would hold out for some time; yet here was Caesar, where they could defeat him for good.

Caesar immediately invested Gomphi, building a fortified camp and ordering his men to make siege equipment including ladders. He pointed out to his men the twin objectives of a well-stocked and rich town along with the need to strike terror into the neighbouring towns. The opportunity for plunder was obvious. On the very day of his arrival, his forces began their assault starting in mid-afternoon. By sunset, they carried the town and began collecting plunder. Now well supplied and carrying their loot, Caesar's army marched away to Metropolis, the next town in their path.

Initially, Metropolis closed its gates and manned the walls, depending on the rumours about Caesar's weakness. Raising signals and sounding horns, Caesar called Metropolis's leaders to the walls; his men paraded captive citizens of Gomphi, who were known to the Metropolitans. They told of the results of their opposition to Caesar. Metropolis opened its gates to Caesar's army. The men paid for supplies and maintained perfect discipline. All the towns in Thessaly opened their gates except for Larissa, held by Scipio's strong army. Finding a suitable site in the Thessalian plains, rich with ripening crops, Caesar set up his camp near Pharsalus and waited for Pompey's arrival. Within a few days, Pompey and his army joined with Scipio's forces at Larissa, and he marched to Pharsalus and camped near Caesar.

The Battlefield Emerges

It was 4 January (solar calendar, 6 November) that Caesar had sailed from Brundisium to land in Epirus. By mid-April (solar calendar, mid-February) Caesar hemmed in Pompey near the shores of the Adriatic. On 9 July (solar calendar, 7 May), Pompey delivered the double attack that forced Caesar to march into Thessaly. Caesar established his camp at Pharsalus on 1 August (solar calendar, 30 May); Pompey followed by 3 August (solar calendar, 1 June). In short, Caesar and Pompey had danced around each other for some seven months and accomplished nothing. Caesar's soldiers were as tired as were Pompey's soldiers; neither side had any intention of compromising: the time had come for a decision. The problem was Pompey's; Caesar was ready for battle from the beginning of the war but Pompey had avoided an engagement, believing Caesar's support would evaporate. Pompey had avoided battle in Epirus assuming time was on his side. When that proved wrong, he was able to upset Caesar's position and strategic plans by a bold and adroit manoeuvre. Now that Caesar was in Thessaly, the time had come to finish him off.

Caesar remained ready for battle. He had absolute trust in his army; he had created this army and led the cadres which formed the army's core for almost ten years. Caesar knew by name all of the old soldiers and he depended on them to train new recruits and bring them up to his standards. They trusted and revered him and understood that with their help and hard fighting Caesar could not lose. Caesar intended to reward their faith.

Pompey was now ready for battle. If he did not fight, his army, of many disparate parts, might disintegrate. The Romans knew a homogeneous force was always stronger than a force made from diverse pieces. Pompey had pulled his army together to make it as strong as possible, but it remained many pieces. When he marched his force from Epirus into Scipio's camp, Pompey announced Scipio was an equal commander in rank and honour. The official trumpet that blew when Pompey came would blow for Scipio; two, not one, great tents housed the high command. Still, this did not sit well. The high-ranking senators and important equestrians were upset that battle was not immediately joined so they all could return to Italy to assume the different posts over which they still squabbled. The Roman aristocrats in Pompey and Scipio's camp fought over who should get this house of Caesar's supporters and who should get that house, what honours belong to which noble, and who should succeed to Caesar's office of High Priest. Above all, they clamoured to finish Caesar off, so they could return to Italy and get back to business as usual.

Chapter 12

Pharsalus

Note: the exact site of the Battle of Pharsalus is unclear in the literary sources. In the late nineteenth and early twentieth century, there was a lengthy scholarly row about where the battle took place. The site of the town Pharsalus was not in doubt nor the River Enipeus: the question was, did the battle take place north or south of the river. In my opinion, the investigations of John Morgan, 'Parapharsalus – The Battle and the Town' (*American Journal of Archaeology*, Jan. 1983, pp 23 – 54), cleared up the matter. I am sorry to say the *Barrington Atlas*, usually particularly good, is confused on the geography here. For good maps and battle descriptions, see Si Sheppard, *Pharsalus 48 BC*: Osprey Campaign, 2006. In my narrative, I describe the landscape as presented in Morgan's article.

Manoeuvring for Advantage

It was 1 August (39 May, solar calendar), when Caesar chose a site for his camp on the north side of the River Enipeus, near the crossing of the main route that led south to Pharsalus and north to Larissa. Wide fields of ripening wheat spread across the plains surrounding the camp. Three- and four-miles distance, low but rather steep hills rose to the northwest. Caesar spent a few days allowing his supplies to catch up replenishing his stores. During that time, his men's morale improved as Caesar talked with small groups and individuals, reminding them what they were accomplishing.

A few days after Caesar set up camp, Pompey arrived and marched his army to the lower reaches of the hills to Caesar's northwest, building his camp on a rising plain that was bordered by the hills. After Caesar pulled his army together, he decided to test Pompey's frame of mind. He drew his army out of camp, put them in battle formation a short distance from camp, and waited to see what Pompey would do. Pompey did nothing. The next day, Caesar again drew his army out and assumed battle formation, and again, Pompey did not march out to take up Caesar's challenge, but he sent out his cavalry to harass Caesar's men. Caesar had only a little more than 1,000 cavalrymen. As a force multiplier, he trained young, athletic men to fight as light infantry alongside the cavalry horses. With practice, the horse and foot learned to fight against cavalry forces many times their number,

The next day, Caesar again marched his army out in battle formation moving further toward Pompey's camp until his army reached the foot of the hill on which Pompey camped. Pompey sent out his infantry but stationed his formation on higher ground, so if Caesar attacked, it would be at a significant disadvantage. Pompey's cavalry, many more than Caesar's, often attacked, only to skirmish with Caesar's horse and foot. Pompey lost many more men than Caesar, including one of the Allobrogian brothers who had deserted Caesar. On the following day, Pompey drew his army out in battle order some distance up the slope, putting an attacking force at a significant disadvantage. Caesar declined the opportunity.

Caesar told his officers that he had enough of this dance and said that Pompey was not going to surrender the advantage of higher ground. Rather than being yanked around by the great Pompey, Caesar declared they would break camp and march north, collecting supplies and cutting Pompey's communications. Perhaps, then, Pompey would come out to fight or allow Caesar's manoeuvring to wear him down to collapse. He gave the order, 'Break Camp' and the soldiers began rolling up their tents and storing gear. Suddenly, a lookout sentry called for attention and pointed across toward Pompey's camp. Pompey had led out his army down the hill, to form up in battle order in a space acceptable for battle. Caesar immediately called his men to order: 'We will change our plans; we see before us the opportunity for battle; we must be determined; we will not easily find another chance like this.' He directed his men to drop everything and put on their arms and armour. They formed up in battle order at the gates and Caesar prepared his army for battle.

Considerations for Decisive Battle

Pompey, pressured by the senators with him and his officers, decided it was time for battle. He believed his forces had weakened Caesar's army in the battle for the lines and now could overwhelm him by the weight of numbers. He informed his staff of officers that Caesar's battlefront would disintegrate before his infantry force closed with Caesar's. When they asked how that was possible, he described his tactical plan: with his larger force of cavalry, much larger than Caesar's, he would assault Caesar's right-wing, open because there was no anchor on Caesar's right. His cavalry would repel Caesar's horse and then roll up his infantry line from its rear. Pompey told his officers that he had discussed this with his cavalry commanders, and they had agreed this was practical.

Pompey set the following day for the battle and told his friends, followers and supporters, now was the moment for which they had waited; now was the time to defeat Caesar and destroy him. Labienus added to Pompey's message: the army Caesar has out there, that is not the army that conquered Gaul. Rather it is only raw recruits who Caesar picked up to replace his old soldiers, all of whom were dead from battle or pestilence. Pompey's officers and men were confident in their coming victory.

And so, 9 August arrived (7 June, solar calendar). Here, at this decisive turning point, we need to consider how Caesar intended to win because if he lost, he would be undone and all his efforts from crossing the Rubicon would simply be vain. He, his family, his friends and his supporters would not survive. To merely trust in the fighting abilities of his men was not enough. There was something more needed: it was Ptolemy I Soter who said, 'I'd build a bridge of gold for a retreating enemy.' Indeed, many said during the Greek and Persian Wars of the fifth and fourth centuries, that the golden archers of King Darius won more battles than any other soldiers. This referred to the golden daric coin minted by the Persian Great King and used to bribe many Greeks. Caesar was generous with money; the question was, how to use it?

A Roman army was tied together by interlocking chains of command, with a single commander-in-chief as the final authority. To bribe an officer at a given level to prematurely pull out of line would run into the problem that other officers and the soldiers could ignore the order. To corrupt the unit, one would have to bribe most of the officers; this plot would leak, and besides, the men might not obey. Auxiliaries were often bribed but, then again, Roman commanders never really trusted them in the first place. Bribing a Roman army to turn tail was unlikely to succeed.

But other actions were worth many *denarii*. Information was always valuable. Which units were strongest? Which officers were cowardly? And, most important, what was the battle plan? Officially there was no traffic between Caesar's and Pompey's camp; in fact, since sutlers, merchants, and tradesmen were constantly at the camps' gates, covert communications continued between both sides. Pompey's policy held that Caesar's people were criminals; prisoners from his side were killed. Caesar, on the other hand, stated clearly that his argument was with a political faction in the senate, and so was forgiving. What better way was there to stay in Pompey's camp and yet retain Caesar's favour with a few choice bits of information? Whoever won, it didn't matter to the informant. Thus, Pompey's battle plan came to Caesar.

The Armies Deploy

Information given by covert methods may be correct or purposfully incorrect. Either way, such information is useful, either pointing at one course of action or hiding another course. Caesar considered his options while he watched Pompey's army deploy. To the repeated fanfares of horns and trumpets, out marched the commander's guard, elite soldiers with shining armour, helmets with plumes, and shields painted in vivid colours carrying the commander's personal standard. Following the guard, came the commander, gorgeous and brilliant in magnificent armour, bareheaded, so all can see him. His staff, equally resplendent followed him. Then with many more horns and trumpets sounding fanfares came the legions, exiting the camp in perfect order, century following century, each with a standard, forming into cohorts marching under their standards, forming into legions, each with a golden eagle.

On Caesar's left, up against the banks of the Enipeus River, Pompey stationed the I and III Legions. These legions had been Caesar's but by order of the senate, he granted them to Pompey. Caesar was sure they would do their duty but no more. Behind these two legions, Pompey took station. The Syrian Legions came next under Scipio. The Spanish cohorts brought by Afranius combined with the Cilicia legion held, from Caesar's perspective, the right-wing, Domitius commanding. These legions, posted on the wings and in the centre, Pompey considered his strongest. Between the wings on either side and the centre, Pompey placed the motley collection of cohorts that made up the majority of his infantry. All told, Pompey's battle line held a hundred and ten cohorts. Seven more cohorts garrisoned the camp and important places on the supply route. In total, Pompey fielded 45,000 fighting men. Pompey had a further 2,000 men, old soldiers, and their relatives who maintained personal loyalty to him; these he distributed throughout his battle line to strengthen his soldiers' resolve. Pompey's cavalry, under their many standards, formed on Caesar's right, exiting the camp by a different gate. Formation after formation filed out and mixed within the units of horse were all of Pompey's archers and slingers. These were units of different nations, with different dress, and various forms of weapons and armour formed upon Caesar's right. Caesar saw an enormous cavalry force, the information was correct and he was now confident in his plan.

Caesar gave the signal and horns and trumpets sounded. His troops placed themselves in deployment order, century by century, collecting into cohorts and cohorts into legions. There were eight legions that had fought in Gaul, VI, VII, VIII, IX, X, XI, XII, XIII, and one more, XXVII, formed by

Mark Antony from his naval troops in the summer of 49. Unlike Pompey's legionnaires, Caesar's had packed all their parade accoutrements. They marched out in battle trappings but without decorations. Spreading across the field, the renowned X Legion moved to Caesar's far left, anchoring the line on the Enipeus' banks, directly opposite Pompey's I and III Legions, which Caesar had raised and commanded before they became Pompey's. On the far right, there was the IX Legion, badly hurt in the struggles near Dyrrachium. Caesar stationed the VIII Legion as support for the IX, so together they might fight as one. He deployed his army in three lines, each legion with four cohorts in the first line, four in the second line, and two in the third. The two cohorts of each legion in the third line were the most experienced and toughest fighters in the legion.

Caesar had eighty cohorts in his battle line, 22,000 men, along with seven more cohorts to guard his camp. His left was under Mark Antony's command, P. Sulla commanded on the right, and Gn. Domitius commanded the centre. Caesar told his staff he would station himself with Mark Antony. As the formations deployed, Caesar quickly withdrew six select cohorts from the third line and organized a fourth line on his right behind his thousand horsemen, opposite the massive cavalry force facing Caesar's right. His orders clearly stated: no unit, not the third line, nor the whole army would attack until Caesar gave them their specific signal.

Caesar, once his force was deployed, rode along his front lines reminding his men of how much he did for them, how much he sought peace not war, and how hard he worked to keep casualties to a minimum, not only his side but also their brothers in arms on the other side. When Caesar reviewed the cohorts of the fourth line, he added that the outcome of the day's battle rested in their courage and ability. The army received his words with enthusiasm, and they clamoured for the fight to start. Caesar ordered his trumpeter to sound the attack. Many horns and trumpets took up the call.

Combat

The space between the battle lines was narrow. Should both armies charge, they would meet in the centre. But Pompey ordered his line to receive Caesar's attack, so Caesar's men would be fully involved in combat when Pompey's cavalry on his left wing swept Caesar's right wing away ready to roll up Caesar's line. As the signals sounded, G. Crastinus, First Centurion of X Legion, called on his comrades in his reinforced century, 120 volunteers, 'One battle remains! Caesar will recover his dignity and we, our liberty.' Looking directly at Caesar, he continued, 'I do today, Conqueror, actions which, be I alive or dead, will deserve your gratitude!' He and his century charged forward, out from the right wing, beginning battle. The whole battlefront charged forward with Crastinus. But, as they charged across the field with their pilums at the ready, the centurions saw Pompey's men were not moving. At midfield, the centurions halted the charge, letting the men catch their breath and redress their line.

After a short time, the first centurions of Caesar's legions, standing a few feet to the front of the battle line, signalled each other and as one man, the legions again charged. Approaching Pompey's line, Caesar's soldiers hurdled their pilums, drew their swords, and crashed into the waiting line. Pompey's men, well trained and disciplined, parried the pilum storm, threw their own pilums, and drew their swords, receiving Caesar's men without their line breaking and giving as good as they got. As Caesar's legions charged across the field, Pompey's cavalry with all his archers and slingers in one massive formation, charged Caesar's thousand horse and light troops. Caesar's cavalry, mindful of their flanks, slowly gave way to Pompey's superior force, then pulled out of line. Seeing Caesar's cavalry disengaging, Pompey's horsemen, now confirmed in their sense of triumph, broke up into separate units and charged toward the rear of Caesar's legions.

Caesar, keeping a close watch on the manoeuvring on his right, waited until Pompey's cavalry units had committed to their advance, gave the signal for his fourth line of six cohorts to attack. With horns blowing and insignia flashing in the sun, the six cohorts of exceptional fighters rushed upon Pompey's horse, repelling them at first contact. The cavalry units turned and fled the field, galloping off to high hills. They left the archers and slingers defenceless; Caesar's cohorts chased them down and killed them all. The advance of the fourth line continued, they reformed and manoeuvring around the end of Pompey's lines, they crashed into the rear of the formations fighting Caesar's legions in front.

When Caesar saw his fourth line moving into Pompey's rear, he gave the signal for his third line, waiting patiently, to join the battle. Advancing all along the battle line, the exhausted first and second lines pulled back, allowing the fresh third line access to the battlefront. They smashed into Pompey's wearied and drained troops who gave away and began retreating. Pompey saw his cavalry disintegrate and then saw panic take hold of the strongest part of his line. He rode his horse off the field, back to his camp. On entering his camp by the praetorian gate, he ordered the centurions to prepare the camp's defences and told them he was going to alert the men at the other gates. Rather than that, Pompey went to his headquarters where he waited on events.

Pompey's line bent and broke, with some legions holding ground and others disintegrating, their men fleeing in terror. The legions which held together retreated back to their camp, but they were few. Others headed to a series of hills. It was now noon, and Caesar's soldiers had been under arms for more than six hours. They were fatigued, but Caesar called on them to finish their enemies and his men rallied. They put themselves back into formation and prepared to assault Pompey's camp. The seven cohorts stationed in the camp were ready for Caesar's attack; Thracian and other tribal units gave support. Arrows, spears, and pilum swept the camp ramparts, killing some, wounding more, and forcing the garrison to retreat. Pompey's men, escorted and guided by military tribunes and centurions, abandoned the camp and made for the high hills nearby where they joined those who had fled the battle. Caesar's cavalry gave chase, catching L. Domitius who had fallen from exhaustion, they finished him off.

Battle's Aftermath

When Caesar's soldiers advanced into the camp, Pompey took a horse, ripped off his insignia and consular trappings, rode out of the decuman gate, and headed toward Larisa. Once in Larisa, Pompey fell in with some of his subordinates, changed horses, then continued at speed on his way. Riding through the night, Pompey collected an escort of some thirty men. They soon arrived at the sea, found a cargo ship in which he and his men sailed away. Pompey said to his escort, often and clearly, that his trust was betrayed because those parts of his army in which his trust was greatest were those who first broke and ran.

Caesar's men were shocked at the sights inside Pompey's camp. Soldiers' huts covered with fresh turf; food set out, ready for the victory celebration, officers' quarters with tables set with silver plate. Pompey's camp was quite different from Caesar's austere business-like camp. Caesar rode into Pompey's camp and instructed the centurions to keep the soldiers from plundering the riches in front of them. Calling his soldiers together, he reminded him that while they had defeated the enemy, those defeated soldiers were nearby in the hills and many victories had been lost because plundering had become more important than fighting.

The defeated army concentrated on one high hill, the men forming themselves into centuries and cohorts. They soon found there was no water on the hill. Caesar started to construct earthworks surrounding the hill, but the defeated Pompeians began moving off the hill along a ridge leading to the route toward Larisa. Caesar reacted quickly dividing his force, sending some legions back to Pompey's camp; others, he sent to his own camp, and he kept four legions in hand and pursued the Pompeians by an easy route below the hills. After marching for six miles, he manoeuvred his men between the hill on which the Pompeians now found themselves and the river, toward which they were headed. Caesar told his four legions that he knew they were exhausted, and the sun was near setting, but a little more work would end the war. His men dug fortifications that cut all the ways from the hill to the river. The Pompeians would get no water this night.

Seeing that they would go without water, having many wounded and everyone thirsty, the Pompeian commanders sent a delegation to Caesar, saying if they were allowed to take water up the hill, they all would surrender in the morning. Caesar agreed. During the night, a few men of the senatorial order disappeared from the hill into the darkness. At dawn, Caesar ordered all the Pompeians to come down off the hill, bringing their weapons but throwing them down into a pile at the hill's foot. They all came and without bitterness, knelt before Caesar, with tears in their eyes and outstretched hand, pleaded for mercy. Caesar received their petition with grace, told them to rise, and introduced them to his men as fellow comrades in arms. He told the surrendered Pompeians that they were safe, and their property remained for them in their camp. Caesar then ordered the men whom he had sent back to the camps to return and those who were with him to go to the camp for a well-earned rest. Later that day, Caesar rode into Larisa.

Results

Caesar's accountants took stock of the battle's cost: he lost about two hundred soldiers in the fighting but that included thirty centurions. Even the brave Crastinus fell, struck by a sword in his face. Caesar's men killed about fifteen thousand Pompeians and captured a total of 24,000 men. Even Pompey's outlying forts easily gave up. Of course, Caesar counted only his Roman soldiers but included Pompey's auxiliary men in these totals. Caesar's army captured 180 standards along with nine eagles. That indicated Caesar defeated and destroyed nine legions. This was a great victory.

Section IV

War in the East

Chapter 13

Caesar in Egypt

The End of Pompey

The Battle of Pharsalus fragmented the senatorial faction; however, like a hydra, the splinters could each grow into a powerful organization. Caesar had won the battle; his problem was how to crush those who refused to accept his victory. Rome and Italy, he held; Gaul would remain his, no matter what, but the real problem was the fact that Pompey had pinned him in Epirus for too long. He had taken Spain, but Pompey had many friends there. If he didn't appear there soon, the province would slip away, and Africa was in the same condition. The West was calling him.

Wealth and power were in the East. Asia, Syria, Palestine, and the richest prize of all, Egypt was his for the taking. Solidifying the West but losing the East would return him to the same place where he was a little less than a year ago, and, if that happened his tough loyal soldiers would certainly lose heart. Moreover, Pompey was somewhere nearby. Caesar needed Pompey, as a prisoner if necessary, but better, as a friend and supporter if that could happen. The shattered senatorial faction might regenerate under Pompey but without him, they were a diffident mob of argumentative people: good for debate, bad for action. So, Caesar's objectives were two: grab the East, particularly Egypt, and run Pompey to the ground.

Caesar rode at the head of his cavalry guard, following Pompey's trail. He had a legion follow so it would be there if needed. The news came from Amphipolis; Pompey had decreed the conscription of all young men, Greeks, and Romans. Whether this was an effort to construct a new army to fight for Macedonia or a smokescreen to hide Pompey's flight, no one knew. In actual fact, Pompey had sailed to Amphipolis and spent an evening in conference planning the future. Pompey collected money to continue his flight and hearing Caesar was drawing near, he sailed away toward Mytilene. A storm boiled up, keeping Pompey in port for two days; on the third day, the weather moderated, Pompey acquired a few more ships, all small, and sailed to the Cilician coast and beyond to Cyprus.

While in Cyprus, Pompey received word that the town council of Antioch had mobilized a militia and proclaimed all the senatorial rebels were outlaws. They specifically ordered the exclusion of Pompey. The town council of Rhodes issued the same decrees. Rhodes refused admittance to both former consuls of the Lentulus family and their party of senators and magistrates. Pompey saw the direction in which the wind was blowing and decided his objective should be Egypt. Many senatorial leaders were headed toward Africa, others were going to attempt to take back Spain. They all needed money; if he could seize Egypt, he could supply money and build a new base from which to oppose Caesar. Pompey requisitioned the funds from the companies collecting state revenue and convinced some people to lend him large sums. He took on board his ships many strongboxes of bronze coins, to pay soldiers. Having enrolled some 2,000 trusted slaves from his friends, Pompey armed them and sailed for Egypt.

Pompey's small fleet anchored off the port of Pelusium because nearby was the boy King Ptolemy's camp with his advisors and army. Because Pompey was instrumental in keeping the boy king's father, Ptolemy XII, in power, he expected a warm welcome. From his flagship, Pompey sent messengers to the boy king, explaining what he needed. When they arrived at the camp, the messengers found many soldiers and officers whom they knew and who had served under Pompey in the east. After the wars in the east had concluded, these men had gone to Egypt and served Ptolemy VII. Now they served the boy king who was involved in a war against his sister-wife, Cleopatra.

The young Ptolemy's advisors, high officers, and courtiers saw Pompey as a threat: if Pompey did prevail over Caesar, he would replace them with his own friends but should Pompey lose, then they, as his allies, faced death. The answer was simple: kill Pompey while he was at his weakest. The king's assistant, Achillas, and his assistant, a man who had served under Pompey, L. Septimius, went by boat to Pompey's ship. They told Pompey that the king would receive and support him, but he had to come with only a few associates because the king needed to present his new alliance with Pompey as an accomplished fact. Pompey, who trusted Septimius, agreed and took a small boat to shore, landing inconspicuously. There, Achillas and Septimius killed Pompey. The former consul, L. Lentulus, arrived from Cyprus the next day and Achillas killed him also.

While Pompey was looking for a site to build his new base, Caesar arrived in Asia. He brought back treasures appropriated by the senatorial faction, particularly those of the Temple of Diana at Ephesus. Word quickly spread of marvellous happenings foretelling and celebrating Caesar's great victories. All adorned the victor with glory or so said his supporters. After a few days spent firming up his position in Asia, Caesar received information about

Pompey passing through Cyprus. Since Asia was closed to Pompey, Caesar suspected he was headed toward Egypt. If Pompey could command Egypt's resources, he would reignite the civil war. Caesar assembled a fleet from Pompey's former forces, ten large warships from Rhodes along with a few warships from the Asian fleet. He drew a legion from Thessaly and another from his legate, Q. Fufius in Achaea. In total, Caesar had some 3,200 foot and 800 horse at hand. Caesar believed he did not need a strong force to go anywhere because the news of his victories was everywhere. When he landed in Alexandria, the officials presented him with Pompey's head. Pompey's murder by people who he had helped was an unpleasant surprise. When Caesar marched from the docks, he had his twelve lictors leading his procession. Egyptian soldiers, seeing Caesar parading through Alexandria, rioted, claiming this was an insult to royal dignity. Caesar removed the lictors to appease the populace, but every day disturbances broke out in different parts of the city, resulting in the deaths of many Roman soldiers. Caesar found dealing with the Egyptians distasteful.

Egypt

Difficult as the Egyptians were, this was not new. Romans had dealt with the Egyptians for over a century. Unlike Greece, Pergamum, and Syria, the Romans had not absorbed Egypt into their direct administration. There were many reasons for that which all added up to the fact that the Egyptian elites managed to outmanoeuvre Roman elites. This did not mean Romans were not in Egypt, rather they became part of Egyptian politics which provided more ways to avoid direct Roman rule. Egypt was wealthy yet like a broken reed; if leaned on, Egypt pierced the hand. There was great beauty yet deadly danger lurked in dark spots.

There were two different Egypts. The first and most visible to the rest of the Mediterranean world was a Macedonian kingdom. Royal in spirit, Greek in thought, it centred on the world-city of Alexandria. Here, trade from Britain, Spain, North Africa, and the rest of the inner sea crossed paths with goods from India, the East Indies, and China. A myriad of people knew Alexandria. Learning, research, and discussion made up a vibrant intellectual centre. War was generally someone else's problem.

The other Egypt was an ancient, introverted temple complex, centred in Memphis. Here, the ancient civilization continued. Today, the sights of ancient Egypt are up the Nile, south toward the cataracts, Upper Egypt. However, the rich farmlands of the delta were also important; given its productivity, Lower Egypt was often more important at times rather than the upper realm. The ancient temples and their surrounding towns have disappeared into the wet soil but they were there in large numbers. Here, the ancient priesthood maintained their hold, as they had for millennia. Wealthy, secretive, and able to solve problems of ambition and greed without recourse to outside powers, the priesthood was always an unseen factor in Egyptian politics.

The king, always of the House of Ptolemy, was a Macedonian prince who ruled through Greek officials, but was also a god and Pharaoh of Egypt, manifesting his will through his priests. The Royal officials were literate and trained for their tasks. They generally stayed away from the priesthood's holdings. The priests were dedicated to the ancient gods, especially the more important ones, and were no strangers to the Mediterranean world, knowing the languages and politics of all manner of people. The cults of Serapis and Isis along with Hermetic mysteries had spread across the sea and needed to train personnel to manage their temples. Many priests, select and observant, moved along all roads near the Mediterranean. They had many secrets and they kept them well.

The House of Ptolemy had too many ambitious and able members. The game of musical thrones went on for decades. In the last decades of the second century, Ptolemy IX Soter II started his first reign of about ten years. But Cleopatra III wanted her son, Ptolemy X Alexander, to be king. For twenty years, the two kings intrigued and fought each other for the throne. Ptolemy X Alexander, in an effort to borrow money in Rome to reclaim his kingdom, wrote a will that on his death, his kingdom would become Rome's. He was killed soon after.

Ptolemy IX Soter II held the throne until 81 BC; he worked to keep the Romans happy, and the Roman politicians worried about a proconsul being a master of Egypt having too much power. When Ptolemy IX Soter II died, his daughter, Cleopatra Berenice III became queen. However, Ptolemy XI Alexander II, son of Ptolemy X, was in Rome. Sulla wanted him to be king of Egypt and sent him to Alexandria where he married Cleopatra Berenice II and became co-ruler. Within twenty days, the new king murdered the queen. But Berenice was very popular with the people of Alexandria; they rioted, invaded the palace, dragged Alexander II to the gymnasium and killed him. The Alexandrines, anxious lest the Romans came to take an empty throne, recalled a son of Ptolemy IX, who became Ptolemy XII, New Dionysus. During the sixties of the first century, politics at Rome began to revolve around the question of the annexation of Egypt. Crassus the Rich wanted to annex the country and he was supported by one of the aediles, Julius Caesar.

To counter these moves, Ptolemy XII passed out a great deal of money to all sides in the Roman government. He found his greatest supporter for Egyptian independence in Pompey. Crassus, Caesar, and others still pushed hard for Egyptian annexation. In the years of the Alliance of the Three, Ptolemy XII promised to give to Pompey and Caesar 6,000 talents for recognition as king of Egypt. As consul of the year 59 BC, Caesar managed a Senatus Consultum through the senate recognizing Ptolemy as king and a law recognizing Ptolemy as Friend and Ally of Rome. But Ptolemy did nothing when the Romans annexed Cyprus and so forced the king to leave Egypt, in 58 BC. He ended staying in Pompey's villa near Rome.

Egyptian politics swung this way and that for two years. If the money lenders wanted to be repaid, then the solution was to return Ptolemy XII to the throne. In the consulship of Pompey and Crassus, Pompey sent instructions to the proconsul of Syria, A. Gabinius to bring Ptolemy back to Egypt and secure his throne. Gabinius marched an army to Egypt, defeated Ptolemy XII's enemies, and placed him securely on the throne in 55 BC. In order to secure the succession to the throne, Ptolemy raised his eighteen-year-old daughter, Cleopatra VII, to co-regent. In his will, he stipulated that her eldest brother rule as co-equal.

Ptolemy XII died in early 51 BC; Cleopatra succeeded him as sole ruler but in 18 months, a clique behind Ptolemy XIII, twelve years old, pushed her out. Three people led the clique, the eunuch Portheinos, Ptolemy's 'nurse,' a military officer, Achillas, and the intellectual Theodotos of Chos. During the civil war in autumn 49 BC, the Roman counter-senate in Thessaloniki, on Pompey's recommendation, recognized Ptolemy XIII as the legitimate ruler of Egypt. So, after Pharsalus, Pompey had believed he would get a warm welcome from Ptolemy XIII's officials.

Caesar in Egypt

Caesar despised the men who sought to buy his favour with the head of his friend and fellow noble Roman. He found their failure to maintain order stupid. They were only murderous ineffective fools. His chosen solution was to call into Egypt the new legions he had organized from Pompey's troops. Worse, he was unable to leave Alexandria because the etesian winds were blowing, not allowing any ships to sail away. Caesar was well aware that when he was consul, he had overseen the senate's decree and assembly's enactments which made king Ptolemy XIII a Roman ally. Now, as proconsul of Rome, he stated his pleasure, that King Ptolemy and his sister Cleopatra disband their armies and submit their dispute to him.

Ptolemy's 'nurse' (translated as tutor), Pothinus, ran the Royal administration. His view of his position was simple: whatever Caesar decided, he would be out of power, and then his enemies would eliminate him. Even worse, his effort to curry favour with Caesar by killing Pompey turned sour. His answer was simple, crush Caesar. He sent secret messengers to the army at Pelusium, appointing Achillas commander and ordering the army to come to Alexandria. This was not a weak force. The fighting core of the army was made up of Gabinius' soldiers that he had marched to Egypt, putting Ptolemy XII back on the throne. Old but experienced, these men had become part of Alexandria society, marrying local people, training their sons in their trade. Added to this basic force, there were mercenaries from the Syrian wars with brigands, along with escaped slaves and exiles. There was 2,000 cavalry, originally raised by the Romans but added to Ptolemy XII's force. Altogether, Achillas' army was 22,000 strong.

Caesar intended to use Ptolemy XII's will, as the basis of his decision, which detailed the succession: the eldest of his sons and the eldest of his daughters should become the next rulers of Egypt. Caesar was ready to recognize Ptolemy XIII and his sister Cleopatra as king and queen of Egypt. Believing his judgment would resolve the causes of discontent, Caesar was most upset to hear that the Royal army was marching toward Alexandria. His force was small and might easily become lost in Alexandria's streets and alleys; he pulled his forces back into the confines of his base in a corner of the royal palace from which he had access to the harbour and into the city. He alerted his men and officers about difficulties to come. He also went to King Ptolemy XIII, telling him to send officials to Achillas, informing him that no further action was required.

The king sent the high officials, Dioscorides and Seapion, both experienced and able men to Achillas; but when the courtier conducted them into Achillas' presences, Achillas immediately ordered them seized and killed before they could say anything. Both were assaulted, one dead on the spot, the second, seemed dead but was drawn off by his friends wounded but alive. Since Achillas continued his march, Caesar took charge of King Ptolemy to ensure the soldiers in the coming army were rebels against their legitimate ruler. Achillas' men paid no attention to the king's government. Considering that the number of soldiers available to Caesar was so small, Achillas pushed forward his attack into the city. Throwing his elite troops against Caesar's residence-headquarters, Achillas nearly drove Caesar out into the open. Caesar launched a cohort through a side street and hit Achillas' force on their flank, pushing the enemy back. Manoeuvring his cohorts through the streets near his headquarters, Caesar tied down Achillas' attacking force.

Not only was Caesar hard-pressed in a tactical sense, but he also faced a decisive strategic menace. From his headquarters to his back and right, spread the royal palace, providing a secure rear; to his left and front, stretched out the harbour in which, there were the fifty heavy warships sent to support Pompey, quadriremes, and quinqueremes, all armed and ready to sail. More, twenty-two decked warships were on patrol duty in the harbour and seafront. Should Achillas' forces seize these ships and row them into the harbour, they would cut off Caesar from any communications beyond Alexandria and he would face defeat. The struggle for the harbour was a battle of numbers against training. Numbers began to overwhelm Caesar's soldiers. He ordered his men to set the ships in the harbour on fire. This was done and a huge fire flared up, burning the fleet along with many cargo ships.

Out from the harbour ran a causeway to a small island that dominated the harbour entrances. Here, on this island stood the great lighthouse, the Pharos. Caesar embarked his staff and a select team of soldiers in small boats and rowed to the island. There was a village on this island but the inhabitants kept clear of Caesar's men. Caesar ordered the construction of a strong position near the lighthouse and secured his communications with the world beyond. He immediately sent for supplies and reinforcements. While Caesar was busy, the fighting in the town died down because, in the confines of the narrow streets, neither side was able to gain an advantage: casualties were few and both sides withdrew to guarded positions. Caesar returned to his residence, and as night fell, saw to it that his men strengthened their positions. Near the residence building, there was a theatre; fortifying the two buildings, Caesar constructed a citadel and extended his strengthened lines to the main port and the rest of the docks nearby. Now, he could withstand any attack.

Achillas received the younger daughter of King Ptolemy, Arsinoe, who sought his support in her bid for the throne. From the palace, Pothinus sent messages to Achillas, informing him of Caesar's weaknesses but Caesar's men captured some of these messengers and on the basis of their evidence, Caesar executed Pothinus and took over control of Ptolemy XIII. Secure in his base, Caesar summoned the fleets of Rhodes, Syria, and Cilicia along with archers from Crete and cavalry from the king of the Nabataeans. His engineers began fabricating artillery; he ensured a good supply of food and raised auxiliary troops to support his legionnaires.

The Battle of Alexandria Begins

Caesar's engineers stiffened his defences by rounding out the lines to eliminate awkward twists and turns. The soldiers battered through building walls to make runways along the inner walls and punched access ports through the outer walls to allow the shooting of arrows and throwing of stones against any attacker; they also demolished any structure that blocked their lines of sight. Caesar's concern was to isolate his holdings in his part of the palace and along the wharves into one unified command by occupying all the area from the harbour south to the gardens and parklands which bisect the city in those parts. His crews built high towers and raised platforms to hold artillery to target missiles across the open spaces of ground fronting his lines allowing his forces to support each other all along the lines. That the enemy might try to set the city on fire was not a concern since the buildings and houses were built of paving stone and terracotta, using arching instead of timber trusses. The real problem was fodder and water which was in short supply. Both were readily available in the parkland to the south.

The Alexandrians quickly prepared for a massive attack in the near future. They sent out a summons throughout the kingdom, recruiting as many men as possible and shipping large amounts of weapons into the city where fabricators working in shops produced more weapons. Moreover, they armed the adult slaves, wealthy owners supplying them with food and pay. Alexandrian recruits manned the outlying fortifications; the regular troops, organized in cohorts stayed in central locations, ready for battle. They built a triple barricade facing Caesar's fortifications some forty feet high and deeper into the city, they also built watchtowers ten storeys high with artillery on top. Some of these towers sat on wheels, pulled by oxen along straight streets, back and forth.

The Egyptian forces in Alexandria surprised Caesar with their resourcefulness and cunning. They maintained constant pressure against Caesar's lines while they accumulated an overwhelming force. At large public meetings, the leaders told how the Romans had swallowed and enslaved country after country. Gabinius had invaded a few years before, but King Ptolemy sent him away. Then Pompey came, thinking to take Egypt for Rome. Pompey's death did nothing to frighten Caesar, the leaders reminded the crowds. He is here. If Caesar succeeds in staying, Egypt will fall to the Romans. Now is the time to attack! Because the storms of the season have cut him off from supplies and reinforcements, we can defeat and kill him and his men.

Chapter 14

The Battle of Alexandria

Caesar in Danger

Caesar found himself in serious danger. The trip to Alexandria had become a disaster and he faced threats that were worse than any he had faced in Gaul, Spain, or Epirus. He was as bad off as when he was captured by pirates in his youth, but the enemies he faced now would surely kill him if they had a chance. He had landed on 2 October, which was at the end of solar month of July. The heat was heavy. First, he received the news about Pompey's murder which did not help his plans at all. Then came rioting and constant disturbance and, even worse, he could not sail away because of the adverse winds. Now he was in the middle of a full-scale siege war and was at the losing end of the struggle. It was mid-November, mid-September by the solar calendar, a whole month and a half wasted and his opponents in the empire were regaining strength.

Worse, his enemies in Egypt were growing stronger; Ptolemy's younger daughter, Arsinoe, fearing that her older sister, Cleopatra, had allied with Caesar, colluded with her eunuch tutor, Ganymedes, to kill Achillas. She took control of the insurrection with Ganymedes as army commander. He was a competent military commander and he immediately increased the soldiers' pay. Organizing a council of war, the leaders of the insurrection looked for a quick way to destroy Caesar. Ganymedes pointed out Caesar's greatest vulnerability was water; the question was, how to deprive him of access to it.

Under Alexandria ran a series of subterranean channels carrying water from the central canal that brought Nile water into the city and distributed the water to the city gardens and parks that surrounded monuments and holy places. Royal buildings and private houses connected to these channels and received water in any amount. Since the Nile carried a lot of silt, a series of cisterns both large and small allowed the silt to settle and so the outlets provided clear water. The Nile provided vast quantities of water, there was no central location controlling the system or even an accurate idea of what channels went where. How to cut Caesar and his forces off from water was going to be difficult.

Ganymedes devised a way to contaminate Caesar's supply of water. First, he blocked all of the channels they found in the area they occupied which flowed into Caesar's area. Then, operating a series of water lifting wheels, they flooded the cisterns nearest Caesar's lines with seawater. Soon, Caesar's troops, using the pipes and cisterns near the Alexandrian lines, found their water was brackish. Then they found the water in the centre of their area was also brackish but even worse, the water that was brackish became undrinkable.

Caesar's soldiers discovered that soon all the water would become undrinkable and they panicked. They expected Caesar to give the order to abandon Alexandria and embark on their ships. The officers saw a more difficult problem: if they abandoned their positions, the Alexandrian insurgents would know and attack immediately and probably would overwhelm the Romans. Caesar discussed the problem with his engineers; they pointed out that the channels through which the water ran leaked a lot. In the generations since Alexandria was built, a mass of sweet water underlay the city. Wells could easily access sweet water.

Caesar assembled and addressed his men, leaving sufficient forces to guard their defences. He told them that underneath them, there was plenty of sweet water, getting it would begin immediately. Even, however, if they could not find good water in the ground, they could send ships along the coast for water. They had done this before, but they could not abandon their positions because, by their numbers and hatred, the Alexandrians would break in and kill many. Further, loading ships from open boats was difficult at the best of times, and that was not now. To survive, they must stand and win. Caesar then ordered his chief centurions to drop whatever they were doing and organize crews to dig wells, working through the night. By dawn, they had a great quantity of sweet water at hand. The soldiers' fears were calmed; the business of war resumed.

The next day, there appeared the sails of a fleet coming to reinforce Caesar. Domitius Calvinus had assembled this fleet which brought XXXVII Legion, raised by Pompey, along with a good supply of wheat, arms, and artillery. They made the African coast a little to the west of Alexandria. Because of the constant east winds, they could not sail into Alexandria's harbour but were able to firmly anchor in safe waters. The fleet commanders sent a fast boat to Caesar, requesting water. Caesar mobilized his fleet, and, commanding from the flagship, sailed toward Calvinus' ships. Caesar's ships carried their normal contingent of rowers, but Caesar was loath to leave his fortifications unmanned and so brought no troops. He sailed along the coast to a peninsula some eight miles west of Alexandria. Landing on shore, Caesar sent the rowers out to collect water which he transferred to Calvinus' ships.

Some of the crews went looking for plunder and ran into Egyptian horsemen. From these prisoners, the Alexandrian command found out that Caesar was with the ships, and that he had no combat troops on board. They immediately ordered their fleet to sail from Alexandria and intercept Caesar. Soon, the Alexandrian ships were in Caesar's sight. With no troops on board and night coming on, Caesar ordered his fleet to land and set up a defensive position. While his fleet was landing, a Rhodian combat ship on the right-wing became separated from Caesar's formation. The Alexandrian commander sent four quadriremes and some open boats to capture the isolated Rhodian. Caesar could not let the enemy capture his isolated ship and ordered a number of Rhodian warships to rescue their compatriot. The hard-fought battle ended with the capture of one quadrireme, the sinking of a second, and heavy casualties to the Alexandrian fighting men. The fall of the night ended the engagement.

The next morning, Caesar's fleet rowed into Alexandria's harbour, towing the cargo ships against a light headwind. The arrival of Caesar's reinforcements and supplies was a severe blow to the Egyptian forces. Almost in a day, what looked like a coming victory faded into a draw. The Alexandrians redoubled their efforts to destroy Caesar. The first action they took was to strengthen their barricades cutting off Caesar's position from the rest of the city. Then they increased their harassing fire from their towers; Roman officers and men died unexpectedly. Ganymedes called his officers to a meeting and pledged to rebuild their fleet because now, the only way to defeat Caesar was to sever his supply lines. With more men, Caesar needed more food and fodder and the Alexandrians needed to organize a force to halt any resupply for Caesar. Most of the people of the city and coast were well-practised in seamanship, they eagerly volunteered to work on repairing old and building new ships.

The wrecked ships Caesar had burned in the harbour supplied parts and pieces; the Alexandrian brought old warships, layed up for years, and guard ships used to enforce customs due into the harbour. They needed wood so the Alexandrians dismantled colonnade roofs, took the structural beams from gymnasia, and unroofed public buildings to build ships and fabricate oars. They did not build fine, seagoing ships because they planned to fight in the harbour. But, in a few days, there floated in the harbour twenty-two quadriremes and five quinqueremes. To these, the Alexandrians added a large number of open boats, each manned by skilled fighters. They rowed their ships around the harbour, changing formation and practising combat manoeuvres, showing that their fleet was formidable. Caesar now commanded nine Rhodians, eight Pontic, five Lycian, and twelve ships from the Asian fleet. These included ten quinqueremes and quadriremes, but the rest of his fleet were open boats. He saw the enemies' fleet and prepared to attack.

Caesar Attacks

Caesar faced an intricate strategic problem: if he stayed on the defensive, his enemies would gain momentum and perhaps generate the force to defeat him before more reinforcements arrived; if however, he attacked, then should he lose, he surely would be in deep trouble and if he won, the victory could not be decisive because the Alexandrians could just pull back to their basic positions. On the other hand, by attacking, he would have the initiative and perhaps find some advantage to weaken the Alexandrians. His fleet was prepared and Caesar, standing on the deck of his flagship, gave the order to attack.

The fleet formed up, rowed out of the palace harbour and swung around the Pharos lighthouse. Once clear of the Pharos, Caesar's formations took their places for battle; on the right rowed the Rhodian squadron and on the left were the Pontic ships, about four hundred paces separating the two lines, allowing for deployment. Caesar followed behind these two squadrons, leading the rest of the fleet, ready to order them to bring support where they might be needed.

The Alexandrian fleet was coming out, ready to fight. Their first line held twenty-two ships; the rest followed in a support position behind. Surrounding these main warships, a cloud of small boats of different sizes, armed with fighting men and fire weapons, were planning to create diversions and pick off weakened ships. The entrance channel of the Eunostos Harbour passed through a region of submerged rocks and both fleets stopped before entering this channel. For some time, the fleets faced each other, waiting for the other side to begin moving into the channel. Whichever side rowed first into the channel would be at a disadvantage, faced by the full force of the enemy and hemmed in by dangerous rocks.

After some time, the Rhodian flagship lowered a skiff which rowed over to Caesar's ship. On the skiff was Euphranor, commander of the squadron; he approached Caesar and told him that he wanted to lead his squadron into the passageway. He and his men would hold firm until Caesar could reinforce them and that way, Caesar would prevail. Euphranor was an accomplished and experienced commander who had the respect of the

Romans and Caesar agreed with his plan. When Euphranor returned to his ship, Caesar signalled the battle to begin.

Four large Rhodian ships rowed through the channel before the Alexandrians reacted but soon the Alexandrian ships surrounded the Rhodian ships. The skills of the Rhodian pilots and organization of the rower crews were such that even against great odds, the Rhodian ships always presented their fronts to attacking ships, never allowing a broadside strike nor losing a bank of oars. The rest of Caesar's fleet joined the combat. The battle pivoted on soldiers' fighting strength and determination, not seamanship nor subtlety. On the rooftops of the city, crowds of people observed the ongoing struggle. Caesar encouraged his men, telling them that his and their fate rested in their hands. Eventually, the Alexandrians pulled back, retiring to their harbour but leaving three major warships sunk along with a quinquereme and bireme captured by the Romans.

Now that he had blunted the Alexandrians' desire for sea combat, Caesar looked to his next move, which was to take the island which divided Alexandria's harbour in two. In doing so, he would begin a strategy of levering the enemy forces out of the city by taking strategic strongpoints, one at a time. The island dominated the harbour and waterfront of the city. On the island's east side sat the Pharos, the great lighthouse, already in Caesar's control. Extending west of the Pharos a narrow causeway led to the main island, upon which sat a fairly large village of two- and three-storey buildings. The island was long and thin, running east to west; the waterfront extended, rocks in some places, sand in others, allowed landings along its whole perimeter. A long and broad causeway ran to the island from the city. This also allowed landing access. Caesar's position in the city was well fortified and secure: now he could amass a large body of troops.

He collected a large number of cargo ships and open boats and loaded on these ten cohorts of infantry, a cloud of light troops, and some squadrons of Gallic cavalry. To begin, he launched an attack on the far side of the island with some decked warships. Once that attack drew the islanders' attention, Caesar sent his flotilla toward the island's near side, the boats landing their soldiers on a broad front. The islanders met the attack with courage: they held the beaches and repelled attacks from the roofs of buildings. Their five warships, supported by open boats pursued Caesar's smaller boats and defended the more open access points. But soon Roman organization and discipline prevailed. Once a squad of Roman infantry found their footing, more came to reinforce them and they pushed the islanders back.

When the Roman infantry reached open ground, they formed up in battle formation and attacked. The islanders could not face the infantry assault;

they broke and ran to the built-up area. Once their battle line failed, the islanders' naval forces abandoned their stations, left their ships, and joined their compatriots in the built-up areas of the island. These buildings, some three storeys tall, were easily defended and Caesar's soldiers had no siege equipment. Yet the islanders, after the Romans killed a few, started to panic. Then panic spread and masses of men fled from the buildings, headed for the causeway, or swam the eight hundred paces to Alexandria. Caesar's men captured some 6,000 of the islanders.

Clearing all opposition from the island, Caesar considered where he might make further gains. Letting his forces plunder the island, he ordered all the buildings on the island demolished. A causeway connected the island to the lighthouse; the islanders had abandoned it. Another causeway led from the island to the city and here, the Alexandrians had built barricades and guarded the structure. Caesar decided he needed to launch an attack to seize the causeway because he saw that by holding both causeways, and he already held the one to the lighthouse, he would stop the many attacks of small fire ships against his fleet.

In the early morning, some of Caesar's warships rowed near the causeway to the city. Suddenly, artillery shots and arrow storms swept the causeway and the troops on guard there broke and ran. Another wave of ships pushed forward and landed three crack cohorts on the causeway. They pushed forward and established a bridgehead on the city street running along the docks. The troops holding the causeway's end constructed a barricade blocking access from the city to the causeway. While these troops were defending their position, Caesar had his engineers fill in the spaces under the bridges which allowed ships to move under the causeway. Using stone and mortar, they completely blocked the openings so no ship could row into Caesar's harbour.

While the engineers and workmen blocked the openings, the Alexandrians regrouped and rushed out, forming a battle line facing the Roman barricade. At the same time, they sent out boats to hinder the ongoing work blocking up the openings under the bridges. The fighting grew hot, the Alexandrian foot attacking the barricade and their boats shooting at the soldiers, engineers, and workmen on the causeway. Caesar and his officers were occupied with encouraging his soldiers in the fighting and they did not see their own ships approach the causeway. On their own, the men of Caesar's fleet sailed across the harbour to reinforce the fighters on the causeway. After the boats reached the causeway, rowers and sailors scrambled onto the causeway in order to help their side. Once on the causeway, they shot arrows and threw stones, driving off the Alexandrian boats from the causeway. The sailors' assaults at first were effective, driving the boats away. Intent on continuing raining their barrages on the boats in front of them, the sailors failed to see some other boats unload a squad of Alexandrians further down the causeway, out of direct sight of both the sailors and Caesar with the engineers.

Without any warning, these squads attacked the sailors on their flanks where no one was looking. The sailors were not in military formation nor were they disciplined as infantry: they panicked and started to flee toward their ships. Seeing the effect of their small unit attacking the sailors, more Alexandrians climbed up onto the causeway and joined the attackers. Those sailors who remained on the boats, seeing the panic and blood, started to withdraw their gangways, preparing to push off, in order to keep their boats out of the Alexandrians' hands.

The noise of this commotion came to the three cohorts defending the barricade at the causeway's end. Under attack from a rain of missiles, hearing the confusion and screams of pain behind them, and seeing the panicking sailors running toward their boats, which were pushing off from the causeway, the infantry understood that the enemy was going to cut them off and surround them. They quickly abandoned the barricade and moved on the double toward the boats. Some did not get the word quickly enough and the Alexandrians cut them down. Others reached the boats, often to have the press of men, sailors, and infantry, swamp and sink the boat. Still, others, stripping off their armour and holding their shields above their heads, jumped into the water and swam to the boats.

Caesar was encouraging his men at hand when he too was swept up in the confusion. In danger along with the rest, he turned and hurried to his ship. Many men followed him and swarmed onto his flagship. Knowing what was about to happen, Caesar dived off his ship and swam to another ship further off. The mob in their panic capsized his ship and everyone was dumped in the sea. Once he landed, Caesar sent a mass of small boats to rescue his men. In total, Caesar lost about 400 infantry and a few more than that number of sailors. The Alexandrians were elated. They occupied the causeway, building fortifications and reinforcing them with artillery. The Romans still held the island, but the causeway and its arched passageways fell to the Alexandrians. Caesar's harbour remained open to their enemies.

Treachery and Deceit

Rather than becoming downcast by their repulse from the causeway, Caesar's soldiers wanted revenge. Day and night they launched murderous raids against the Alexandrians, sometimes catching their enemies in the middle of one of their own operations and other times hitting them when they were at rest, believing they were safe. Constant disruption, whole sections of Alexandria cut off and occupied by combat forces did not sit well with the business interests and aristocratic leaders who supported the Ptolemaic dynasty. They advocated making a deal with Caesar. After all, Caesar had a civil war to fight with turmoil spreading in Asia, Africa, and Spain. If he were satisfied with the administration in Egypt, he would leave. Others had enough of Arsinoe and her eunuch commander, Ganymedes, and preferred a more stable court. Important Alexandrians had sent secret messengers to Caesar, sounding him out; they wanted to receive their rightful rulers, Ptolemy XIII and Cleopatra VII.

Caesar, however, faced a problem: Cleopatra, already in Caesar's heart, did not want to return to the situation she was in before Caesar's arrival: at war with her brother's supporters and pushed again into exile or worse. Since his sister insisted on staying with Caesar, the adolescent boy-king believed Caesar was pushing him out of power for Cleopatra's benefit and did not want to go. Caesar insisted, no doubt thinking having his enemies together in one group made their defeat surer. Caesar told the youth, if he really wanted to stay in the palace, he should order his supporters to make peace.

Ptolemy XIII did no such thing. Once joining the Alexandrians, he threw himself into the struggle against the Romans. The Alexandrians found their new leaders were no more effective than their old ones. News had come of an approaching Roman army, something they believed unknown to Caesar because of their blockade of his position. Marching south from Cilicia and Syria, the army was supplied by convoys along the coast. The Alexandrians decided to intercept a large convoy in order to weaken the coming army before it arrived. The Egyptian command placed scout ships near Canopus to find the fleet so they could set up an ambush.

Caesar heard about the coming army soon enough and saw the Alexandrian fleet getting ready to sail. He readied his fleet, appointed Tiberius Nero as commander, and sent it out to fight. At the fore was the Rhodian squadron with Euphranor in charge. Reaching Canopus, Caesar's ships found the Egyptian fleet: both fleets assumed battle formation. With Euphranor's ship leading his squadron, the fleets clashed. Euphranor's ship rammed and sunk a quadrireme and pushed forward to strike another, but his squadron was unable to support his attack because of the press of ships. The Alexandrians surrounded Euphranor's ship and sank it, killing all on board. The Romans thwarted the Egyptian ambush but at a high coast.

At the time of this sea-fight, a strong army supporting Caesar approached Pelusium, one of the two keys to Egypt, the other being Pharos at Alexandria.

As Pharos defended the sea approach so Pelusium defended the land route, and the Egyptians had placed a strong garrison in the town. Leading the Roman force was a wealthy citizen of Pergamum named Mithridates, a friend of Caesar's. He was a seasoned military commander, whom Caesar sent into Cilicia and Syria to raise troops when the Alexandrian war heated up. Mithridates had collected troops from what was left of Pompey's armies. Antipater, a leader of a Jewish faction in Judea joined Caesar's side and brought powerful units of Jewish fighters to assist Mithridates. This army quickly advanced and surrounded Pelusium. Assaulting the town in relays, Mithridates' soldiers overwhelmed the defences in a day and took the town. He placed a garrison in Pelusium and marched south into the delta, approaching the temples and residences of the native Egyptian priests.

When the advisors of King Ptolemy heard about Mithridates' route, they drew together a large formation of troops and marched to intercept him. Since he was marching down into the delta, the Egyptian commanders planned to block Mithridates from crossing a large branch of the Nile. King Ptolemy's forces sailed down the west branch of the Nile, the vanguard reaching the river before the main body came up, and immediately attacked Mithridates' force. But the Roman army had constructed a strong camp; the Egyptian troops attacked, Mithridates counter-attacked, killing most, only a few reaching their flotilla on the Nile. The survivors of the battle joined together with the main body and prepared to attack again. Suddenly, they found Caesar and his army in their rear.

Caesar Victorious

For half of a year, Caesar was trapped in Alexandria. Adverse winds, ambitious leaders clashing with one another, riots, and siege, all had kept him from more important business at hand: defeating the senatorial faction. Spain was tottering, Africa was in the hands of Pompey followers, the Balkans and Asia Minor were in upheaval. Caesar's efforts were needed elsewhere than where he was, buried in an ancient palace, fighting an enemy whose defeat really meant nothing. We have only to look at the timeline of his actions to see how out of kilter his war-winning strategy had become.

Caesar had arrived in Alexandria on 2 October (28 July); the Alexandrian War began about 6 November (1 September), depending on which action might mark the war's start. The war continued, holding Caesar at a disadvantage without interruption through 10 December (4 October) when the XXXVII Legion arrived. From 10 December through 20 December, Caesar fought for advantage, uniting the newly arrived legion with his forces. He gained control of Pharos Island but lost the causeway on 6 and 7 January (29-30 October). On 6 February (27 November), Caesar sent his fleet to intercept an ambush against the supply fleet supporting Mithridates of Pergamum's arriving army. Mithridates took Pelusium on 6 March (25 December) and marched south into the delta. He fought and defeated King Ptolemy's vanguard on 15 March (3 January). Caesar was in a difficult position: his solution was to reinforce his actions and work toward the complete submission of Egypt.

After he had repulsed the Egyptian attack and disrupted their retreat, Mithridates sent a message to Caesar advising him of his situation and Caesar prepared to march to join him. King Ptolemy and his advisors also knew about Mithridates' defeat of their vanguard. They had already collected a large force and began shipping it up a branch of the Nile. Caesar did not want to meet them while they sailed up the Nile, instead, he sailed across the Mareotic Lake and then up a canal. He landed and marched toward King Ptolemy's army. They had camped in a strong position, fronting the Nile, a marsh, and an irregular height. This position had long been used as a military base, Flavius Josephus (*War of the Jews*, 9, 4.) called it the Jew's Camp, indicating that units of Jewish mercenaries had occupied the position.

Caesar's army marched toward King Ptolemy's camp and when he was about seven miles from the camp, the Egyptian commanders sent all their cavalry and a select unit of light troops to block his advance. Between Caesar's army and the king's camp ran a canal with very high banks. The Egyptians stationed their cavalry and light troops along the canal, blocking Caesar's advance. Roman soldiers were not going to let an advantageous position stymie their attack: the legionary troops cut down tall trees, long enough to reach from bank to bank and they started across the canal, trusting to their shields and armour to allow them to ignore light archers and slingers. Caesar's German cavalry found a spot where the banks were lower and swam across the canal. The heavy infantry pushed across the canal; the Egyptian troops turned to flee only to run into Caesar's German cavalry. Only a few Egyptian horse and foot regained their camp.

The Roman army reformed and advanced to Ptolemy's camp. Caesar thought the Egyptian army would collapse when they saw the strength he had brought against them but this would not be the case. Standing in serried ranks, Egyptian heavy infantry lined the camp ramparts, which oversaw an effective defensive structure set in a strong position. Caesar decided an immediate assault would not succeed. Instead, he set about constructing a camp near Ptolemy's camp. Nestled as Ptolemy's camp was between the

Nile, a marsh, and an irregular height, the only easy way in was through a nearby fortified village, linked to the camp by strong bastions.

The next morning, Caesar's legions attacked the village; he used his total force, only a small number of men might have carried the place, but Caesar wanted to be sure the Egyptians knew what was facing them. His troops carried the village, the defenders fleeing across the connecting bastions into Ptolemy's camp. Caesar ordered his men to follow immediately. His troops halted at the camp's fortifications, carrying on the fighting with missiles and slung stones. Other units penetrated the open space between the camp's ramparts and the Nile, shooting at everyone they saw. The best Egyptian soldiers were in the units defending the way from the village; the soldiers defending the ramparts facing the Nile were not effective but other troops approached carried on a flotilla rowing on the Nile which provided a strong crossfire of arrows and slung stones against the Romans. Caesar saw that the height, which had a strong garrison, was now almost unoccupied, the soldiers either joining the fighting elsewhere or viewing the struggles at closer range.

Caesar's soldiers were fighting well; the Egyptian soldiers held their positions with skill and determination; their front was not going to break without a harsh and costly struggle. Caesar decided the loosely occupied height provided an opportunity to unhinge the Egyptian defence. He called together several crack cohorts, placed them under the command of Carfulenus, an experienced and popular officer, and sent them off to take the height. Moving around the camp's ramparts, the cohorts scaled the height, fighting uphill against a few but determined enemies. Killing or pushing the Egyptians aside, the cohorts reached the top of the height and gave a great cheer. The Egyptians in the camp had no idea what was happening, but all saw that one side of their camp had fallen to the Romans. Panic and confusion spread among them.

Down the height the cohorts rushed, killing and wounding many Egyptians. With the confusion getting worse, the Romans broke into the camp from all sides, the Egyptians fleeing toward the Nile. Over the ramparts they swarmed, the first over getting crushed by the next, and then by the one after, as they fought to escape the Romans. Between the soldiers killed by the Romans and those who died in the debacle of an escape, the Egyptian army was lost. King Ptolemy joined those fleeing. He gained a boat on the Nile but then, masses of men swimming in the river overwhelmed the craft in their efforts to get aboard. The boat sank and King Ptolemy drowned. His army was not only defeated but destroyed.

Caesar, surrounded by his German cavalry, quickly set out overland toward Alexandria. He arrived before the gates of the quarter of the town garrisoned by his enemies. King Ptolemy's commanders had drawn all the soldiers out of Alexandria to fight Caesar; now those people who remained were not interested in continuing the battle. They surrendered to Caesar, expecting, and receiving his magnanimity. He accepted them as his clients, promising protection and they pledged their loyalty. Coming to his own quarter, he opened the blockaded streets. His army, his compatriots, and his servants cheered him and celebrated his victory.

The war was over. Caesar now had to stabilize Egypt and ensure the government remained loyal to him. He proclaimed Cleopatra and her younger brother, Ptolemy XIV, joint rulers of Egypt five days after his victorious entrance into Alexandria. He sent younger sister Arsinoe into comfortable exile. Caesar's army controlled Alexandria but the crux of power in Egypt, as the Ptolemaic dynasty well understood, was down the Nile in the temples and residences of the ancient priesthoods. The Macedonian kings had also to be Egyptian Pharaohs, in traditional costumes celebrating traditional rituals. Pharaoh oversaw the appointments of priestly administration, hopefully following priestly opinion. Caesar saw the need for a meet and greet of Queen Cleopatra with her high priests; meetings which needed to include him. That way he could make substantial agreements for Rome's support for their function and their loyalty to Cleopatra. Together, the Roman warlord and Macedonian queen spent a month sailing on the Nile, certainly not a 'pleasure cruise' however pleasant it may have been.

Julius Caesar.

Gnaeus Pompey.

Mark Antony.

Queen Cleopatra.

Marcus Cicero.

Gaius Octavius.

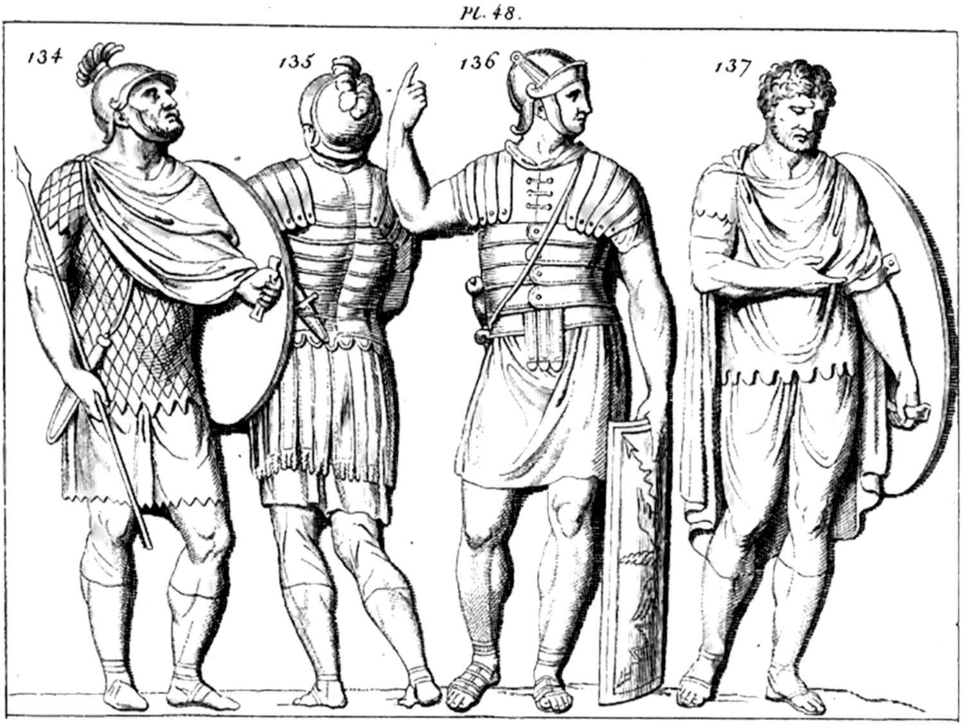

Caesar's soldiers.

Aquafer.

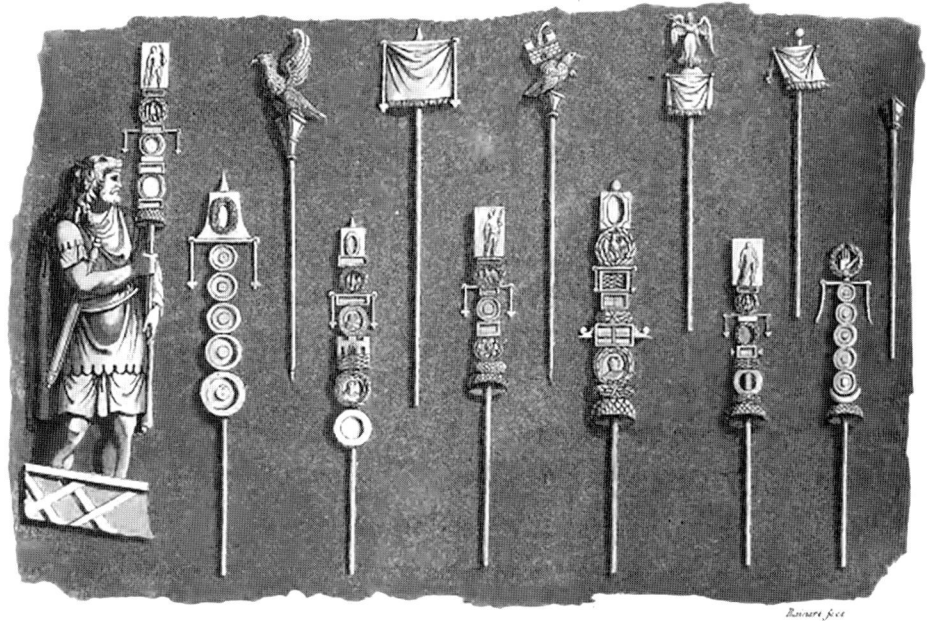

Standards.

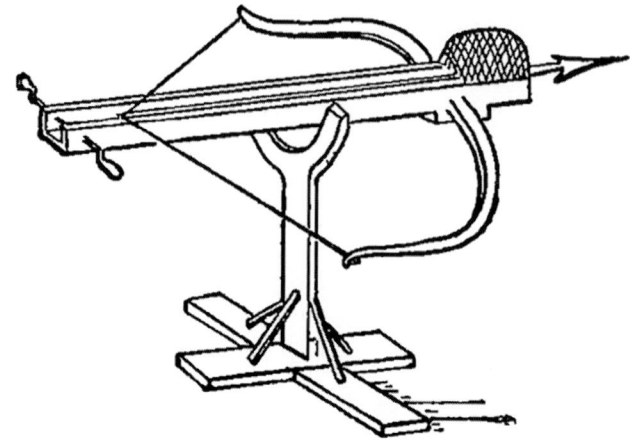

Scorpion.

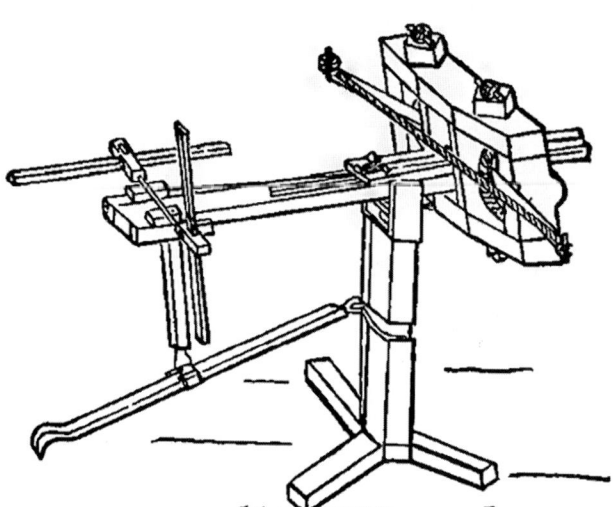

Torsion projector.

Large projector.

Warship.

Remains of a Roman street.

Remains of an *insula* in Rome.

Great Alexandrian Lighthouse.
(*Adobe Stock*)

Merchant trade ship.

Reading texts.

Taking notes.

Bread from time of Roman Empire.

Chapter 15

Victory Fades Away

Caesar's Dilemmas

During the seven months Caesar was occupied in Egypt, he was aware that the senatorial faction was building a base from which they could regain power, that serious disputes had arisen among his own supporters, and there were dependent states seeking to gain from Rome's weakness. Now that he held Egypt firmly in his hands, he was ready to march off to extinguish the wildfires which had broken out. In November the People of Rome had elected Caesar Dictator II for a year; but Rome was never stable, and many provinces were in upheaval. Africa was in the power of his enemies, Spain was sinking into chaos, Illyricum was rent by fierce battles, and foreign powers threatened the Eastern frontier. Different factors dominated each situation but behind all the problems was one factor: lack of leadership. Caesar needed to decisively settle arguments, disputes, and misinterpretations, all at once. But, of course, he could not be in more than one place at a time, so he had to prioritize his moves. The problem areas he faced: Africa was the main base of his enemies; Spain was the source of silver and troops; Illyricum was the passageway from Greece and the east to Rome; and the eastern frontier where many foes of Caesar and of Rome lurked. Each area had unique and complex problems.

Senatorial Africa

After he won the Battle of Pharsalus, Caesar's strategy was sound. He pursued the heart of the senatorial faction, chasing after Pompey as he attempted to repair his broken forces. Pompey had to hurry because Caesar was always close behind. Pompey's senate and followers gravitated toward Africa, but they were without decisive leadership and had to rebuild their forces. Pompey headed toward Egypt because he believed he had great influence there, supporting as he did King Ptolemy XIII and his court. By uniting the wealth of Egypt and Africa, he and his faction could block the grain shipments to the City of Rome and undercut the Caesarean faction. Caesar sought to capture Pompey and force some kind of settlement, and by coming to Egypt with a small but strong force he thought to grab Pompey who came with only his staff. Both strategies were sound, but both came to nothing when the Egyptian king's favourites thoughtlessly killed Pompey.

In Africa before Pharsalus, the senatorial governor, Varus, maintained the provinces for Pompey but he followed the directions of King Juba whose light horse and foot archers dominated the field. After Pharsalus, the scattered forces of the Republicans and their leaders collected there. Scipio and Pompey's sons, Gnaeus and Sextus, the indomitable Marcus Cato, and many loyal and experienced military officers joined together. As their first move the senators and King Juba purged all those they suspected of supporting Caesar, killing some, driving others away, and expropriated property, goods, and money. Because Caesar was tied down in Egypt, no opposition appeared to threaten senatorial Africa and that allowed the Republicans to organize and strengthen themselves.

King Juba presented the only difficulty, elevating himself from client king to equal ally and protector of the Romans. He coined Roman money bearing his name and indicated that only he should wear purple and Roman commanders should lay aside their purple. For the time being, the Roman leaders ignored Juba's pretentiousness and endeavoured to work out who would replace Pompey as supreme commander. Scipio claimed the position because, during the campaign in Thessaly Pompey, Scipio's son-in-law recognized him as equal commander. The governor, Varus, claimed the command because he ran the province in which the war would happen. The fact that he appointed himself did not strengthen his argument. The army officers and most of the experienced military men preferred Marcus Cato to take charge: while not a military man, he had the determination and drive to bring victory.

Cato, however, stood aside and recognized Scipio as supreme commander, not because he thought Scipio had military talent nor because he agreed with Scipio's policy but because looking at the legalities, he agreed Scipio had the law on his side. Still, Cato had sufficient prominence in senatorial circles to convince Scipio and anyone else to follow his ideas. This included King Juba, who Cato set right on the proper relations of a client king to the People of Rome. King Juba did back down regarding his pretentions especially after he was given permission to charge the costs of his army to the Roman treasury along with an increase in territory once the war was won. Soon the Republicans set up a new senate of three hundred in Utica, filled out with the addition of rich Roman equestrians.

All the senatorial leaders pushed forward the preparations for war. Cato especially strove to build a new and massive army to oppose Caesar. Every possible man found himself impressed into service, including freedmen and Libyan natives. The recruiters took so many men that a significant number of farms were untended. The result was impressive: fourteen legions marched under their orders, two already raised by Varus, eight formed out of the wreckage of Pompey's legions reinforced with local conscripts, and four raised and trained in the Roman manner by King Juba; there was a cavalry force, 1,600 strong formed of Gauls and Germans; King Juba's massive light cavalry and foot archers were reinforced by his 120 war-elephants. Their navy consisted of fifty-five warships. All in all, a formidable force would now face Caesar. Certainly, this was a large enough force to defend Africa and perhaps invade Italy.

Their main weakness was lack of money. They managed to raise a substantial sum by requiring the newly made senators, the richest men in Africa, to tax themselves but there remained shortfalls. Yet here the senatorial faction developed a powerful opposition to Caesar.

Spanish Chaos

When Caesar had left Spain in 49 BC, after his victory over Pompey's legions, he appointed Q. Cassius Longinus propaetor in Further Spain. Cassius Longinus had a reputation for avarice and arbitrary actions, but Caesar owed him for favours received and did not think he could cause too much trouble in Further Spain because most of the inhabitants he would deal with were Roman colonists, many of whose families had lived in Further Spain for generations. About this, Caesar was wrong. Cassius Longinus had four legions at hand: II, XXI, and XXX Legions and a local legion. The II Legion and the local legion were raised by Pompey and had surrendered to Caesar; the XXI and XXX came from Italy with Caesar. Cassius Longinus believed (with good reason) that he was unpopular with the Roman people in Further Spain's towns because of his constant unscrupulous extractions. He awarded the men of the legions 100 *sesterces* each and more to the officers to buy their loyalty.

With the coming of winter, Cassius Longinus went to Corduba to hear cases as chief judge. Not only were cases won by bribery but false accusations, brought by Cassius Longinus' agents, were only dropped through donations to the chief judge. Many large sums which changed hands were hidden in creative accounting. The propaetor was powerful and rich and inspired fear, but even those who worked and profited with him loathed him. He was feared, but also hated. Orders arrived from Caesar, who was opposing Pompey in Dyrrachium for Cassius Longinus to collect his troops and land in Mauritania in Africa. There, joining with King Bogud, he was to attack King Juba of Numidia and apply pressure so Juba would stop sending reinforcements to Pompey. Longinus was overjoyed. He called for new taxes to support this expedition and set about to rake a goodly amount off the top. Soon, a plot to kill Cassius Longinus emerged among those whom he believed were his friends. The plot failed. Many were executed, and more had to pay money for them and their families to survive. Cassius then raised the new V Legion, intending it for the protection of his property and self.

A few days after the attempted assassination, official word came of Caesar's victory at Pharsalus. Cassius Longinus still intended to invade Africa; he increased the tax rates and ordered the legions to collect at embarkation ports. The local legion mutinied, marched to II Legion's camp and the two formations joined together and appointed a certain T. Thorius their leader. They marched to Corduba and organized a base of action against Cassius Longinus. The civil disruptions spread with Cassius Longinus ravaging Corduba's hinterland. The opposing forces camped against each other, neither side ready to attack the other but both refused to leave. Demanding help from King Bogud and M. Lepidus, proconsul in Hither Spain, Cassius intended to crush his opposition. Both Bogud with his troops and Lepidus, with three and a half legions, arrived on the scene. After a brief investigation, Lepidus understood the problems.

Trebonius came to Further Spain as the new governor. Cassius packed up his belongings, including treasure chests of coin and silver, and embarked on a cargo ship to avoid any involvement with investigations. The season was unfavourable for sailing, yet to stay was not safe. Sailing around Spain to the mouth of the River Ebro in fair weather, Cassius Longinus did not want to land. But the seas soon ran high, the wind picked up and the ship was lost. The ship's sinking and loss of Cassius Longinus ended any investigation and, of course, made any accounting of Longinus' money impossible. This was certainly the best result that anyone could hope for by the Roman administration.

Cassius Longinus was gone but the damage he did to the people in Further Spain remained. For years, Pompey and his agents managed Spain and as far as the Roman community was concerned, they did well. Caesar had sent Cassius Longinus and he was a disaster who drove many old families into poverty and upset many long-established social relations. Caesar was not popular with many important families but at this point, they had no choice.

Success in Illyricum

At the time Caesar and Pompey were sparing in Thessaly, Pompey's fleet attacked Brundisium but Caesar's commander, Vatinius, repulsed the fleet, capturing a quinquereme and two smaller ships. Soon came tidings of Pompey's defeat and the fleet sailed away while its commanders considered what to do. At the same time, Caesar had two fleets, one at Messana in Sicily and the other in the Vibonensis gulf of southern Italy. Pompey had sent G. Cassius with a strong fleet of Syrian Cilician and Phoenician ships, to eliminate Caesar's fleets. Cassius destroyed the fleet at Messana with fire ships, and damaged part of the fleet in southern Italy, but legionnaires recovering from wounds or sickness launched several ships and counter-attacked Cassius' fleet. They captured his flagship, a quinquereme, took another quinquereme, and sank two triremes. But then word came to Cassius about the defeat in Thessaly, and he also sailed away to consider his options.

When Caesar was manoeuvering against Pompey in Thessaly, he sent his *quaestor*, Cornificius as *propraetor* to manage Illyricum. The land was devastated by the operations of Caesar and Pompey; the townsmen supported Caesar, the tribes in the hills supported Pompey. By delicate and careful administration, Cornificius settled the land, launching a strong attack against the more predatory tribes' hill forts but making deals with the more reasonable tribes. After Pharsalus, many of Pompey's supporters took refuge in Illyricum. Caesar was concerned they might overpower the province and he recalled Gabinius from exile, assigned to him troops, and directed him to support Cornificius. This is the same Gabinius former consul, who had returned Ptolemy XII to power and was convicted of corruption and exiled. However, ill fortune or age had caught up with Gabinius, the winter was harsh, supplies non-existent, and defeat reoccurred. Sick and beaten, he retreated into Salona, on the Adriatic coast, where he died.

At Brundisium, Vatinius received messages from Cornificius, requesting reinforcements and supplies because he had reports about Octavius making treaties with the hill tribes, attacking towns from the sea, and besieging strongholds with land forces. The winter was harsh and Vatinius was sick; still, he worked on through, mobilized forces, and tried to gather a fleet. Since Caesar's fleets in Sicily and southern Italy were damaged, Vatinius sought to bring the fleet in Achaia, but the fleet was not prepared to sail. Vatinius instead ordered metal rams attached to fast boats; there were many fast boats, but they were not built strongly enough to be fighting ships. Added to his regular warships, Vatinius had a passable fleet. These he filled with older veteran legionnaires who were in Brundisium because their units had sailed to Greece, and they were on the disabled lists. Vatinius set out for the coast of Illyricum.

Octavius was attacking Epidaurus when Vatinius' fleet found him. He abandoned the siege and sailed off to the north expecting Vatinius to pursue his fleet and prepared to ambush him. Collecting his fleet in the shadow of Tauris Island, Octavius waited for Vatinius to arrive. Soon, Vatinius sailing at the head of his fleet approached Tauris. The seas were high, the weather stormy and Vatinius' fleet was strung out in line ahead. Suddenly a ship appeared bearing down on his flagship. The ship's yardarm was at half-mast and fighting troops lined her decks. Vatinius ordered his sails lowered and his troops at the ready; he raised the battle flag, instructing his fleet, in line astern, to do the same. At the same time, Octavius' fleet emerged from behind Tauris in line ahead and then formed a line of battle.

Vatinius' ships took up their battle formation, facing Octavius' fleet; his ships were fewer and smaller than those of Octavius and rather than some finely thought-out plan, he trusted to audacity. His quinquereme charged Octavius' quadrireme. Octavius turned his ship to face Vatinius' charging warship and both ships smashed together head-on. Octavius' ram broke off and the two ships timbers locked together. Other ships from both sides joined the battle, forming a mass of interlocking ships. Vatinius' troops, hard fighting veterans of Caesar's armies, readily jumped from their ships onto Octavius' ships, spreading blood and killing men in their paths. Octavius' flag quadrireme sank, along with many others, captured or rammed, holed, and sunk. Vatinius' men killed many of Octavius' men, the others jumping off into the sea. Octavius escaped his doomed ship in a small boat, but masses of men swimming nearby overwhelmed the boat, and Octavius was dumped into the sea. Wounded, he managed to swim to a light galley where he found safety. Storm and night ended the battle.

Octavius and what remained of his fleet sailed off into the storm. Vatinius collected his fleet together where Octavius had anchored the night before. He captured one quinquereme, two triremes, eight biremes, and many of Octavius' rowers. The next day, Vatinius had his ships, his own and those he captured, repaired, and the following day he set off in pursuit of Octavius. He sailed to Issa, one of Octavius' main bases only to find that Octavius, his remaining ships, and soldiers had departed from the area, intending to sail to Africa to join with the senatorial forces there. Vatinius returned to Brundisium in triumph, having cleared the route between Italy and Macedonia of Caesar's enemies.

Trouble in North Asia

At the time the troubles in Alexandria brewed up, disturbances erupted on the eastern frontier. Caesar had placed Domitius Calvinus in charge of Asia and the adjacent provinces. King Deiotarus of Galatia came to Calvinus as spokesman for the client kings of eastern Asia Minor. He urged the Roman governor to protect his kingdom of Galatia, the kingdom of Lesser Armenia, and Ariobarzanes' kingdom of Cappadocia from the ambitions of Pharnaces, king of the Crimean Bosporus. Pharnaces was a son of the Great Mithridates, rewarded by Pompey with the throne of Bosporus. Deiotarus said that if the threat of Pharnaces remained, the client kingdoms could not pay the tribute required by Caesar. He added that more important than sending the funds to Caesar, the prestige of Rome was at stake. Calvinus sent an official embassy to Pharnaces demanding he withdraw his troops from Lesser Armenia and Cappadocia and stop damaging the Roman people by his ill-considered actions.

To back up his demands, Calvinus marched with the XXXVI Legion toward Pharnaces. Since he had already sent two legions to Caesar, Calvinus requested Deiotarus send the two legions which Deiotarus had raised from his own resources using Roman instructors. Also, both Deiotarus and Ariobarzanes added a hundred horsemen each to Calvinus' forces. Further, Calvinus sent orders to bring up the legion forming in Pontus and sent an officer to recruit auxiliary troops in Cilicia. These forces quickly assembled at Comana, a base in Pontus facing Lesser Armenia. While he was forming up his army, Calvinus received Pharnaces' reply to his demand: King Pharnaces had pulled out of Cappadocia but had recovered Lesser Armenia which he owned by hereditary right from his father. Since there was a dispute about this, the king continued, the issue should remain open until Caesar decided the issue. The king pledged to do whatever Caesar wanted.

Calvinus, however, believed Pharnaces pulled out of Cappadocia because he knew the positions in the eastern part of Cappadocia were hard to defend, while Lesser Armenia, closer to Pharnaces' supply bases, was far more defensible. Also, surely Pharnaces' scouts told him that Calvinus sent two legions to reinforce Caesar in Egypt; the king seemed certain Calvinus was weak. So, the Roman commander put on more pressure and Calvinus replied to Pharnaces, 'If a matter is "open" then it ought to remain as it was', and repeated his demand to evacuate Lesser Armenia. Putting his forces in march formations, Calvinus set out to attack Pharnaces.

The Roman army marched along a high wooded ridge that extends into Lesser Armenia from Pontus but also marks the border of Cappadocia.

By keeping to the high ground, Calvinus avoided an unseen attack and by marching along the Cappadocian border, he could draw supplies from friendly areas. Pharnaces kept sending messengers offering rich gifts and suggesting other solutions. These constant discussions were efforts to buy off Calvinus and opportunities to keep track of his line of march. Calvinus refused to accept any gifts, saying his only purpose was to safeguard the interests of the Roman People and protect the lands of Rome's allies. His army marched long distances every day until he approached Pharnaces' town, Nicopolis in Lesser Armenia. The town sat in a well-watered plain a fair distance from the mountains on Calvinus' route.

Calvinus ordered his troops to construct a camp on mountain slopes about seven miles from Nicopolis; to advance on the town, he needed to march his army through a narrow valley. Pharnaces set up an ambush at the head of the valley, stationing select infantry and all his cavalry to attack Calvinus when he marched through the valley. To make the scene more complete, Pharnaces had cattle placed here and there in the valley complete with peasants attending to them. The thought was that Calvinus' men would scatter and forage in the valley, then Pharnaces' men would attack and catch them while they were scattered.

While he prepared for his ambush, Pharnaces kept sending messengers to Calvinus talking about peace and friendship to put Calvinus off his guard. But Calvinus took these communications seriously and decided he would do better staying in his camp and allowing Pharnaces to withdraw in his own way. Fearing his ambush was revealed, Pharnaces pulled his troops back to his camp. The next day, however, Calvinus broke camp and marched through the valley, setting up camp near Nicopolis. As the Romans were completing their camp's defences, Pharnaces marched out of Nicopolis and assumed battle formation. This arrangement was in an eastern style, different from those the Romans usually encountered; the front was one long straight line of infantry connecting the centre and two wings. Behind each wing and behind the centre, three lines gave support. A single line of fighting men joined the wings and centre so, from the front, the formation appeared as one massive block.

Observing Pharnaces' manoeuvre, Calvinus completed his camp after posting men on the ramparts to keep watch on the enemy. After the Romans had completed their camp, Pharnaces withdrew back into Nicopolis. The next night, couriers brought messages from Caesar for Calvinus; a spy of Pharnaces acquired a copy of the dispatch and brought it to the king. The dispatch, issued at the time of crisis in the struggle for Alexandria, ordered Calvinus to send more reinforcements to Caesar and march into Syria to provide more support. Pharnaces saw victory in this message: Calvinus must withdraw and that would make his forces vulnerable to attack. The next morning, the king instructed his sappers to dig two straight trenches, four feet deep, extending out from the town's walls. These trenches were distant one from one another just the width of his deployed army. Once his men finished the trenches, the king posted his infantry between the trenches while he placed his massive force of light cavalry outside the trenches.

Calvinus was more concerned about Caesar's difficulty than his own problems. If Pharnaces defeated him, it would be important for local conditions, but he certainly could withdraw. If someone defeated and killed Caesar, then the senatorial faction would win, and he would be a fugitive of a lost cause. He could not trust Pharnaces to make any kind of agreement and certainly, the king would attack if given an opening, so the only solution was to defeat the king. He deployed his army near his camp and he posted the XXXVI Legion as his left-wing, the Pontic legion as the right-wing and put the two legions of Deiotarus in the centre. He formed the two centre legions deep and narrow, hoping their depth might give them strength. Since the king's army was already deployed, the signal for the attack came quickly.

Calvinus' soldiers charged toward Pharnaces' line. On the Roman right-wing, the XXXVI Legion smashed into the king's cavalry outside the trench and pushed to Nicopolis' walls, turning left, they crossed the trench and attacked the king's infantry in their rear. On their left-wing, the Pontic legion was not as bold, keeping away from the king's infantry but the soldiers swung around to attack them in the flank. Pharnaces' cavalry hit the Pontic force's flank and his infantry attacked their front when they tried to cross the trench. The Pontic legion disintegrated. In the centre Deiotarus' two homemade legions crumbled in the first assault. Pharnaces' army, freed on its own right and centre turned against the XXXVI Legion. The well-trained legion, commanded by experienced and able officers, formed an all-around defence, pushed their way off the battlefield and fought their way up into the foothills where the king's men gave up the pursuit.

Still, Pharnaces had won a significant victory. The Pontic legion was a loss; Deiotarus' two legions were gone, most of the men killed. The only bright spot was the XXXVI Legion which lost merely some 250 men, unfortunately including many senior officers. Calvinus collected the remnants of his army, formed around his one remaining legion, and marched away through Cappadocia into Asia.

Pharnaces was elated, not only had he repulsed Calvinus, but he believed Caesar was headed for defeat and death. He marched into Pontus and seized the land, setting himself up as his father's successor; he would become the new Mithridates the Great. He stormed many Roman towns, killing and plundering their citizens, sparing the young and good-looking so they would become slaves and eunuchs.

Chapter 16

Veni, Vidi, Vici

War in the East

Control of events slipping out of his hands, Caesar had to carefully consider his next moves. Whatever he did, it would take many months. His choice was critical: if, on one hand, he went to Rome, he could manage the city and Italy but his enemies, in Africa and across the Mediterranean, would spread their influence on the empire's periphery, in Spain, Asia, and Macedonia, blocking food supplies and trade. Given enough upheaval in the provinces, the city would welcome the senators back. If, on the other hand, he marched to Africa and fought his enemies there, like the monster Hydra, at each defeat the senators would simply go on to organize new centres of opposition. He would end up chasing them to one place while they undermined him at another. He could not win such a struggle.

Another option beckoned: Sulla, then Pompey, had gone off to the east, conquering the evil monster Mithridates, setting the east in order and returned, triumphant against the foreign enemy. Pharnaces, Mithridates' son, was causing trouble. This was nothing which in normal times, the eastern legions could not easily handle but the times were not normal. Rather than fighting a war of Roman against Roman, Caesar decided to march north against a foreigner threat. Leaving the XXVII and XXXVII Legions along with many cohorts in Alexandria, Caesar marched toward Syria with his faithful veteran VI Legion. Egypt, he knew was secure. If the rulers of Egypt remained faithful, the Roman army would protect them; should they fail to support Rome and Caesar, the army would destroy them.

Caesar left Alexandria at the end of April 47 BC, (mid-February solar calendar), reaching Ake Ptolemais around the first week of June (fourth week of March solar calendar). He soon took ship to Seleucia Pieria, arriving mid-June (early April solar calendar). In Syria, he received the latest news from his supporters in Rome. The administration in Rome was corrupt, overly expensive, and unable to accomplish important tasks. The college of tribunes was seriously split, the two factions facing each other in a stand-off, and the garrison was undisciplined and overindulged by their commanders. Caesar saw the problem: lack of leadership. But rather than panic, he kept to his plan, settling the eastern provinces and dependent states. Syria, Cilicia, and Asia had remained peaceful during the civil war, so Caesar thought he could manage any disagreements quickly. Bithynia and Pontus were going to take more time because Pharnaces occupied Pontus where he should not be; his victory over Domitius Calvinus allowed him to believe his forces were equal to Rome's.

In Syria, Caesar arrived in Antioch where he rewarded individuals and towns who helped their local communities and the Roman administration; he held hearings to settle disputes, giving swift judgments based upon evidence; he received neighbouring kings, princes, and potentates, taking them under his personal protection provided they guarded Roman Syria. He pronounced these allied rulers, Friends of Caesar and the Roman People. After he managed the Syrian administration, Caesar appointed his friend and relative Sextus Caesar as governor and commander of the Syrian legions. At the end of June (mid-April solar calendar), he sailed in his fleet to Tarsus. Caesar met with local leaders and allied rulers as he had in Syria and strengthened the ties holding the province of Cilicia together.

As soon as Caesar completed settling Cilicia, he set out to deal with Pharnaces. He marched through Cappadocia to Mazaca as fast as possible. He called together all the local leaders to make sure his supply of food and necessities was secure. The Cappadocian royal house was large and quarrelsome, but they had loyally supported Roman interests. Caesar intended they should do well and not fall out among themselves. Caesar honoured King Ariobarzanes but made his brother, Ariarathes, lord of part of Lesser Armenia under Ariobarzanes' suzerainty. Lycomedes, a member of a cadet branch of the royal house, who had a strong historic claim to the throne, Caesar installed as high priest of the goddess Bellona and master of her temple at Comana, a position second only to the king of Cappadocia.

His supply was secured, Caesar marched on to the border of Pontus and Grecian Gaul (Galatia). The Tetrarch Deiotarus met Caesar at the border. Deiotarus held almost all of Galatia, but the three other tetrarchs opposed him as best they could. Without dispute, however, Deiotarus was king of Lesser Armenia, awarded him by the Senate of Rome for services during the Mithridates Wars. But Deiotarus met Caesar dressed as a suppliant, begging for pardon because of his support for Pompey in the civil war. A large crowd of high-ranking officials and important local men accompanied him. He excused himself by saying that he faced overwhelming power and had not the right to judge disputes among the Roman People but obey the orders given him.

Caesar would have none of his excuses: Deiotarus merely took the expedient way out of a problem when he ought to have remembered Caesar's great acts of goodness. Nevertheless, Caesar forgave him because of the friendship he and his supporters had shown him in the past. As to the dispute among the tetrarchs, Caesar would see to that later. He told Deiotarus to put on his royal robes and be forgiven. Then Caesar ordered him to hand over his legion, trained in the Roman way, along with all his cavalry for the campaign against Pharnaces.

Pharnaces

Once he had marched to Pontus, Caesar gathered his force together. It was not strong, the VI Legion was by now about a thousand swords, battle and hard travel having taken their toll. But these were the hardiest men and best fighters in all of Caesar's army; they were veterans of many battles, skilled at killing. Caesar also had the two legions which Calvinus had commanded in his expedition to Pontus, XXXVI Legion, and the Pontic legion; their commanders had brought them up to strength, but they were no better than they were under Calvinus. Deiotarus' cavalry was, however, strong, and skilled. Pharnaces' representatives soon approached Caesar. They offered peace since King Pharnaces would do all that Caesar might request and handed over a golden victory crown. Further, they went on, King Pharnaces refused to grant Pompey's demand for troops, unlike Deiotarus who sent troops to Pompey; yet Caesar had forgiven Deiotarus.

Caesar answered the representatives: he would be more than forgiving of Pharnaces if he carried out Caesar's instructions. But the king needs to be mindful of the fact that not sending troops to Pompey as a favour to Caesar was over-shadowed by his severe injuries to many Roman citizens in his power. Since it was not in Caesar's power to bring back the dead or restore mutilated manhood, he did forgive Pharnaces. These are Caesar's orders: Pharnaces must immediately withdraw from Pontus, release all the slaves which his minions and their families held, and restore property and positions to those injured by his actions. Caesar had the golden victory crown returned to Pharnaces' representatives, saying, 'If he does these things Caesar demands, then he might send a victory crown and gifts that victorious commanders are pleased to receive from their friends.'

To all Caesar's demands, Pharnaces readily agreed. Everyone interested in the political world around them knew there were many reasons requiring Caesar to return to Rome. Pharnaces assumed a full assurance of complying with Caesar's demands would send Caesar off toward Rome and actual fulfilment of the demands was not going to be necessary. Caesar was more than Pharnaces' equal in chicanery: without forewarning, he marched against his stronghold, Zela.

Near the Galatian border, Zela was surrounded by hills easily fortified. One of these hills, the highest, was the site of a significant Roman defeat during the Mithridatic Wars. Pharnaces rebuilt the fortified camp that had been on the hilltop and occupied it with his field force. Caesar reached the area and set up camp about five miles from Pharnaces' camp. He scouted out the land around and located a site that had many of the same defensive qualities that protected Pharnaces' camp. Separated from Pharnaces' hilltop by a deep ravine, the same steep ascent to grapple with his forces was matched by an ascent to the site Caesar found. The problem with the site was whether Caesar could occupy and fortify it quickly enough before Pharnaces successfully attacked.

Caesar, in his camp five miles away, ordered his men to collect the timbers required by a fortification brought to him. The area was well-wooded, and the materials arrived quickly. Before dawn the next day, Caesar led all his legionaries out of camp, marching toward the site near Pharnaces' camp. They had left all their baggage and heavy equipment behind. Silently, they occupied the hilltop at first light. Following them after dawn, the army slaves brought the wood and fixtures to finish the fortified camp; Caesar did not want the soldiers, engaged in excavating the ditches and ramparts, interrupted in their work.

When Pharnaces' lookouts saw Caesar's army building a camp less than a mile from their position, they alerted all the people in their camp. Pharnaces ordered his army to stand to arms in formation in front of his fortifications. Caesar found Pharnaces' actions odd: his deployment might be simply a morning ritual; he might think he was threatening Caesar with an immediate attack but if that were the case, the time it would take for Pharnaces' army to descend to the ravine bottom and then ascend the hill upon which Caesar's camp sat would be measured in hours, plenty of time for Caesar to deploy. Caesar had his men continue their fortification work, leaving only his first line on picket duty, to spot any sneak attack by some small group.

In fact, Pharnaces started the descent of the steep hill, intending to attack Caesar. And, as he watched Pharnaces' army struggling down the hill, Caesar stood amazed. Perhaps Pharnaces thought the whole crew working on the camp were slaves, not realizing Caesar's soldiers did their own digging; maybe he believed his own propaganda, that his army had defeated twenty-two strong foes and was invincible; he might think he was facing Domitius Calvinus; Caesar looked on, planning for the deployment of his soldiers. As Pharnaces' troops reached the ravine bottom and began to mount the slope reaching to his camp, Caesar had moments of doubt; what if this manoeuvre was a blind, that the real attack was coming elsewhere?

And sure enough, over in a dip on another side, dust clouds rose in the breeze. A large force of scythe-chariots was bearing down on Caesar's camp. The horns blew the alert and then form-up signals. The men, in a sudden panic, gathered themselves together when the chariots struck. In no organized formation, nevertheless, they hit the attacking chariots with storms of flying pilums, transfixing the horses, and killing the drivers. But the chariot attack was nicely timed: as Caesar's men watched the chariots turn and flee, Pharnaces' men were at the hilltop in line of battle. Raising the battle cry, Caesar's soldiers attacked. Without formation or tactical direction, the men fought as individuals and small groups; valour took charge because the organization had failed.

Bitter hand-to-hand combat decided the battle. The veterans of VI Legion on the right-wing began to push Pharnaces' men over the hill's lip and down the slope. Then the Pontic legion on the left-wing also began to prevail followed finally by the centre units. Pharnaces' troops, many killed, and more wounded turned and fled down the hill, followed by Caesar's legions. Rather than stand and fight, which would avail them nothing, Pharnaces' men tumbled down the hill, many escaping by running away, along the ravine. Caesar's men kept right on, making their way up the slope to Pharnaces' camp. Here, the guards fought briefly to protect their camp, but the legionaries pushed them away and took the camp. Pharnaces escaped his total defeat with a few horsemen.

Caesar was thankful for his victory; he had beaten a foreign enemy, revenged criminal actions against Roman citizens, and recovered Roman lands. He gave all the royal plunder in the camp to his soldiers. He sent VI Legion home to Italy for their rewards and sent Deiotarus' men back to him and left XXXVI Legion and the Pontic legion with Caelius Vinicianus to protect Pontus. With his cavalry in light order, Caesar set out for the provinces of Galatia, Bithynia, and then Asia. He organized and settled the administration in each of these provinces. In Asia, he honoured Mithridates of Pergamum for swift and successful action in Egypt, naming him king of the Crimean Bosporus and awarding him the tetrarchy of Galatia that Deiotarus had seized a few years before. With the war with Pharnaces over and the east from Egypt to Bithynia settled, Caesar headed to Rome.

Rome Without Caesar

After Caelius and Milo failed in their attempt at insurrection, Italy remained quiet for several months. Uncertainty plagued business and trade, those who supported one side or the other could not sell their property because of the fear that should the other side win, they would confiscate the land without recompense for any purchaser.

After Caesar's victory at Pharsalus, no official statement appeared because Cato's fleet at Corcyra blocked the sea lanes. While rumours of Caesar's victory quickly spread, few believed them. Soon, however, the facts became known and all of a sudden all were Caesarean. The senate quickly decreed many honours for Caesar: he was appointed consul for five years and awarded a triumph over King Juba for a victory not yet won. Caesar appointed Antony as Master of Horse although Antony had never been praetor and so was constitutionally ineligible. Caesar overruled the objections. In the exercise of his powers, he sent nominations to the governors of the armed provinces; he left the unarmed provinces for the People's nomination. As Dolabella said to Cicero (Cic, Fam., XI, 9, 3.). 'It remains to fall in with the existing constitution rather than, while hankering after the old one, to find ourselves with none at all.'

Rome was in turmoil. The city's economy had stalled, and questions remained about debt, property and crime. Caesar appointed Mark Antony as his boss of the city but another important Caesarian, Dolabella went to Rome and stood for the tribuneship, having himself adopted by a plebeian so he was eligible. Dolabella secured the election by presenting himself as a strong supporter of the lower orders. The senate had decreed that no new laws were to be passed until Caesar returned. Antony ordered nobody could carry arms on the streets of Rome, but Dolabella and his supporters disregarded both. He proposed to the assembly the repeal of Caesar's debt compromise and removing tenant obligations to pay rents. The tribune Trebellius, also a Caesarian, supported the creditors (many of whom were also of the lower orders). The two sides often fought in the streets and the frequent murders and robberies were often a result of these political disputes, or made to appear as such.

The Senate authorized Antony to station troops in the city but Antony discovered he had serious problems with his soldiers. With the exception of one legion, all the troops who returned from Thessaly became involved in a mutiny. They demanded their prize money which Caesar promised them, and they wanted discharge. Antony had to go to Campania to deal with the legions; he sent Lucius Caesar to act as governor of Rome but Lucius was old and ignored in Rome. When the soldiers heard that Caesar had left Egypt, only to go to Asia, they agreed to nothing. Antony, failing to bring order to the legions, went back to Rome. Seeing that Dolabella's support was strong, Antony supported his position on the issues. This did no good because the tribune's supporters did not care what Antony did and the senate blamed Antony for adding to the disorder. Antony changed course, secretly letting Trebellius know that now, he had Antony's favour. With Antony looking on, pretending to be impartial, Trebellius' mob attacked Dolabella's mob and Dolabella counter-attacked. Buildings burned and men died, leaving blood on the streets. Alarm over the violence became so widespread that the Vestal Virgins removed the treasures from their temple to a safe place.

The Senate called on Antony to clamp down on the fighting mobs and authorized him to use his loyal legion to do it. When the disturbances were raging, Dolabella announced the date for the popular assembly which would pass his proposals into law. On the appointed day, Dolabella's followers barricaded the streets leading into the forum; they refused passage to anyone they thought would oppose the bill. Antony, however, was ready, when the sun rose, he led his troops down from the Capitol, fought his way into the forum, broke up the legal tablets holding the bill's text, grabbed the most obstreperous partisans, dragged them up the Capitol steps, and threw them off the Tarpeian rock.

Antony's action did little to deter Dolabella and his followers, but the news of Caesar's imminent arrival did.

Caesar in Rome

Caesar won the Battle of Zela on 2 August (21 May, solar calendar). The next day, he set out with a light cavalry formation, arriving at Deiotarus' fortress of Blucium on 9 August (28 May, solar calendar). After giving Deiotarus a hard time, Caesar left for Bithynia, arriving on 17 August (5 June, solar calendar). Brutus was in Bithynia and defended Deiotarus' actions. After settling affairs in Bithynia and Asia, Caesar arrived in Athens on 14 September (1 July, solar calendar) and on 24 September (11 July, solar calendar) he arrived in Tarentum.

Once he landed in Tarentum, Caesar made his way toward Rome, meeting and greeting Cicero whom he treated as a friend. Caesar knew that Cicero was not a powerful man yet the lucidity of his thoughts and political expertise made him influential. Showing friendship to the old senator cost him nothing and might reap rewards. Caesar's problems remained ahead. When he arrived in Rome the tribunes settled down. Caesar did not look for blame, he well knew there were serious, almost intractable problems but he could do little until he had crushed his enemies. Antony was loyal and useful; Dolabella was bright and adventurous. There was room for both in Caesar's administration. Both, however, found themselves caught in a problem of their own making. They had bid large sums of money at the auctions of confiscated properties of Pompey's followers, expecting that they were not going to have to pay the sums to take over the properties. Caesar said, pay up. How much actually paid is lost in their account books; still, they had to pay something.

Caesar was planning his next campaign, the conquest of the senatorial faction in Africa. He needed money and soldiers; the legionary mutineers were among his best soldiers, tough independent men, they always fought well but they wanted their cash rewards and Caesar knew if they got it, they would not want to go to war for some time. He would see to it that they would go to war without their rewards by the simple tactic of promising more but giving them, nothing now. Good men, hard fighters, but not so bright.

Carefully planning how to manage this problem, Caesar first sent Sallust (that cynical historian of the Catiline and Jugurtha Wars) to the mutinous legions. Calling an assembly, Sallust announced that Caesar would pay each man 1,000 *denarii* after the coming campaign in Africa. The mutineers told him plainly, it was cash they needed, not promises. The XII Legion threw stones at him, forcing him off the tribunal. Sallust quickly left for Rome. Riled up, the legions broke camp and went to Rome to demand their money from Caesar personally. They encamped on the Field of Mars, demanding Caesar come to them.

Workmen erected a tribunal on the field; soon, Caesar and his entourage came to the camp. Mounting the tribunal accompanied by officers trusted by all, Caesar saw the thousands of soldiers whom he had led for many years. Master of the public meeting, skilled since youth in managing a crowd, Caesar was ready for them. Quietly, agreeably, he asked them what they wanted so he could give it to them. In this way, his ploy began: the best way to handle a crowd is to lead them using shills – an accomplice or confidence trickster – among them. Caesar knew these men; he knew who to trust and who was not his friend. But, of course, some of those who appeared among the most disagreeable were, in fact, his agents.

They had done their job: they had convinced the leading mutineers since they were necessary to Caesar for the coming battles in Africa, they ought to demand release from their service. That way, Caesar would see he must pay them now. In answer to Caesar's question, the mutineer spokesman said they wanted to be disbanded. Caesar replied, 'I dismiss you.' Silence. After a few moments, Caesar continued, 'I will give you what I promised after I have conquered with the aid of others.' Silence. Some of the officers on the tribunal, within the hearing of all, begged Caesar to say something soothing to his long-time compatriots. Caesar turned and faced the crowd; he spoke, 'Quirites' (meaning not soldiers under arms but simply common citizens). The gravity of what they had done sank in. They were no longer Caesar's soldiers; now they were no better than the mobs in the streets.

Some yelled out, 'take us back' – no doubt Caesar's friends, well-coached. Many begged reinstatement. Caesar turned and began descending the tribunal's stairs. Then, some cried out that he should punish the ringleaders, that he shouldn't go yet. Caesar stood still. He returned to the tribunal and said he would not disband all of them and he certainly would punish nobody. But the X Legion, who he had favoured repeatedly, were the leaders of the mutiny, they alone would he disband. He continued, saying when he returned from Africa, he would give them all he had promised and, further, he will give land to them all when the war is over. The soldiers cheered ecstatically.

The men of X Legion requested that instead of disbanding, Caesar should decimate them. Again, this is a nice act of street theatre. No one was going to decimate (kill one man from every ten) such a strong formation but the request added to the drama. Of course, Great Caesar gave way, allowing them to stay in his command. Caesar did not punish anyone for the mutiny, but images of faces remained in his mind, and names on a list were in his files. The legions marched away from Rome toward their ports of travel.

That left the problem of Rome. Caesar had all sorts of reforms that would finally settle the ailing Republic, but first he had to defeat the senatorial faction. Using all the means at his hands, Caesar would keep Rome quiet until he could come back. 'Abolish all debts,' was the cry on the streets. This Caesar met head-on; he too had debts, he was going to pay them as all good people should. However, since the confiscation of so many properties of Pompey's followers had lowered property values generally, Caesar decreed that for the purposes of accounting, property values were those recorded before the current unpleasantness. Moreover, all interest accrued from the beginning of the war was remitted. And, as a sop to the poor, Caesar allowed tenants not to pay a year's rent up to 500 *denarii*.

Then Caesar raised money. He borrowed from individuals and towns with the implication that if there was no payment, things would be tough after Caesar secured his victory. If Caesar lost, the funds were lost with him, so the creditors' best bet was that Caesar should win. He freely passed out honours: governorships, priesthoods, magistrates' offices, and positions in the senate. Calenus and Vatinius became consuls for the last weeks of the year, doing whatever Caesar wanted. Caesar had replaced the Republican constitution with a personal military dictatorship. Now, he had to secure his position.

Section VI

War in Africa

Chapter 17

The African War Begins

Caesar's Campaign Plans

While Caesar was still struggling in Alexandria, he knew he would have to fight in Africa. After more than a year's thought, he developed a comprehensive and subtle plan to bring destruction to his enemies. Rome had invaded Africa numerous times since Regulus landed in 255 BC during the First Punic War. With some 200 years of warfare, Caesar had a good understanding of the African military landscape. The problem with Africa was the dearth of water and food. Too big a force, and no matter how strong they are, they will fail, defeated by supply problems, especially water. Too small a force, and no matter how well supplied, the local enemy will overwhelm them.

Caesar's solution was to design a campaign that started slowly, initially seizing a base area with access to the sea and a moderate water supply and available food.

Caesar Lands in Africa

Once Caesar brought his legions to order after their mutiny, he sent them back to camp, so their officers would reorganize their formations, switching men around in the conuberniums (eight men 'tent-full'), centuries, and cohorts; this was necessary to break up the most toxic cliques and restore the centurions' authority. After the reorganization, the centurions drilled the soldiers in their new positions until they moved quickly, without error. Caesar had faced his soldiers on 22 October (7 August solar calendar); he left Rome a month later, after organizing the administration to his satisfaction. In the middle of the next month, 17 December (1 October solar calendar) he reached Lilybaeum, Sicily. Here, he heard all the rumours about the amazing forces the senatorial faction had assembled: uncountable numbers of cavalry, four legions raised by King Juba, clouds of light infantry, ten powerful legions commanded by Scipio, 120 war elephants, all guarded by several fleets of warships.

Caesar was unimpressed with these numbers. He understood that large forces, containing many different commanders and types of people are more likely to hinder operations than defeat a determined enemy. Moreover, this was going to be a different type of war from his struggles against Pompey. Then, Caesar fought fellow citizens who might become his friends or, at least, accept his leadership. These men he was going to fight had had their chance of surrender. Now they were outlaws and deserved nothing. He assembled a fleet of warships and transports for his army, now made up of six legions, including four of new recruits and his veteran V Legion, Alauda, made up of Gauls, and he gathered 2,000 cavalrymen. As each legion arrived, Caesar embarked them on warships and the cavalry on transports, sending the soldiers to separate landing points where they could construct camps and continue training. Caesar stayed at Lilybaeum, selling choice properties of his enemies to buy more supplies; just before he sailed, he gave detailed instructions to his governor of Sicily, the praetor Alienus, detailing how his troops were to be made ready for the coming campaign.

Sailing from Lilybaeum in a fast ship on 25 December (9 October solar calendar), Caesar joined a few warships and transports. The rest of his fleet, with his infantry and horse, were scattered around western Sicily and nearby islands. In three days, Caesar reached the African coast; his objective was to conduct a reconnaissance in force so when he brought his army to Africa, he would have a secure base and know the enemy he would face. He sailed along the coast, past Clupea, then Neapolis and anchored off Hadrumetum, where his spies had found a serious weakness. The town was commanded by C. Considius and nearby Cn. Piso led a contingent of about 3,000 Moorish light troops based on Clupea.

Caesar waited at anchor for a day, seeing if conditions changed. They did not; the troops landed, 3,000 foot and 150 horse; each man selected for this mission by Caesar himself. They constructed a camp, ensured the local area was secured; Caesar demanded good behaviour from his men, forbidding any plundering or mistreatment of local people. Considius manned Hadrumetum's wall and massed a force to defend the gate, a total of about 8,000 fighting men. Ignoring Considius' forces, Caesar rode around the town with his personal guards, seeing the lie of the land, and returned to his camp. An officer approached Caesar and suggested they send a message to Cansidius, pointing out the difficulty of his situation. Caesar agreed. A prisoner was sent to Hadrumetum with a sealed message for the commander there. Considius' guards brought the prisoner directly to him but before the prisoner, who was carrying the message in his hands could speak, Considius demanded to know who gave him the letter. The prisoner replied, 'Imperator

Caesar'. Considius responded, 'There is only one imperator of the Roman People. That is Imperator Scipio!' At which time Considius ordered the man executed immediately.

Considius did not break the seals on the roll but sent it off, unread, to Scipio along with a report of Caesar's landing and what troops he had with him. Of this, Caesar's camp had no knowledge. They waited a night and a day. Caesar had no intention of attacking Hadrumetum's strong walls; scouts reported large cavalry forces were arriving to support Piso. Caesar had hoped Hadrumetum would surrender and so provide a secure base to deploy his army but that did not happen, so Caesar decided to move further south. He broke camp and started to march away. The town's garrison marched out and occupied the abandoned camp, supported by a large force of King Juba's cavalry. They began to follow Caesar's force, thinking that they were vulnerable.

As the Numidian cavalry approached, Caesar ordered his infantry to turn and face them and his cavalry to attack. A thirty-man squadron of Gallic cavalry dispersed 2,000 Numidian horse, driving them into the town. Caesar returned to his march. Now, the Numidians closed again and retreated, repeating the tactic. Caesar responded by posting some veteran infantry cohorts in his column's rear and a flanking cavalry unit. Keeping these forces in close order, Caesar slowly marched along, ready to repel any attack.

After marching south for some time, representatives from nearby towns and fortresses came to Caesar, pledging loyalty and offering supplies. By day's end, his army reached the loyal town of Respina. Caesar established a camp and organized a supply dump and storage for his soldiers' baggage. Once the soldiers had built a secured base, Caesar marched his army a short distance to Leptis Minor, arriving on 1 January (14 October solar calendar). Envoys from the town pledged to Caesar their loyalty and support. In return Caesar posted guards at the town gates, commanded by centurions, to prevent his soldiers from entering the town or bothering any of its citizens. This was an independent town that commanded a wide beach, good for landing and unloading a fleet. The soldiers built a camp near the town on the shore. Caesar was waiting for his fleet to bring the main force and needed to secure an extended area to stockpile supplies and hold troops.

While Caesar's men were building their camp, a squadron of his fleet arrived, sailing along the shore. Caesar ordered them to anchor off but not to land for a while. Rather than overload his base, he preferred to let the numbers of reinforcements be imagined rather than counted. Certainly, his enemies were nearby; this fact quickly became obvious when a company of rowers had come onshore to draw water and a formation of Moorish horse emerged out of a wadi, killing some and wounding many of them. Caesar explained to all that his fleet was lost along the shore here or there. This was for the ears of senatorial agents collecting information. In reality, Caesar's fleets remained stacked up in their stations, waiting for his call.

Once initially settled, Caesar sent orders for reinforcements to several bases which held his fleets of warships, transports, and cargo carriers. In Sardinia, Sicily, and other islands, his commanders immediately released their fleets. At the same time, Caesar unloaded the ships at anchor near Leptis and sent the cargo ships back to Sicily to pick up more men and materials. He gave ten warships to Vatinius, ostensibly to search out his lost fleets. The rest of the warships, he assigned to the praetor Sallustius Crispus and sent him to take the island of Cercina in order to seize the great amount of corn stored there. By taking or wasting it, he would deprive the senatorial force of its use. Caesar interviewed each officer separately in his tent, making sure each man knew only what he needed to know.

The next day 2 January (15 October solar calendar), after sending out his ships and scouts, Caesar organized his army. With his reinforcements, he now commanded almost 10,000 men. He established a garrison at Leptis Minor of six cohorts under Saserna and marched back to Ruspina where his original force kept their baggage and those recently arrived placed theirs. Caesar and a large force of soldiers in light order scoured the area, taking all the corn, draught animals, and carts back to Ruspina. With his supplies secured, Caesar placed a legion to garrison Ruspina. At the head of seven veterans cohorts, all of whom had previously served on warships under Sulpicius and Vatinius, Caesar marched two miles to Ruspina's harbour. There, he boarded Vatinius' fleet, which had secretly returned; he stayed on board that night, conferring with his scouts, spies, and messengers.

Labienus Against Caesar: the Battle Near Ruspina

At the break of dawn, lookouts on Caesar's ship saw an approaching fleet. His reinforcements arrived on schedule and he ordered Vatinius' ships to land their troops. Since they had embarked the night before, they were unclear about what Caesar was doing but then, everyone else in Caesar's forces was in the dark. Caesar made certain his enemies were going to get absolutely no information about his strategic and tactical plans simply by telling no one about his plans. His seven cohorts drew up under arms on the beach, awaiting the arrival of the reinforcements. Soon, the newly arrived ships came into port and disembarked their large force of infantry and some cavalry. Caesar marched them to Ruspina where they set to work, extending

The African War Begins   169

the base camp. Once the camp was well-along, Caesar organized a foraging party and set out into the hinterland.

Moving some three miles from his camp, Caesar's scouts returned from the more distant countryside, telling him that the enemies' forces were approaching, and looking closely at the horizon, there was a distant but large cloud of dust rising into the sky. The time for battle had come. Caesar had prepared for this engagement, plotting tactics to counter the light but very numerous forces of the Africans and devising alternative strategies to weaken and then destroy the Republican force in Africa. With the dust cloud getting closer, Caesar ordered his cavalry force to come, along with his archery corps, followed by the infantry cohorts. He deployed thirty cohorts of infantry, 2,000 cavalry, and 1,500 archers (I follow Stoffel in these numbers). Caesar gave the order to don helmets, bring weapons and shields to the fore, and prepare for battle.

The dust cloud approached, generated by a large number of men and animals, spread across a wide area. Soon the mass of men and beasts became visible: a long straight line of close ordered troops, and on each wing, there were masses of cavalry. It was an immense force. This was the army of Titus Labienus, a noble equestrian Roman, friend of Pompey, and former assistant of Caesar during the conquest of Gaul. Labienus knew Caesar well; Caesar had entrusted him with the command of his army in Gaul when Caesar was in Rome. Together, they had developed the tactics needed to defeat the Gauls. He had great respect for Caesar's abilities and the feeling was reciprocated.

But when Caesar marched against Rome, bringing his army into Italy at the start of the civil war, Labienus said that action was criminal. He understood Caesar's ambition was to become the autocrat of the Roman Republic. He joined Pompey. The senatorial faction often ignored his advice and Caesar beat him, his cavalry, and the whole senatorial faction at Pharsalus. Labienus knew a defeat is never final until the last man is down. He sailed to Africa, joined with the senators there, and proceeded to devise a way to defeat Caesar. Well-trained heavy infantry made Caesar strong, however, Labienus knew those men; he had commanded many of them and the civil war was a hard slog. Many had mutinied, which meant that many more were dispirited. Face them with an enemy who they could not defeat, and they would fold.

While the senators had legions of heavy infantry, Caesar's soldiers would crush them because they had more experience, were tougher, and were far more aggressive killers. What about masses of soldiers, each one not a particular danger but coming as an overwhelming force? This, Labienus suggested to the senators' war council, was the solution to Caesar's heavy infantry. Use King Juba's light infantry and cavalry and throw them against Caesar's legions, repeatedly. Make Caesar's soldiers feel that the fight will never end. Caesar was very aware of Labienus' tactical abilities and of the nature of North African local troops. He also knew his own weaknesses and these challenges called for new tactics so Caesar devised a new tactical system.

Men who have trained for a job and been trained by men who had done the job for years, don't like to change what they do. His best troops had mutinied (and why not, they are freemen and the wars have dragged on, and on), he had to bribe them with bigger promises than the extravagant promises he had already made and could not pay. Caesar, therefore, designed 'punishment' for these men, reshuffling them between units and then drilling them in strange and difficult manoeuvres. If Caesar's new tactics failed, he would lose but losing is not what Caesar was about.

Caesar commanded his thirty cohorts to advance forward in a single line, all six centuries of each cohort following each other in a single file of centuries, across the enemy front. Each century was eighty men wide, with the enemy to their left as they marched across the landscape. Groups of archers filled in different openings in the formation and about 1,000 cavalry took up position at the beginning and end of the line.

This was a strange formation, but he had his soldiers train for this with all the 'punishment' drilling, which his men now discovered had its uses. Once extended out into the plain, the line halted and turned left to face the enemy, each man in his correct position, forming a long and solid line across the field. Still, the enemy masses of infantry and horses came closer. The enemy cavalry on each flank spread out far beyond Caesar's line. Caesar's cavalry gave way before their enemies' onslaught, not wanting to be overrun, nevertheless maintaining a threatening pressure.

The enemy centre approached the line of cohorts: suddenly, out of what now was seen as a mass of light cavalry, light infantry ran forward and hurled their spears at the Roman line. With strong helmets, sound armour, and large shields, Caesar's infantry easily avoided the flying spears, then, grabbing their heavy pilums, the engaged centuries attacked. They threw their pilums and smashed those in front of them with shields and swords. The enemy horse fled but the infantry stood their ground. The attacking centuries drove the Moorish infantry back but by doing so, they exposed their flanks to the spearmen on their sides. Caesar expected this to happen and had added an order to the trumpets' signals, 'Go no more than four feet beyond the line of the standards.' The horns sounded; the troops withdrew back to their lines. Then Labienus' cavalry struck, surging through the dust, two masses, one on either end of Caesar's line, swept around into the rear of Caesar's cohorts. Caesar's cavalry forces were too small to block their enemies' masses and their horses remained weakened by the sea voyage; they slowly gave way while Labienus surrounded Caesar's cohorts.

Directing his cavalry from their midst, bare-headed, Labienus cheered on his men and, now and again, turned about and insulted Caesar's soldiers. 'Do you know what you're doing, recruit? You all are in a deep mess! I see your misery!' One soldier stood forward, facing Labienus, yelling, 'I'm not a sorry sod, Labienus, I'm of X Legion!' Labienus replied, 'I do not see the standard of the Xth.' The soldier responded, 'Now you understand where I came from.' As he spoke, he threw off his helmet, threatened Labienus with the point of his pilum, then lowered the weapon, stabbing Labienus' horse in the chest and, as the horse collapsed making Labienus fall on the ground, the soldier continued, 'Dear Labienus, you see that a soldier of the Xth has attacked.'

Still and all, Caesar's soldiers were shaken and unnerved. Surrounded, dodging spears, waiting for orders to get them out of this mess, they began to feel helpless. Seeing the attack develop as he expected, sitting on a horse in the midst of his cavalry formation beyond his line, Caesar gave a sign to the trumpeters to sound his order. As the notes rang out, his soldiers understood more about the 'punishment' drills: the cohorts jolted to attention, dressed their ranks, spaced their files, and every other cohort turned about. Then, as one, the cohorts attacked in two directions, straight into the massed enemy. Caesar's two cavalry formations, one at each end of the line burst out of the enemies' lines, so the whole of Labienus' force was split in half, causing confusion and disruption. The horns sounded again; Caesar's troops returned to their battle formation. Holding that formation, Caesar marched his soldiers back toward their camp.

More enemies arrived on the field, M. Petreius and Cn. Piso led 1,600 Numidian horse supported by light infantry. They charged into the battle, giving fresh heart to Labienus' forces. Regrouping their cavalry, the enemy charged to the rear of Caesar's column as it withdrew. Caesar ordered the column about and, together with his united cavalry force, struck and pushed the light troops back. Then Caesar resumed his march. Again, the enemy attacked, but this time, they came only to launch missiles not to engage in hand-to-hand combat. Caesar's troops, foot and horse were exhausted, and the sun was about to set. Caesar went among them, telling them how they were winning a great victory; that the numbers of enemies killed were enormous while their casualties were mostly wounds with very few deaths.

One more time, he went on, they needed to attack. Choosing the strongest cohorts and encouraging the horse, he waited until the enemy's approach was half-hearted and their missiles shot inaccurately, then he gave the order to attack. The enemy scattered. Caesar resumed his march and his army reached camp. The enemy forces then returned to their camp.

Plans Come Together

The battle took place on 4 January (17 October solar calendar), the next day many people came to Caesar's camp. They had deserted the senatorial faction's army and wanted to join his side. Many of these deserters were officers close to the senatorial command and brought information about Labienus' and Scipio's strategic plans. Caesar's spies had been correct in their description of senatorial plans. Moreover, the misinformation his agents had spread about his armies' problems, untrained recruits, dissatisfied veterans, had done its work. Caesar's soldiers had stood up to Labienus' mobs. But now, Caesar would have to face Scipio's original strategy. Besides the masses of Numidian auxiliaries, the senators had drawn out of Pompey's defeat units of German and Gallic cavalry 1,600 strong. They had raised 12,000 heavy infantry trained in the Roman manner and allied with King Juba, had at hand, heavier infantry, masses of light foot and horse, and many war elephants. While he avoided defeat, Caesar still faced a powerful enemy; on the third day after the battle, word reached him that Scipio was leaving Utica with his army.

Caesar's priority now was to secure his base. He set his men digging. Engineers designed and gangs of soldiers built the camp ramparts higher and stronger; new ramparts extended from the town of Ruspina to the sea on one side and from the camp to the sea on the other. Access to the waterways was a necessity for victory. From the ships, Caesar took rowers and sailors, armed them as light infantry, and stationed them on his ramparts. He had the ships' artillery offloaded and installed on bastions of his camps' ramparts. Ships carrying large numbers of archers arrived and these, too, Caesar assigned to defensive positions. He also imported skilled workmen, to manage foundries making iron bullets for slings, arrowheads, and pilums, along with woodworkers to fabricate stakes, gates, and palisade parts. Such work required the importation of quantities of metals and timbers.

His troops soon occupied a strong position that had one major weakness: food was going to become a problem. The senators had collected all available food supplies and labourers before he came. There were few fields available in the drylands and none were being worked. The only food at Caesar's hand was what he brought in by ship. Caesar had carefully rationed his stocks but eventually, they would run out. The key to his success was keeping the sea lanes open and already some of Caesar's cargo ships were lost after small boats attacked them, capturing some, burning others. Caesar sent out warships to patrol the sea lanes leading to the harbour near Ruspina.

Scipio reached Hadrumetum on 9 January (22 October solar calendar) and set up camp to collect his supplies in a stockpile. A few days later, leaving this camp at dusk, he reached Labienus with his Numidian auxiliaries and Germanic and Gallic cavalry. Together, these commanders set up a strong camp within a few miles of Caesar's fortifications. Squadrons of cavalry patrolled around their camp, riding at odd times close to Caesar's ramparts, killing any of Caesar's soldiers who were out foraging for fodder. The pressure Scipio's men applied was telling in Caesar's camp. The ships Caesar had ordered to sail from Sardinia and Sicily were still in port because of bad weather and the animals were all suffering severely from lack of food. Veteran foot and cavalry, who had been through similar situations, collected seaweed along the shore, washed it in fresh water, and gave it to the animals to keep them from dying.

Caesar had anticipated a situation where his forces were isolated from the sea lanes and faced by a strong senatorial force. He had an answer. To the west of the Roman province of Africa sat Juba's kingdom of Numidia but to the west of Numidia, there were the kingdoms of Mauretania. The new king of the eastern part of the kingdom, Bogud, was ambitious. Rather than attack his brother, King Bocchus II of the western part of the kingdom (both were sons of Bocchus I), Bogud would like to defeat King Juba and seize Numidian lands to his east. But Juba was strong besides being imperious and presumptuous. Bogud would have to pick his time carefully. Juba was going to march with another army into Roman Africa to support the senators in their war against Caesar. Bogud thought this was a war Caesar would eventually win, so once Juba was committed in the east, Bogud would attack the western part of his kingdom.

In the middle of January 46 BC, Caesar appeared pinned and open to defeat. Yet he found some satisfaction in his position. He understood that supplies and reinforcements would come; he knew where Scipio was concentrating his forces; he assumed Juba was marching to reinforce the senators, but Bogud would soon strike him in the rear. There were many moving pieces and Caesar was juggling them all: that is what he did well.

Chapter 18

Caesar Builds a Strong Base in Africa

The Senators Plan Caesar's Destruction

Fateful decisions faced the senatorial leaders in Utica. Only they stood between Caesar and the destruction of the Republic. Caesar displayed his usual arrogant disregard of law and tradition when he crossed the Rubicon with his military force. This was clear proof that he intended to replace the liberties of free government with a monarchy with himself as king, regardless of the title he chose for himself. Pompey, against the advice of many, fled Italy, thinking to collect the resources of the east and defeat Caesar between his forces in Spain and in the east. Caesar outmanoeuvred and outfought him. Then Caesar was in Alexandria, surely a morass which would swallow him, but he walked out of that swamp stronger than ever. Now, the last battle was upon them. They strove to do everything in their power to bring an end to Caesar's career and kill him.

Marcus Porcius Cato was the leader of the senators. In his late forties, austere, shrewd, commanding, and uncompromising, Cato had hated Julius Caesar for decades. What was a serious political disagreement for Pompey, Scipio, and Labienus, was for Cato a deeply personal affront. For all the senatorial leaders, the struggle was a matter of life and death, for Cato it was a fight with a metaphysical darkness. While Cato never took military command, he understood military affairs better than many commanders. Now, with Caesar holding a small toehold on the eastern shores of the African province, Cato believed this was the time to destroy him, throw everything at him, overwhelm his soldiers and kill him.

At Utica, Cato swept the streets, picking up any able-bodied man, freedmen, Africans, even slaves, sending them as reinforcements to the military commanders. He was concerned, however, about King Juba's troops. The king had already sent large contingents of troops who fought well against Caesar. If his kingdom were safe, Juba would continue to send countless men, mostly light cavalry, and infantry but also some legion-sized formations of heavy infantry. Cato knew about King Bogud in eastern Mauritania. Caesar no doubt had already offered the king inducements to attack Numidia. To keep King Juba from this distraction on his west, Cato pressured Gnaeus Pompey, eldest son of Pompey the Great, to organize an expedition to attack King Bogud. Reluctantly, young Pompey did so.

Uncompromising and demanding, Cato had taken young Pompey to task for not being like his father: Pompey the Great raised, organized, and led a victorious army as a teenager, yet here was Gnaeus Pompey, thirty years old, and unable to attack King Bogud. Africa was nothing like Picenum nor was this civil war anything like the Social War, Pompey explained but it did not matter to the obstinate Cato. Pompey collected thirty small ships of diverse types including a few with rams, loaded them with 2,000 fighters, all slaves or freedmen. Their arms were of many types and some of the men had nothing.

The fleet sailed to a Mauritanian frontier town, Ascurum (location unknown). King Bogud had been waiting for the right time to strike into Numidia; he concentrated troops along his eastern frontier but kept them out of sight. Among the towns holding these forces was Ascurum. Pompey landed, disembarked his troops, pulled up in battle order, and advanced toward the town. There was no reaction; Pompey moved to invest the walls. As his troops approached the town gates, suddenly the gates opened and out charged strong units of Bogud's royal army. They smashed Pompey's force, who fled back to their ships. Gnaeus Pompey had enough of Cato and his unreal demand. He sailed his fleet directly to the Balearic Islands, carrying on the war against Caesar in ships, on his own.

Just like Cato, King Juba feared and hated Caesar. He appreciated the need to crush Caesar while he had few forces and serious supply problems. He marched from Numidia when Scipio had left Utica; his forces were strong, and he made haste to join with his allies. But King Bogud heard that Juba had left Numidia, he marched. Rather than try to turn local tribesmen into soldiers, he hired a Roman, Publius Sittius, and his army of mercenaries. Sittius was a prominent equestrian who had supported Catiline. When Catiline's revolt collapsed, Sittius was in Mauritania trying to gain support for Catiline's efforts. He sold his holdings in Italy and Spain, settling in Mauritania. There he built a private army which he used to raid and plunder. His support for Caesar was well-known.

Sittius led his troops against Cirta King Juba's richest town. After taking several large tribal villages in the area, Sittius offered terms to the Cirtans, they should all leave the town and let him occupy it. The Cirtans refused and Sittius easily took the town while his men killed all the inhabitants. After looting the dead town, he pushed further into Numidia, plundering the countryside and towns as he advanced. Word spread as the smoke from fires rose high in the sky. Soon, breathless messengers told King Juba about the invasion, just as he was about to unite with Scipio. Juba recognized Caesar's hand in this invasion and faced the dilemma: continue to push against Caesar or save his subjects. But there was really no answer other than turn around and defend his kingdom because the very instruments needed to defeat Caesar, his massive army, contained the men whose families and homes were under threat. Certainly, they could not take the long view. Moreover, if he lost his lands, would the senators fight for it or make a deal with whoever held the land? Juba turned his army about and marched toward Numidia. Further, he recalled his forces under Scipio's command, leaving only thirty elephants.

The Senators Start their Attacks

The senatorial commanders planned to take the initiative by launching offensives in many direction, hoping to weaken Caesar by many small attacks. When Caesar had landed, Cato and his supporters said Caesar was not leading the expedition in person; regardless of the truth, the rumour seemed serviceable to deflect help that might come from the Caesareans in the province. Caesar, hearing of this, wrote letters to the towns of the African province, announcing his presence. Refugees came to Caesar's camp, to escape harsh treatment by the senatorial faction. Important people in their own towns, they brought stories of cruelty and pain inflicted by Caesar's enemies. In the second week of January (toward the end of October solar calendar), Caesar announced he was changing his plans: he had planned to stay in his camp-fortress over the coming winter and begin offensive operations in the spring; now he decided to order his troops to come as soon as possible. He immediately sent a message to Alienus and Rabirius in Sicily by swift boat telling them to embark as large a force as possible and dispatch it to him now. They should pay no attention to weather or other excuses.

Caesar said in his message to them and in other messages to Italy, that the rebel senators and their followers were laying the African province waste, destroying farms and fields, villages, and towns. Even the very well-off were in chains and their children seized as hostages and sold into slavery. In their camp-fortress, people could see the smoke rising from burning farms and villages; Caesar was constantly looking at the sea, waiting for his troops. All the while, he did not neglect his soldiers, continuing training and building towers, strengthening ramparts, and constructing breakwaters in the sea.

Scipio knew Caesar had never fought elephants. He decided to make the beasts the spearhead of his attacks. Unfortunately, the thirty elephants left with Scipio were rideable but untrained for war. Scipio determined to train them to face Caesar's soldiers. He lined up the elephants facing front. They then walked toward a line of slingers, who pelted the beasts with stones. When the elephants turned aside and began to run away from the slingers, another line of men hit them with larger and more painful missiles, forcing them to turn around again and advance toward the line of slingers. The men all saw the elephants as useful tools on a battlefield, but likely to be dangerous to both sides in a battle. And, of course, with such poor training, they were right.

South, along the coast from Ruspina and beyond Leptis Minus, is the town of Thapsus, held for the Republican faction by the former praetor Vergilius. The traffic toward Caesar's camp was obvious. Vergilius fitted out a swift ship along with several long boats thinking to capture or sink some of Caesar's ships carrying supplies and reinforcements. His attacks were unsuccessful, Caesar's ships were able to repel his attacks. Still, he kept up the effort, hoping for a win. He attacked a transport carrying men and officers of the V Legion. The military tribunes in charge, the brothers Titus, opposed Caesar. An important centurion, Salienus equally dissatisfied with Caesar, suggested they all surrender to Vergilius, saying they all might get better rewards from Caesar's opponents than what had come from Caesar. After the ship surrendered, Vergilius took them to Scipio, who put them under guard. Scipio did not need fractious unreliable soldiers. Within two days, he put them all to death, allowing only the execution of the elder brother Titus before his younger brother.

Under Scipio's direction Labienus invested Leptis with his cavalry forces. Caesar's commander, Saserna held the town with six cohorts; he had strengthened the fortifications and mounted many projector engines of several types; he easily repulsed Labienus' men. But Labienus continued to attack the town until one day a cavalry squadron concentrated before the main gate. A shot from a scorpion hit the squadron leader and pinned him to his horse. Labienus decided his demonstrations were not worth the cost.

Representatives of the small town of Aeylla (location unknown) came to Caesar, promising to follow his will in all things and requesting a garrison of his soldiers to protect them from Scipio. They told him they would provide all the supplies needed by the garrison. Caesar sent the former aedile C. Messius with a garrison for Aeylla. Word of the Aeyllans' decision quickly reached Hadrumetum; the commander there, Considius Longus, had a garrison of two legions and 700 cavalry. With eight cohorts, he marched toward Aeylla, trying to forestall Messius. But Messius reached the town before Considius, who was not about to try to attack the town lest he lost many men. Instead, he turned his forces about and returned to Hadrumetum.

After communicating with Labienus, in a few days he received a powerful cavalry contingent and marched back to Aeylla to invest the town.

Scipio Faces Caesar

Once encamped, Scipio started to march his troops out about 1,000 feet from his camp and formed line of battle. When sunset approached, he returned them to camp. He did this action many days in a row. Caesar made no response. Scipio saw Caesar's lack of response as indication of trouble in the camp. Scipio marched out his whole army, elephants armed with towers leading, taking up positions close to Caesar's ramparts. While the infantry formed up, Scipio deployed his cavalry and light troops, extending across the front of Caesar's position.

When Scipio advanced toward his enemy's camp, Caesar was sitting in his headquarters tent, doing the endless paperwork of army management. Lookouts came with reports of Scipio's advance, he simply looked up and directed some centurions to see to it that the foragers who were beyond the ramparts return to the camp in a manner to suggest they had finished their work, not as if they were fleeing an enemy. Once they returned, they were to man the walls. The cavalry guarding the gates were to hold their positions until the enemy came within missile range. Should the enemy advance further, they were to retire inside the gates as if their shift were ending.

Rather than engage Scipio in battle, Caesar had decided to wait until sufficient reinforcements arrived in order that he would not only be victorious but overwhelmingly so. Scipio kept his troops positioned in front of Caesar's ramparts for a few hours, to demonstrate his contempt for Caesar, who was hiding behind his ramparts. One by one, Scipio returned his units to his camp. In the camp, he held a parade, informing his troops of how much better they were compared to Caesar' army of raw recruits. Soon, they all will have victory! Caesar, after Scipio left, ordered his army to return to their duties, the foot foraging, strengthening the fortifications, and the cavalry, scouting and guarding the camp.

Scipio received no news from Caesar's camp; he did what he could to hinder Caesar getting any information from his own camp. What he did not know was how information leaked out of his camp. The horsemen Caesar used to patrol along his ramparts, watching for infiltrators, often skirmished with Labienus' cavalry. At times, when the German and Gallic squadrons ran into the similar squadrons of Caesar, they conversed and pledged good faith to each other. Information changed sides. Added to the collaboration of his Gallic and German cavalry, many of Scipio's allies, the Gaetulians (a general name the Romans gave to the many Berber tribes), deserted him to go to Caesar's camp. Caesar took them in; he awarded several of their leaders' letters of recognition and allowed them to return back to their villages in order to convince their compatriots to raise troops to defend themselves from the dictates of others.

While Caesar dealt with Scipio's manoeuvres, Sallust sailed at Caesar's direction to the Cercina island. When he arrived, the population came out to welcome him. The senatorial commander, C. Decimus, who only had a garrison made up of his household slaves, fled on a small boat. Decimus had been stockpiling grain for Cato. Sallust was pleased with the large supply of grain at hand; he loaded several cargo ships in the harbour and sent them to Caesar. At Lilybaeum, the pro-consul Aliennus sent his second convoy of warships and transports, carrying XIII and XIV Legions, 800 Gallic cavalry, and 1,000 slingers and archers. With a fine wind, the fleet arrived at Ruspina harbour in three days. Caesar was overjoyed with the simultaneous arrival of supplies and reinforcements. Morale in his camp rose; after a brief rest to shake off the effects of seasickness, the new troops replaced the soldiers who had come with Caesar at work on the bastions and ramparts. Further: vital information came, P. Sittius had captured one of Juba's main fortified magazines.

First Engagement

In the senatorial camp facing Caesar, the commanders questioned their enemy's inactivity. Why did not Caesar attack? He always sought the initiative, why not now? The lack of action caused acute anxiety about what Caesar would spring upon them. To find out what was happening, Scipio chose two Gaetulians who he particularly trusted and sent them into Caesar's camp as deserters. Crossing the lines between the two forces, guards took the two men directly to Caesar. They told him they had words for him if he would allow them to speak without punishment. Caesar readily accepted the condition. Telling him that Scipio had sent them to his camp as spies, what Scipio was particularly interested in was whether Caesar had dug traps or trenches to block the elephants in front of his gates. Besides that, Scipio wanted to know what Caesar's tactics would be to face the elephants. More important to Caesar they went on, many of their fellow countrymen supported him as did many of the soldiers in IV and VI Legions. Caesar received the men into his service, enrolled them in the unit organized for refugees from Scipio's camp, giving them pay for the length of service with Scipio. And indeed, the next day quite a few deserters from the IV and VI

Legions came to Caesar's camp. Representatives from the town of Thysdra also arrived. They told Caesar about 300,000 measures of grain (two and a half modern carloads of wheat grain) were in storage in their town stockpiled by merchants and large landowners. They requested a garrison to protect their holdings. Caesar said he would send soldiers soon, but they need to be patient.

They needed patience because Caesar was going on the offensive and needed all his forces. He sent his fleet back to Lilybaeum to pick up the rest of his legions and bring them to him. But now, with the addition of two experienced legions to his force of veterans, he would attack. In the darkness of early morning on 25 January (7 November solar calendar), Caesar ordered his scouts and camp messengers to his tent and gave them instructions for the day, sending the scouts out to determine the best paths to where he was going to lead the army and the messengers to inform the centurions to wake up the men and have them ready to march. No one else had any idea about his plans. In mid-morning, he marched his army out of camp, in the direction of Ruspina, still within his fortified area but in a different direction than one might expect.

Ruspina sits on a peninsula which bulges out into the Mediterranean Sea, about three miles wide by around three miles from base to point. Facing the peninsula's base, a flat flood plain extends for about twelve miles into the hinterland, following the path of a dry river. All the land is flat; a rolling height some four to five feet is the largest 'hill'. Bordering the flood plain on all sides, a mixed topography of watercourse furrows marks the landscape. The differences in height of these formations were no more than a few feet; there are no real 'heights'.

Passing by Ruspina, Caesar marched out of his fortifications along the sea on the southern side. Marching around a wide radius, he turned from south to west, to north in about an eight-mile march. He headed toward a chain of higher ground surrounded by dried water channels. On each of these prominences, old fortifications remained in various stages of ruin. But on the furthest prominence, that nearest the plain, Scipio had refurbished the fortifications and placed a garrison. Caesar, with his guards, rode by each of the other forts; he stopped before reaching the last one, and observed Scipio's garrison. He sat quietly, observing the lay of the land. He then ordered the soldiers to reconstruct the forts, which by simply picking the displaced stones, they did in a half hour. Then he ordered his legions to construct ditches and ramparts leading from his position overlooking Scipio's fort through the line of forts back to where they had started their march.

Scipio and Labienus saw Caesar's advance. They understood his objective was to extend his lines to construct two fronts at right angles from which he might attack from different directions. To stop him, they had to move. They marched their cavalry out of camp and deployed them in the plain about a mile from their camp and then deployed their infantry about four hundred paces from their camp. With this force, they threatened Caesar's troops constructing their new lines. Caesar paid no attention to Scipio's moves. He stayed with his troops encouraging their efforts. Soon, however, Scipio's line approached within a mile and a half of Caesar's earthworks. Rather than stop work and pull back, Caesar ordered a squadron of Spanish horse, backed up by a small unit of light troops, to attack Scipio's fort at the extremity of the line of prominences.

The horsemen overwhelmed the Numidians, killing some, capturing others. Labienus, seeing the outpost fall, led all his right-wing cavalry, a core of Gallic and German warriors surrounded by a cloud of Numidians, to restore the situation. Caesar, once Labienus had advanced some distance from his main body of troops, launched his cavalry left-wing against Labienus' force, to cut him off from the rest of his troops. Between the two converging wings, there was a large fortified villa, surrounded by walls with high towers on each of the four corners. Labienus, on the far side of the villa, did not see Caesar's horsemen coming toward him until the horsemen in the rear fell to Caesar's squadrons. In the middle of the shrieks of pain and surprise, the Numidians broke and fled but the Gauls and Germans stood their ground. Caesar's horse backed them against his fortified lines and in a hard-fought engagement, killed them all.

When Scipio's legions saw the collapse of their cavalry wing, they broke formation and retreated into their camp through all the gates. After Scipio's army fled the field, Caesar had the recall sounded and drew his cavalry back within his fortified lines. Riding among the dead Gauls and Germans of Labienus' cavalry, Caesar recognized many of the soldiers: those who formed part of Labienus' personal guards, some who were known as particularly ambitious adventurers, others who had become prisoners and changed sides for their own freedom, all large and skilled fighters, all equally dead.

The Stand-off Continues

The next day, Caesar marched his army out onto the plain in battle formation. Scipio remained in his camp. From the dry watercourses at the edge of the rough ground, Caesar advanced his formations toward Scipio's camp. Between the two armies sat the small, fortified town of Uzitta; here

Scipio drew water for his forces and centred his quartermaster's operations; he had to defend the town. He marched out of his camp to face Caesar. Deploying the infantry in the usual three lines, before them he stationed the cavalry in squadrons and between the horse units stood the armoured elephants equipped with fighting towers. Caesar assumed Scipio was marching to engage him, so he halted his army and finalized deployment. Instead, Scipio side-stepped toward the town, so his centre stood behind the town, and he stationed his cavalry and elephants as two wings, one on either side of Uzitta.

Caesar kept his position until the sun rested near the horizon. Scipio was not going to advance, and Caesar saw no reason to attack with an army necessarily fragmented because of the town's position. With a strong garrison of Numidians in the town and the two wings of horse and elephant, the chances of error in manoeuvring became high. His men had been in line of battle under the hot sun since the morning without food. Caesar returned within his fortified lines.

While Caesar and Scipio drew down their confrontation, another struggle continued. Battles continued to rage between Caesar's commander, Messius, who defended Acylla with three cohorts and Considius who was besieging him with eight cohorts and Numidian and Gaetulians mercenaries. Many of the besiegers' assaults failed; large machines approached the walls to break into the town only to collapse in flames. News of Caesar's success in the cavalry battle came. Because Caesar prevailed, Considius was out on a limb and easy pickings. He pulled out, burning his gain, spoiled his wine and oil, and marched roundabout to avoid any contact with Caesar's forces, returned his cohorts to Scipio and went to Hadrumetum.

The weather often disrupted sea traffic between Sicily and Caesar's base at Ruspina. Varus' fleet, commanded by Octavius captured a trireme lost in a gale. Onboard was a troop of veterans commanded by a centurion and some new recruits. Varus kept the men under guard and sent them to Scipio. Received by Scipio on a public tribunal, they found themselves lectured on how the deceiving and lying Caesar had forced them into his service. Scipio invited them to join his army, thinking, it seems, that they would be grateful. The centurion of the XIV Legion answered Scipio. Politely but firmly, the centurion rejected Scipio's offer and his characterization of Caesar. From a friendly expression, Scipio's face grew dark. With a nod, he signalled his guards. They killed the centurion in front of everyone. Scipio then condemned the rest of the veterans to death, which his guards immediately carried out. The recruits he drafted into his army. Caesar was most upset when knowledge of this incident came to him.

Besides attacks from his enemies, Caesar's army suffered from damage falling out of the sky. An unexpected storm hit Caesar's camp in the night; a downpour of rain accompanied by hailstones pelted men and equipment. Caesar had kept his expeditionary force as small as possible. The usual accompanying impedimenta, wagons, slaves, and sutlers were still in Sicily. The rains, flooding, and hail ruined temporary shelters, food, and put out all the fires. That night the men wandered around the camp with their shields held above their heads. Most amazing of all, the spear-points of V Legion caught fire but did not burn.

Clearly, the African campaign was a hard fight.

Chapter 19

Difficulties in Africa

Caesar's Offensive Continues

Caesar and his soldiers put their camp back in order after the storm; the only good news was that their enemies were as inconvenienced as they were. News came about King Juba; after the cavalry engagement, Scipio had sent a message to the king, telling him to come and join in Caesar's destruction. Seeing his position enhanced by being part of the army that defeated Caesar, Juba left his commander, Saburra with a large army to counter Sittius' raids, and marched toward Scipio. He led three of his own legions, 800 standard cavalry, a large formation of irregular horse, a similar formation of light infantry, and thirty elephants. He saw himself as the supreme commander in the campaign and intended to take full credit for the victory. He reached Scipio's camp and set up a separate royal camp.

The rumours which spread about the army Juba was bringing emphasized the vast numbers of legions, irregular troops without numbers, and masses of battle-trained elephants. The reality was quite different. To Caesar and his soldiers' eyes, it was simply more of the same. To Scipio, however, they were the tools of victory. The day after Juba arrived, Scipio held a parade on the contested ground, with music and cheers, sixty elephants, all the heavy infantry, the different units of cavalry, and the mass of light troops promenading on the field. They advanced further toward Caesar's lines than before and then, they turned around and went back to their camps. Caesar was unimpressed.

Here were almost all of the forces which the senators could raise to defeat him. Now Caesar began to plan their destruction. He had his soldiers extend his fortified lines further toward Scipio's and Juba's camps. There was a higher rough patch near Scipio's camp which Caesar wanted to occupy before Scipio understood what he was doing. Labienus, a better commander than Scipio, saw exactly what Caesar had in mind and since his camp was closer, he intended to upset Caesar's plans. The route which Caesar had to travel to reach the site crossed a dry watercourse with steep banks. Beyond the watercourse, there was an ancient densely planted olive grove. Labienus placed a powerful cavalry unit backed up by veteran light troops, out of sight in the ravine. Further in another direction, he stationed another cavalry force so once Caesar faced the ambush in the watercourse, this second cavalry unit would hit him unexpectedly. This was a clever double ambush. Caesar sent out a reconnaissance party of horse to explore the dead ground in front of him and Labienus' troops thought this was Caesar's main force. The trap sprung but it caught nothing. Rather, Caesar's cavalry charged, pursued, and slew some of Labienus' cavalry as the rest of them along with Labienus fled the area. Caesar's men dislodged Labienus' force from the rough patch and held it.

Caesar quickly fortified the hill and expanded it into a good-sized camp. From this new main camp, he organized his legions into work crews to dig fortified lines from this camp to Uzitta, so each line would reach a corner of the town's fortifications. The passageway this created would allow his assault troops access to the town without exposing their flanks to the clouds of irregular cavalry or direct attacks from Scipio's cavalry. Also, the passage would ease the way to his side for deserters from the senatorial side. And more importantly, the low ground supplied the opportunity to construct more wells because water was scarce. As always, a strong veteran formation kept guard at the front of the works as it pressed forward because the enemy's African cavalry and light troops were constantly skirmishing with Caesar's forces.

Late in the afternoon, when Caesar had begun to withdraw his men from their labours, the combined senatorial commanders launched a full-scale assault with all their cavalry and light-armed troops against Caesar's legions. Caesar's cavalry faltered under the unexpected attack, giving ground. But not Caesar. He quickly turned his legions about, assumed battle formation, and attacked. With the legionaries coming into battle, Caesar's cavalry turned about, reformed, and charged the Numidian horse, a massive but disorganized force. The Numidians scattered and fled, suffering many causalities. Wind-driven dust and the setting of the sun put an end to the engagement. In the confusion, many troops of both the IV and VI Legions deserted Scipio and came over to Caesar. Even worse for Scipio, the cavalry which had fought for Curio but was captured by Varus and forced into the senatorial cause became uncertain of who was going to prevail in the end and many joined Caesar.

Caesar Fights at Sea

While Caesar and Scipio were duelling over the plain between them, reinforcements sailed from Sicily with IX and X Legions on board. Varus, at Utica, had beached his fleet for the winter but the senatorial command had received word about the fleet bringing Caesar's legions and decided to attack it. Varus launched his fifty-five ships with Gaetulians as rowers and officer cadets from Utica as marines. Sailing from Utica, the fleet arrived at Hadrumetum, waiting for Caesar's ships to come into range. Caesar at Ruspina, although he was unaware of Varus' moves, ordered out L. Cispius' fleet of twenty-seven ships to patrol the sea lanes between Ruspina and Thapsus to guide the transport fleet into port. Just in case some of the transports sailed toward Hadrumetum, Caesar also sent thirteen warships under Aquila to patrol off that port. Cispius easily reached their station off Thapsus, but an ill-wind kept Aquila's ships from rounding the headland before Hadrumetum. They found shelter in a cove and waited out the storm. The transport fleet anchored out at sea just off Leptis to avoid the severe weather; the men of IX and X Legions disembarked themselves, going ashore to find food and a little loot leaving the transports defenceless.

A spy found a way to get word to Varus about the defenceless transports off Leptis. Before the sun rose, finding the weather had moderated, Varus sailed his war fleet out of Hadrumetum's inner harbour. Aquila was still at anchor in his protected cove. In the early morning, before anyone knew he had sailed, Varus' fleet bore down on the nearly empty transports and their guard ships. They set the transports on fire and seized two quinqueremes which surrendered without a fight because there were no soldiers on board.

Smoke on the horizon and breathless couriers told Caesar what was happening. He was inspecting his new fortifications about six miles from his harbour. Giving his horse its head, he raced toward Ruspina where he commandeered a light sailing ship and sailed out, instructing all his ships to follow. As he sailed out further, Caesar saw the large enemy fleet sailing some distance away bearing toward Aquila, who was returning to port. Caesar ordered Aquila to fall into line behind his fleet and follow in pursuit of the enemy.

Varus, his victory achieved, knew Caesar would soon counter-attack to avenge the damage he had sustained; he was sailing back to Hadrumetum. Caesar sailing in his light craft, directing the large warships in his wake, coming up on one of the captured quinqueremes, directed some of his leading warships to take the ship. This they did, easily recovering the ship and its crew, along with Varus' 130 men prize crew. Further, Caesar's ships also took one of Varus' triremes with its crew and marines because the ship had fallen behind the body of Varus' fleet as it hurried toward Hadrumetum.

While Caesar's ships picked up prizes, Varus sailed the rest of his fleet around the headland, making harbour, and rowed into the inner harbour. Once Caesar's fleet resumed the pursuit, the winds were wrong to round the headland. Riding out the wind at deep-water anchor through the night, at dawn Caesar sailed into Hadrumetum's outer harbour. His men burned all the cargo and transport ships, threatening the rest of the ships in the inner harbour. After waiting to see if Varus was going to start a naval engagement, when nothing happened, Caesar returned to Ruspina.

The IX and X Legions marched from Leptis to Caesar's camp near Ruspina. These two legions had ignored discipline by leaving their transports and warships undefended and then they caused trouble for Caesar's allies. Moreover, these were the same legions that mutinied in Italy and Caesar was none too happy to see these men. The day after the two legions arrived, Caesar held a parade for all military tribunes and centurions of his army. After a speech about the duties of command, Caesar openly dismissed both the military tribunes and the centurions from IX and X Legions for their corrupt and self-serving approach to command. These men, Caesar placed under guard and sent off with no more than one slave each back to Italy.

While Caesar was receiving reinforcements, King Juba received unwelcome news. The Berber communities the Romans called Gaetulians had followed Caesar's suggestions brought by their countrymen who Caesar had accepted into his camp and then sent home. None of them supported Juba but his fighting men were too strong to oppose without help. Caesar, by reputation remarkable, gave his promise to aid their communities in any struggle against the king, and so induced them to revolt. Suddenly, King Juba faced a war on three fronts. Sittius still caused trouble in the western parts of Numidia; he was facing Caesar beside Scipio, and now the Berbers were rebelling. Juba detached six cohorts from his army and sent them back to Numidia to oppose the Gaetulians.

Scipio Avoids Battle

Caesar's lines reached the point where they were just out of spear-cast range from Uzitta's walls. Here, Caesar constructed a camp large enough to hold five legions. While the legions marched in, engineers built strong emplacements for projector engines on the side facing the town. Behind earthworks and palisades, large stone-throwing ballistas flanked by man-killing scorpions (unseen but gives a bad sting) flung barrage after barrage, shattering walls and cutting down men. At night, by the lights of cooking fires and lamps, lit to show the lanes in the camp, about 1,000 noble Gaetulians horsemen came to the gates, joining Caesar.

During the day, while Caesar's engineers were setting up his camp, Scipio saw one of his commanders, M. Aquinus, holding a conversation with C. Saserna, one of Caesar's officers. Scipio sent word to Aquinus, saying such conduct was inappropriate and should stop at once. Aquinus sent the messages back with the response that, on the contrary, he needed to conclude his business. King Juba saw the discussion. He assumed he was the supreme commander of the army and sent a royal messenger to approach Aquinus and in the hearing of Saserna, said 'The king forbids you to hold this conversation!' Aquinus withdrew back to Scipio's lines, preferring not to enrage Juba. But the story of the encounter, a barbarian king giving orders to a noble Roman, did not sit well on either side. Even worse, Scipio as a symbol of his authority wore a cloak of purple until King Juba told him, so it was said, that only Juba could wear purple. Whatever was said, after Juba came, Scipio wore only a white cloak.

The day after Caesar's artillery began shooting at Uzitta, his enemies determined they needed to support the defenders of the town. Scipio, Labienus, and Juba joined together their entire force and pushed forward to a strategic prominence, deploying their armies against Caesar's fortifications in the plain. Caesar quickly responded with a counter deployment, moving his forces outside the lines and preparing for battle. He expected his enemies would attack. On horseback, Caesar went to each of his legions, encouraging his men, telling them of his confidence in their loyalty and fighting skills. This done, Caesar gave the signal, and all his troops assumed battle readiness. Caesar choose not to advance: Uzitta held battle-hardened cohorts which could easily challenge those in front of them; rough patches of ground would break up any advance by his troops; and anyway, let Scipio and his forces make the first move and so be at a disadvantage.

Indeed, Scipio had arrayed his troops in attack formation. His centre held all his and Juba's legion in line, behind he placed all of Juba's Numidian foot, ordered into formations so seen from a distance, they might appear as legions. Cavalry and elephants made up the wing on Scipio's right. The elephants with light infantry in support were in front, the entire force of standard cavalry was stationed behind the elephants forming the core of the right-wing. Beyond the cavalry, Scipio deployed Numidian light foot and horse a mile or more further from the cavalry on the right. The plan was for the light troops to out-flank Caesar's left by a significant distance, so as they pushed into Caesar's rear, the standard cavalry formations would follow while the elephants pinned Caesar's troops in place. On Scipio's left-wing, he reinforced the town with some elephants and light troops, assuming the fortifications would hold any attack by Caesar.

Caesar was ready: he formed his battle formations to meet Scipio. On Caesar's left-wing (Scipio's right-wing), he placed X and IX Legions; in his centre, from his left to right, stood XXV, XXIX, XIII, XIV, XXVIII, and XXVI Legions; his right-wing, facing Uzitta and Scipio's few troops, he placed some crack cohorts of his veteran legions along with some eager cohorts of recruits. Caesar reinforced his left-wing by forming from the legions in line, a third line of cohorts, extending to XXIII Legion in his centre. While Caesar was confident that his right-wing, based on fortifications, was strong, his left-wing dangled out into nothingness, outflanked by Juba's massive force of light horse. At the extremities, he stationed his whole cavalry supported by V Legion. Units of archers were stationed throughout his wings, particularly the left. Only some 300 paces separated one army from the other through the deployed expanse.

And then, they stood and waited. Caesar was not going to attack at a disadvantage. It became clear, neither was Scipio. At the tenth hour, as the sun moved toward the horizon, Caesar had enough and began drawing his soldiers back into camp. As the troop formations unfolded and marched back as columns through the fortifications, the massed group of Numidian light cavalry facing Caesar's right-wing moved toward his camp, while Labienus' cavalry on the left-wing held its ground, keeping the attention of Caesar's legions. Seeing what they thought was an opening, some formations of Caesar's cavalry charged the Numidians. The Numidians turned about and fled; Caesar's horse with their attached light infantry gave chase, but once Caesar's horse rode into a morass, the Numidians turned about and attacked. Too far away for support from their own lines, the horsemen turned around and rode back from where they had come, thus leaving their light foot in the lurch. The Numidians cut down as many of the foot as they could catch. The result for Caesar was, one missing horseman, many wounded horses, and twenty-seven light troops dead. As night came full-on, Scipio, back in his camp with his troops, celebrated this victory.

The next day, Caesar ordered his army to extend his fortifications. His soldiers dug fortified lines deep into the plain blocking Scipio's ability to send out raiding parties in an effort to harass Caesar's operations. In turn, Scipio built counter fortifications, to keep Caesar from hemming his forces from strategic ground. While the digging continued, there were constant cavalry skirmishes. In the very day after Caesar's cavalry unit abandoned their light troops supports, a unit of Caesar's cavalry, disgraced by their fellows' misadventure, ran across a formation of 100 or so Numidian horse while out foraging toward Leptis. They drove into them, killing many and capturing the rest.

Famine Forces Manoeuvre

Slowly, another problem had emerged which Caesar had to solve or lose the war. He was always aware of possible supply difficulties, but they had become acute. When he first landed, he had a small army and brought in supplies by ship. At that time, the senatorial commanders had already swept the land for food, locking it up in their granaries, impressed most of the farm workers into their armies, and destroyed what they could not take. In three months of campaigning, Caesar had called in reinforcements and received large numbers of deserters from his enemy's armies. When they came, his legions had left their army slaves behind; but the young men who did the fighting picked up slaves and camp followers in their normal activities. In naval actions, Caesar had lost a large number of transport-cargo ships and, in turn, had destroyed many of the enemy's transports. There were many mouths to feed and little food. The only good news was that his enemies had the same problem.

Strategy shifted from trapping and destroying the enemy to finding food and denying it to the enemy. Success ensured victory; failure meant defeat and death. We need to understand that the men who made up Caesar's army were young, energetic, unscrupulous, and without pity. Trained killers, human life meant little to them. Their job was to kill and destroy and they were good at it, finding enjoyment in their accomplishments. At the best of times in the classical world, following the path of a marching army, you would find a trail of robbed and murdered men and raped women and girls. Where an army was hungry, most others were starving.

In this part of Africa, many outlying settlements stored their food in specially constructed underground pits. Caesar's spies located a number of these settlements. Just after midnight, Caesar sent two legions with a small cavalry scouting unit toward one of these settlements about ten miles away. Late in the day, they returned to camp, carrying a lot of grain. Of course, the people who lived in the settlement were deeply distressed by this requisition; if they objected too much, the soldiers killed them and more, if the soldiers found their women, after raping them, they would drag the more attractive ones back to their camp. Since the enemy was in the same business of collecting food, the soldiers would not leave the seed corn behind and so unless the villagers could find an unplundered place to go, they would starve to death.

Labienus' spies told him of Caesar's foraging expeditions. He decided to lay an ambush to clip Caesar's wings and take the grain he was collecting. Seven miles from his own camp, Labienus marched with a large number of light foot and horse to camp unseen but just off Caesar's route. Caesar's agents kept him informed about Labienus' actions and Caesar planned a counter-ambush. Waiting for a few days to lull Labienus' troops, before dawn Caesar led a cavalry formation and three veteran legions out of the rear gate of his fortifications, sending the cavalry on ahead. His cavalry advanced along their regular route. Spotted by Labienus' men, they kept moving along as if they had no worries. As Labienus' troops prepared their attack, Caesar's heavy infantry fell on them, killing more than 500 in the first rush and throwing the rest back in flight. Not to be undone, Labienus charged Caesar's horse with his whole cavalry. Caesar's horse gave way to Labienus' onslaught, but Caesar brought up his heavy infantry and Labienus' cavalry pulled back. Caesar's cavalry suffered no loss. King Juba, embarrassed by the flight of his light foot, crucified those who fled the battle.

After reviewing information collected by his scouts, Caesar decided on a plan to weaken Scipio and the senatorial organization in Africa. He ordered all his troops in camp to pack up and be ready to march. He picked out men who weren't up to the physical demands of hard marching and used them to garrison Ruspina, Leptis and Acylla. Cispius and Aquila were to take their fleets to blockade Hadrumetum and Thapsus. Caesar then had his camp set on fire, marching his army in battle formation out of the rear gate of his fortifications before dawn. He concentrated the impedimenta at the back of his column, guarded by the left wing. Before dusk, the army reached the small but well-fortified settlement of Aggar, solid friends of Caesar and stout defenders against attacks from Caesar's enemies. In the plain by Aggar, Caesar ordered the construction of a single camp; then organizing a foraging party, he personally led his men around the local farmsteads. The foraging was good. They returned to the camp with large amounts of barley, oil, wine, figs, and even a little wheat.

When Scipio learned that Caesar was on the march, he pulled his whole army out of their camps and followed behind him. Finding Caesar's new camp, Scipio settled his forces in three separate camps about six miles from Caesar's camp. Scipio's scouts brought him information about a well-stocked settlement about ten miles distant, called Zeta. Scipio immediately sent two legions to gather supplies. A spy brought the news of Scipio's move to Caesar. Finding his enemies closer than he would have liked, Caesar abandoned his new camp and marched into rougher country to build another one. Zeta was some fourteen miles distant; Caesar organized a powerful striking force in mid-afternoon and hurried toward the place. When he arrived at Zeta, Scipio's legions having secured the settlement were off foraging farmsteads. Before Caesar could organize an attack against the legions, scouts informed him that strong reinforcements for them were in their way. Rather than fight an immediate engagement, Caesar took Scipio's commanders prisoners, installed his own garrison under Oppius, and marched back to his camp leading twenty-two of Juba's camels, carrying all sorts of goods.

On their way back to camp, Caesar's column had to pass Scipio's camp. The senatorial commanders knew they were coming; Labienus and Afranius hid in rough country with a mass of cavalry and light troops ready to ambush Caesar's train. Suddenly, as Caesar passed, Labienus' cavalry rose up and charged the column's rear. Hearing the commotion, Caesar directed his cavalry to distract the enemy horse with an attack while his infantry piled their burdens and fell into fighting formation. His foot advancing and horse harassing, Caesar easily pushed the enemy light troops back. Satisfied with repelling the sudden attack, Caesar resumed his march. Then, there they were again; light foot and swift horse, harrying Caesar's column. Again, Caesar stopped, his cavalry swept the enemy horse away and his infantry pushed the enemy foot back. The march resumed. Out of rough ground, the enemy light troops continued: attack, retreat, attack again, retreat. Caesar understood the tactics. The enemy were not trying to kill armoured soldiers, rather they kept on wounding horses. Without cavalry, Caesar would have to make camp. But this was a landscape without water. His army had no water supplies. If he camped, within a day without water, Caesar's force would die.

The sun had sunk toward the horizon, and Caesar's army had gone hardly 100 paces in four hours. Caesar sent his horse back to camp on their own. Employing the same tactics he had used in his first battle in Africa, he ordered the soldiers into tight defensive formation. Marching slowly but steadily, ignoring for the most part the enemy attacks, Caesar made his way toward his camp. Should the enemy approach too closely, three or four legionaries would turn, transfix the attacking troops with heavy pilums, and the enemy would flee. He finally entered his camp in the first hour of night, losing no one in the whole engagement and only ten wounded.

Caesar Retrains his Troops

For the moment, Caesar's camp had enough food and access to water, but he was deeply troubled. A gang of barbarians had chased him and his legions around and while the losses were minor, he did not have a solution for the tactic at hand. Worse, what were Scipio's legions like? He had not yet met them in battle. Juba's legions would scatter like leaves in a wind, but Scipio had a hard-bitten staff, good soldiers and deeply committed men. His legions might be very good. No military decision was sure. Caesar resolved to follow his path forward though developing a new training programme. He brought skilled gladiator instructors into his camp and training ground. Fighting in line as heavy infantry took a certain skill set but Caesar's soldiers needed other skills. The gladiator instructors taught man on man combat; how many feet to pull back from the enemy; the manner of turning about and attacking; how to restrict the space of the enemy's movement, charging foreword, feint attacks, the best time to throw their spear. By training these 300-men units, one for each legion, Caesar raised his own light troops.

The rest of his legionaries Caesar kept in heavy infantry training, ready to meet Scipio's legions. The other problem which disturbed Caesar and his men were the war elephants. When Caesar and his army were pulling back, fighting the light troops, Scipio deployed his legions in front of his camp which was normal, but what caught Caesar's and his troops' attention were the sixty or so elephants posted in front of the legions. Already, Caesar had found a solution regarding the elephants. While still in his camp near Ruspina, he received in shipment from Italy a number of war elephants. His men became familiar with the beasts, finding their vulnerabilities and slowness of movement. The instructors provided the elephants with armour so the soldiers could find where the animals were still unprotected. Equally important, Caesar kept the elephants with the horses, so they became used to the smell and trumpeting. The fact that the elephants were normally docile impressed the soldiers.

Caesar kept his eight legions busy with training and foraging, marching them about from spot to spot. The desert was different from anywhere the men had fought. Used to the climate after three months, having met the enemy in different combat situations and now trained in the new way of fighting, Caesar looked forward to battle.

Chapter 20

Decision at Thapsus

March toward Thapsus

Three months in the desert: hard fighting, little results, hunger, thirst, strange people, Caesar's soldiers were not happy and neither was Caesar. Personal relationships on a team, man to man, group to group, are never easy but privation and lack of success intensify animosities. Caesar understood such animosities can tear an organization and especially an army apart. Caesar had rethought his strategy: the failure to handle the Numidian light troops would lead to his defeat and destruction. His new units of gladiator-trained fighters might solve that. He was not particularly worried about Scipio's elephants, his knowledge of their use in Rome's history telling him they were a double-edged sword. Supplies, however, were the main problem: that and bringing Scipio to battle.

Caesar needed to bring his army together. On 21 March (22 January solar calendar), Caesar held a full lustration; this was a purification ceremony. As High Priest of the Roman People, Julius Caesar presided over the sacrifice of a pig, ram, and bull. The animals in procession circled around the whole army three times and then were slaughtered and became part of the ceremonial feast. The army had a new beginning: all former wrongs and enmities were gone now, and the army was a band of brothers that together would conquer. After the purification, Caesar continued training by marching the troops from one spot to another; his soldiers foraged but Caesar's real reason for marching was to watch the enemy following them. After two days of this, Caesar marched his army close to Scipio's camp and deployed for battle. Scipio did not react. Seeing no response, Caesar returned to his camp as the sun set. Previously, representatives from Vaga, near Zeta, came to Caesar requesting a garrison and promising supplies. Before Caesar could organize a relief party, a spy informed him that Juba had wind of Vaga's efforts to defect and quickly marched to the place and took it. Juba's men killed all the inhabitants and destroyed the town.

His army united, his supporters massacred, his enemies avoiding him, Caesar began his offensive. He struck camp and marched to the town, Sarsura. Scipio had placed a garrison of Numidians to guard Sarsura's stock of supplies. Labienus followed Caesar and when he marched far from his old camp, heading toward Sarsura, Labienus let lose his light cavalry and infantry to harass Caesar's rear. Labienus' men cut the main body of troops off from the train of supply carts of sutlers and merchants; he imagined Caesar's legionaries were fatigued because of their heavy packs when the marching soldiers made no move against their harassers. Taking greater risks by coming closer and closer to Caesar's troops, the Numidian troops scented blood.

That was just what Caesar wanted. He had 2,400 soldiers, 300 from each legion, trained in gladiator tactics, ready to counter-attack the Numidian light troops. Caesar's cavalry, wheeling around, joined with these contingents of his shock infantry; they all bore into the Numidians, cutting down many and pursuing the rest. Labienus, surprised and upset at the turn of events, beat a fast retreat. Once the Numidians were at a distance, Caesar's troops returned to their march. Labienus followed but at a distance, not wanting to close to combat range.

Arriving at Sarsura, Caesar's men took the town and ordered his soldiers to kill all of Scipio's garrison, even the commander, P. Cornelius, who fought gallantly before Caesar's men cut him down. Caesar seized all the grain in the town, distributing it to his men. Then he marched to the town of Thysdra, garrisoned by Considius with a powerful force and his personal guard of gladiators. Caesar studied the lie of the land and the town's fortifications. There was no water source nearby and the fortifications were well made and fully manned. Caesar settled into a new camp some four miles from water to give his men rest, but then before dawn the next day, he marched his army out of the camp and returned to the campsite at Aggar. All this time, Scipio's army, followed along behind Caesar. When Caesar went into camp, Scipio went into his.

Reinforcements arrived for Caesar; these were the balance of his legions, those recovered from sickness or on leave. One convoy brought them all, a total of 4,000 legion infantry, 400 cavalry, and 1,000 light infantry slingers and archers. These filled out Caesar's legions and force structure. He had as many trained soldiers as he could feed and manoeuvre in the desert and he was ready for battle. At that time, an opportunity to weaken King Juba arose. Representatives came to Caesar from the town of Thabena, a Numidian seaport. They had massacred the royal garrison and requested soldiers to defend them from Juba's army; they appealed to Caesar to accept them as friends and allies of the Roman People. Caesar approved of their actions, sending Marcus Crispus with three cohorts, archers, and artillery engineers to hold the town.

Behind Scipio's camp, there was a fortified settlement, Tegea, in which Scipio had posted two thousand light cavalry. When Caesar had advanced his legions toward Scipio's camp, Tegea's commander, Pacideius, stationed his horse in line to the right and left of Tegea. At the same time Scipio led his legions out of camp and stationed them about a mile from his camp's ramparts, along the edge of broken ground. As the day progressed without Scipio's men making any movements, Caesar decided to cause him a little trouble. He directed an arrack by a 400-man unit of his standard cavalry against the far wing of light horse near Tegea; he added light troops, slingers, and archers to support his horse. At full gallop, Caesar's cavalry struck the wing of light horse, scattering it. Their commander, Pacideius, redeployed his horse in open order, expanding their flanks to envelop Caesar's cavalry.

Caesar rode over to the legion nearest to Tegea and ordered 300 foot, trained in gladiator tactics, to march at the double and support the cavalry. While Caesar's cavalry was fighting Pacideius' horse, Labienus sent cavalry reinforcements to replace those who were wounded or exhausted. Caesar's 400-man cavalry unit had to give ground, facing the increased pressure from the mass of light horse pushing them back. He sent another 400-man cavalry unit to support the already engaged unit. The arrival of the 300 specialty foot and fresh cavalry unit rallied the original unit, and all joined together to deliver a devastating charge against the Numidian horse, killing many, wounding more, and driving them back deep into broken ground. When the sun was setting, Caesar led his troops back to camp in battle order with no serious loss. Many of the Numidian horsemen were dead and their commander, Pacideius, was severely wounded in the head by a pilum which pierced his helmet.

Scipio was afraid of Caesar's army. He would not face Caesar in battle on level ground. This was no surprise, but Caesar now intended to force Scipio into battle and destroy him by threatening something Scipio had to defend. Nearby on the coast, south of Leptis, was the senatorial stronghold of Thapsus. Caesar had investigated the site, noting strongpoints and vulnerabilities. Water was available; ships could provide supplies and taking the town would seriously inconvenience Scipio and worse, make him look weak in the sight of the local powers along with the commanders in Utica.

Just after midnight on 4 April (5 February solar calendar), Caesar and his army marched away from his camp at Aggar, reaching Thapsus, sixteen miles from Aggar. He immediately began to construct earthworks which blocked the exits from Thapsus while also building a new camp and strongholds at commanding points. A competent commander, Vergilius, and a large garrison held Thapsus. Rather than lose men battling Caesar, he decided to hold fast; he always could bring in supplies by sea, despite Caesar's blockade if necessary. Besides, there was the question of which side would win the war. When Scipio found Caesar had gone and was heading toward Thapsus, he mobilized his army and followed. He well understood that Vergilius was a strong supporter of the senatorial position but if faced with obvious destruction, he probably would see the logic of Caesar's cause. Scipio built two camps about eight miles from Thapsus.

The town sat near the sea on a low flat plain; inland, a saltwater lagoon stretched seven miles along the coast. The lagoon blocked a direct route to Thapsus but left a dry passageway along the coast, about 1.5 miles wide at the north and almost two miles wide in the south. In the middle, the passageway was three miles wide. Once Caesar had occupied a good part of the passageway with his earthworks and camp, the only two access routes were at the north or south of the lagoon.

Scipio approached in the north, his shortest route to Thapsus. Caesar had anticipated this move; the previous day, Caesar had three infantry units build a small, fortified camp in the middle of this route to Thapsus. Scipio could either winkle them out, an expensive task, or go around to the southern route. The rest of Caesar's army was camped in the earthworks enclosing Thapsus; if Scipio were to relieve the town, he would have to defeat Caesar; to do that, he had to find an open plain. Taking his army, Scipio marched through the day and night around the salt lagoon; at dawn, he found himself not far from Caesar's earthworks, and a mile and half from the sea. There he started to build a camp.

Battle

In the morning, when Caesar saw Scipio and his army so close, he withdrew his soldiers from the construction work, had them arm themselves, left the proconsul Asprenas to guard his camp with two legions, and marched toward Scipio's camp in open order. Caesar sent word to his fleet, ordered half the fleet to blockade Thapsus; the other half were to sail just off the coast near Scipio's camp, at a given signal, they were to raise a ruckus from the shore, surprising Scipio's troops from their rear. Arriving before the enemies' camp, Caesar saw Scipio's army drawn up before the ramparts. On each wing, stood the war elephants, supported by light troops; in the centre, however, most of the troops were still constructing the camp's fortifications. Caesar deployed his troops in three lines: on his right-centre he stationed the X and VII Legions; the VIII and IX Legions were on the left-centre. On each wing, Caesar placed five cohorts of V Legion to deal with the elephants; for the rest, each wing had a cavalry core supported by light foot with slingers and archers on the outer fringes. Caesar walked around, visiting each formation on foot; he recognized veterans, shared experiences, and encouraged recruits.

While Caesar talked to his troops, he saw Scipio's troops on the camp's ramparts running about here and there, rushing in the gates and out again, an undisciplined chaos. The distraction raised by the ships' crews was taking hold. Caesar's soldiers began noticing the disturbance in Scipio's camp. Officers and Caesar's staff advisors told him the time had come to charge the enemy. The signs from the immortal gods were clear. But Caesar wanted to wait longer, while the distraction created more chaos in Scipio's camp. Caesar had no intention of losing control of his army; standing in front of his battle line, he protested that this was not his way of fighting, he did not want any sort of uncontrolled attack. Suddenly, on the right-wing, a trumpet sounded the attack, followed by a mass charge of the troops. Every cohort charged, ignoring the centurions trying to hold back the front lines, but the soldiers simply swept around them.

While masses of soldiers in his centre surged forward, Caesar on his horse by this time, signalled 'Fortune be yours' and giving his horse its head, charged the enemy front ranks. On the right-wing, the formations of slingers and archers hurled rapid volleys of missiles against the elephants, hitting them with hunting arrows, leaden bullets and stones. The elephants, stung and in pain, wheeled about and trampled the ranks of soldiers supporting them. The beasts pushed their way through the half-finished gates of the camp. The Numidian cavalry on the same wing, seeing the elephants' rout, turned about and fled the field. The legion infantry, moving through the area abandoned by the elephants and Numidians, reached and overran the camp ramparts, killing the few soldiers who dared to stand and fight. Once the right-wing collapsed, the centre and left-wing followed. Scipio's army broke and fled to their old camp in the north.

The elephants on both wings were out of control; soldiers of V Legion had to deal with the problems they created. A particular enraged elephant caught a transport man underfoot and knelt on him. A veteran of the V drew his sword and attacked the beast, but the elephant picked the man up with its trunk. The soldier, seeing he was in trouble, hacked at the truck with his sword. The elephant dropped him, turned around, and went off trumpeting to find its fellows.

Scipio's forces were in total disarray, fleeing Caesar's troops. Seeing the collapse of their field army, many men of Thapsus' garrison exited the town by the water gate, facing the harbour and sea. Wadding waist-deep through the water, they made for land. But Caesar's fortifications enclosed Thapsus in a large crescent, so the soldiers found themselves facing Caesar's camp slaves and youths, standing on top of a rampart, cutting off their access to dry land. These men drove off the disorganized groups throwing rocks and pilums, so forcing them back to Thapsus. The mass of Scipio's legions hastened toward their camp in the north. When they arrived, there were no defenders or commanders to bring order to the chaos. The men discarded their armour and hurried to King Juba's camp, but Caesar's men had already occupied that camp.

Having nowhere to go, Scipio's men collected in a prominent spot, facing Caesar's soldiers. Deciding they had done enough Scipio's men lowered their arms and saluted Caesar's troops, a sign of surrender. But Caesar's soldiers and officers would have none of it, in blood lust, they slaughtered all of Scipio's men they could find, and even attacked some high-ranking civilians on their own side, accusing them of supporting the enemy. Caesar watched as his men continued to slay what remained of the enemy army, saying to his men that they should not kill so many, so we are told.

Caesar was master of three camps; he had routed a powerful army that left 10,000 dead on the field and counted the loss of only fifty of his men along with a few wounded. He returned to his camp near Thapsus. Regrouping his forces and collecting the elephants, Caesar paraded his army in front of Thapsus. He marched sixty-four armoured elephants with towers and troops accompanying them. Caesar sent a personal request to Vergilius, assuring him of leniency, but there was no response from the town, so Caesar withdrew back to his camp. The next day in full view of Thapsus, Caesar offered sacrifices to the Roman gods. He held another parade and standing on a dais rewarded his troops, giving decorations to brave individuals. When the ceremony ended, he marched away, leaving proconsul Rebilius with three legions blockading Thapsus and Cn. Domitius with two legions at Thysdra where Considius commanded. Caesar sent M. Messalla with the cavalry ahead toward Utica, to prepare for his arrival.

Scipio's cavalry, fleeing the battlefield, reached the fortified settlement of Parada on their way to Utica. The residents refused to grant entrance to the cavalry because they already heard about Caesar's victory. Bitter, the cavalry assaulted and took Parada. They then looted all the shops and houses, piled up a large quantity of combustibles in the market square, set it on fire, and thrust into the flames, the bound, alive, and beaten residents of all ages. Having accomplished their vengeance, they rode on to Utica.

The Collapse of Senatorial Africa

At Utica, Cato, and his compatriots, after receiving the news of Scipio's defeat, believed that many of the civilian population supported Caesar and were a danger. They had their soldiers round up all these civilians and imprisoned them in a guarded stockade near the military gate. The members of the town's senate were placed under house arrest. When Scipio's cavalry arrived at Utica, they found the stockade holding civilians of Utica; believing they all supported Caesar, the horsemen stormed the stockade. But the people in the stockade drove back the horsemen with stones and clubs. Unexpectedly repulsed, the cavalry rode into Utica and killed many people they ran into, then broke into many houses, torturing the inhabitants and plundering goods. The cavalry was out of control. Cato tried to stop their depredations, but the cavalry refused to obey; finally, Cato began distributing 100 *sesterces* each to the cavalrymen to get them out of the town. Faustus Sulla also began distributing money; he left Utica with the cavalry and rode toward Juba's kingdom.

Scipio called together the influential citizens of the province including the Roman senators. Since they had all supported Cato and his faction and profited from them, Scipio told them to free their slaves and organize a force to defend Utica. While some reluctantly agreed, more simply thought of flight. Scipio was actually of a like mind. He organized the ships at hand into convoys, assigning them to different destinations and allowing passage to those fleeing. Anyone was allowed to go where they wanted, for a price, of course. Cato, severely depressed by the defeat, planned with L. Caesar to care for his children (he knew L. Caesar would find a way into Julius Caesar's good graces) and killed himself. L. Caesar announced to the citizens of Utica that the war was over and left to find Julius. When Caesar's lieutenant, Messalla reached Utica's gates, he found them open. Posting a guard at the city's entrances, he took it over for Caesar without damage.

Caesar, at the same time, marched to Scipio's magazine at Usseta and found large quantities of food and weapons; moving on, he soon reached Hadrumetum. The town opened its gates and Caesar accepted the surrender of Scipio's commanders and granted them pardon. He sent auditors to inventory the arms, grain, and money stored in the town. The same day, Caesar marched toward Utica, leaving a legion as a garrison. On the way, he met L. Caesar, whom he pardoned as he did many other African aristocrats. He arrived at Utica at dusk. Rather than enter the town in the night, Caesar waited for the morning.

He entered Utica in the light of day. Calling the citizens to an assembly, Caesar made clear his appreciation of his supporters in the town but those who supported the senatorial faction faced punishment. Their lives, he promised them; their property, he was going to sell. However, he told them, if they chose to buy the property back, he would honour and register the title. The 300 who formed the African Senate requested Caesar name a total sum for all of their property. Caesar agreed. The sum was 200,000,000 *sesterces*, payable over three years; the important citizens of Roman North Africa willingly accepted the sum.

King Juba and a small staff fled from the battle, hiding in farms during the day, moving at night. Eventually, they reached Juba's capital, Zama but the town authorities refused him permission to enter. Juba's wives, children, and treasures were in the town; he begged they should join him; however, they seemed reluctant to take the opportunity and stayed in Zama. Neither threats nor pleading accomplished anything and Juba went off to one of his country estates. After the Numidian towns outlawed him, King Juba and his staff fought among themselves in a suicidal pact. A slave finally killed King Juba.

The leaders in Zama sent an offer of surrender to Caesar at Utica. With his personal guard and a cavalry force, Caesar entered the kingdom; he pardoned all who sought him out and when word spread of his clemency, all the kingdom's horse rode to accept Caesar's generosity. At Thapsus, Vergilius kept his walls defended but increasingly bad news trickled in: M. Cato killed himself; Utica surrendered; Juba was wandering around without a force; there was no senatorial army anymore. He accepted the promise of safeguard for himself and his family and surrendered the town and garrison. At Thysdra, Considius with a small force of supporters, mercenaries, and Gaetulians and a large amount of money, secretly left the town. Once they were in open country, many in his company murdered him and his friends to gain possession of the money.

Some of the senatorial leaders including Faustus and Afranius led a force thousands strong. They carried the plunder of Utica and headed for Spain. Sittius, the Caesarian mercenary captain who had taken the western reaches of Numidia, spotted the senatorial party. Laying an ambush, he attacked the senatorial camp at dawn, killing or capturing all of them. In a few days, Faustus and Afranius were dead. While one group tried to escape across the desert, Scipio, his commanders, and staff fled by ship. The weather was stormy, their fleet had to take shelter at Royal Hippo; Sittius's fleet was in the harbour and overwhelmed Scipio's fleet, killing Scipio and those with him. Caesar appointed Sallust proconsul and set him over Numidia.

In three weeks of selecting leaders, punishing opponents, and collecting large amounts of money, Caesar secured the African administration in hands loyal to himself. Caesar also dismissed many older soldiers from his legions. The mutineers particularly found themselves retired; he paid them in full and allowed them to go where they wanted. On 13 June (15 April solar calendar), he sailed from Utica and landed in Sardinia three days later. Settling matters in the islands, Caesar sailed to Italy, reaching Rome on 25 July (26 May solar calendar).

Section VII

The Second Spanish War

Chapter 21

Caesar Returns to Rome

The news of Caesar's victory at Thapsus filtered into Rome about 20 April. Those who secretly hoped for Cato and his compatriots' victory now accepted the inescapable. All Rome rejoiced in Great Caesar's victory. The Senate convened and quickly awarded Caesar new honours. A thanksgiving celebration of forty days would mark the great victory. Caesar would triumph four times; he would have seventy-two lictors accompanying him in his triumph processions, celebrating his three dictatorships. He was elevated to Prefect of Morals and his dictatorship would last for ten years. In the Senate, Caesar would always sit with the consulars and be the first to express an opinion. On the Capitol, his triumphal coach would sit opposite that of Jupiter. At the Senate's order, there would be a statue of Caesar standing upon a globe of the earth and have the inscription, 'Caesar is Divine'.

Caesar arrived at Rome with his entourage and stayed in one of his villas outside the ancient walls. Once settled in, he called for a meeting of the Senate, probably in one of the reception rooms of Pompey's theatre. He assured the Fathers he was not a Marius or Sulla; there would be no massacre. Now that he had supreme power, he said, he needed to act with care and consideration because he would not do those things he had condemned in others. He would only use his great power for their benefit. Caesar explained that his current and future actions were not based on impulse or sudden changes of mind but were carefully considered results of thought-out extended plans. He had not presented his programmes to them yet because he wanted them to work with him to accomplish needed tasks. He was not their master but their champion, not their tyrant but their leader. 'When it comes to accomplishing everything that needs to be done on your behalf, I will be both consul and dictator, but when it comes to injuring any one of you, I am a private citizen.'

Caesar told the senators that he destroyed, unread, all the correspondence found in Pompey's and Scipio's camps. The slate was wiped clean, and they could begin to work together in a new way, united in love for each other and without suspicions. They needed to see Caesar as a father as he will deal with them as beloved children, wishing they would excel yet understanding human weaknesses. Nor should they fear his soldiers; they guarded the empire, his and theirs. Soldiers needed support, of course, but their benefit to all was great. So that is why taxes were raised. But this was for everyone's good. They should rest assured taxes would be fair and would not impact certain people and not others. Money was necessary for the government, but no one would lose money through the wrong action. And so, the Senators needed to consider him, not as a tyrant but as their compatriot, working for the benefit of the Roman People and the empire. After he spoke to the Senate, he called an assembly of the People on the Campus Martius and told them the same thing.

Caesar's Triumphs

The great civil upheaval had concluded. Uncertainty and doubt dissipated in general rejoicing; not that everyone or perhaps even most supported Caesar, but the question seemed resolved and life could return to normal. Die-hard enemies of Caesar spread rumours that Pompey's sons were raising troops in Spain, but the thought of a victorious Spanish army marching on Rome seemed very unlikely. Caesar decided to mark his successful campaigns indelibly on the imaginations of the Roman People with the biggest shows anyone had ever seen. He would hold four separate triumphs marching through the City of Rome for his fifteen campaigns, one following another in short intervals. His triumphs were for his conquests in Gaul, Egypt, Pontus, and Africa.

Early in the morning, the march participants collected on the Campus Martius, just beyond the arched structure called the Porta Triumphalis, near the large square building surrounded by a walled enclosure known as the Villa Publica, an administrative headquarters for conscription and the census. These were the only public buildings on the Campus Martius. Once the marshals had organized the procession, the present and former magistrates proceeded by their lictors stepped off first, with all the senators following. The peal of trumpets announced the coming of the floats as fanfare followed fanfare. Each float held a display illustrating some significant facet of the campaign, piles of arms and armour marking a victory, rich furnishing of some palace, pictures of important people killed or captured, piles of bullion and coins, all the spoils of victorious war.

After the floats marched, the captives and their families followed, each captive, a leader or commander of an enemy of Rome. They all were dressed in their finest clothes but were kept in chains. Some faced, after the parade,

a brutal but fast death at the hands of Rome's expert executioners in the dank prison cell beneath Rome. However, for many of Caesar's captives, there remained just a comfortable exile. Then came Caesar. His seventy-two lictors, many more than any Roman ever had, came first, followed by the triumphant Caesar, face painted red, standing in a magnificent carriage, pulled by four white horses. After the great Caesar marched the legions. They marched to the beat, horns sounding, armour gleaming, standards held high, singing about how wives and daughters need hide because the bald ravisher was in town. The proud and arrogant soldiers let those watching the parade know here was the conquering army of the mighty commander.

The procession marched from the Triumph Gate on the field of Mars down the Flaminia Way through the Flaminia Gate in the Servian Wall into the City of Rome. Proceeding through the Forum Boarium, the parade followed the Tiber passing the end of the Circus Maximus and then turned left to march the length of the Circus and along the Palatine hill to the Sacred Way. Turning left again onto the Sacred Way, the procession marched along the Palatine's side, with its fine houses and gardens, turning left to march past the King's House, the precinct of the Vestal Virgins, and into the Roman Forum. From the Forum, the parade reached the foot of the Capitol Hill, and here, the triumphant Caesar drove his carriage up the winding street to the summit where stood the Temple of Jupiter Optimus Maximus. When Caesar reached this temple, he descended from his carriage and, on his knees, ascended the steps to perform the required rituals for the continued prosperity of the Roman People.

The four triumphs followed each other over several days: the first, over the Gauls and Germans, showed images of battles and sieges, piles of strange arms and armour from Gauls, Britons, and Germans, baskets of bullion, and prisoners, including Vercingetorix. When Caesar's triumphal carriage passed by Lucullus' temple of Good Fortune, the carriage broke apart, almost throwing Caesar on the ground. The crowd took this as a bad omen, but Caesar quickly got a new carriage and carried on as if nothing had happened. The second triumph, over Egypt, carried images of the Nile, the great lighthouse, and gory pictures of the deaths of Achillas and Pothinus, Pompey's murderers. The parade included the prisoner, Queen Arsinoe, Cleopatra's sister. The crowd showed great pity for the queen's plight. The third triumph over Pontus carried 'Vini Vidi, Vici', with pictures of Pharnaces' fleeing troops. The last triumph, over Juba, contained elephants and African warriors followed by the main prisoner, the six-year-old child who had succeeded to the throne. Later, as an adult, he would rule in Africa.

Caesar's Celebrations

Once the triumphs were over, Caesar held a great banquet for the People of Rome. He had 22,000 tables laid with plenty of food and free fine wine. As darkness fell, Caesar returned to his residence, accompanied by twenty elephants carrying torchbearers on both sides of the procession, followed by thousands of citizens. As day followed day, Romans beheld new spectacular events. He held large gladiator fights in the memory of his daughter, Julia. Troops of musicians and dancers appeared in every neighbourhood. In public squares and parks, actors and artists presented dramatic shows. Caesar's engineers constructed a lake on which warships battled with rams and fire. In the Circus Maximus, real battles between prisoners and condemned criminals took place. Each side had 1,000 foot, 200 horse, and twenty elephants. Then, there were beast shows, where hunters killed many lions and giraffes. Huge crowds found great amusement in these entertainments. In the crush, here and there, many died.

Caesar issued rewards and payments to the Roman People and army. Making an issue of a great silk awning protecting spectators from the sun, a group of soldiers complained that such extravagance meant less money for themselves. Dissatisfaction spread among the army. With his own hand, Caesar grabbed the principal spokesman and pushed him into the hands of his bodyguards. Then as high priest, he had him executed and two more of the trouble causers were ritually sacrificed by the priests of Mars in Mars' field.

Caesar's Reforms

While he entertained the Roman People with spectacular shows, Caesar took in hand the massive task of reorganizing the crazy-quilt ad hoc structures that were the administration of the Roman Republic to bring order into the chaos. His actions in this regard were not matters of deliberation. As a family had one head, as an army had one commander, the Republic needed a single, well-informed hand to make Roman administration into a sound and effective system. And that hand was Caesar's.

As Protector of Morals, Dictator, and Consul, Caesar arranged the appointment of new senators, raising the Senate from some 300 members to 1,000. He saw to the appointment, confirmed by the election of the Comitia, of all the magistrates, each holding office for no more than a year but appointed for years in advance. He strengthened the supervision of provincial governors and enforced anti-corruption efforts. Any questions that might arise were his to answer.

Many Romans in the city were receiving supplies of corn subsidized by the government, but the whole setup was corrupt from the start. Some enrolled their slaves and saved money; others freed their slaves and set them up in the system. Some others, not citizens, found ways to buy their way into the distribution. Caesar put an end to the larger-scale fraud in the programme; he turned Clodius' political bribe into government poor relief. He accomplished this by requiring all landlords of tenements in the city to report how many people were in their buildings who received the grain. This number was 320,000. Caesar then sent trusted investigators around to determine which people were really eligible for the subsidy. They removed 170 people from the rolls. Caesar decreed 150 people as the final number of recipients, and the praetor in charge would add new people to the rolls only after those already on had either died or moved away.

Caesar set up a programme in which citizens who had large families received rewards. All seditious activities were outlawed, as was any organization of people which did not have long-standing in the Republic. Jews, however, were exempt from this prohibition. Teams of investigators kept their eyes out for possible violators. Caesar oversaw the confiscation of estates resulting from the civil war: he ensured that only those estates belonging to the guilty parties were confiscated, giving warrants of possession to legitimate owners.

Before the civil war, Caesar had initiated large building projects in Rome to beautify the ramshackle city and provide employment for many citizens. He started the large law court building on the south side of the forum, the Basilica Julia, the new Senate House, the Curia Julia, and proceeded to enlarge the forum to give better access to the Field of Mars. When the war started, work on these projects stalled. After his return from Africa, he again pushed these projects along, adding a new project, the Forum Julia, complete with a large basilica and a magnificent temple to his ancestor, Venus Genetrix.

Soon after the celebrations finished, Queen Cleopatra arrived in Rome, bringing Caesar's son, Caesarion, and an entourage including savants from the Museum, mathematicians, and astronomers. Caesar gave her a large villa on the Janiculum Hill, enrolled her as Friend and Ally of the Roman People, and placed her statue in his temple of Venus Genetrix. Caesar had sent for a team of experts to work on one of his most important reforms, that of the chaotic Roman calendar, and Cleopatra had come too. From Caesar's perspective, her coming was very opportune. Not only was she good company, educated and aware, but being the savants' employer, the Egyptian queen would see to it that they worked with Caesar. In almost two years of ruling Egypt, she was secure enough to leave her capital and country for an extended period, showing her political ability.

Caesar was about to begin the calendar reform, which became the longest lasting of his achievements. This calendar is the same one used today as part of the 'common' era, with some adjustments made fifteen centuries later. The calendar of the Republic was an ancient lunar system knocked together into the shape of a solar calendar. It had ten months, running in length from twenty-eight to thirty-one days, for a total of 355 days. To keep the months in sync with the seasons, thus the solar year, Roman priests, every other year, inserted the month Mercedinus after 23 February or, adding 22 or 23 days to the month, and then returned to the remainder of February's days. Because of the civil disruptions during the Late Republic, the month was not added, resulting in chaos. Months were distant from the seasons; years were cut short; festivals became inappropriate.

Caesar would change that. He brought order into this chaos and made a lasting improvement to the Roman concept of time. Caesar had discussed timekeeping in Alexandria with the Museum's mathematicians and astronomers. The Senior Astronomer Sosigenes brought a small staff of experts with him; he developed a new Roman calendar for Caesar that would not shift seasons through centuries. The years, they calculated, were three hundred and sixty-five and a quarter days long. They kept the Roman ten months but added two additional months, one soon called after Julius Caesar (July) and the second name after his heir, Caesar Augustus (August). The mathematicians shifted the number of days from other months, and every fourth year, they added a day to February. This is the Julian Calendar, after an adjustment by Pope Gregory XIII, 1582, still used today.

Julius Caesar Rules the Senate and People of Rome

After a couple of months, once Caesar had returned to Rome, freedmen, ordinary citizens, and senators saw an efficient administration, less corruption than usual, and prosperity spreading through the city and across the empire. The government had improved. But the government was Caesar. He listened to concerns and might even change a ruling or regulation, but the decisions were all Caesar. Dictator, consul, commander of victorious armies, no one could win an argument with him nor could any group overturn his decisions. Caesar had to take stock of what he had accomplished and where his accomplishments would go at this stage of his life.

Caesar Returns to Rome 211

Caesar, now, was the Republic; he saw Marius' collapse; he remembered, not fondly, Sulla's dictatorship. The failure of Sulla's attempt to reform the Republic gave the young Caesar his opportunity to start in politics. After Crassus' disaster in Syria and Pompey's failed campaign in the Balkans and unfortunate death in Egypt, Caesar alone held the prize. He did take control of the state; he made things better. But, the question came to him: how to make this permanent? Simply setting up a system and then walking away failed for Sulla. The best answer was a successor and a line of successors.

Caesar's loyal and able people managed his affairs as he directed. Caesar, however, kept no subordinates who were his equal in matters. None of them could replace him; Mark Antony, his right-hand man, lacked that sense of balance that allows those subtle nuances which help people change their minds. Others, while certainly nuanced, lacked the stature to command Roman aristocrats. Caesar's answer was a dynasty of related people revolving around the House of Julia.

It is essential to understand that Caesar was not interested in 'social justice' of any sort. He was interested in efficient administration, clear rulings, and accommodations that accepted human nature as the Romans saw it. Class warfare and democratic rule, those concepts were foreign to Caesar. If bread and circuses kept the rabble quiet, so be it. What Caesar wanted was a strict but malleable rule. His successors needed position, power, and skill. There were several possibilities; Caesarion was one, a toddler now, but children grow. His mother, who Caesar trusted, made a good advisor and role model for the man the child would become. He could not, of course, rule in Rome, but he could manage the east. By having a strong allied Ptolemaic Egypt (Caesarion was also a Ptolemy) dominate the east, the threat of another politician using the east as a springboard to power in Rome became less. But who should rule in Rome?

Caesar had several relatives with families. Most noticeable was his sister's grandson, Julia, whose daughter married into a cadet branch of the House of Octavia. Caesar's grand-nephew was Gaius Octavius Thurinus. Gaius Octavius's father entered the senatorial order as a new man in 69 and rose to praetor and governor of Macedonia. He died suddenly in 59 when his son was four years old. Atia, daughter of Julia, the grand-nephew's mother, took the matter in hand and raised her son and his two sisters as Roman aristocrats. Gaius studied Latin, Greek, and oratory and, the Octavians being bankers, he had a good head for numbers. When his grandmother Julia died in 52, the eleven-year-old Gaius gave a funeral eulogy and came to Julius Caesar's attention. When young Gaius turned 15 and received the *toga virilis*, Caesar had him elected to the priesthood in the College of Pontiffs. During the

Festival of the Latins, Caesar appointed young Gaius, Prefect of the City, an honorary position with a high profile. When Caesar returned to Rome after the African War, young Gaius was always close to him. He accompanied Caesar in his triumphs and joined him in the theatre and shows. Caesar even allowed Gaius to act as an intermediary, able to grant access to Caesar.

Caesar goes to Spain

Problem after problem came to Caesar. He handled them all, a few critical issues and many minor difficulties that meant nothing except profit to one or two individuals. Caesar had set his government in motion and his subordinates could handle all these issues. The brothers Pompey gathered soldiers and expanded the territory they controlled; they readily repulsed the force Caesar had sent against them. Caesar decided he would rather lead an army in the field than deal with all the detailed work of civil administration. After seven months at Rome, he headed for Spain.

Chapter 22

Caesar's Second Spanish War

The Sides Engage

The collapse of the senatorial faction in Africa was almost complete. Only Cn Pompey's sons, Gnaeus and Sextus along with Labienus and Varus escaped the debacle. They and their few troops made their way to Spain. Caesar, after settling Africa, went to Rome where he received honours, celebrated triumphs, and reorganized the administration. Rumours came of a rising power in the west. A new Pompey had come and would restore the Republic. Caesar did not think much of the brothers Pompey nor Labienus, but the danger, if not terribly serious, was obvious. A mere nine months after his victory at Thapsus, Caesar was back in Spain, ready to take the field.

Spain was unsettled before Pompey came. The administration in Further Spain collapsed under Q. Cassius' corruption. Several legions, originally raised by Pompey before the civil war, were in open mutiny. They expelled Caesar's governor, Trebonius, and appointed Scapula and Aponius as authorities. Before Caesar won the war in Africa, Pompey's son, Gnaeus, had landed in Further Spain. The legions there elected him their commander. By winter's end, those who survived the defeat in Africa filtered into Further Spain, including Sextus Pompey. By that time, Gnaeus Pompey had thirteen legions, four composed of veterans. Gnaeus Pompey went around to each community, pressuring them to provide supplies and recruits. Some communities sent what Pompey wanted to avoid trouble. Those communities who decided to resist often found themselves sacked and plundered. The few communities that successfully resisted, sent appeals to Italy, begging for help.

Caesar was aware that the Pompeians were expanding their holdings in southern Spain. He sent a fleet and troops from Sardinia, but they were unable to make any headway. The Pompeians ruled most of the communities in Baetica with only a few exceptions. In November of 46 (Caesar's calendar corrections and reforms now take hold), Caesar marched from Rome with eight legions and 8,000 cavalry to crush the last outpost of the senatorial faction. He reached Saguntum on the seventeenth day from his departure.

Ten days later, slowing his pace because of health difficulties, Caesar reached Obulco, thirty-five miles east of Corduba. He had sent instructions ahead to his commanders that he had come and expected them to send a cavalry force to him, but they said he had come too soon for them to collect the horsemen. Caesar waited for a month (December 46 – early January 45 BC) for collecting his troops, allowing his centurions to recruit more men, and filling his supply magazines.

The Pompeian faction held the compact and rich lands of Further Spain which centred on the large town of Corduba and the fertile lands along the Baetis River (Guadalquivir). Sextus Pompey held Corduba with a strong garrison, using the town as a headquarters and supply centre. Brother Gnaeus was besieging Ulia, a town that had refused to join their cause. When the townspeople learned of Caesar's arrival, they secretly sent a delegation to Caesar, asking him to relieve the town. Caesar was aware of Ulia's loyalty to him and the Roman People. He immediately ordered six cohorts of foot and accompanying cavalry to hurry to the town. Just before Caesar's column reached Pompey's outposts, a tempest and gale struck. It was so dark, that no one could recognize the man standing next to him. The horsemen took a single file formation, followed by a few of the infantry, and rode in the rain between the outposts of the besiegers. When they approached the town, a sentry asked who they were; one of the soldiers told him to shut up, 'Right now, we are trying to get to the gate so we can take the town.' The rain, the wind, and the snappy answer discouraged the sentry from looking closer. Reaching the gate, they gave the password, and the guard admitted the relief force into the town. Their accompanying infantry went to different sectors while the cavalry went back out of another gate, raised a shout, and charged the besiegers' camp; at the same time, the cohorts waiting beyond the siege lines attacked and Pompey's troops scattered. The siege ended.

The reason the relief force did so well so quickly was that Gnaeus Pompey had pulled most of his troops out of their positions near Ulia. While the relief force was on its way, Caesar moved against Corduba with a strike force: a special unit of heavy infantry, accompanied by a train of horses led by a few cavalrymen. Once they were in view of Corduba in the distance, they all took to horseback and sped toward the town. Observers on lookout towers gave the word, and Sextus Pompey sent a large force of foot out of the gate to deal with the coming cavalry, so Pompey thought. But, once the horse came near the defending troops, the heavy infantrymen dismounted, formed a battle line, and massacred the defenders. The surprised Sextus immediately sent to his brother the message to come to Corduba to save it from Caesar's attack. Gnaeus Pompey withdrew most of his troops from Ulia.

Caesar approached Corduba with his main force along the south bank of the Baetis River on 10 January. The Baetis is a large and swift river and access to Corduba was by a large stone bridge. Caesar bypassed this bridge, marching further to the east rather than trying to storm it, as it was well defended. He pitched his camp down the river, planning to cross beyond the direct sight of Corduba's garrison. The Baetis river runs to the west. A little better than two miles from the stone bridge, the river flows through a sharp bend; here islands and bars break the river's flow. Caesar had his engineers design woven mesh bags to hold river stones; having his men manufacture many of these bags, they filled and lowered them into the water between different islands and exposed bars in the riverbed. On to these piles of bags, his men placed timbers spanning the distance from one pile of bags to the next and so built a bridge for men, animals, and wagons. Caesar reinforced his camp on the south side of the river to hold supplies and guard the crossing. On the north side of the river, he constructed another camp to safeguard the northern end of his bridge and to threaten an advance against the northern side of Corduba. Then, switching direction, he sent his men, on the south side of the river, to build a camp threatening the south entrance of the stone bridge. Caesar had all three camps connected by earthworks and watchtowers.

Sextus Pompey, in Corduba, watched Caesar's lines grow with trepidation. He had no idea what Caesar planned to do. Gnaeus Pompey, arriving on the south side of the river, grasped Caesar's intent. Riding at the point of a lengthy line of legions marching along the roads, Gnaeus saw Caesar's works extending toward the stone bridge. Obviously, Caesar did not suppose he could starve Corduba out because everyone knew about the immense warehouses full of grain and there was a large river of running water within easy reach. But what Caesar was doing was to cut off Corduba from supplying anyone south of the river, particularly Gnaeus' tens of thousands of men coming up. Gnaeus quickly made camp; then he sent out teams of excavators digging trenches to block Caesar's men from extending their trenches. As a few days passed, first one side then the other would prevail. The men became more determined, massing in scrums, pushing their opponents into the river, stabbing, slashing, smashing each other as one side tried to gain the outside flank by digging out ramparts of the earth to over-top the others' ramparts. Mounds of dead matched mounds of earth. As more days passed, Caesar tried to lever Gnaeus' troops out of the labyrinth of trenches and ramparts and onto the open ground. That was not going to happen. Caesar saw that he was wasting time and men; it was time to change his approach to the problem of destroying Gnaeus Pompey. If Gnaeus was dug in and had a line of supply back toward his strongholds, he was immovable. Only by getting Gnaeus out in the open and outmanoeuvring him was Caesar going to crush him.

The Struggle for Ategua

At dusk, Caesar brought his troops to the ready, set his three camps' fixtures on fire, and marched south from Corduba and the Baetis River, leaving fires burning through the night. He headed toward the fortress stronghold of Ategua, Gnaeus' main base and magazine. The lands south of Corduba, beyond the Baetis' flood plain, rise in a series of rolling hills, high, without rough areas. Just downstream from Corduba, a tributary enters the Baetis flowing from the south; this is the stream Salsum (Guadajoz). Twisting around hills through valleys, the Salsum flowed down from the uplands. Near where the Salsum turns sharply from the southwest to the northwest, sits Ategua on a hilltop.

Caesar marched his legions, the III, V (Alaudae), IV, X, XXVIII, and XXX through the hills and reached the town of Ategua in the morning. He set his soldiers to work, building a wall of contravallation with high wooden towers and stockades along with a platform for machinery. On nearby hilltops, ancient fortifications stood or lay in ruins. Many of Caesar's soldiers set themselves up in winter quarters in these structures, rebuilt and roofed, which served as outposts to warn of coming dangers. Gnaeus Pompey's spies told him where Caesar was going. While Gnaeus waited for all his troops with their pack mules and carts to come to Corduba, he dispatched a few specially trained cohorts of foot and squads of horse to harass Caesar's forces. Thinking his outposts would give warning of any attack, Caesar believed his position was secure. Morning mists, however, provided cover for Gnaeus' vanguard of assault troops as they crept up to Caesar's outposts. Gnaeus' men struck out of the fog, overwhelming the outposts and killing most of their garrisons.

His forces concentrated and his advanced attack successful, the following night, Gnaeus burned his camp and set out to relieve Ategua. He followed the Salsum river, marching on the left (southwestern) side because Caesar's army was on the right (northeastern) side of the river. He camped near the settlement of Ucubi, to the southeast of Ategua. By the time Gnaeus had settled in his camp, Caesar finished the preliminary construction for his assault against Ategua. The hills around Ategua twist and turn all routes through them and block lines of sights. There is a plain along the Salsum River, at closest about a mile from Ategua. Gnaeus camped on the opposite side of the river from Ategua up on a prominence where Gnaeus could see both Ategua and Ucubi. His men dug in, fortifying his camp.

Gnaeus had a problem with his troops. He had the eagles and standards of thirteen legions but only two legions, deserted from Trebonius, were trained and blooded. A third legion was made up of Roman settlers with some veterans; there was a fourth, raised by Afranius which Gnaeus had brought from Africa. Runaway slaves and native troops made up the rest of his legions. His cavalry and light troops were good but few. Caesar's troops, on the other hand, were his usual mix of hardened veterans and eager recruits, something which was obvious to anyone who saw them march by or encountered them informally. Just as with his father, Gnaeus was loath to feed his men into the jaws of Caesar's killing machine. More importantly, he intended to avoid the fate of his father's army.

About four miles from Gnaeus' camp, on the same side of the Salsum River, was another of Caesar's outposts, known as the Fort of Postumius. Gnaeus saw this fort as easy pickings. It was on the wrong side of the river, at the end of a difficult march through the confusing country. Caesar, he figured, would not attempt to relieve the place. That night, Gnaeus marched out of his camp around midnight and by dawn was ready to attack the Fort of Postumius. At sunrise, Gnaeus' troops raised a shout and shot a massive volley of missiles. Many of the unsuspecting defenders were killed or wounded. The defenders quickly rallied. They returned fire and sent a messenger to Caesar. Not the cautious commander Gnaeus took him for, Caesar set out with three tough legions and marched straight to relieve his beleaguered garrison. Arriving at the fort, he went directly to the attack. Gnaeus' troops fled after Caesar's first assault hit them, killing and wounding many. Several of Gnaeus' men surrendered, including two centurions and eighty shields were found on the ground.

The next day, Caesar received cavalry reinforcements when Arguetius arrived with crack cavalry units from Italy and auxiliary forces raised in Saguntum. That night, after Caesar routed his troops at Postumius' fort and Gnaeus saw the arrival of Caesar's reinforcements, he knew that his position was vulnerable to a quick strike by Caesar, cutting him off from supplies and help. He burned his camp and marched toward Corduba. An auxiliary commander attached to Caesar, King Indo launched his Spanish cavalry at Gnaeus' retreating column but fell foul of one of Gnaeus' well-trained legions who cut the auxiliary cavalry to pieces. Caesar passed off King Indo's defeat as an opening for opportunity. The following morning, one of Caesar's cavalry commanders extended his patrol close to Corduba, thinking the defenders would expect Caesar's cavalry to be shaken by yesterday's defeat. He found a supply train of pack animals trekking toward Gnaeus' camp. The cavalry force seized fifty of the animals with their packs and minders, returning with them to Caesar's siege camp near Ategua.

During these days, there was a small but steady movement of deserting officers from Gnaeus' side who brought reports of rising desperation in Gnaeus' camp. They worried about Caesar's agents spying and undermining confidences in the brothers Pompey. Midnight after the capture of the supply train, the defenders of Ategua launched an attack against Caesar's lines, shooting fire missiles at the siege works without success. In the morning, a cavalry patrol found two men near the camp who claimed they were slaves. When the patrol brought them into Caesar's camp, some of his soldiers recognized them as deserters from Trebonius' army. They suffered immediate execution. Later the same day, a party of messengers from Corduba came to Caesar's camp, claiming they were lost and thought this was Gnaeus' camp. Caesar's men cut off their hands and threw them out of their camp.

That night just before midnight, Ategua's defenders launched firebrands and missiles as usual. They had the habit of continuing to shoot their munitions until they were out of projectiles for the night and then remain quiet. Caesar's men would then go to work, repairing the damage. This time, though, they waited for the dust to settle, then suddenly, they launched another barrage, causing many casualties. In the morning, the defenders emerged from a gate and attacked the men of the VI Legion who were extending the earthworks. Attacking from higher ground, these attackers thought they had the advantage; the veterans of the VI taught them they were wrong. Suffering heavy casualties, the defenders retreated into Ategua. The following morning, Gnaeus directed his men to construct a fortified causeway to the River Salsum. A scouting squadron from Caesar's forces investigated what Gnaeus' men were doing but they failed to see one of Gnaeus' larger cavalry units until too late. They had to flee, leaving three men dead.

On the same day, Caesar's men found another spy and executed him immediately. In the siege lines facing Ategua, a group of Caesar's soldiers thought they could talk their way into Ategua; making their way into the town through a sortie point, they contacted several of the townspeople who returned to their camp and told Caesar they accepted his authority, but Gnaeus' heavy infantry dominated the town. Caesar made an agreement, sent the townsmen back, and told them to support the attacks on his camp so Gnaeus' commander would not suspect their lack of loyalty. That night, all the townsmen supported Gnaeus' soldiers when they bombarded Caesar's lines. Caesar's side returned fire, targeting individuals on the walls and the fortifications themselves. One large ballista, shooting rounded stones of more than 100 pounds each, aimed at a tower on which the defenders manned a large projector machine. Suddenly, the tower walls collapsed, bringing down the projector, the crew of five, and the machine operator. During the shooting storm, Caesar ordered his infantry to brace to receive an assault coming from the town; his soldiers, expecting a sally, formed up in a strong cordon around Ategua's walls but no attack came.

The Struggle for Ategua Ends

As the defenders and townspeople of Ategua continued to keep Caesar's troops occupied, Gnaeus completed his fortified lines to the River Salsum. Because Caesar did not oppose the construction of his earthworks, Gnaeus assumed Caesar was overstretched and showing weakness. To demonstrate his superiority, Gnaeus sent out large cavalry formations sweeping away any of Caesar's scouting units they found. In the sight of both camps, a wing of Gnaeus' horse found a patrol of Caesar's cavalry supported by some light foot. The size of Gnaeus' contingent induced Caesar's soldiers to move their position. Gnaeus' horse pursued and some of Caesar's men stood to, blunting Gnaeus' attack but they found themselves overwhelmed. After this success, Gnaeus' troops pushed after Caesar's troops until Caesar's men reached level ground and took up battle position. Then, Gnaeus' men pulled back rather than engage.

Caesar's cavalry reformed in his camp, to refit and reorganize after the previous action. Out from the town, the light foot emerged and began to attack. Rather than pull back, the horsemen dismounted, deployed in battle formation, met, and cut their way through the enemy troops, killing 120, stripping the arms of others, and wounding many. Caesar's men lost three soldiers with twelve infantry and five horsemen wounded. Later in the day, Ategua's defenders again took to their walls and began bombarding Caesar's lines. Once the defenders had the attention of Caesar's men, they brought up to the top of the wall the men with whom Caesar had met. Gnaeus' soldiers killed the townsmen and threw their bodies off the walls onto the ground before Caesar's men. Caesar and his men reacted with shock.

As the sun was setting that same day, a messenger from Gnaeus secretly entered Ategua. He brought orders that in the coming night, the garrison should launch a missile storm then advance out of the gate with torches, setting fire to Caesar's towers and ramparts. Once Caesar's works blazed away, the garrison was then to retire to Gnaeus' lines, evacuating Ategua. In the dark of night, the walls of Ategua lit up with the flair of fire as missiles shot out into Caesar's camp and his lines enclosing the town. Hour after hour, the missile rain continued. Caesar's soldiers stayed out of the line of fire, expecting the defenders to eventually tire of the exercise. In the dark before the dawn, the gate which faced Gnaeus' camp in the distance, opened and out rushed the entire garrison, carrying brushwood and packs of wood to fill in the trenches. Using long hooks, they demolished the huts Caesar's soldiers had built for the winter, setting fire to the straw-thatched roofs. Further, much of the silver and clothing which Gnaeus' men had taken from the town was spread around so Caesar's soldiers would scramble after it rather than opposing Gnaeus' soldiers. Gnaeus had stationed his army that night just across the Salsum River in battle formation, ready to move to gather in the garrison troops.

The sudden attack surprised Caesar's men but well trained as they were, they assumed battle formation quickly, faced and repulsed the garrison's attack, pushing them back into Ategua. In the morning Caesar had the few soldiers his men captured executed. A refugee from the civilian population of Ategua brought the story of how the murder of citizens ended: Junius, a covert agent of Caesar, confronted the garrison commander when the killings started, protesting that people who gave the protection of their altars and hearths should be so treated; this action polluted these who did the killings! At that, the commander relented and stopped the killings.

Once the next morning's activities were proceeding, some of the garrison officers in Ategua talked together. Their problems had become acute: killing the suspected informers and throwing them off the walls was a mistake, not only upsetting Caesar's men but also their own soldiers. Then, their effort to break out failed. Now, they faced Caesar's soldiers who were in no mood for mercy. They decided to see if Caesar was open to negotiations; Tiberius Tullius and Cato Antonius went out of the gates to talk with Caesar. Tullius gave an impassioned speech about what a shame the misunderstandings and civil wars had led to this confrontation. He begged for mercy. Caesar promised that, as always, he would show mercy to fellow citizens when they surrendered but first, they must surrender unconditionally. Returning to Ategua's gates, Tullius and Antonius did not agree on how to approach their commander, since they did not receive a clear answer from Caesar. Tullius thought Antonius was going to denounce him to the commander and have him executed. As they walked through the gates, Antonius grabbed Tullius to drag him to the commander as a traitor. Tullius took his dagger, slashed Antonius' hand, and ran back to Caesar's lines.

The garrison's hold on Ategua was weakening and cohesion among members of the garrison themselves was fading. Some soldiers killed people who tried to flee the town, other soldiers deserted. Caesar's patrols arrested a messenger from Gnaeus to his commander in Ategua. Reading the message, Caesar sent him on his way. The message told of Gnaeus' and Labienus' decision to abandon their relief effort and that killing citizens of allied towns was very stupid. Battle and missile exchanges flared on and off but the news that Gnaeus was going to march away left only one end to the siege. Caesar received a message from Munatius, commander of Ategua's garrison, offering to surrender and give Caesar the loyalty he had given Gnaeus before Gnaeus abandoned him. Caesar replied, assuring Munatius that Caesar always kept his word. On 19 February Caesar took possession of Ategua.

Gnaeus Pulls Back

Fugitives from the surrender of Ategua quickly found their way to Gnaeus' camp and told him about the loss of his largest stronghold and magazine of food and weapons. Gnaeus had taken pains to keep unwelcome news about defeats and desertions from his men, but this was too big a defeat to hide. Over the following days, numbers of officers and veterans defected to Caesar. Gnaeus evacuated his camp by the Salsum River, pulling back six miles to Ucubi which became his headquarters and supply dump. He built a main camp and several small forts surrounding the town and camp. Caesar broke camp and marched to the Salsum River; he established his main camp on the far side of the river from Gnaeus' point of view. He then constructed a bridgehead on the other side of the Salsum, across a ford and temporary bridge.

Gnaeus sent strong cavalry units to harass Caesar's bridgehead troops. Coming on without warning, they cut down several light troops and wounded more. These attacks provided cover for Gnaeus to infiltrate spies through Caesar's lines. That night, Caesar's men captured four infiltrators, three slaves and one veteran. Caesar had the slaves crucified and the soldier beheaded. The next day, Gnaeus' cavalry ambushed a watering party, killing some, capturing others while losing twelve who surrendered to Caesar's forces. The news filtered back to Caesar: when Gnaeus set up his HQ in Ucubi, he held an assembly of citizens, telling them to make a list of known supporters of Caesar and give the list to the town garrison commander. A few days later, Gnaeus had more than 200 citizens brought out of the town. He had seventy-four beheaded and ordered the rest back into Ucubi; most bolted and ran away, 120 joining Caesar. Beheaded or fled, Gnaeus got rid of them.

Chapter 23

The Struggle Ends

Caesar closes in on Gnaeus

After Caesar had occupied Ategua, members of a delegation from Ursao, trapped in the siege, asked for an escort back to their town. Caesar gave them an escort of local Roman businessmen and senators, then sent them on their way. Ursao was an important town, under the direction of the administration sitting in Ategua, supporting Gnaeus and the Senatorial faction. Caesar thought sending the envoys after their experiences in the siege of Ategua, would at least bring up questions about which side Ursao should support. Reaching Ursao, Caesar's escorts stayed outside of the town's walls while the delegates entered through the gates. Inside the town, the two factions argued over the information the delegates brought. Those supporting Gnaeus were most unhappy, some of the more involved filtered out of the town; when the delegates rejoined their escort, Gnaeus' supporters attacked the escorts and killed them. Only two men survived and managed to return to Caesar and tell him what happened.

The citizens of Ursao met in assembly and appointed investigators to go to Ategua to find out what happened. When the team of investigators returned, they reported to the assembly that the delegates' account was correct. When their conclusions became known, groups formed, shaking their fists at the head of the senatorial faction in the town. Some even threw stones at him. They all shouted that he had caused the destruction of them all! Once his compatriots rescued him, the faction leader requested to go to Caesar and make things right. Given permission, he set out and contacted Gnaeus' forces. He collected a personal force of hard men; secretly at night, he brought them into Ursao. They killed all the leading men who supported Caesar and seized control of the town.

Once his agents secured Ursao, Gnaeus sent a letter to his commanders there, explaining his strategy; he had no doubts about his forces' superiority over Caesar's, but Caesar refused to fight without overwhelming advantage of the ground. If they did fight, Gnaeus would end the war quickly. The reason Caesar was able to persevere was that he took strongholds full of supplies. Gnaeus made it clear he would protect all his strongholds and so bring Caesar to battle when he ran out of supplies. That way, he would win. Some days later, Caesar's scouts managed to acquire a copy of this letter: there was nothing surprising here; Gnaeus was correct. Caesar intended to take his strongholds, one after another until Gnaeus met him on level ground or starved hiding in the hills.

While Gnaeus planned Caesar's defeat, Caesar put further pressure on Gnaeus' lines. He continued to build earthworks along the Salsum, advancing his lines toward the bend in the river where it flowed north and turned west. From that point, Caesar could march south without having to cross the river. Gnaeus' cavalry and light troops continued to harass his troops with arrows and spears. Their repeated attacks discouraged the troops who tried to build the works and defend them at the same time. From the far side of the Salsum, soldiers of V Legion saw their compatriots withdraw from the missiles of their enemies.

Two centurions crossed the Salsum and rallied the soldiers. With the centurions at their head, they charged up a hill causing the enemy cavalry and their light troops to retreat. As they continued advancing up the hill, the cavalry reformed and threw a heavy missile volley. One of the centurions fell victim to a missile and the other took up the charge. The enemy surrounded and killed him. A cavalry formation on the other side of the river saw the brave man fall and then the enemy soldiers began to strip off his awards; they charged over the river and up the bank, scattering the enemy horse, chasing them to their own ramparts. In their eagerness to raid the enemy's camp, Caesar's cavalry formation found itself trapped against the enemy's earthworks by his cavalry, supported by light troops. Hemmed in as they were, Caesar's cavalry escaped by determination and hard fighting. There were many in the formation with wounds yet, except for the two dead centurions, there were no fatalities.

The next day, Caesar marched his army east along the Salsum for about four miles, and following the river around a bend, keeping to the river's right, he had a clear path to Gnaeus' stronghold of Soricaria (modern Castro del Rio?). The town had a strong garrison and Gnaeus' spies had informed him of the move, so he sent troops to reinforce the place. Caesar camped within striking range of Soricaria and began building earthworks to cut the town off from communications with Gnaeus' forces. Caesar's extended lines threatened to cut Soricaria's access to the fortress of Aspavia which guarded the road to Ucubi. If Gnaeus did not stop Caesar's excavations, he would be admitting defeat at Soricaria. There was a high hill that dominated part of the way to Aspavia. Gnaeus sent some strong units to occupy the hilltop.

When Caesar saw Gnaeus' troops scrambling up the hill, he sent a force to forestall them because if Gnaeus held the promontory and dug in, Caesar would need to find a different way to blockade Soricaria. The forces clashed on the hillside. Caesar's men pushed Gnaeus' forces back in hard fighting, killing 323 light troops and 138 legionaries. The numbers of Caesar's casualties are not given.

The following day, 5 March, Gnaeus' troops returned; while Caesar's men continued to extend their fortified lines, Gnaeus' cavalry launched raids, throwing spears and shooting arrows while their infantry stayed on high ground, avoiding any direct engagement with Caesar's forces. One man, Antistius Turpio from Gnaeus' army, strode out from Gnaeus' lines and challenged any single soldier of Caesar to a duel. Q. Pompeius Niger, a Caesarean from the town of Italica in Spain took up his challenge. The men on both sides stopped their work and formed two audiences as if in an amphitheatre to see this spectacle. The duel went on some time, weapons and shields flashing in the sun as the fighters displayed their skills. No doubt the end of the duel would conclude the day's endeavours except for the fact that down from a hill, a large cavalry squadron, seen but assumed to be watching the duel, suddenly attacked Caesar's light troops protecting the earthworks.

Caesar's cavalry drove them off but when that cavalry unit retired to Caesar's camp, Gnaeus' mounted force followed, continuing to harass Caesar's troops. But when they reached Caesar's camp, the light troops, whom they had harassed for days, suddenly formed up, raised a shout, and charged the enemy horse. Gnaeus' cavalry lost several men, panicked, and fled back to their camp. Caesar was pleased with his men's steadfastness and courage, saving a situation that might have become out of hand. He awarded the Cassian formation 3,000 *denarii* and decorated the formation's commander with five gold torques. Officers and men from the other side kept joining Caesar's forces; they all brought rumours of dissatisfaction among Gnaeus' troops.

When Caesar had pushed Gnaeus' army off the hill and isolated Soricaria, dismay and trepidation struck Gnaeus Pompey and his staff officers. Caesar was clearly backing them into a corner. Gnaeus marched deeper into the hill country leaving Attius Varus in charge of the fortifications. Establishing a new camp in an olive grove near Spalis, Gnaeus had no intention of leaving supplies for Caesar. The garrison soldiers in Ucubi burned the stockpiles of supplies and the town, then marched to join Gnaeus. Since Spalis refused to open its gates to Gnaeus, he stormed and burned that town, after plundering all the goods and food. Caesar marched out of his camp and followed Gnaeus deep into the hill country coming to the stronghold of Ventipo where he set up for an assault, but the town capitulated. Moving on, Caesar took Carruca. Then he proceeded into the plain near Munda and established his camp near Gnaeus' camp.

Battle of Munda

The next morning, Caesar was about to march out of his camp to take some more strongholds; news brought by his scouts, however, thwarted his intention. Gnaeus' army was in full battle formation and had been before first light. Gnaeus and his staff were very aware of the precarious nature of Ursao's support for their side; since most of their stockpiles of food and weapons were within the town, its defection would damage their cause significantly. All wanted the war to end and Gnaeus told the townsmen that Caesar would not fight because he was afraid that his army of young recruits would evaporate. To prove his point, he stood his army in battle formation, under the walls of Munda, challenging Caesar to attack.

Just as previously, Gnaeus would take high ground advantage so Caesar would have to attack uphill, so now Gnaeus carefully chose his ground to put Caesar's attack at a significant disadvantage. With the town walls to his back, Gnaeus placed his troops in a way that Caesar's soldiers must wade through a marsh, then cross a small river, which would give Gnaeus an opportunity to grapple with Caesar's army when the army was disordered from crossing the river. But the plain was wide and open, the day was sunny, and the enemy was in sight. The horsemen saw great cavalry country in front of them; the infantry saw the end of the war by the end of the day. A battle was always a question, no one ever knew what the outcome would be, yet now was the chance they had not seen through the whole campaign. The time to fight had come. Caesar's army, in battle formation, marched toward Gnaeus' forces deployed under Munda's walls. As they approached the river, they expected Gnaeus to advance toward them, expecting Gnaeus' troops to catch them while crossing the river but his army did not move.

Gnaeus stationed his troops on the steep rocky ground that sloped up to Munda's walls, ready to descend quickly against Caesar when he crossed the river. But this was bluff. Gnaeus did not expect Caesar to attack. When Caesar began marching across the plain, heading for the river, Gnaeus lost his nerve. He would stay under Munda's walls. The first round went to Caesar.

Gnaeus' battle line held thirteen legions, screened on their flanks by cavalry and 6,000 light troops. Auxiliary troops were about as many, but the truth was, most of these soldiers were not able to stand up to a trained Roman

Legionary. Caesar fielded eighty cohorts, the four veteran legions, III, V, VI, and X, and four of recruits, who by now were also experienced, along with 8,000 cavalry. Having crossed the river, Caesar's army approached the slope on which Gnaeus' army stood. The way was steep and rocky. Caesar, on the battlefield, saw the problems facing his men; he ordered the advance halted and the men to form proper ranks and files. The men grumbled at the halt, thinking they might not conclude the fight this day but their officers assured them: fighting was near. The men of X Legion, on the end of the right-wing, shifted into correct formation immediately; III, V, and VI Legions followed, as then did the auxiliary and the cavalry to the end of the left-wing. The signal raised, the horns sounded, and the battle cry was given. Caesar's soldiers advanced into battle.

The enemy was brave, but they were not trained to real war as practised by Caesar's men. Just before the first clash, Caesar's soldiers threw a volley of pilums, smashing many an enemy soldier; as the fronts engaged, further volleys from the men behind the first line caught more enemy soldiers before they were aware of them crashing down. The enemy fought with slashing assaults and wild yells, but they became hemmed in by repeated pilum volleys. Spread apart, Caesar's soldiers pushed in and compressed their lines. Huddled together in a solid mass, the flying pilums knocked them down like a strong wind in a field of tall grass. On Caesar's right-wing, X Legion, with years of experience and faultless skills, pushed their opponents back and back, until Gnaeus' officers decided they had to stop X Legion's advance. They began to pull a legion out of their right-wing to transfer it as support for their left-wing, so Caesar's right-wing would not outflank it.

However, pulling the legion out of Gnaeus' right-wing disrupted his line; Caesar's cavalry broke into and applied pressure against the forces on the right, who gave way so both Caesar's right and left wings crashed into Gnaeus army. The screams of the dying, swords beating on swords, attempts at rallying fighting men, sounded louder and louder as Gnaeus' army collapsed. Many of the defeated soldiers fled into Munda. The field was Caesar's.

Aftermath

Gnaeus' forces lost 30,000 men dead, including Labienus and Attius Varus. Among the dead were some 3,000 upper-class Romans, from Rome and Spain. Caesar lost about 2,000 cavalry and infantry. Of course, these numbers would not include auxiliary troops. Caesar received thirteen legionary eagles from the defeated army plus the usual standards and rods of office. The survivors of the debacle found safety within the walls of Munda. Gnaeus and his army commanders avoided Munda, riding off to find sanctuary. A young officer rode to Corduba and informed Sextus Pompey of the defeat. Sextus divided up the available funds among his cavalry, announced he was going to have peace talks with Caesar and fled. Gnaeus Pompey was wounded. He escaped with a small escort of foot and horse, making for the naval base of Carteia south, near the straits. Eight miles from Carteia, Gnaeus had enough of riding a horse. He dismounted and had a message sent to Carteia to dispatch a litter to carry him to the town where he found a place in a house. Each member of the Senatorial faction in the town received a message from Gnaeus to see him. Each was surprised that the others were there. When they came together, they inquired what Gnaeus would do next. In fact Gnaeus broke down and begged for protection.

At Munda, the survivors of Gnaeus' army waited to see what was going to happen. Caesar directed his men to blockade the town. His soldiers gathered up shields and pilums for a stockade, with dead bodies as a rampart, and on swords buried in the muck, with their points sticking up, they placed severed heads, facing in all around the town. Keeping the battle's survivors locked up in Munda, where they had plenty of food and water but could not cause any trouble, seemed a good idea to Caesar. He went to Corduba.

Many refugees from Gnaeus' legions and camp followers had made for Corduba. When they saw Caesar and his legions approaching they occupied the bridge, repulsing Caesar's leading body of scouts and guards. When Caesar approached, their spokesman told him they were the few survivors of the battle, accompanied by the hectoring of his compatriots. Rather than confront them directly on the bridge, Caesar marched to the crossing he had made when he brought his army to Corduba and camped on the other side of the river, opposite Corduba's walls. Despair spread throughout Corduba when people realized those in power were now powerless and Caesar's murderous army was at their gates. Fighting broke out between the factions and some of those deeply invested in the senatorial group killed themselves. The sound of the commotion reached Caesar's camp.

Two legions took shape in the town: some of the refugees from the battle were joined by former slaves, freed by Sextus comprising XIII and IX Legions. The men of XIII intended to defend Corduba at all costs; those of IX looked toward accommodating Caesar. Both started fighting each other while some men of IX seized some walls and towers, sending representatives to Caesar, imploring him to send his legions into the town. When Sextus' supporters found out about their defection, they started to set the town on fire. Caesar entered Corduba and joined the fight. When the struggles ended, 22,000 were dead.

With a trusted garrison in Corduba, Caesar marched his legions toward Hispalis. On the road, he met the town's representatives who assured him of their loyalty and begged his forgiveness. When he arrived at Hispalis, Caesar sent Caninius into the town with a guard and set up camp near the town. While the occupation of the town seemed easy, inside the walls there were strong differences of opinion. A firm ally of the brothers Pompey, (at this distance from Rome, Senatorial and Caesarean factions meant little; the disagreements were about who was in charge here in Spain), a certain Philo was well connected to the Lusitanian tribes. Secretly leaving Hispalis, he joined with the Lusitanian warlord, Caecilius Niger, who commanded a formidable body of mercenaries. Philo returned to Hispalis with these men, penetrated the town at night, and killed the garrison and many of those opposed to him. He closed the gates and set up the town for defence.

The overthrow of the friendly administration in Hispalis angered Caesar but rather than launch an assault against the town and risk the danger that the Lusitanians might set it on fire and destroy the fortifications, Caesar withdrew all immediate threats to the town. According to the plan which Caesar and his staff developed, they pulled away from the sentries who watched the town, allowing the Lusitanians to believe they had an opening to raid the countryside. At night, the mercenary force moved out of Hispalis to plunder ships in the River Baetis. Once they secured their loot, the mercenaries set the ships on fire to distract Caesar's soldiers so they could return to Hispalis. What they did not know was that Caesar's cavalry was waiting for them. The cavalry cut down all of them. The next morning Hispalis opened their gates to Caesar.

As Caesar was dealing with the problems in Hispalis, representatives from the town of Carteia arrived and announced they had Gnaeus Pompey in custody. They offered him to Caesar as an apology for denying him access to the town during the war. Once Hispalis was settled, Caesar set off toward Carteia. On his way, the town of Asta surrendered but Caesar attacked other towns which tried to hold out. In Carteia, disagreements broke out about Gnaeus' fate: he had many supporters in the town. Fighting broke out and Gnaeus with many supporters fled Carteia, capturing twenty warships and put to sea. Caesar's naval commander, Didius, brought forth his fleet, attacking Gnaeus' warships. Some of Gnaeus' ships surrendered, the rest caught fire and burned. Gnaeus and his personal guards escaped in a light craft, reached the shore and set up a defendable position. Caesar sent a strong cavalry force and a couple of cohorts of infantry in pursuit and after a long struggle of hiding and seeking, with Gnaeus travelling by litter, he was found, alone and hidden in a cave. His captives quickly beheaded him, and on 12 April brought his head to Hispalis.

After he had defeated Gnaeus' fleet and heard that Gnaeus was dead, Didius beached part of his fleet for refit and took up station in a local stronghold. The band of Lusitanians who had tried to protect Gnaeus, reformed. They attacked Didius' base, trying to burn the ships but Didius' force defended the beached ships. The Lusitanians split into two groups, the first to burn the ships, the second to deal with the defenders. When the first group gained the ships and set some on fire, Didius advanced from the stronghold and attacked the second group which was waiting for him. They fled, allowing Didius and his guards to chase them and lead them into an ambush. Didius fought bravely but was cut down.

Fabius Maximus commanded the force blockading Munda. The thousands of trapped soldiers in Munda could not agree on what they should do, some wanted to surrender, others thought they ought to try to escape. The two groups fell to fighting and some tried to break out; in the fracas, Maximus managed to take the town. Fourteen thousand men surrendered, then Maximus marched off to Ursao. With the only water source for miles and timber a long way off, with strong walls and natural fortifications, Ursao could hold off an enemy for a long time. Still, that would accomplish nothing so the town surrendered.

With the war over, Caesar started to settle outstanding issues and raise money through confiscations and selling prisoners. Those towns in rebellion, Caesar fined and confiscated lands; the towns which supported Caesar, he rewarded with prospects of Roman citizenship and immunity from taxation. Reforming the administration, setting up new colonies, granting petitions, and introducing new legislation, while effective, did not remove old loyalties to the House of Pompey. Sextus Pompey hid in the north and collected a force of fugitives and mercenaries. Returning to the south, he managed a guerrilla war, even holding off Caesar.

As long as local forces held him in check, Caesar did not see him as a major problem. He spend most of his time in Hispalis, then went to New Carthage to establish a colony. Caesar's seventeen-year-old nephew, G. Octavius had come to Spain and accompanied him. From New Carthage, Caesar went to Tarraco and then in the middle of September (45 BC), returned to Rome.

Chapter 24

The Civil Wars End

During the seven months of his Spanish campaign, Caesar pondered his path forward through the morass of Roman politics. Once the fighting was finished, he travelled to various places in Further Spain, settling issues that had arisen. On these trips, Caesar took Octavius with him. Now, he had his mind made up and decided how he was going to reform the Republic. His idea was to establish an overseer who was not going to be a king, sticking his fingers into everything, but a distant authority like a father, guiding actions in general directions and correcting blatant abuses, but letting people find their way within this framework. These reforms revolved around methods of operation; they were not structural changes. This overseer was a special person, semi-divine, set above the society. Moreover, the office of overseer was going to last generations, descending through a family dynasty of semi-divine rulers.

The foundations of Caesar's concepts rested on his understanding and faith in religion. Modern secularists describe the political actions of both Caesar and Octavius as purely Machiavellian or motivated by some sort of class consciousness. Such mindsets are alien to the classical world. Roman religion was a powerful and intellectual series of concepts based on a deep emotional foundation of family, clan, and community. Roman religion's heart is the image and concept of the gods' favourite society, the People of Rome. Caesar, the descendant of Venus, patrician, aristocrat, favourite of fortune, and ever victorious, saw his victories and current position as the gift of Jupiter the Best and Greatest.

When Caesar arrived in Italy, he went to his estate near Labicum. On 13 September 45 BC, he composed a new will, naming Octavius as his principal heir and adopting him as his son. He sent instructions to his supporters in Rome, telling them how the Romans should receive him. When Caesar entered Rome, the magistrates and senators greeted him. Caesar was honoured and feared as no one had ever been before. The senate, tribes, provinces, and allied kings vied to grant extravagant honours. He should have a crown of oak signifying he was his country's saviour; the Senate and People of Rome proclaimed him the father of his country, dictator for life, consul for ten years, and his person was sacred and inviolable. He should conduct government business on a golden and ivory throne. When he held sacrifice, he should be in the dress of a triumphal victor. The month of Quintilis became July. Temples were dedicated to him. Statues of Caesar would be in the processions of statues of the gods in the circus at the start of the chariot races. A statue would be on the Capitol with the kings of Rome, and another in the temple of Quirinus, the deified Romulus, with the inscription, 'To the unconquerable god'. Further, the senate granted the personal prefix 'Imperator' to Caesar as his name, and this prefix would descend to his children and their children. Caesar alone was to command all the armed forces and appoint subordinate commanders. He alone directed the administration of public funds.

There were rumours that Caesar would be crowned king, but he said he would have none of it. The word was inauspicious. Caesar sat on a golden and ivory throne before the rostra in the forum while the magistrates led by the consuls and the senate, all in their robes of office, presented honours to Caesar. He accepted all, except the office of consul for ten years. Caesar extended his hand but did not rise, showing his dominion over the magistrates and senate.

Within three weeks of his return, Caesar held a great triple triumph for his victory in Spain. He allowed his subordinate commanders, Q. Maximus Fabius and Quintus Pedius, to celebrate with him. After the triple triumph, Caesar held another great feast with shows, gladiator fights, and races during the fifty days of thanksgiving. This was the first Roman triumph over Romans; these enemies were neither enemy nor barbarians. They were Romans with just as good pedigree as those they fought against. Caesar decided that he was at war with his Roman opponents, but they ceased to be Roman by opposing him. He was the chosen of the Roman gods to reform and restore Roman glory.

Caesar and the Quest for Power

When Caesar was born, Marius was consul. Caesar's aunt was Marius' wife. As a toddler and a pre-adolescent, the Roman society in which he lived experienced upheaval and violent disruption. When he was about twelve, Sulla marched into Rome and became consul. When he was about seventeen, Sulla became dictator, and four magnificent triumphs marched through Rome. This was followed by continuing war, slave rebellions, intrigue, and murder. Caesar saw waste, inefficiency, stupidity, and blind ambition. As a young man, he had the solution: a strong leader with a strong army reorganizing the Republic using reason and common sense. Of course, that was what Marius, Sulla, and many others tried, but Caesar thought they didn't know what they were doing. Caesar knew better. What he needed were a political position and a powerful, loyal army.

As the first step toward his goal, Caesar won the praetorship by proposing popular positions and spending a lot of other peoples' money. Roman politics remained disordered at the time, with institutional struggles between orders and personal fights between influential individuals intersecting at different points, often producing strange results. Playing the game, Caesar received the administration of Further Spain. He had a contact with a prominent citizen of Gades, Cornelius Balbus. This man supported Pompey, from whom he received Roman citizenship. Working with the new governor, he brought to Caesar's attention numerous issues in the administration of Further Spain. Caesar was pushing forty and was simply another Roman aristocrat of middling achievement. Caesar intended to change that.

First, Caesar demanded that a particular hill tribe relocate their settlements from heights down into the plains as a precaution against their plundering raids. As expected, they refused and began preparations for defence. But then, Caesar attacked neighbouring tribes when these neighbours tried to move away from Roman domination. This allowed the first tribe to set up ambushes to trap Caesar's force. Caesar found this an excellent opportunity to crush them. He continued to pursue this enemy to the sea. Rather than surrender to Caesar and ending up in Roman slave markets, these people took to the sea and sailed to an island. Caesar had rafts constructed and sent a striking force across to the island, but while some soldiers landed, rough sea forced the rest of the force to return to the mainland, and the tribal refugees cut down those who had landed. Not willing to face defeat, Caesar sent to Gades for ships. He loaded his force into the fleet when the ships arrived and landed them on the island. The refugees, facing starvation or slaughter, surrendered without a fight. Sailing further in his fleet, Caesar reached Brigantium, on the northwest corner of the Spanish peninsula, taking the settlement into the Roman dominion. Returning to the Roman towns of Further Spain, Caesar settled several financial problems that many of the Spanish towns had with Rome, lowering debts and easing loan terms.

During his campaign in Further Spain, Caesar began to develop his skills in handling an armed force. His strategy was simple: where is the enemy? March to him. Caesar's strength depended on the tactical skill of his soldiers. Kill as many enemies as possible, and the rest will flee, then give chase. He was very aware that things don't always work according to plan, so he always looked to alternative ways to hit the enemy. His watchwords were be confident, fight until victory. Of course, Caesar needed an army of brutal, ruthless soldiers to do these things. To train them, he required harder, more ruthless officers. Such men were available, and Caesar would pay their price. These were good pay, opportunities for loot, and those joys of victory: rape and murder. In truth, Caesar and his army were a fearsome collection of very nasty men.

His administration of Further Spain was a great success; he quickly returned to Rome, where he faced the choice, have a triumph or run for consul. Caesar became a great friend with Pompey, the most important Roman military commander, and Crassus, the most prominent financier and banker in the politics of the time. The three of them took over the Republic's administration against strong opposition when Caesar was consul. And so, in a few years, from a minor noble, Caesar had become a military leader and essential politician. But this was just the beginning, what he needed was a large, loyal and strong army.

The nearest open frontier of Roman domination was to the north of Italy. Toward the end of Caesar's consulate, the Gauls and Germans became more agitated than usual. Caesar knew about Gaul and worked with many important figures from Gaul and Germany. He needed military forces to bring peace and Roman justice to this land; he was granted them by the People and Senate of Rome and the right to raise more. Here was his army. Gaul was rich in land, men, and precious metals. Many Gauls lived in hill-fortress towns, and most of Gaul was a settled land of farms, pastures, and forests. This was a prize worth taking, and so Caesar did.

For eight years, Caesar battled the Gauls, Germans, and even Britons along with political battles in Rome to keep his position and influence. The political alliance of the three fell apart. Crassus sought an army and extensive conquests in the east. His campaign failed, and he died. Pompey drifted away from Caesar into a faction of his own making. But through it all, Caesar built his army: a disciplined force of savage killers and marauders, able to defeat any force in the Mediterranean world at the time.

Now was the time to march on Rome. If Caesar did not bring his army, others would take it and disperse it. Caesar wanted a second consulship, but he would not surrender his army. This was against the basic political understandings of the Republic: thus, a Gordian Knot – Caesar knew that it was to be cut by the sword. He pretended to want peace more than his enemies pretended that they could find common ground with him. Both sides knew there could only be war. His enemies would kill Caesar, or Caesar would replace the Republic with his own rule. So began the civil war.

The Reign of Imp. Julius Caesar

After his inauguration of the New Republic, Caesar held all the levers of power. He dismissed his military guards, replacing them with ordinary civilian escorts. He appointed himself and Antony as consuls for the coming year and Lepidus as Antony's successor as master of horse. Antony and Lepidus managed Caesar's supporters, but Caesar wanted to expand his power base. He recalled all exiles except those guilty of major crimes. Many former Pompeians found employment in the new administration. To allow Roman citizens, particularly freedmen and their families, a fresh start, Caesar established Roman colonies in the old sites of both Carthage and Corinth. Caesar received a house on the Palatine from which he conducted business.

Some hoped Caesar, like Sulla, would soon leave power, but that was not to be. Instead, Caesar intermixed his Caesarian faction with the Pompeians who would work with him. If he were eliminated, the political structure would shatter into chaos. That is why he did not fear assassination, but we should also consider Caesar's health. Many modern commentators speak of Caesar's epilepsy. This is improbable. The neurological condition diagnosed today as epilepsy should not be confused with the ancient 'falling sickness'. During his last time in Rome, Caesar is said to have fallen several times (?), and some have said he had the 'sacred sickness'. This is a significant symptom of ill-health. On his march toward Further Spain during his last campaign, Caesar was very sick for a while. He was 56 in 44 BC and had led a very hard life. This might be symptomatic of some circulatory difficulty; whatever it was, Caesar knew he had maybe five years left.

He wanted to solidify his administration and pass it on to Octavius as soon as possible. That meant he needed to organize a lasting administration and appoint people to permanent posts. To accomplish his objective, Caesar had to deal with two problems. One was the loyalty of his Pompeian supporters; he needed people he could trust, including Brutus and his friends along with Cicero. The second problem was easing out of power a certain person in the Caesarian faction who had done him service but did not have the temperament to manage a complex government. This was Antony. Loyal and dedicated, Antony had lost a brother in the civil war, fighting for Caesar. Still, Antony had a nasty habit of taking what he wanted without thinking about how people reacted. Antony easily slid into corruption as an administrator, and Caesar had enough of that.

Caesar planned to finesse the issues. The east, as usual, was under threat by the Parthians, and the tribes to the north of Macedonia were causing trouble. Rather than stay in Rome and deal with the minutiae of administration, Caesar much preferred marching at the head of a powerful army, ready to meet a formidable enemy; he had planned a great eastern expedition in Spain. In the winter of 43 BC, the Roman army concentrated in the east. This moved the legions away from Italy and so away from those who might oppose Caesar's policies and actions. Further, setting up new camps and bases in the east gave the boys something to keep them busy. More importantly, however, he intended to set up an administration in Rome and then leave, allowing a secure transition of power from himself to Octavius. In late winter, 44 BC, he again reshuffled people and offices. Antony remained consul as Caesar's colleague, but Lepidus would become a provincial governor leaving vacant the office of master of horse. Caesar intended that office, very important when the dictator was absent, to go to Octavius and Domitius Calvinus, an experienced, loyal follower of Caesar. That way, if Caesar died on the campaign, Octavius would succeed Caesar.

By March 44 BC, a strong army awaited in the east; Caesar had set up the politics as he thought best and was ready to leave. Three days before he was to depart Rome, he held a senate meeting to clear up final details. Some sixty senators, we are told, had been conspiring to kill Caesar for weeks. Did Antony know about the conspiracy and decide to stand aside? Indeed, with Caesar suddenly dead, he might try for the top position and push aside 'that boy'. Brutus and his fellows planned to restore the Republic after the tyrant's death. In the end, Octavius showed them all just what power was all about.

Appendix I

Caesar's Siege of Massilia and Vitruvius' *On Architecture*

The architect Vitruvius was employed by Caesar Augustus as advisor and perhaps designer of his many building projects. Well educated, practised and practical, Vitruvius complied a manual of architectural practice; he probably translated a number of Greek building manuals and adapted them to Roman taste. This has long been and remains a useful text and guide to classical design and methods. With what we can find about its manuscript history, it seems the work was never lost.

Book 10 of *On Architecture* deals with military machines and war; Chapter XVI talks of 'Measures of Defence'. In Chapter XVI, there is a section about a siege of Massilia in which the town defenders repel an attack using mines, trying to dig under the walls into the town. Some commentators have placed this event in the sequence of Julius Caesar's siege of Massilia during his Civil Wars. There is a problem with this idea, Caesar's *Civil War* has a long section on the siege of Massilia but does not mention anything about the use of mines. Further, the operations described by Vitruvius are extensive and do not fit the ground of Massilia in Caesar's time.

The answer to this question rests in the manner of textual transmission. All the other sieges recounted in the section are in the eastern Mediterranean during the wars of the Hellenistic kings. Vitruvius mentions an Alexandrian architect and engineer, Trypho of Alexandria as the defensive designer in the siege. We hear absolutely nothing of this in any of the civil war histories. Therefore, I think the connection of this incident in the context of Julius Caesar's civil wars is a mistake and the name of the besieged town is wrong. There was a Trypho of Alexandria who lived through the Roman civil wars, but he was a grammarian. That this error was in the first published copy of Vitruvius is unlikely because it was clearly wrong; perhaps when a copy of the manuscript transferred the text from old papyrus to vellum, the copyist could not quite make out the information and transferred the siege to Massilia. Possibly this was a siege of Miletus during the Hellenistic age.

Appendix II

Queen Cleopatra and Julius Caesar

The House of Ptolemy had ruled Egypt for 300 years, ever since Commander Ptolemy, friend and relative of King Alexander, received the assignment to the Egyptian satrapy when the Royal Macedonian council reorganized the empire. Soon, he became King Ptolemy the Saviour, repulsing attempts to remove him from Egypt and redirecting Alexander's coffin from its trip to Macedonia to his capital, Alexandria Next to Egypt.

Macedonian Egypt was a significant power in the eastern Mediterranean for generations, but then came the Romans. They smashed the other Macedonian successor states, leaving Egypt as the only independent considerable power in the Mediterranean. The House of Ptolemy had its difficulties, murderous inter-family intrigues, bitter revolts up the Nile, but the riches of Egypt always saved them. Dealing with the Romans was not difficult; the Romans came with their hands out, they always left happy. On the other hand, the people of Alexandria were not always pleased with how the Ptolemies gave their money and goods to the Romans.

The new Pharaoh in 80 BC, Ptolemy XII, had no secure claim to the throne, so he boosted his titles with claims to divinity. He was the 'New Dionysus' and participated in religious ceremonies, playing the flute as the incarnation of Dionysus. The Romans found this laughable and called him the Piper. Rather than look west for support, Ptolemy XII turned deep into Egypt. His cousin, Petubastis II, high priest in Memphis, was also a relative in the House of Ptolemy, and Ptolemy XII worked at being Pharaoh and Macedonian King. When Petubastis II died, Ptolemy appointed his son to be high priest, Petubastis III, and, having fallen out with his wife, married a woman of the house of the high priest. By his first wife, he had a daughter, Berenice IV; by his second wife, he had three children, Cleopatra and two boys named Ptolemy.

When Sulla's dictatorship ended in 78 BC, the three most potent Roman magnates gathered decisive power into their hands. Pompey, Crassus, and Caesar formed a governing alliance. Crassus wanted to take Egypt over as a Roman province, collecting the Indian Ocean trade and Egyptian grain into his hands. King Ptolemy, seen by his enemies as a lightweight, cleverly outmanoeuvred Crassus with strategic bribes to essential senators. He also gave critical support to Pompey in the war against Mithridates. Pompey became more potent in Rome and valued King Ptolemy's gifts and help with his victory behind him. The citizens of Alexandra did not like seeing their taxes and trade given to Romans, but, at this time, the alternative was direct Roman rule.

In 60 BC, the three Roman magnates formalized their alliance with Caesar's daughter marrying Pompey. Together, the three offered King Ptolemy the title 'Friend and Ally of the Roman People' if he paid 6,000 talents (a year's income for Egypt). The king borrowed the money from the Roman banker, Gaius Rabirius Postumus, and paid Caesar. Other Romans were looking for a piece of the Egyptian pie. Cyprus, an Egyptian holding under King Ptolemy's brother, was a choice plum, and Clodius Pulcher saw the land as a haven for pirates. The Romans annexed the island, and Ptolemy's brother killed himself rather than exile. King Ptolemy did nothing, and the Alexandrians rebelled and deposed him in favour of his eldest daughter, Berenice IV.

King Ptolemy went into exile, taking along his daughter, eleven-year-old Cleopatra. Ptolemy went to Athens with his daughter and entourage, talking to influential people who could help him regain his throne. His answer was Pompey, and so to Rome he went. He stayed at Pompey's villa in the Alban Hills for almost a year. The Roman senate would not support Ptolemy's return to Egypt but did not forbid it. Ptolemy went to Ephesus, where he raised 10,000 talents to pay Gabinius to lead a Roman army to Egypt and place him on the throne again (55 BC). Roman opinion-makers pictured Ptolemy XII as a lightweight, calling him the flutist because he played an instrument at the festivals he instituted as the New Dionysus. He was shrewd and committed to the independence of his house and country.

Ptolemy XII died in 51 BC. His will, recognized by Pompey and the senate, appointed his daughter, Cleopatra VII, and her younger brother, Ptolemy XIII, as the new rulers of Egypt. At first, Cleopatra ousted Ptolemy and ruled alone, but a court faction rallied behind Ptolemy and turned the tables on Cleopatra. In the spring of 49, while Caesar consolidated his hold on Italy, Pompey sailed to Alexandria and requested aid from Ptolemy XIII (about 12 years old). The royal government gave Pompey a strong cavalry unit and fifty large warships. At this time, Cleopatra (about 20 years old) was trying to raise an army in Syria to overthrow Ptolemy.

After his defeat, Pompey returned to Egypt at the end of September (near the end of July solar calendar), intending to rebuild his forces using Egyptian resources. Still, Ptolemy XIII's advisors thought killing him would please Caesar, who also was coming. Presented with Pompey's head, Caesar expressed his sorrow and marched into the palace as a Roman master. Ptolemy's courtiers began to view Caesar as an enemy. Mindful of Roman agreement with Ptolemy XII's will, Caesar summoned Ptolemy XIII and his sister, Cleopatra VII, to the palace. He made it clear he would iron out their differences and set up a stable administration. The summons went out on 9 October (4 August solar calendar). Ptolemy arrived on 14 October (4 August solar calendar); his supporters, however, would just as soon not see Cleopatra, except after she met with an unfortunate end.

Cleopatra was aware of her precarious position, but unlike most Macedonian-Greek Egyptians, she lived in Rome and interacted with Caesar. The Romans, she knew, appreciated boldness but Roman boldness was something that succeeded. No doubt, with the help within the palace, she arranged to meet Caesar unconventionally. Recruiting a handsome and well-known delivery man, she had an exquisite rug brought to Caesar in his office area of the palace as the sun set. Apollodorus unrolled the carpet, and there was Cleopatra. She came because Caesar had summoned her. Caesar was enchanted.

Caesar and Cleopatra

After this meeting with Caesar, Cleopatra had a long and eventful career; possibility and supposition often fill the voids in her story. Plays, novels, and movies portray Cleopatra as everything from an innocent young girl astonished by the old rake to a manipulative shrew who took the kind older man for a ride. That all aside, we can draw some conclusions based on what we know. When Apollodorus unrolled Queen Cleopatra in front of Caesar, she was a little over twenty. As a young teenager, she had been in Rome and had seen and probably had talked with Caesar. As a royal Ptolemy, she was married to her brother and understood the joys of human reproductive methods. Caesar, famous for his many female conquests, was now about fifty plus and did not need another lover, although an attractive woman would be nice. The one thing both Cleopatra and Caesar had in common was an inordinate passion for political power. Whatever else they might have found pleasurable that evening, their main concern was plotting a future together as allies. Cleopatra would have allied with Pompey, but he was dead. Her only hope was Caesar. On the other hand, Caesar needed to secure Egypt for its wealth and trade routes. By joining together, they could satisfy both their desires.

Once he had pacified Alexandria and seen to Ptolemy XIII's demise, Caesar worked to secure Cleopatra's domination of Egypt. She was not only a Ptolemy but was also a member of a high priestly family and so was in a position to become High Priestess of Egypt; Caesar was High Priest of Rome and presenting themselves as a couple, with an infant on the way, they became the divine rulers of Egypt with their child uniting Egypt and Rome. This is why the couple took their trip up the Nile: to present the new divinities to the many great temples that sat on the sacred river. With Caesar's army holding Egypt and Cleopatra as high priestess and goddess, the land was secure for both of them. Caesar and Cleopatra formed a strong alliance and, we may assume, an emotional bond.

After Caesar returned to Rome, Cleopatra arrived with personal staff, Museum savants, and Caesarean. Clearly, Caesar was not unhappy to see her and their son. He gave her a large house and reformed Rome's calendar with the help of the Museum savants. She left Rome soon after Caesar's murder. Caesar may have visualized a future with his adopted son, Octavius ruling Rome, Greece, and the west while allied with his son in Alexandria ruling the east but there is no longer any evidence. The struggle between Antony and 'that boy' Octavius opened an opportunity for her to choose sides and influence the outcome in her and her son's favour. She allied with Antony, who had no love for Octavius and knew both Cleopatra and Caesarion. An independent eastern empire suited Antony. Caesarion was Caesar's son and so Antony fought to protect Caesar's 'true' legacy. Unfortunately for the eastern empire, 'that boy' did well. The young Julius Caesar destroyed the empire of Cleopatra and Antony.

That left the question of Caesarion. Octavius claimed that Caesarion was an imposter, not the son of Great Caesar. Politics demanded such a claim because accepting Caesarion as the son of Caesar undermined Octavius' position. Yet, Octavius had seen the infant, was himself close to Julius and so would know Julius Caesar's opinion which appears to be that Caesarion was indeed Caesar's son. When the young Julius Caesar landed in Alexandria to settle the aftermath of the Actium War, he somehow disposed of the seventeen-year-old Caesarian. The official story was that that the young Caesar had him killed.

Appendix III

The Museum and Library at Alexandria

Collecting facts out of the body of Classical literature is a matter of time and effort; interpreting those facts takes imagination and discernment. But there is more: there are the dreams of lost grandeur and wonder. Would it not be amazing if we had a complete copy of Livy? Even better, how about the complete works of Tacitus? Or Aristarchus' astronomy? Sophocles' plays? And on, and on. One of the great dreams of modern times is the lost Library of Alexandria and of its host city. Our interest here is the question, did Julius Caesar burn the Library of Alexandria? To look at this question, we first need to understand what was this library? And then ask the question, how did Caesar burn it? That there was a question at the time is made clear by the compiler of Caesar's *Alexandrian War* who said, 'For Alexandria is not burnable because the buildings there are constructed without wood, put together with solid construction and roofed with fired clay or paving stones.' (Bello Alexandrino 1.1).

We must ask, what were the Museum and Library of Alexandria? Modern commentators understand these institutions were very important in Hellenistic intellectual achievements. They idealize these institutions as some kind of altruistic achievements of the human spirit's search for knowledge. In part that may be true of those employed in the institutions, but the purpose of the Museum and Library, in the cash and carry world of Hellenistic Civilization, was to make money. Education is good business, as Harvard and Yale, Oxford and Cambridge, and your local public and private school systems know only too well. The administrators of the schools, the teachers, the maintenance staffs, the suppliers of materials, books, papers, etc. all have their hands out. And this is how it has been since the beginning of professional instruction, starting with the sophists.

The Museum

So, let us look at the Museum. Now the word Museum (Greek, Mouseion) means place sacred to the Muses; these are deified personifications of the human impulse to accomplish intellectual and artistic endeavours. Like all mythology, explaining the inexplicable does not require consistency or logic to reveal truths. The ancient Greeks had a number of interpretations of who were Muses. Popular perception viewed the Muses as the offsprings of Zeus and Mnemosyne (memory); they are Calliope, epic and rhetoric; Clio, history and records; Euterpe, making music with instruments; Thalia, light poetry and comedy; Melpomene, serious dramatics; Terpsichore, dance; Erato, serious poetry; Polyhymnia, prayer and hymns; Urania, mathematics and astronomy.

Since the Museum was dedicated to the Muses, we may expect the organization of departments revolved around the Muses' subject matters. Agreeably, current instructions of higher education have similar curriculums: literature of many types, history, mathematics and physics, sciences of many types, religion, and the performing arts. While not included in the Muses, physical activity, running, jumping, and physical games were also included in Alexandrian education. Certainly, Alexandria's Museum was not the first institution of this type in the Greek world, but it was the best for centuries.

What we see in the Museum is a school of higher education, training young men to become experts in chosen fields where there was good employment or business prospects. While the Muses may be for self-improvement, their gifts can readily earn money. And, of course, being students in such an institution costs dearly. Which brings up the question of its physical plant. Interestingly, the Polish Archaeological Expedition have uncovered a site in central Alexandria which reveals a campus-like area which fits the requirements of such a school in Kom el-Dikka. Here are found lecture rooms, walk-ways, a small but exquisite theatre, and a full-sized bath complex. The 'common eating hall' we hear about, is the cafeteria (hopefully better appointed than current examples). The remains are dated to late antiquity but, like all educational establishment, there is constant rebuilding requiring further investment, with cash passing through the hands of administrators. Next to the campus, there are large houses in which teachers and students could live. Certainly, it is not beyond possibility that this is, indeed, the Museum.

The Library

The next question is what was the Library? We first hear about book collections in Greece in the time of Peisistratus, particularly the works of Homer. Then we find the works of the First Sophistic which leads us to the Academy and the Lyceum. Both dealt with significant numbers of written works. Also, we may be sure the dramatist, musicians and speech writers had collections of works. Above all, however, there were state archives, records of laws, property ownership, citizen rolls and the like. These were mostly on papyrus rolls and formed the material basis of books.

So, for almost three centuries the Greeks were dealing with the problem of manufacturing and storing books. They knew that other peoples of the Near East also had collections of scrolls, many of a religious nature, some of practical How to Do It texts. Techniques of storage were common. Books, including papyrus, have four major enemies: first is dampness which will quickly deteriorate the fabric of the pages; second are pests which find the pages easily digestible and eat their way through the book; third is fire which quickly destroys any amount of books in its path; and fourth is time itself. Books deteriorated on their own. Papyrus was notorious for its ability to fall apart after time. The reason is the glue used to hold the strips of the papyrus plant together degrade and the dry papyrus filaments pull apart. In this condition, there is little chance of saving the book. In the age of the Museum, all these things were well known.

Ptolemy II spared no expense building his library. If it was to last, he needed to defeat the book enemies. Considering the construction problems of satisfying the specifications for keeping books safe, it is quite certain that the images often passed off as the Library of Alexandria are fantastic. The idea of having book stalls set in stoa type walkways is definitely wrong. Bad weather, rain, and heat are very damaging. There was no sunlight shining in from massive windows. Direct sunlight damages books. In an age before eye spectacles, the best way to read was with indirect lighting, either shaded windows or a carefully constructed oil lamp with shaded light. The papyrus was a cool light sepia brown with letters in dark brown (almost but not quite black). Tables, chairs and lamps sat in open spaces between the stacks. The stacks themselves were vertical bins holding square wicker boxes with the scrolls stored vertically. On the box side were the cataloguing information and the authors' names. Storing scrolls horizontally will, in time, hasten the break-down of the papyrus fabric. A large hall with a solid roof was suitable with small, shaded windows.

There are a few good examples of classical library buildings recovered in excavation-restoration efforts. The most complete is the Library of Celsius in Ephesus. Here is a large masonry building, purpose built, with double masonry walls for ventilation, with a large room some 55 feet wide by 30 feet deep of two or perhaps three storeys tall. An interior walkway ran around the building as a second floor, leaving the central space open. For the size of the room, the windows are not large. Along the walls, there are niches for cabinets holding book boxes. There also may have been free standing cabinets with shelving for book boxes on the main floor. The building was solid, with little chance of accidental fire, sitting on a firm foundation. In Timgad, Algeria there are the foundations of the Library of Rogatianus. This is a purpose built complex, some 80 by 77 feet centred on a semi-circular room with a number of wing rooms. It was well constructed to judge by the foundations, which is all that is left. Other library remains include Hadrian's library at Athens, also a substantial building.

The conclusion: Ptolemy II's library was a substantial masonry structure with thick walls, heavy fire-resistant roof, smaller windows, and deep foundations. If Kim el-Dikka was the Museum, then the Library was where the Cathedral of St. Marks stands, because of the solid masonry foundation on which the church sits.

Caesar in Alexandria

In book III of his *Civil War*, Caesar tells us of his landing at Alexandria. The news of Pompey's death including Pompey's severed head surprised him. Even worse, the sudden upheaval and threat of attack by Commander Achillas pushed Caesar off balance (Civil War, III, 111). With only a few thousand men, Caesar faced 20,000 Ptolemaic troops. As Achillas sent his soldiers to occupy the city, Caesar saw the greatest danger to his men and himself as the Royal Fleet sat in the military harbour. There were the fifty quadriremes and quinqueremes returned from the campaign in Greece and a further twenty two warships as harbour protection, all armed and fitted for battle. If Achillas seized these ships, he would cut off Caesar and his forces from any relief and destroy them all. To forestall them, Caesar saw to it that the whole fleet burned. (Civil War, III, 112).

Alexandria was a major port designed by skilled engineers and built by master craftsmen. The war fleet had its own harbour; fire, especially catastrophic fire, was a serious concern to the builders, not only to protect the fleet but also the city in troubled time. Engineers designed the port to protect the city, not threaten it when it burned. Instead, the danger to the library was the rising in the city. To construct the battle towers and fields of fire necessary to beat Caesar, the Alexandrines tore up and removed many buildings. A solid structure like the library was a choice strongpoint for the insurgents who would have removed all the books to make way for their immediate needs. If that was the case, then fire and flood struck the library. On the other hand, the war damage in Alexandria was quickly restored under Cleopatra and then Antony. Books were replaceable and the library was still a going concern under the Emperor Claudius (reign 41-54) who sponsored an addition to the structure and there is an inscription celebrating a library director, Tiberius Claudius Balbilus around 70 AD. The library continued to exist as an institution until the crisis of the third century and came to an end in some physical or political catastrophe.

The Wreck of Classical Literature

Some commentators have said that the Museum and Library at Alexandria suffered a decline of intellectual activity after the Age of Augustus but compilations such as Strabo's Geography, Pliny's Encyclopedia, and Plutarch's works shows us deep interest and solid achievements were on-going. To current intellectual judgement, there was a shift away from 'important' topics to pseudoscience speculation. The limitations placed on Classical sciences because of the lack of technological sophistication which might have allowed finer measurements and greater perception were final. Classical mathematics and physics were at a plateau and would not go any farther until a new whole magnitude of technical skill arrived. Still, the savants of the Mediterranean world during the high and later Roman Empire investigated not the physical but the spiritual frontiers of human existence.

During the Hellenistic Age, there were one or two great libraries, in the High and Later Empire, academies and libraries proliferated. We must remember that the literature produced by these academies is today the foundation of Judaism, Christianity and Islam. Every week, billions of people find consolation and hope, attending meetings in assembly buildings which have grown out of the many traditions of the ancient world.

In the antagonistic human and natural environments of the ancient Mediterranean, life, never easy, became harder as the third century gave way to the fourth and fifth centuries. Scarcity, want, invasion and poverty threatened. The losses to the body of Classical literature did not come about because of carelessness, stupidity, or bigotry. Rather, rational people had to make decisions about the allocation of resources in a time of political and ideological upheaval and declining prosperity. What was most important at a critical moment decided that this work would survive and others were discarded. The decline of economic wherewithal, caused by many reasons beyond our current knowledge, shrank the libraries and book collections in both east and west. The Classical literature we have left is a fine library for an academy of higher education. Our books include examples of this and that and a number of complete works by important authors.

What did in the ancient books was that fourth book enemy, time. The papyrus deteriorated. A papyrus book a hundred years old was on the way out. The only way to preserve the text was to transfer it to vellum, an expensive and time-consuming task. There are no primary copies of Classical literature surviving that have come down through the years as an ancient papyrus book. Archaeologists have discovered a few hidden in the dust of time, but most of the Classical literature that we have survives because concerned people took the time and money to preserve it.

Appendix IV

Caesar and his Army

'It is by proper maintenance (of supplies) that armies are kept together.'
Julius Caesar, Dio, 42.49.5

Caesar's Army

The Roman army was old. From the time of the kings, the Romans organized their young men into combat units and marched them out to fight for the glory of Rome, for land, for plunder and for status. War was at the core of the Roman state; successful war brought lands, slaves, and peoples into Roman hands. But more war required more armies, and the Roman secret of success was to turn their defeated enemies into Romans in order to conquer more lands and people to make more Romans. After the expulsion of the kings, for some four centuries the Roman army pulled together a vast collection of provinces across the Mediterranean Sea. In this process, the Roman army and state changed. Rome herself changed. Soldiers of Rome were part of Rome; they were not robots or mercenaries but free men and elite citizens. Roman society was always a hierarchy; soldiers had a high status and expected their interests to be served.

The army of Julius Caesar was something unique in Roman experience. There were others like it, now and again, but none with an edge so sharp. Like the Army of Northern Virginia, Caesar's army was a personal instrument of its commander. His army had weaknesses, but Caesar's strategy was to hide the faults and emphasize the strength. The organization of Caesar's army was like all the Roman armies of his time. But Caesar made his army different, a product of tradition yet unique, as this appendix will show.

The Tent-Full

We will start at the sharp edge, the squads of men who did the actual fighting. This was the eight men conubernium, meaning 'tent-full,' a group of eight fighting men who shared a tent and a mule to carry heavy equipment, including their tent and cooking apparatus. This was standard practice in the Roman army. This group was self-chosen for the most part, old friends and relatives who knew each other's qualities. When, in the course of events, a new member came, he was hazed until judged fit or expelled. The usual result was many tent-fulls tightly locked together and some made up of the rejects of other tent-fulls, tied together in their rejected status.

Competition being a factor in Roman life, each tent-full kept an eye on their fellow groups, either as friends or rivals. Each tent-full had at least one servant to handle the mule, do the cooking, and mend the clothes. This person was often a slave, sometimes a woman. Besides the mule each tent-full, perhaps in partnership with another or more tent-fulls, had a wagon pulled by horses for their personal belongings, such as money, loot, relatives, and slaves. Adding up all the wagons into a train would hinder the army's mobility so for the most part, the wagons, their goods, and personnel were kept at a fortified base camp. There were a lot more people and animals than on the registers of the legion. The tent-full was responsible for ensuring their members were proper in their dealing with fellow soldiers, kept their equipment in order, followed orders, and were good team members. One man was recognized head of the tent-full and he represented the needs and interests of its members to the commanders.

These men were about sixteen to twenty-five years old. There was a solid minority of veterans, who were the cadres of the legion. They might reach forty years old but front-line soldiering was tough work, and by forty very few men were up to it. The cadres in Caesar's army knew each other from years of service. They either got along well or avoided those they disliked. In Pompey's army, with a few exceptions, most of the men were new to the legion if not to the business of soldiering. After a bloody encounter, the tent-fulls had to reform. In Caesar's tent-fulls because a core of men had served for a long time, shifting about was smooth, for the most part. For Pompey's men, not having served together for a long time nor being used to the shock of combat, such change was disruptive and increased tensions between the soldiers.

The Organization

Ten tent-fulls made a century of eighty men. Each century was under the command of a centurion; an officer who had special insignia and carried a swagger stick which indicated he was allowed to hit the men when they displeased him. Each centurion had five under officers: an assistant commander, the optio, (chosen by the centurion), a standard bearer who carried a long pole holding the number of the century and the cohort to which it belonged, a signaller who sounded a horn, and a guardsman who assigned sentries and kept order in the century. In formation, the centurion and standard bearer stood in front of the assembled century and the optio stood in back. Two centuries together formed a maniple and three maniples formed a cohort, which then consisted of six centuries and so, 480 men, plus twelve more for officers. Each tent-full of eight was a unit which, combined with other tent-fulls, formed ranks or files in their assigned position in their cohort. The centuries took their place in the cohort by numerical order, one to ten, according to the commander's assignment.

The position of a cohort depended on its number, from first to tenth. The number represented the legion commander's judgement of the relative effectiveness of each cohort, the lower the number the better the cohort. The highest-ranking centurion was the centurion of the first century of the first cohort: he was the Primus Pilus. The lowest level centurion was that of the tenth century of the tenth cohort. Between these two centurions there were ninety-eight more, each a graded position. Caesar's top centurions had been with him for years; they knew him and understood how he manoeuvred his formations. Caesar's forces moved as a smooth mechanism. Pompey's centurions came from many sources, some had a long history with him, others came with the legions Pompey acquired from Caesar, still others came with various Roman nobles, landowners, and professional mercenaries. Complex manoeuvres were far more difficult for Pompey than Caesar.

Food and drink

A soldier needs clothes, food, shelter, and hygienic facilities. In the Roman army of the Late Republic, the group of eight, the conubernium (tent-full), mended their clothes, cooked their food, managed the tent, and carried their baggage. Of course, they did not do these things themselves. Each tent-full was given a servant and a mule, but the men were not without their own resources and could acquire others. Also, they shared a wagon with other tent-fulls or, if they could afford it, they had their own wagon, cook, washing woman, and driver. These wagons generally stayed near the legion's base camp; when Caesar's legions were on the move, the tent-full had only their mule and one servant. The mule pack contained a hand grinder for grain, a bronze cooking pot, a flat iron plate or stone, and a spit for roasting, along with tent materials and personal items.

Most food consisted of wheat grain, 60 to 70 per cent bulk and calories. Added to the wheat were root vegetables, legumes, beans, peas, and lentils; meat was issued in moderation, usually pork or beef sausages, ham, bacon, and salt pork. Mutton and beef in different forms were not unknown. To flavour the food there was salt, herbs, and garlic. Olive oil was necessary for most cooking and has added value as a condiment. Beverages were equally important. Water was always necessary and in large amounts. Different milks, from cow, sheep, or goats was drunk at times, but more often turned into cheese. While cheese is not mentioned in the literature, cheese squeezers are found on military sites.

Once they gain what they need, soldiers want entertaining and stimulating beverages. Water in quantity is always necessary but fermented liquid gladdens the heart and raises morale. The Romans had a large wine industry and vineyards existed in Italy and throughout the empire. Once the harvest was in, the grapes were processed a number of times in different ways, producing the juices for different types of wine. First, the grapes were trodden by foot providing 'free-run' juice. This was considered the optimum wine making juice, used for making the best wines. Second, the grape mass was placed in a press, made from wooden beams placed side by side, the grape mass between them; then, using a pulley system, the beams pressed together, causing the juices to run down a channel into a container. This was done twice; then water was added to the press and a third pressing was made and kept separate. The wine makers quickly transferred the grape juices to large earthenware jars (*dolia*) often set in the ground where fermentation occurred, lasting two weeks to a month. The wine was then transferred to storage amphora to age. The wines from the sequence of pressings were different: the 'free-run' wine was choice, stored to age; the pressed wine was set for stock trade; and the third pressed wine was 'sour' (*posca*). Flavourings, including honey, were common. Also, different wines were fortified and so made much stronger. This would produce a much tastier *posca* wine for the soldiers.

Soldier Life and Food preparation

In camp, the soldiers and their servants took the unprocessed raw materials and turned them into palatable meals. There were two meals a day, *prandium* (breakfast) and *cena* (dinner) in the evening. Young men, strong and active, have a great appetite. They don't require subtle or delicate flavours but without hearty meals of savoury and bold character, they are not pleased. Taking the raw grain, shelled and crushed, the cook made the dough into flat, thin cakes, and allowed them to sit for a morning or a day. Spread out on a hot flat rock sitting over a fire, the cakes were covered with cheese, bacon, vegetables, or sausage. This is a sort of Bannock bread. Using an iron plate, the cooks made a type of flat bread, with meat, cheese, or vegetables. Meat roasted in religious ceremonies or salted for storage also added to meals. Each 'tent-full' was responsible for providing their own meals; this did not mean they could not cooperate together. Some tents had men who cooked very well, others had flavours and unusual ingredients; tent mates and comrades ate together, enjoying each other's company.

On the march, food was simple and eaten quickly, 'hardtack' biscuits and sour wine. The biscuits were mass produced and stored in supply camps, passed out to soldiers at the beginning of the march, a supply following in wagons as the legions advanced. At the end of each day's march, most soldiers would construct the new camp, other soldiers and their servants set about cooking the evening's food. Breaking up the biscuits into bits, soaking them in water and a little wine and adding tidbits of vegetables and preserved meat, they prepared a quick stew. No doubt, hunks of cheese and tasty morsels appeared at dinner along with a bit of strong drink.

Along with food and companionship in camp, we need to remember that Classical civilization was addicted to music. As far as actual remains of the sound of Greco-Roman music, we have very little. But all those poems, prayers, and acclamations we find in Classical literature were sung. Song and, as night followed day, dance was important in the lives of the ancient Greeks and Romans. We can picture Roman soldiers spending their evenings singing both happy raucous songs and deeply devout hymns as individuals with an audience or as choirs. We can imagine a camp in evening, the men, tired and well fed, all a little intoxicated, dancing in circles around fires in quick, complex steps, singing songs of accomplishment, poems to love and desires.

Supply Trains

Soldiers' lives revolved around their camps. On the march, camp life was spartan and simple. In reality, most of the soldiers' career was spent in base camps which were actually mobile towns. Like all towns, a large amount of food stuffs, animal feed, and fuel arrived every day. A large settlement sat outside the camp's fortifications housing as many or more people than were in the legion. Here were the tents, huts, and houses of retired soldiers and their families, hostages with their retinues, and slave dealers with their stocks. Nearby stood the warehouses of sutlers (*lixae*) and paddocks of animal breeders.

The camp and its surroundings formed a collection point for supplies coming in from the countryside. When a legion marched off, the men carried supplies for a number of days. Each man needed some three pounds of food a day, minimum. If the legion was marching to another camp, they could travel light. Otherwise, not many days behind, a wagon train had to follow, bringing sacks of food, oil, and fodder. If we consider three pounds a day typical (it was probably more) and a legion at full strength of 5,000 people (usually, it was less), we are talking about seven and a half tons of food a day. Given say, 500 pounds per wagon, that is fifteen wagon loads a day to feed the legion at a minimum. Add cavalry and pack animals, and the number easily doubles. So, for a month's worth of supplies, we see 450 wagon loads, per legion. And that does not include the food to feed the men and animals transporting the goods.

More important than food was water. Men can starve for a while; thirst puts them out of action within a few days. Leather sacks, small and large were used to transport water but in hot dry weather, they emptied quickly. Lines of march had to follow water courses or dig wells at each stop. Roman engineers were expert at well digging, finding locations for wells, and digging them deep. Still, there were places without enough water and there, whole legions did not march.

In the late Republic, local authorities maintained base camps at strategic points through their territories. They collected taxes in kind and kept the warehouses full. Still, a marching army was a collection of hungry young men, looking for a meal and entertainment. Roman citizens were hard pressed when the army crossed their path, we can only imagine what happened to subject peoples. And, even if the army officers could maintain discipline, their passage was as if they were swarms of locusts.

Logistics Management

Man-management is an art, but the management of labour and material is a science, and no inexperienced youth was going to be able to handle the job. The legate depended on an older experienced man, the *quaestor*, who was responsible for supplying the soldiers, paying the man, moving the impedimenta, and making sure the legion had horseshoes, spades, swords, cooking pots, and tents, rope, etc. The *quaestor* handled the cash boxes, bookkeeping, auditing, accounting for revenue and expenses, complete with contracts, receipts, and debts. Since he handled the affairs of up to 5,000 fighting men along with dealing with the mob of camp followers, he needed a large staff. Slaves and freedmen served this purpose well along with a few friends. This was clearly a business in itself.

If the legion was on detached duty such as a garrison, the legion's *quaestor* collected the provisions, most often in conjunction with the local civil authorities. Large field armies of more than two or three legions were under a commander-in-chief, a great nobleman and political heavyweight. He brought his own *quaestor*, someone he knew and trusted. He also brought his own bookkeepers and auditors. The *quaestor* was deeply involved in soldiers' pay as well as supplies because both rested on the same figures, how many mouths are there to feed and hands wanting money. Caesar used experienced businessmen to act as his chiefs of supply and rewarded them well.

The Commanders

The commander-in-chief of a Roman army in the late Republic held the office of consul or proconsul; he was the *dux belli* with almost unlimited powers of peace or war, of managing legions of citizens and auxiliary troops. He appointed, with senate approval, if possible, a legate to command a legion. Under the legate, there were six military tribunes, who acted as the legate's staff, assistants, and overseers of the management of cohorts, centuries, and tent-fulls. The military tribunes helped hold the legion together. The legate and military tribunes were young Roman aristocrats, the sons of rich landholders or of successful businessmen. We should not think of these young noblemen as effete or uninterested in their position.

Roman education for their male children separated out those who did not have the abilities and aptitude for fighting or command. Those who were not right for the hard tasks of war found themselves in priesthoods or as takers of omens. For those who had the capacity for exercising power, the army was the place to start. These young men learned how to handle slaves and underlings by gaining their affection along with delivering punishments, inducing them to work hard and with diligence. Man-management of slaves is hard, with just the right balance of carrot and stick, a skill that has no general rule but depends on each individual on both sides of the equation. To deal with proud Roman citizen professional soldiers was even more difficult, which is why Roman aristocrats thought this type of military duty was important for their ambitious young men. The six military tribunes were at the start of their political careers, they needed to figure out how best they could handle the myriad problems of thousands of obstreperous fighting men. If they didn't learn how to do the job, back to Rome they went and received some obscure priesthood.

Caesar as Commander

In organization and supplies, Caesar's armies were similar to other Roman armies of his time. Leadership made the difference between his army and those of his opponents. Caesar was an excellent tactician. The purpose of armies and combat was victory and the way an army won was by killing their enemies. He inculcated this idea in his subordinate commanders, his centurions, and his soldiers. He trained his men in the skills which produced large numbers of dead enemies. Each man had to have mastery of his weapons and the skill to kill. The manoeuvres of his centuries, of his cohorts, and legions were optimized to bring the enemy into the range of his men's weapons. Then they killed without mercy. Caesar's strategy was simple: where is the enemy? How do I get to him? Whatever miscalculations or errors of judgment he made – and he made a lot of them – were corrected by the killing spirit of his troops. Of course, commanding a large body of trained killers was tricky. Powerful violent men want what they want. Caesar had no problem with that. He paid them well and let them have their fun. Plunder, rape, murder; well, that was tough for their playmates.

Caesar's accounts of his campaigns clearly describe his tactical methods. Studied and taught since their appearance, they describe how Caesar won his wars. Analysing Caesar's campaigns through the lens of modern tactical thought shows how Caesar mastered military art. The author of *On Tactics, A Theory of Victory in Battle*: Naval Institute Press, 2017, B.A. Friedman, US Marine Corps, compiled a list of eight tactical tenets. All are consistent with Caesar's operations.

1. Manoeuvre was integral to Caesar's tactics. His army was almost always in motion. Except for the campaign in Epirus, where he put Pompey's army under siege, Caesar kept his men in motion.
2. Mass, Caesar often marched with his forces separated but he always fought united. He did not need to outnumber his enemies as long as his troopers had the mass at the point of contact in order to shatter their line.
3. Firepower, Caesar made sure his soldiers were well supplied with their heavy pilums. Just before the battle lines collided, his soldiers halted and threw a barrage of their heavy spears to strike the enemy just before his soldiers charged their enemies at the sword's point.
4. Tempo, timing of operations, and within operations was always critical. When to move, to attack, to withdraw, all needed to be quicker than the enemy, to anticipate his moves and to move when he did not anticipate.
5. Deception, Caesar used spies, lies, and feint manoeuvres to keep everyone guessing; at times, he alone knew what he intended to do and not only his army, but his staff were unaware of his objectives.

6. Surprise, Caesar's enemy faced a confusing cloud of misinformation and fragmentary sightings of his actions. When he was ready; when he had massed his forces; there he was, ready for battle.
7. Confusion was Caesar's enemy in his own operations and his friend when inflicted on his enemies. His orders were clear, his subordinates followed them, and his soldiers obeyed their officers.
8. Shock: Caesar's main tactic in battle was to shock the enemy army so hard that it disintegrated. He accomplished this in many ways; his soldiers were well trained and practised in lethal skills; he organized them into groups which willingly supported each other, competing in the killing arts; rewards for success were generously given and allowed and prosperous retirement was promised.
9. Moral cohesion, this is probably the single most important quality for which Caesar strove. Victory will hold any army together. Keeping the army together in reverses and defeat is necessary to a winning force. Caesar was hardly perfect. He made many mistakes, but his armies' cohesion saved many times and his ability to develop new more successful operations rewarded his soldiers faith in him.

This is not to say Caesar ran perfect campaigns; he did not. While his overall strategic vision was excellent, his plans of operations often led him into deep trouble. The worst move he made was trying to trap and besiege Pompey's forces in Epirus. The Emperor Napoleon I pointed out that this was a rash move in the extreme and the resulting failure of Caesar's lines was only surprising in that it took so long for Pompey to try to break out. Pompey's attack by sea and land was well done and smashed Caesar's operational set up, leaving his army shattered, without supplies. Caesar, of course, mentions little of the resulting predicament because he was too busy to sit and compose notes just as he neglected to record his defeat in his effort to take Dyrrachium. Because of the trust and faith his soldiers had in him, he managed to recover from the debacle. But his end was close at hand if his efforts failed.

This was the worst miscalculation in Caesar's civil wars but the mess in Alexandria was almost as bad. Coming to Egypt in order to capture Pompey, Caesar found himself embroiled and then trapped in Alexandria for months. He managed to turn the tables on the Egyptians, but it was a close-run thing. Caesar's ability to escape from bad positions was remarkable. Then again, he believed he was on a divine mission to reform the Roman state.

Caesar Master of War

Caesar taught himself the art of war in Gaul. After his experiences as propraetor in Spain, he had an idea of where he wanted to go with his soldiers. It was his campaigns in Gaul that gave him a master course in combat. He did not do this alone. When he went to Gaul, besides a strong military staff, Caesar brought a number of successful businessmen who were expert in buying and shipping materials. These people worked with Caesar's *quaestors* ensuring supplies for his soldiers. As his campaigns continued in Gaul year after year, Caesar and his logistics teams developed efficient practices in material management. We need to understand that Caesar's actions collecting supplies were a great cost to communities from which the supplies came. Caesar was far more interested in providing for his army and paying them than worrying about villagers.

Appendix V

Warships in Caesar's Time

Sea Power in Caesar's Civil Wars

The Romans were well aware of the practices involved in the exercise of sea power. As Caesar's civil war brewed up, both he and Pompey prepared fleets for combat. The ships upon which power rested followed designs originated and improved centuries before. Everyone concerned about sea war knew each type of ship and its capabilities. The basic strategy of sea power at this time was to block the movement of men and supplies into important ports. To stop ships leaving a port in small numbers was impossible and it was hard to bottle up a fleet, but stopping a fleet from entering a port by forcing it into battle was well within possibility.

The tactics of sea war were limited by the ships' capacities for manoeuvre and sea worthiness. In some ways the ships were exceedingly well suited to battle, yet they had weaknesses. They could carry hundreds of men, large projector machines, and use themselves as rams, yet they could stay at sea only for a limited time and even inclement weather made them dangerous for their own crews. The first action of a war fleet was to find a base where the ships could land so their crews could collect water and food. This base also needed to provide protection from storms. A harbour in a port was the best place to stay but a sea commander could improvise a temporary place to stay on a uninhabited section of coast.

Romans classed their ships by purpose and propulsion method. Cargo ships were large with a small crew, moved under sail, and used boats to pull into port. They could stay at sea for many days as they sailed along coasts. Warships were known by the number of men in a vertical line who rowed the ship. The smallest was called a bireme, having two men on a oar or one man with an oar above a second man with an oar. Next was the trireme with three men in a vertical row, one at the bottom, a second above him, and the third, sitting in an outrigger above and out from the second. Then came the quadrireme, two banks of oars with two men per oar, followed by the quinquereme, perhaps one row of three and one of two rowers. These were the main large warships. There were others, sevens and so forth but these were not used in Caesar's Civil Wars.

After the Bronze Age collapse (about 1200 BC) and the emergence of Iron Age society in the eastern Mediterranean, seafaring slowly recovered in the form of trade, piracy, and colonization. 'Round' ships carried merchandise and armed 'long' ships carried warriors. Phoenicians, Greeks, and Saite Egyptians sailed across the Mediterranean. By 600 BC, there was a main type of warship which the Greeks called the penteconter. The word indicates fifty oared; modern experts describe an oar-propelled ship with two banks of oars on a side: twelve on the deck and eleven below in the hold. These were warships, used in attack and defence. Besides the power of the fighting men on the ships, which included the rowers, penteconters used rams to breach their opponents' hulls.

A large battle took place in the Tyrrhenian Sea about 535 BC between the Phokaian Greeks, who were escaping Persian domination, with Carthaginian and Etruscan fleets. In this battle of Alalia, the Phokaians defeated the much larger allied fleets using ramming tactics. The success of rams to break into the hold of an enemy's ship provided the impetus for adding a third rank of rowers. When this third rank emerged is difficult to say; there are representations of possible three-banked Phoenician ships in Assyrian palace sculptures from around 700 BC. But, as H.T. Wallinga points out in *Ships and Sea Power Before the Great Persian War*, the trireme appears as a major force at the time of the Persian Cambyses' conquest of Egypt (525 BC).

Soon we hear of large Persian fleets of triremes sailing in the Aegean Sea, manned by Phoenicians, Egyptians, and Greeks but under Persian royal command. Thenceforth, triremes are the warships of choice in Mediterranean Sea fights until the wars of Alexander's successors. However, there were other designs. The Carthaginians developed the *quadriremes*, probably a large ship with two banks of oars with two men to an oar. Dionysius I of Syracuse (r. 405-367 BC) generated the *quinquereme*, (three banks of oars, two oars with two men, one oar with one man?); followed by Dionysius II of Syracuse (r. 367-357; 346-344) use of *hexaremes* – 'sixes'. When Alexander's commanders began fighting for mastery, new ship designs proliferated, accompanying but not displacing triremes.

Ship Construction

The problem facing the warship designers, then and now, is the ideal calculation of speed and sturdiness. A heavy ship can be very hardy but slow; a fast ship needs to be light but that means the ship is delicate. The trireme was used in the Mediterranean from the 520s BC to Constantine's war with Licinius in 324 AD, when we hear of three Athenian triremes coming to the support of Constantine's fleet. That is about 850 years. In that time, shipbuilders tried many different ways of putting the ship together and adjusted designs as they learned more about seamanship. The triremes used in the Persian invasion of Egypt and those used by the Athenians in the Peloponnesian War were quite different from Hellenistic and Roman triremes by the simple exercise of building and rebuilding the ships over decades and centuries of experiences.

The trireme's structure was the result of taking a long pentenconter and constructing an outrigger above the top row of oars and so building another row of seats for oarsmen. The Greeks called this structure, *parexeiresia* (a place that sits besides), and this turns a long pentenconter into a trireme. Different triremes were built to suit different purposes; some were fast and very light, others were heavier and made for ship-to-ship combat, still others were fitted out to carry horses and supplies.

All were constructed along similar lines (Morrison and Coates, *The Athenian Trireme*, gives an excellent account). An oak keel for support when the ship was drawn up on shore, formed the basis on which the hull, boards bent and fitted together with mortise and tenon joints, made a smooth outer surface. A light wood was used, from pine or fir trees. The builders made the internal fixtures, such as the ribs giving strength to the hull and the seats for the oarsmen, out of mulberry or elm. A thick cable ran the length of the ship which the crew could tighten to pull the ship's structure together providing rigidity. They coated the whole exterior with pitch, to fill joints and protect the wood from rot and sea worm. Masts and yards made from pine or fir trees with sails of papyrus or linen propelled the ship with the wind. Oars made from young fir trees pushed the ship about when rowed.

Crew

The oared Classical warship moved by muscle power. The Athenian trireme had 170 oarsmen. Each man had an oar and a seat; the three men above each other had to work in unison and each group of three in the ship had to row in time with each other. As Morrison and Coates relate when the reconstructed trireme, *Olympias*, rowed into the sea, this was harder than the ancient texts might indicate. In a ship about 115 feet long, with 170 rowers pulling oars, giving orders, and keeping time was difficult. The *Olympias* used a loudspeaker system, something beyond Thucydides' understanding. But obviously the ancient Greeks had effective means of keeping their rowers in time. The *Olympias*' directors did work with whistles (pipes?) and tried to communicate with the rowers by having two rowing masters across the ship communicating by visual signals.

This is all too complex for an ancient class of warships. Looking at films of the *Olympias* under oar, it is clear that the rowers are wrong. Young college-age folks are too healthy, too intelligent, and too eager to make good long-term oarsmen. Their rowing discipline is not good. Yes, they tried really hard, but they simply miss the mindset of poor, farm raised, hard working men almost on the point of real poverty. In the ancient ship, discipline was harsh at the best of times and without exact timing and coordination, the ship and crew were in danger. The files of three men policed themselves and if not, the crew was happy to help out. The crew wanted their drachma a day and to keep themselves safe.

The rowing crew was managed by a rowing master and his assistants. He gave the orders to start, stop, turn, speed up and slow down. Exactly how he gave his orders is unclear, perhaps some sort of visual signalling method because the crew of the *Olympias* at the bow or stern could not hear spoken or sounded orders from a director situated in the middle of the ship. Timing for the oar strokes proved difficult to achieve but the young adults pushing the oars on the *Olympias* had little practice keeping time, given popular music styles. The ancient Greeks, however, practised group dancing. Dancers usually do not sing but they run through the music in the head as they move to the tune. Members of the crew not at oars could easily sing or hum the music while the rowers followed the music like a dancer. (The author of the chapter on the *Olympias*' sea trials made the comment, 'there is no clear evidence that the ancient Greeks ever hummed in our sense' but equally, there is no clear evidence that the sun rose every morning.) The *ryppapai* in Aristophanes' *Wasps*, as mentioned by the authors, worked well. Besides the rowers, Athenian triremes had a sail crew, normally about ten men who raised and lowered the sail and minded the rigging.

The main director of the ship's seagoing operations was the man at the helm; his place was in the stern, handling the double rudders. He commanded the ship's crew; under him, five officers were responsible for communicating his directions for the working of the ship. There was the officer in the bow who made sure the helmsman's directions passed to the people in the bow area; the rowing master saw to the oarsmen; an executive officer managed the wages and costs of the ship; and a shipwright saw to the physical structures. Besides the ship's crew, there were fighting men included in the ship's company: ten *epibatai*, elite solders, and four archers. The archers' task was protecting the helmsman and the soldiers protected the ship. These numbers are an ideal case, each ship might be a little different. The Athenian trireme carried some 200 men and was a formidable, well trained fighting machine.

Caesar's Fleets

Caesar's civil war started without much warning. Crisis was often the cry in Roman political disputes but for years these ended in some minor occurrence, a riot or minor blood bath. Only when Caesar began marching into Italy did anyone understand that this was not just another manoeuvre by a faction, rather war was at hand. There was no time to construct new fleets of ships; the war would start with what was in the harbours. The question became, who was able to grab the most. Pompey, once he went east, had the advantage with the Syrian and Egyptian fleets at hand. However, these did not threaten Caesar because, after the taking of Italy, he marched west. The ships toward which the civil war sailors looked were of three types: triremes, quadriremes and quinqueremes.

A quadrireme was a heavy ship, not fast; rather with its weight and oar thrust, it generated strong momentum which allowed it to ram enemies without suffering damage to itself. With a broad deck, it carried wooden turrets armed with projector machines and a larger contingent of marines than the smaller and lighter triremes. Next came the quinqueremes which were larger than the quadriremes, and so heavier with more men. There was another class of warship, with the outrigger strengthened to allow a second oarsmen, thus making a 'six' but these were not used in this civil war's battles.

Sea battles during the late Republic were fought by amateurs who had little experience handling ships in battle. The rowing masters knew how to handle the oars and the helmsmen knew how to handle the ships; exactly how to manoeuvre them in battle was the problem. Following the battle narratives, fleet management appeared centred on keeping ships together in some sort of mass. Single ships, most often triremes, executed complex manoeuvres now and again, but fleet actions depended on luck, weight, and marines' fighting skills.

Sea Battles

During the third century BC, in Hellenistic times, Philo of Byzantium compiled a manual of military and engineering methods. Much of his material came from Alexandria, during the reigns of Ptolemy II and III.

His section on naval warfare is particularly pertinent to the battles Caesar's forces fought. The following is a summary of Philo's description of how to defend a besieged town from a naval attack.

> *'If a stronger enemy approaches your fortified town from the sea, sail out to meet him. Collect your best fighting men on your largest and strongest ships, ordering them to defend their ship and not try to board the enemy's ships. Sail toward the enemy's fleet in a crescent formation: fast attack ships and light boats stay on the two wings ahead of the main body; armoured ships and cargo ships collect in the centre, defending the access to the town's harbour. As the enemy approaches, shoot fire missiles at his ships and rain arrows on his crews and soldiers. Repel any attempt to board your ships but ram and set afire the enemy's ships. When you have repelled the enemy's attack, concentrate your fleet around your heavy ships and advance against his fleet. Attack the enemy, forcing him to flee and then send ships to shatter the steering oars and break up the rowers' oars.'*

Caesar's sea commanders followed these tactics, knowing of them either directly or more probably indirectly from a common source.

Appendix VI

Projector Machines in the Late Republic

Missile Shooting Mechanism

In the accounts of combat in the Ancient Greek and Roman world, we hear about missiles, both large arrows and heavy stones, flying through the air and striking targets with effect. These missiles are thrown from machines worked by crews. While archaeologists have never found any of these devices intact, bits and pieces have been recovered and there are representations in carved pictures of military actions. Most important, however, are a small number of treatises which describe the construction of these machines, some even having diagrams.

There remain four works describing the projector engines. The most important is Heron of Alexandria's *War Machines*, written during the late first century AD. Heron compiled information about mathematics, mechanics, and pneumatics from many sources. His *War Machines* evidently rests on the work of Ctesibius, a mechanic who worked under Ptolemy I and II. While Heron described some projectors which are simply large bows set in framework often mounted on stands which shot large arrows, he went on with an account of torsion engines; large structures, shooting either great bolt-like arrows or stones. These mechanisms were powered by twisted springs of hair holding shafts on either side which when released, sling forward with great force.

Second, Biton of Pergamum (ca. 240 BC) wrote an artificer's manual, a concise collection of instructions and measurements. He describes both 'big-bow' models and torsion machines. Then, Philon of Byzantium wrote about a generation after Biton; he gives the dimensions for arrow and stone-throwing engines, with formulae for establishing size of projectile in relation to size of torsion spring, along with discussion of faults in some machines and suggestions for innovations to improve the weapons. The fourth writer was the famous architect, Vitruvius, who worked with both Julius Caesar and his heir, the later Augustus. In his *De Architectura*, he devotes book X to machines, including two sections on projector machines. Like Biton, they tend toward practical construction designs rather than full descriptions.

In the texts of Herodotus and Thucydides, we hear about arrows and spears but no mention of projector engines. In the compilations of Diodorus of Sicily, we catch echoes from Philistus, a friend and historian of Dionysius I, ruler of Syracuse. Philistus wrote a series of books relating the wars of Dionysius at the beginning of the third century. In 399 BC, Dionysius called to his city many skilled artisans and designers to build weapons for the wars he intended. He paid them well. Diodorus states, 'In fact, the catapult was invented at this time in Syracuse since the ablest skilled workmen had been gathered from everywhere into one place.' (Diodorus of Sicily, XIV, 42.1) Understanding that Diodorus' source was Philistus, we may presume the clear statement came from Philistus. (Marsden *Greek and Roman Artillery, Historical Development*, pp. 49-50)

Diodorus uses the Greek word for catapult in his text and I suspect his source wanted to say that this invention was something special. Still, the earliest securely dated references to the torsion engines include the fragments of a comic play about Philip II of Macedonia by Mnesimachus; Aristotle's *Athenian Constitution* which describes young citizen soldiers being trained in the operation of catapults; and the accounts of Alexander's campaigns include catapults in both the Macedonian and Persian Greek forces. By the death of Alexander, torsion projector machines were widespread.

These authors tell us that initially, someone developed a large bow, attached it to a framework with a sliding arrow holder which allowed the archer to rest the slider end on the ground. Using the weight of his body, the operator pushed the slider, thus pulling the bow string back, locking the slider into place. Then the operator released the bow string with a trigger of sorts. This was called a *gastraphetes* 'belly shooter'. Later, someone attached a ratchet to the frame holding the slider and produced an early cross-bow. Briton tells us that Zopyrus of Tarentum improved the 'big bow' by setting it on a stand and served the weapon with a crew, who could pivot the weapon side to side and up or down.

The Torsion Engine

Fabricators could make bows only so big. By developing the double torsion springs, the 'big bow' machine became the catapult projector, a far more powerful launch platform. The first torsion projectors shot arrows: *katapelti oxybeleis*, (catapults for sharp missiles) perhaps developed under Philip II of Macedonia; then Alexander's engineers produced *katapelti petroboloi* (catapults for rocks). Within about thirty years, Demetrius Poliorcetes was shooting three talent stones (180 lbs) from large machines. By 280 BC, an engineer, Ctesibius, working in Alexandria generated formulae which calibrated the size of spring, structure, and missiles to produce the most effective mechanisms.

The torsion engine was a wooden structure reinforced at weak points with bronze connectors. Two sinew rope springs, each in a box-like structure sat side by side with the projectile throw-way between them. Solid bronze bushings held the spring on top and bottom. On the extremity of each bushing, a bronze bar held the lengths of sinus ropes threaded through the bushing and over the bar and back through the other bushing and around its bar. Once the area within the bushing was filled with rope, the operator, using a bronze wrench-like tool, twisted one of the bronze bars until the rope was taunt. Then, as he twisted the bar further, the rope contracted and tightened up. With two arms inserted into the two twisted rope springs and connected by a heavy bow string, the machine became a large crossbow with a much more powerful 'bow'.

Machine builders had to reinforce all the parts because the repeated shootings severely shook the machine. Once the projector was placed and sprung, the operator consulted a table which showed the relationship between the projectile weight, the diameter of the bushings, and the distance the projectile would travel. Then, given the projectile's weight, the crew director could aim and elevate the machine to hit his target. After each shot he could adjust his aim.

With use, the spring stretched and weakened. For quite a number of shots, simply turning the bushings hold the spring ropes would keep the projector going but eventually, the rope frayed. Of course, a competent engineer would have a number of spring boxes ready to go and simply replace the boxes with worn out springs off the framework and replace them with new springs. This was a swift and simple process.

Appendix VII

A Short History of the Roman Republic to Caesar's Civil War

The city of Rome had kings at first. L. Brutus established liberty and the consuls. Dictators lasted only briefly nor did the rule of the ten men last more than two years. Neither Cinna, nor Sulla dominate for long. Both Pompey and Crassus lost to Caesar; Lepidus and Antony fell to the arms of Augustus who, during civil disruptions under the title of first citizen, accepted supreme power.
(Tacitus, *Ab Excessu Divi Augusti*, 1.1)

Tacitus' opening words for his history *From the Death of the Divine Augustus* gives a short account of the Roman Republic. For more than four centuries, the Romans managed their affairs through discussion and deliberation in a series of interconnected institutions they called *res publicae* or 'matters of the people'. Our earliest detailed description of the government of the Roman People comes to us as a large fragment of Polybius' *History*. He describes a well-run state with firm social distinctions, the orders of Roman society, as they were known. While the distinctions were solid, people could pass through them, leaving one order and entering another. The quality which determined which order one was in rested on a mixture of heredity and wealth.

We always must remember the states around the Mediterranean during the Classical age were designed to serve the transcendent powers which were beyond human capacities. The deities of earth and sky, the forces of life and death, and the fertile powers of growth and prosperity were at the centre of state functions. Aristocrats were the best because they descended from the gods. The commoners were common because they grew out of the soil. In between were people who held the favour of the divine to one degree or another. At the bottom were the scum of the earth, living only to serve their betters. This was not mere theory; it was an accepted fact.

Crises Begin to Weaken the Republic

Polybius' *History* runs to 146 BC. The Roman state was still successful and expanding Roman territory at his conclusion. Cracks in the state structure begin to appear with the eruption of the First Servile War in Sicily (135-132 BC). Once the Carthaginian threat was removed from Sicily after the Second Punic War, Roman land speculators bought many tracts of land, organized large estates and marketed them to rich Roman *equites* looking for profitable investments. The Roman victories over Macedonia, Syria, and Greece brought masses of slaves on the market. The Sicilian estate owners bought up slaves for minimal amounts and worked them to death. Slaves were so plentiful, owners found replacing them was cheaper than caring for them. They worked in chains during the day and slept in underground pits. In 135 BC, the slaves in Sicily revolted, killing plantation managers and owners, taking, and sacking towns. The slaves established a state under a king and organized an army of about 70,000 men. After defeating local authorities, the slave kingdom survived an attack by a regular Roman army led by a consul. Finally, in 132, after he crushed the disturbance in Rome, the consul Publius Rupilius smashed the revolt, crucifying some 20,000 prisoners.

This disturbance in Rome was a result of the slave revolt. Tiberius Gracchus, an aristocrat, ran for the office of tribune on a platform of reform. Many of the great slave holding estates were set up on *ager publicus*, land owned by the Roman state and seized years before from enemy states who were now Roman allies. By paying a nominal fee, estate owners acquired large tracts of land upon which they organized large scale slave agricultural businesses. This had spread throughout much of Italy as well as Sicily. Gracchus connected this growth of slave estates to the decline of traditional family farms of Roman citizens from which Rome had drawn her soldiers. Now, he pointed out, there was a shortage of soldiers as well as a large population of Roman citizens who owned nothing but their names on the citizenship rolls, the proletariat. Just recently, an eastern potentate, the king of Pergamum had willed his state, large and rich to the Roman state. Gracchus proposed to use the wealth from Pergamum to finance his land reforms.

Gracchus proposed the voiding of the leases and the dividing up and redistribution of the estate lands into small farms and granting those farms to those citizens who had no property. Many aristocrats and rich commoners strongly opposed Gracchus' efforts. Not to be thwarted, Gracchus brought his proposal before the Plebeian assembly, but another tribune, Marcus Octavius, vetoed the proposal. Gracchus appealed the veto to the Plebeian assembly on the grounds that a tribune who worked against the welfare of the People ought to be removed. This was done and the proposal was made into law. The opposition, however, claimed this was unconstitutional because it would give final power to a temporary assembly. The issue came to a head when Tiberius Gracchus ran for re-election. A mob formed which slaughtered Tiberius and 300 of his followers. This was the disturbance in which Publius Rupilius was involved.

It was the first time in memory that legitimate violence was used to settle a political dispute. The senatorial interests believed they had put an end to popular radical efforts to gain power. But ten years later in 123 BC, Tiberius' brother Gaius Gracchus became a tribune. His main objective was to eliminate the extraordinary powers the senators used to legitimize their use of force as a constitutional action. He proposed and saw passed the laws in the Plebeian assembly. As a further reform, he proposed Rome's Italian allies become Roman Citizens. He ran for a third term in 121 but was defeated because his sponsorship of the allies was very unpopular. A huge riot broke out; a mob killed Gaius Gracchus and some 3,000 of his supporters. The administration established a land commission which divided up some estates on the *ager publicus*, giving the lease holders compensation; many families settled newly created farms. The immediate problems were ended but not solved. The Republic muddled through until new major issues arose starting in 113.

The Frontiers in Flames

The Roman lands around the Mediterranean were warm and fertile. To the north, tribes and clans fought for land and food. From the North Sea came the Cimbri, moving south toward the sun and sea. In 113 BC, the Cimbri reached the Danube in Noricum, threatening the Taurisci who requested help from Rome. The next year a Roman consular army arrived in Noricum and ordered the Cimbri to depart. Instead, the Cimbri defeated and destroyed the Roman army. The Cimbri seemed about to threaten Italy, instead they marched around the Alps into Gaul. In 109, they invaded the new province of Gallia Narbonensis, defeating the local Roman force; in 107, the Romans lost a consular army along with the commanding consul in Gaul.

While the northern frontiers of the Republic burned, on the southern shores of the Mediterranean in the Kingdom of Numidia another challenge to the Republic emerged. When the Numidian king died, he divided his land between three sons and the Romans were to guarantee the settlement. One of the sons, Jugurtha wanted the whole kingdom. In 111 BC, claiming that Jugurtha bribed the commissioners sent to enforce settlement, the tribune Gaius Memmius pushed the assembly into declaring war on Jugurtha. The Romans sent a number of armies to set Jugurtha to right, but between bribes and defeats, they accomplished nothing. Finally, in 109, the senate appointed the plebeian noble, Quintus Metellus as commander in Africa and Metellus chose the former tribune and senior army commander, Gaius Marius as his subordinate. In Africa, Metellus and Publius Rutilius Rufus (a noted disciplinarian and strategist) put the army through retraining, imposing strict discipline.

The Roman army fought well enough and boxed Jugurtha into corners a number of times, but Jugurtha proved very adept at manoeuvre and counter-attack. As the war dragged on, politics in Rome heated up. The tribal assembly, in 107, removed Metellus from command, replacing him with Marius. Even though the assembly usurped the senate's prerogative in this matter, the senators accepted the decision. When, in the same year, Marius returned to Rome, he won election to consul. Collecting a staff, he quickly returned to Africa and immediately renewed the war, with his *quaestor* Lucius Cornelius Sulla as second in command. After hard fighting, Marius defeated Jugurtha's armies but could not stamp out Jugurtha' guerrilla force. Working together with Sulla, Marius detached many of Jugurtha's supporters with bribes and had them deliver the king to him. The war ended.

The northern tribes, however, continued to cause trouble. The new consuls of 105 decided to crush the Cimbri and their allies. Gathering a huge army of 80,000 fighting men, strongly supported with supplies, the two consuls marched their separate ways into total defeat. Rome was open to the enemy. The enemy did not march straight to Rome, seeing the Romans as a broken power. Rather the Cimbri advanced deeper into Gaul, fighting and plundering while their allies consolidated the lands they had already won.

The Ascendancy of Marius

The terror caused by the march of the Cimbri toward Rome shocked the senate and people. In desperation, they proclaimed an emergency and chose Marius as consul for 104, without the ten-year interval as normal. Further, they elected Marius consul each year following for a total of five years. Marius was going to build a new Roman army, well trained, and effective. Up to this time, the Romans conscripted their soldiers from landowners who had to supply their own weapons and armour. As the Gracchi pointed out, the base from which this force drew had shrunk. Many of the conscripts were not the best material, their weapons were obsolete, nor were many interested in fighting. Marius changed all this.

The major change Marius brought was ending conscription and replacing it with a voluntary system which allowed young men of the *capite censi*, those with no property other than their names on the citizen roles (proletariat), to join the army and receive pay for their service. He standardized training and discipline, equipment and weapons, leadership, and supplies. Previously, the main tactical unit was the maniple, two centuries of eighty soldiers joined together. Marius joined together six centuries into a cohort as the primary manoeuvre unit. With eighty men in a century, this was a united force of 480 soldiers, allowing field commanders a more concentrated punch. Ten cohorts made a legion. Each century, each cohort, each legion had its own symbol and identity, all collecting around the aquila, the eagle of the legion. The army received the volunteers and if accepted the new soldier was to serve for many years. When he was released, he would receive land or money to set himself up on his own.

Marius created a standing professional army. Before, legions formed under the command of the consuls and those appointed by him. They were numbered as first, second, third, sometimes fourth legions and the next consuls could disband them and organize new legions. Now, the legions stayed in existence, and had an identity of its own. And while each year had two new consuls, the legions often stayed as standing troops year after year. The legionary became a fixture of the Late Republic.

While Marius and his staff hurried the organization and training of their new army, the Cimbri, moved off through Gaul into Spain. Turning about, they gathered many allied tribes and moved toward Italy. Marius was ready. In 102, during a complex campaign, his Roman army defeated the tribal allies, one at a time. By the end of the year, only the Cimbri remained. The next year the tribe outmanoeuvred a defending force and reached the Po. Marius marched to them and destroyed them. After his great victory, Marius was unrivalled in Rome, consul in command of his new victorious legions. Following his victory, Marius proposed to grant Roman citizenship to the Italian allies' legions, saying in the middle of combat, he could not tell who was a citizen or Italian.

Marius was elected consul in 107, 104, 103, 102, 101, and 100; his eminence was overwhelming. His political power, however, rested on the assembly and many senators were suspicious of his ambitions. The traditional Roman fear of over-powerful citizens concerned many citizens. The Cimbri War raised a number of popular officers, among them Cornelius Sulla, a patrician without an estate. Roman politics revolved around the rivalry between the assembly and senate on many issues but most incendiary was the question whether the Romans should allow their Italian allies to have citizenship.

Leaders in both the assembly and the senate were at odds with one another over the citizenship question, as were the leaders of the allied states. The alternative to Roman citizenship, establishing a state of Italy independent from Rome, appealed to many. The Romans dithered year after year. In

91, many Italian towns renounced their alliances with Rome and began to construct a new state, Italy. The Romans saw these actions as rebellion and launched a bitter war to crush those towns. This was the Social War or war against the allies (*socii*). At the same time, other towns stayed in the Roman alliance and the Romans granted citizenship to the citizens of the loyal towns. The war was bloody. The Romans achieved victory in 87; the result, however, was that the citizen population in all the Italian towns became Roman citizens, some 500,000 Italians.

Wars and Civil Strife

News of the Cimbri wars, Jugurtha's victories, and the rebellion of Rome's Italian allies spread through the east. Roman power, seeming so solid for generations, now had begun to crumble, or so it seemed. Ambitious and coveting eyes saw great opportunities on the horizon. The commercial classes, in old Greece, along the coast of the Aegean Sea, and in Asia Minor had found Roman businessmen harsh and arrogant. On the sorth coast of the Black Sea, sat the kingdom of Pontus, ruled by an ancient Iranian dynasty. King of Pontus, Mithridates VI, decided the time had come for Roman dominance of the east to end. In 89, he picked a fight with the Bithynian king; because of the Social War, Rome had only two legions in the east and these marched to support the Bithynians. Mithridatates defeated and scattered them. The towns of Asia Minor opened their gates to the Pontic forces. Now, Mithridates decided, he could eliminate all the Romans in the east.

Choosing a date in the middle of the next year, Mithridates sent secret envoys to the towns in Greece and Asia Minor to inform them of the day when the local people would rise up and kill all the Roman businessmen, their families and servants. In truth, at that day's end, some 80,000 Romans and Italians were dead. Mithridates expanded his kingdom across the Aegean to include much of Greece, including Athens. When the news of the massacres reached Rome, both the assembly and the senate were horrified; that Roman families died was bad, that they were killed at the behest of an eastern despot was worse.

The Social War was winding down. At the head of the Roman army marched Cornelius Sulla. A former subordinate of Marius, Sulla was a successful and popular commander. He was elected one of the consuls for 88; he initiated laws capping interest payments and regulating debt collecting which were popular. The Republic turned to him to deal with Mithridates. Marius had put himself forward for the task, but Sulla was both younger and more popular with the young soldiers. At the same time, the Romans needed to bring a quick end to the Social War and granted citizenship to surrendered communities. Only Nola, inland from Mt. Vesuvius, refused to accept terms. Sulla planned to march to Nola, crush their rebellion, and then transfer his army east.

In Rome, while Sulla was still at Nola, his consular colleague, Q. P. Rufus, in agreement with Sulla, worked to stymie legislation designed to quickly organize the Italians into Roman citizenship. The tribune Sulpicius, with the support of Marius, began demonstrations which became riots. Sulla returned to Rome to quell the disturbances but found himself trapped by the mob and had to find refuge in Marius' house. There, he had to agree with tribune Sulpicius' legislation. After Sulla returned to Nola, Sulpicius called a meeting of the assembly to void Sulla's command over the army and appointed Marius instead. To confirm his legislation, he had the assembly remove senators from the senate until no business could be done because of the lack of a quorum. Violence broke out in the forum when some tried to lynch Sulpicius, and his bodyguard of gladiators killed some of them.

When the envoys came from Rome to announce the change of command, Sulla's soldiers stoned them. Sulla proclaimed an illegal faction had seized power in Rome acting in an unconstitutional manner. He took five of his six legions and marched on the city. The bands of gladiators Sulpicius and Marius employed to protect their power fled before Sulla's soldiers who then forced both Sulpicius and Marius to flee Rome. Sulla declared Marius was an enemy of Rome; Marius fled to Africa. A slave of Sulpicius turned him in; after killing Sulpicius, Sulla had the slave freed for locating an enemy of the state and then executed for disloyalty. Once he settled Roman politics to his satisfaction, Sulla departed for the east and Mithridates. This was the first time a Roman commander brought troops into Rome to solve a political problem. Everyone understood this was a bad precedent.

When he was sure Sulla was occupied with fighting Mithridates, Marius returned to Rome in late 87. He allied with a radical reformer, Cinna, and took control of the city. Both were elected consuls for 86, Marius for the seventh time. They declared Sulla's enactments void, condemned him to exile, and killed many of his supporters in Rome. Under the administration of Marius and Cinna, the two issued edicts having the force of law rather than legislating through the assembly. They also appointed magistrates to high office without bothering about elections. Marius died within a month of taking office; his son, Marius the younger, joined Cinna as leaders of the Republic. They sent an army under Flaccus to relieve Sulla of his command.

Word soon came to Sulla about all these matters. When Flaccus arrived, Sulla attempted to undermine his authority. Many of Flaccus' soldiers joined Sulla until Flaccus marched north to face Mithridates. Rather than continue the war against Mithridates to its conclusion, Sulla made a hurried compromise peace and turned toward Rome. When he reached southern Italy, many of his supporters came out of hiding and went to his camp. These included Marcus Crassus and Metellus Pius, each at the head of their own armies. Further north, Gnaeus Pompey raised three legions, defeated Marian forces in his area and marched into Sulla's camp where Asia hailed him as imperator. Sulla marched toward Rome facing the forces of the younger Marius. When he was defeated in a battle, Marius sent a message to Rome for his followers to kill Sulla's supporters. Senators and priests fell to the weapons of the Marians.

A general war broke out throughout Italy with Sulla's supporters defeating the Marian forces. Sulla marched toward Rome; after hard fighting in front of the Colline Gate, he marched into the city. Sulla's soldiers killed any Marian supporters they found and slaughtered all of the Marian surrendered soldiers, to the number of some 8,000. Sulla became dictator and reformed the Republic, weakening the powers of the tribunes and of the assembly and strengthening the senate. His reforms put the Republic solidly in the hands of the aristocrats. He died in 78, still powerful.

The Rise of Pompey

The defeat of the Marians in Italy did not end their efforts for regaining power. Pompey had put down the Marians in Africa, but significant numbers managed to flee Italy and Africa. They found refuge and built a base in the northwest part of Spain under Sertorius. More, while their own problems occupied the Romans, Mithridates again began expanding his power. Further, the social upheavals generated a climate of rebellion not lost on the large slave plantations in Italy. In 79, Pompey supported Marcus Lepidus for consul, believing he would fully support Sulla's reforms. Lepidus disappointed him, leading a movement to remove the reforms and weaken the senate. Pompey raised troops from his home district, crushed the movement and killed its leader, Marcus Brutus, father of the Marcus Brutus who helped kill Caesar.

The senate gave Pompey the task of hunting down and eliminating Sertorius in Spain. Raising legions for this campaign, Pompey fought in Spain for five years, organizing the Spanish communities for the Republic but holding them in his hand. In 71, the third great slave uprising hit southern Italy, under Spartacus' leadership. More than 120,000 slaves rebelled, building their own kingdom. Pompey marched from Spain and Marcus Crassus from Rome to crush the uprising. Crassus had defeated the most important slave forces by the time Pompey arrived.

Both powerful Roman leaders saw that Sulla's reforms had not settled the Republic's problems. Pompey and Crassus formed an alliance, and they were elected joint consuls for 70. They worked on updating the corn dole, restored some powers to the assembly, and kept the senate's influence in bounds. One problem which influenced all their problems still increased; the pirates in the Mediterranean aided Mithridates, brought help to the slave rebels, supported the Sectorians in Spain; all this along with plundering trade ships, kidnapping the rich, looting ports, and demanding protection money from everyone. Despite strong opposition, the Romans awarded Pompey extraordinary powers to deal with the pirates; he had 500 warships, oversight command of the whole of the Mediterranean, and of all land within fifty miles of the coast. He could commandeer what ever resources he needed. With a master plan, Pompey eliminated the serious threat in forty days.

The next year, 66, the Republic granted another extraordinary command to Pompey. He was to finish the Mithridatic Wars and settle the disputes among the lands of Asia Minor. Even since Sulla left the east to return to Rome, Mithridates had pressed against Roman restrictions on his power. Sulla had left a force in Asia Minor under Lucius Murena to kept Mithridates in check. In 83, he deemed Mithridates was not keeping the peace and attacked. Mithridates defeated him the next year and the Romans made peace the following year leaving him dominant in Asia Minor. The Romans then sent Lucius Lucullus to attack Mithridates in 73. Initially successful, Lucullus found himself outmanoeuvred when Mithridates defeated one of Lucullus' subordinates, killing some 7,000 Roman soldiers in 67. The Roman response to this defeat was sending Pompey to finish the war. In the next year, Pompey defeated Mithridates. He pursed him for three years, finally trapping him in a fortress. The rebels killed Mithridates in 63.

Finished with Mithridates, Pompey reordered Asia Minor and marched south, annexing Syria, taking Judaea as a client state, and organizing an eastern frontier for the Republic. Pompey returned to Rome in 62 and celebrated a magnificent triumph in 61. He increased the Republic's revenue by 70 per cent and left a treasury of more than a year's total income.

The Republic Begins to Crumble

While Pompey was in the east, a number of Roman aristocrats, many in the Roman crowd of commoners, and disaffected rural citizens joined in a radical conspiracy to change the nature of the Roman state. Under the leadership of senator Catiline they would march on Rome from the north, a mob would rise up in Rome, and together, their movement would kill the consuls and most of the senate and organize a people's state – or at least that is what Cicero and his supporters said Catiline was planning. Certainly, something nefarious was supposed to happen. Consul Cicero found out about the conspiracy and using the senate decree which instructed the magistrates to take all necessary actions to preserve the state, he ordered the main conspirators executed without a trial. Cicero then sent an army to the mountain town of Faesulae in Tuscany which routed the Catiline army and destroyed the town. The army commanders forced the survivors to build a new town in the valley below their former mountain town, which is now Florence.

When Pompey returned from his eastern expedition, he found a changed political climate in Rome. He and Crassus had attempted a balance between those backing the powers of the assembly and those backing the power of the senate but now, the Catilinian affair had turned feelings against the assembly and the senate was managing policy. Many senators understood that loosening the senate's authority would lead to chaos and decided that doing nothing was better than doing anything. The senate refused to ratify the agreements made by Pompey nor grant lands to his soldiers. They believed Pompey had overstepped his authority and did not want to see him become stronger. Pompey was stuck in an awkward position; if his agreements did not hold, the whole east might erupt in war; if he could not satisfy the desires of his men for what he had promised, his reputation as a military commander would falter.

Pompey gravitated back to Crassus but also invited the young Julius Caesar to join in a three-way alliance. Together, the popular military leader, the successful money manager, and the clever and perceptive young man would turn the tables on the senate. And so, it was. The senate ratified Pompey's agreements: his soldiers received land and both Crassus and Caesar gained what they wanted. The 'three headed monster' controlled Rome (Modern historians call this agreement the First Triumvirate). To ensure Caesar was on board with the arrangement, Pompey married his daughter Julia. Together, the alliance saw Caesar elected as one of the consuls for the year 59. The status quo senators had joined together and had one of their own number, Marcus Calprunius Bibulus, elected as the other consul.

Bibulus' task was to block all of Caesar's initiative, making him look ineffectual and making the 'the headed monster' alliance look incompetent. But Caesar was always effective and competent. The result was that Bibulus locked himself in his house, telling all and sundry that Caesar's acts were illegal. No one paid attention to him. After his successful consulship, Caesar received three provinces north of Italy, facing Gaul. He needed a good military reputation and a strong army for his future plans. He needed to find a reason to fight the Gauls. He had no problem finding many reasons.

Caesar had also supported the radical patrician, Publius Clodius Pulcher, to become a Plebeian so he could run for tribune. Clodius hated the senate and was working to weaken the institution. He caused Cicero much trouble over the fact that Cicero had the leaders of the Catilinian affair executed without a trial. Cicero went into exile and the mob burned down his home in Rome. He pushed Cato out of Rome by having the assembly appoint him on a mission to Cyprus. Then he had the assembly change the grain subsidy into a grant of free grain. Using his mobs for hire, Clodius struck at his enemies, and they were many. He fell foul of Pompey and began giving Pompey's followers trouble. Pompey was not about to sit around and take Clodius' insults; he funded another tough, Titus Annius Milo, to give trouble to Clodius. Now, the street disturbances became twice as troublesome than before.

Pompey began to rethink his alliance with Julius Caesar. Clodius was Caesar's creation, but Caesar could not control him or, perhaps, chose not to control him. There was a plan to remove Caesar from his command, but the three leaders met in Luca and patched up an arrangement. They agreed that Caesar would keep his command for another five years and the consulship of 55 would fall to Pompey and Crassus. In the summer of 54, suddenly a lot went wrong. Corruption scandals erupted, one after another; violence swept across the streets of Rome with fights between Clodius' and Milo's followers. Worse for the alliance, Caesar's daughter, Julia, died in childbirth. Pompey lost whatever connection he had with Caesar.

In 54, Crassus was busy organizing an eastern campaign. He launched his invasion of Parthia in 53. Unfortunately, Crassus had neither the strategic insight of Pompey nor the tactical virtuosity of Caesar. The Parthians drew Crassus deep into the desert, counter attacked with heavy cavalry, and crushed Crassus' army, killing Crassus. In the same year, Milo murdered Clodius, causing more upheaval. With the death of Julia, Crassus, and Clodius the alliance of the three was ended. Pompey joined with the senators to maintain the status quo and bring stability to the Republic. He saw Caesar as a dangerous influence.

Beginning in 51, a number of senators began an effort to remove Caesar from his command so they could clip his wings. Caesar intended to stand for consul in 49 and looked for a bridge between the end of his command and his election to consul. In 50, enough senators agreed to withhold any new official position from Caesar so once he surrendered his military command, he would be a private citizen. Caesar understood this result would mean either exile or death. In any case, his political career would end. Caesar decided that would not happen.

Appendix VIII

The Economy of the Classical World

The Rich Man and his Money

In the first century AD, Jesus of Nazareth told a story discussing fundamentals of the Greco-Roman economy. Matthew (25:14-30) recounts the tale. It runs like this: a rich man was going on a long journey. He entrusted his wealth to three of his slaves and entrusted different amounts to each slave, according to his estimation of their abilities. To one, he gave five talents; to a second, he gave two talents; to the third, he gave one. When he returned, he called his slaves together for an accounting. The slave who received five talents had invested in business and now had ten talents. His master said that he was a good and loyal servant. The second slave was given two talents, he also invested the money and now had four talents. He, too, was told that he was a good and faithful servant. The third slave still had only one talent. He explained that he knew the master was a hard person, who reaped where he did not sow and gathered where he had not winnowed, so he buried the talent until the master returned. The master called him a bad and lazy servant and took the talent from him and gave it to the one who had ten, saying that, at least, he should have put the money into a bank so when the master returned, he would have interest added to the original amount.

This tale comes from the Roman Near East as part of an economic network extending through the Mediterranean west to the Atlantic and east into the Indian Ocean and Central Asia to China. Specific points of the story tell how this economy functioned.

First, slavery was a primary factor in the Mediterranean Classical economy. For millennia before Classical culture emerged, slavery provided the labour base of organized society. Across the Eurasian-African landmasses, slavery was everywhere. No one questioned it; there were no alternative labour options. However, looking at slavery from another direction, there were far worse things than being a slave. A slave had value. Just as an owner cares for his cattle and dogs, he needs to care for his slaves. Healthcare was not a significant problem in the Greco-Roman world: the healthy lived, the weak died, masters and slaves alike. Physicians, many of whom were slaves, cured minor or immediate ailments. The slave owner supplied food, clothing, and shelter for his properties and utilized their labour.

Second, the story is about money and how it is best handled. The people for whom the tale was initially written would understand the term 'talent' was a monetary amount the equivalent of 6,000 *denarii*. Near Easterners might understand 'denarius' as drachma, a Greek equivalent used by Jesus as the standard 'day-wage'. If we choose to understand the amounts as actual cash, a talent is a little less than 60 lbs. of pure silver. The 6,000 coins of silver or 1,500 coins of gold were held in small bags of 100 silver or 25 gold coins, each bag being a 'mina' silver or gold; there were 60 bags per talent. To transport the coins, there were strongboxes, for individual talents, say 70 lbs.; for five talents, say almost 400 lbs.

The tale is not intended as a fantasy, so dealing with a couple of talents or more was not unthinkable. Carrying big boxes of cash is both inconvenient and dangerous. However, there were alternatives – the tale mentions 'tables', which is the term for banks. Bankers in Classical times were men with a counter and enough coins to change money from one currency to another, but they did not have large collections of coins at hand. Instead, these were stored in safe places, such as the treasury of a temple. Handling the transfer of large amounts was done by note. This is made clear when we listen to Cicero's money problems and how he dealt with them.

When the rich man entrusted his wealth to his slaves, it was in the form of notes written in conjunction with his banker. The money was put into special accounts from which each slave could withdraw. And the investments were made by notes. The banker had a 'papyrus' trail to follow the transfers, and, in all probability, no physical coins changed hands. When the slave who buried his single talent hid the note, the result was the money, moved from the rich man's account into the special account, gained no interest from the banker.

At this time, businesses in the Mediterranean were run by families and owned by individuals. Small and medium-sized business operations collected in many towns and in the few large cities. All sorts of businesses grew up. They emerged from an agricultural base of landed estates which produced cash crops. The businesses provided products from necessities to luxury items and provided the services of transportation, construction, money handling, and much more. Their labour was family members who received a cut of the business and slaves whose care and well-being was also necessary for the business to run.

There were less agreeable forms of slavery. For instance, agriculture labourers on large estates who were imprisoned in underground cells during the night and chained during the day; workers in the mines which constantly had to buy new slaves cheaply because miners did not live long; sex workers of all kinds who sometimes did very well but often had unfortunate ends, and gladiators. Even worse, masters could abandon the slave because they were too weak to work. They quickly died, one way or another. So, working with a business family was not all that bad.

Money Made a New Society

With the emergence of urban centres across the Ancient Near East, trade in goods, which had long existed, became an essential part of economic life. Methods of exchange varied according to circumstances, but common understandings of value were necessary for the business to continue. The equation went something like this: a healthy cow is worth X amount of wheat, is worth Y weight of silver, etc. Analytic thought and imagination on both sides were critical to negotiate satisfactory transactions. Among the many commodities traded, slaves were vital because they were the only source of labour for major endeavours and made life easier for the elites.

As the Ancient Near Eastern civilizations extended their influence, trade routes grew across the Mediterranean. But suddenly, a significant technological improvement changed the conditions of trade and life. This was the invention of money. Here, of course, we come upon a subject of great contention. I will speak of money meaning, metal coins manufactured for commerce. The first coins appeared in Lydia, made by King Alyattes, around 580 BC. There are only a few examples of these coins, but that king's son, Croesus (reign about 585-546), issued many coins, probably to pay for Greek mercenaries to defend his kingdom. The technology of coinage spread to Greece and improved. Coins paid for the foundation of Classical Civilization.

The use of coinage caused the structure of society to change. Herodotus tells us that the introduction of coinage generated the start of retail trade; with state-issued coins, many people found different ways of livelihood. Most coin users' livelihoods depended on slave labour. Joining together, these people formed the state, the state's religion, and the armed forces. Their loyalty shifted from family, tribe, and hereditary lords to their chosen leaders and state. They viewed themselves as a nation centred on a ceremonial and market centre, their city. They were citizens of their nation's city-state.

Coins came to Athens during the time of Peisistratus; trade quickly increased in Athens and Peisistratus established the Classical Agora as the main marketplace. After the overthrow of Peisistratus' sons, the democracy under Cleisthenes reformed the currency. By that time, most Greek city-states had their own coinage. The techniques of coin-use changed the way people looked at each other and their world. First, everyone handling coinage needed to understand numeracy and how to relate numbers to things. Second, the existence and gathering of coins allowed people to loan wealth to others, resulting in the capacity to spread wealth to the able. Third, people who run businesses need the skill of literacy. Instead of a small number of rulers and priests, now a crowd of merchants and goods sellers became literate. Coins, wealth, writing: these factors generated new concepts and innovation. Writing in this society suddenly aware of itself brought forth poetry, plays, speeches, then histories and philosophies. All this grew out of market enterprises. The Greeks bought their miracle with coins and loans. Athens developed a precocious capitalism.

In 499 BC, the Athenians involved themselves with the revolt of the Ionian cities against the Persian Empire and drew the attention of the Persian Great King. While they repelled the first Persian offensive, the second, in 480, promised to be overwhelming. The Athenians discovered vast silver deposits which they invested in shipbuilding and commerce. These actions generated the power to avoid inclusion in the Persian Empire. After their victory, the Athenians became a dominant financial centre producing a flowering mercantile and literary culture. For a generation after the defeat of the Persians, the Athenians prospered and did pretty much whatever they wanted in the eastern Mediterranean. In the next era, their former friends and enemies made common causes. After thirty years, these enemies finally defeated Athens. But the 'Athenian Way' had spread throughout the Greek lands, extending to their neighbours.

Included in the 'Athenian Way' was the never-ending propensity to fight wars. All states fought wars, but coinage, finance, and loans became an important part of military undertakings. Furnishing the accoutrements of battle made up a good part of the manufacturing and commercial businesses. Moreover, the fruits of winning a war brought new wealth and slaves into the warrior states' treasury to be distributed to businesses producing more war equipment. While war hindered the economy of the losers and even sometimes meant their extinction, the victors prospered. Further, the animosities of the poor against the rich was often alleviated by paying poorer strong young men to become fighters and thus allowing them entry into more favourable circumstances. Coins and war became a profitable formula. Of course, this was only for the winners.

King Philip II of Macedonia profited most from Athens' examples. Minting coins from his mines, he had the money to pay for an effective army and buy the expertise necessary to turn it into an irresistible force. But rather than conquer towns to plunder, he set them up as autonomous partners in his state, letting them run their affairs as long as they remained loyal. His son, Alexander, did even better, smashing the Persian Empire, marching into Central Asia and India; he and his successors founded commercial towns throughout the Near East, establishing coin-based economic networks bringing prosperity and wealth. As is the nature of wealth, large concentrations grew under the direction of a few, yet still enough spread about, so the eastern Mediterranean lands became more prosperous than ever before.

Economic Growth and Technological Transformation

Slavery and money were the basis of Hellenistic economies. This was a precocious capitalism because while the Classical society spread, it did not develop any further. Technological advances were few and the problem of generating power beyond that of human and animal muscle was never solved. There were some interesting experiments with water and wind but nothing that shook the social fabric. This form of capitalism was indeed precocious because when, for a variety of reasons, the currency collapsed in the third century AD, the free enterprise concerns collapsed with it and were replaced by a state-dominated command economy of the honourable betters telling the humble how things were to be done. At the same time, the slave system also contracted significantly as the former businesspeople either became subjects of the honourable or managed to become honourable themselves.

The question of industrialization is important because only by looking at this possibility can we understand the nature of Classical society. The reality is that Classical civilization was never going to industrialize. There are two reasons for this: one, the ancient Greeks and Romans were not capable of generating the concepts necessary for industrialization; two, they did not have the necessary materials available to them.

First, intellectual depth: Hellenic authors wrote marvellous works of profound understandings which have inspired people across the millennia. Their speculations are amazing and spread across the vistas of possibilities. However, their endeavours centred on questions of quality without much regard for quantities. Hellenic mathematicians laid many of the foundations for the modern mathematical sciences, but the means they used were seriously hindered by their inefficient calculation tools, their clumsy number notations, and uncertain mechanics of proof. The calculation of heat transfer were simply beyond them. Hero's aeolipile, a sphere with opposing nozzles placed over a heat source, spun around with force, demonstrating the power of steam, but the formulation of an accurate description of the forces involved was beyond Classical savants' capacity. This is made clear in the text of Hero's Pneumatics. Here, Hero demonstrates useful techniques and describes the phenomenon observed but absent are any sort of measurements or an accurate concept of cause.

Second, the quality of manufactured materials was not fine enough to give accurate readings for exact measurements. The Antikythera mechanism is a spectacular bronze calculating calendar. Nevertheless, it is typical of Hellenic thought in that while it gives answers, it is not particularly accurate and is based on a faulty understanding of cosmic structure. Alchemists could not find exact weights, times, and sizes to turn their investigations into chemistry. Classical iron was not workable in a way that would form practical fireboxes and boilers. Steel was imported from China. There was a vast knowledge and experience void between though in the Classical World and the type of thought existent where industry began.

Money and the Economy of the Later Roman Republic

When the Athenians began experimenting with their democracy, Rome was a small town in the centre of Italy, in the process of ousting a monarch and establishing a government of the Peoples' affairs without kings, the Republic. The Roman state slowly expanded, an organization of self-sufficient small farmers until the Gallic tribes descended on the town and sacked it a decade or so after Athens's defeat in the Peloponnesian war. The state of sturdy farmers recovered but was divided between aristocrats and commoners. Still, they began to expand, conquering their neighbours only to integrate them into the Roman state. Trade and business existed without coins but with precious metals. The Roman aristocrats did not want a commercial society developing because they believed such activities weaken character and brought immorality. The great wars which began when Pyrrhus invaded Italy in 280 through the Punic and Macedonian Wars ending in 168 BC, changed Rome and Roman society.

The Romans experimented with a silver currency during the Second Punic Wars, finally deciding on a coin weighing 3.9 grams or 1/84 of a Roman pound of silver. Called the *denarius* (tenner), it was given as 10 *as*, (an *as* was worth one pound of bronze). Later, in 141 BC, the coin's value was raised to be worth 16 *asses*. This is the coin of the Late Republic. It remained stable until after Caesar's assassination.

Hannibal's invasion and victories in Italy severely wounded the Roman state. At great cost in men and materials, the Romans took emergency actions to pull their forces together and counter Hannibal's offensive. The Romans needed men, weapons, ships and food, in great amounts. They coined money, dealt with merchants, manufacturers, lenders, and commercial transactions of all kinds. The Second Punic War ended on 202 BC. The Roman aristocracy and senate found themselves in a commercial society; try as they might, they could not reverse the tide of the growing money economy.

Senators constantly complained about people thinking money was more important than tradition; that they were more interested in business success than adhering to Roman values. The senate decreed that no noble Roman could engaged in any occupation other than agriculture. Most Roman aristocrats found these laws easy to avoid. What was a ceremonial centre for an agrarian society quickly became a commercial-financial city.

Conquests led to wealth gathering into Roman hands which then required further conquest to protect what was already conquered. To conserve wealth, the Romans invested in productive activities and, given Roman values and traditions, that meant farmland. Large plantations run by slave labour were quite profitable. The back-breaking labour of small farms brought no such returns and many farmers were glad to receive a handful of cash and go to live by their wits and initiatives in Rome or some town where life was more comfortable. The numbers of large estates grew and small farms shrank.

The Roman aristocracy was large and divided into factions built on family and economic interests. Competition between these factions centred on elections for Roman magistrates, each group trying to make themselves look good and the others bad. There were issues to be sure and each side looked for more. Major social changes caused by the growing proto-capitalistic economy provided many points of disagreement. This came to a head during the Tribunate of Tiberius Gracchus (133 BC) when he introduced his agrarian laws. The Roman traditions of small farms and country living seemed more important to many Romans than looking deeply into problems emerging from the growth of empire and commerce. Particularly important for Tribune Tiberius Gracchus was his efforts to divest many rich Romans of opposing factions of large properties. His enemies also understood the importance of Tiberius' objective; they killed him at the doors to Jupiter's Temple on the Capital Hill.

The Emergence of the Empire

The issues centred on the question, who would dominate Roman politics? The two main groups, each broken into many factions, were the old rich who lived by estates and rents and the new rich who ran the provinces and businesses. The different sides transformed and mutated as their component factions grew and split, changed allegiances and formed new ones. Each group sought the People's support while also maintained that they were the true aristocrats, the Best. This was not one long crisis, it was a desultory civil war, one side or the other often winning but unable to destroy their opponents. In 60 BC, Pompey, representing the traditionalists allied with the financier, Crassus, to bring stability. But Pompey also allied with Caesar, who would support him, when necessary, against Crassus. The alliance evaporated after the Parthians killed Crassus in 53 BC. Pompey supported a more traditional approach to government than the rising financier-business oriented group wanted. Their answer was to go to Caesar.

Caesar, on the other hand, had his own ideas. Since his praetorship in Spain, Caesar had an understanding: the solution to the troubles of the Republic was the rise of a semi-divine moderator who would oversee the operations of the Republic so the different groups and the kaleidoscope full of factions would work together, each following their own interests, to maintain the People and Senate of Rome. For this, he generated a conquering army; for this, he fought an immense civil war; for this, he took power. Yet, he did not convince the factions that he was doing this for their own good. After his murder, the whole structure of the Republic collapsed.

But, his nephew and heir, Octavius now the young Julius Caesar, appreciated the concept. With a different style of action and often a softer touch, the young Julius Caesar became the August One, the moderator of the restored Roman Republic. He emphasized peace and strove to build prosperity by encouraging urban economic development. The empire flourished as no previous society in the Mediterranean had ever done. For better than two hundred years, the empire prospered as towns grew and citizenship expanded.

In around the 230s AD, the system ran aground. Citizenship was not going to expand unless the slaves and serfs were included and that was not going to happen and the military commitments of the empire increased substantially because of stronger enemies in the north and east. The imperial administration tried all sorts of tricks to solve an insolvable problem, only to wreck the coinage which ended the financial business practices which underwrote prosperity. The empire collapsed into a severe depression and did not ever fully recover. A new economic model emerged under Diocletian and Constantine, that of a command economy under the direction of an all-encompassing state.

Appendix IX

Caesar's Commentaries: Sources, Purpose, Composition, and History

Books

A close reading of Caesar's Commentaries demonstrates that all of them are based on a single source: Caesar's military daybook. Most evenings, Caesar wrote, or dictated to a scribe, notes about the day's events, recounting actions, the names of people Caesar wanted to remember, and including reports sent in by subordinates describing operations essential to the accomplishment of Caesar's military objectives. Those looking for hidden mendacities or subtle propaganda will see only mirages. Caesar is brutally honest: he follows the Great Alexander in the Civil Wars by untangling the Gordian knot of Roman politics with the sword. He does not care if people believe he is right; if they cause him too much trouble, they will find themselves dead; otherwise, Caesar will ignore them because it is hard to win an intellectual argument against a man who commands formidable victorious legions. This was a lesson his heir and successor took to heart. It is not necessary to assume Caesar's writings are always correct or accurate, but instead, when Caesar wrote a note, he believed it to be true.

The primary consideration in the analysis of Caesar's Commentaries is how they became books. Books are always about money, publishing is expensive, and bookselling is an art. The book business in the City of Rome was beginning to develop. Publishers produced books as a sideline to their normal activities of making acceptable copies of legal documents, wills, contracts, mortgages, and the like. The skills were the same: someone reading the manuscript and others writing down the text. A will might need only two or three copies; a broadsheet containing a legal text for distribution might need many more. Most books were made from papyrus in scrolls. Discriminating readers preferred the soft feel of prepared papyrus to the harshness of vellum. Further, the scroll lay flat as opposed to using a codex format.

No matter how the book is produced, it must have specific qualities that people read, enjoy, and respect, and this is true not only for Classical

Civilization but for all literate cultural traditions. A book needs a main point; it should include development and must speak to people in a meaningful manner about a human concern. Caesar's notes did not make a book. The notes needed organization and fitting together to some conclusion. This is what a publisher, be he an ancient Hebrew, an Indian savant, an Islamic scholar, a Chinese literati, or a Renaissance businessman, needs to see to publishing.

The trick to publishing is control of cost. Even at a high capital outlay, producing more copies makes each book cheaper than having one book at a time. Then, the question becomes one of finding buyers to shell out coins for the product. Good bookselling induces the public to demand the product, 'having (and hopefully reading) this book makes you better!' Tastes differ, and bookselling finds profit in this fact. There is poetry, philosophy, rhetoric, politics, history, and fiction of one or another type. Intellectual challenge and exciting entertainment are the primary sales points. Then, a never-ending pile of books was made to educate the young. These are not necessarily one for each child, but a master copy made for the schoolroom. With thought and creativity, books can be a satisfying business.

Caesar's Writing

The next question is how Caesar became a published author. Certainly not for money. There were no copyright laws; the publisher could produce books for sale without, or even against, the author's agreement. Caesar must have got something for creating his works and sending them to a publisher who saw money at the end of the process. One answer to our question is Caesar's regard for written records. As consul, he was the first to require the Senate to publish a record of its meetings, the Acta senatus (or Commentarii senatus). Another is Caesar's chosen genera: military history. Romans read a lot of military history; Polybius' extensive and detailed narrative used Latin sources; Livy used more Latin sources than Polybius, and accounts of ongoing wars in Caesar's youth were available. Many Roman men had experiences as officers in the Republic's armies. They enjoyed discussing accounts of different struggles; equally important, the youth needed some idea of what war and command were all about. Roman soldiers, centurions, and officers were literate; training manuals, the stories contained in the Greek and Roman accounts of their wars, even if only recounted through word of mouth, all were important to the ambitious soldier.

As a young propraetor in his early thirties, Caesar took command of the army in Hispania Ulterior and increased it with more recruits. He attacked

Lusitania and continued north, finally reaching Brigantium (modern Corunna) with foot and ships. When he returned to Rome, the senate awarded him a triumph, but his enemies outmanoeuvred him and he could not hold the event. Worse, all sorts of stories emerged out of the woodwork: the war was unnecessary; Caesar just ran a plundering expedition to repay his debts; the enemy was disorganized and untrained, and so forth. He did not have the details of the struggles at hand. He had a hard time remembering who did what. But the military bug bit. Caesar would be a conqueror, and he would have the information to tell everyone about how he did it.

As Caesar was pushing towards forty years old, he became consul in the give and take of the political intrigue infesting the workings of the Republic. As his term moved toward its end, he chose to receive both Cisalpine and Transalpine Gaul as his provinces for five years. Tribes were in turmoil, and Caesar placated the German king Ariovistus to keep him quiet. There should be no doubt that Caesar's objective in this assignment was to go to war in Gaul, expanding the Roman Imperium, gathering wealth for his projects, and, most important, building a formidable army that would match anything Pompey or Crassus might raise.

Here, we run into the man responsible for producing Caesar's *Commentaries* as a book. L. Cornelius Balbus was a Spaniard from Gades. As a young man, he worked with Pompey in the Sertorius War and Pompey was so pleased that he made Balbus a Roman citizen. He came with Pompey to Rome in 71 BC, where he met Caesar, then just thirty years old. When Caesar went to Spain as a propraetor in 61 BC, he took Balbus with him as chief engineer. The two worked well together; in 58, when Caesar as proconsul went to Gaul, Balbus accompanied him. During the years of war in Gaul, Caesar often sent Balbus back to Rome to handle his business affairs. As a senator, Caesar could not deal directly in business but using intermediaries was accepted, and Balbus was Caesar's man in the business.

Balbus' good friend was Titus Pomponius, a wealthy equestrian from a family of businessmen. Pomponius was a real estate investor in the city of Rome and did very well; he chose the nickname, Atticus, to reflect his love of Athens and regard for Hellenic culture. He was the writer and recipient of many letters to and from Cicero which make up a good part of Cicero's published correspondence. Julius Caesar was also friends with Atticus, he was his houseguest when travelling in Greece. Atticus ran a successful publishing enterprise; he trained slaves as scribes and manufactured papyrus scrolls for his books. His list included Plato, Demosthenes, and Aeschines; critics favoured his editions for accuracy and readability. In all probability, Balbus supported the idea of a detailed daybook and Atticus agreed to publish it if Caesar wrote it up.

The War in Gaul

While he prepared for his first campaign in Gaul, Caesar started his daybook. He recorded the names of people, tribes, places; he wrote about motives and movements, so no one was going to criticize his actions without Caesar having a counter-argument. After his first year in Gaul during the winter hiatus, Caesar wrote up his notes into a narrative, describing his political understandings of Gallic politics and his military operations. Rather than using the rhetorical arts and flourishes, Caesar presented his material as simple and clearly as he could. He understood that the best propaganda is straightforward and precise.

Caesar was not the first military commander who wrote up his experiences. In many ways, his narrative reflects Xenophon's *Anabasis* in that the narrative is clear, concise, and accurate. Schoolmasters often used Xenophon's works to teach Latin speakers proper Greek and the *Anabasis* was particularly useful in introducing students to literary Greek. Certainly, the young Caesar when he was learning Greek became familiar with the *Anabasis*.

Balbus had a hand in Caesar's business. He was probably instrumental in convincing Caesar about the benefits of having his account reproduced and distributed. We know it was a success because Caesar did it again next year. The right people read it and recommended it to their compatriots. Six times Caesar wrote up the year and sent it off for distribution in Rome. The point of the work, besides Caesar's review of each year to understand his success and failures, was to put certain facts about his army and his management of the army's operations before certain people. His objective was not to gain popularity, which was a simple matter of spreading money about strategically, but to demonstrate to certain people why they should trust Caesar's army and command ability in any future unpleasantness.

The Civil War

When Caesar mobilized his army in defiance of the expressed will of the Senate in January 49 BC, his *Commentaries* on the War in Gaul had reached book VII, his account of the year just previous was in raw note form but not done. Still, Caesar thought this type of work was valuable because he started a new daybook series. He started the new series with a full description of the issues as they unfolded, as he saw them. He starts in *media res*, like any great epic, because he planned to connect this text with volume VII of his *Gallic War* series. Even without modern numbering, the narratives of the civil war fall into three sections and need separate consideration. The first sections run from the statement of reasons for crossing the Rubicon through the conquest of Italy and Caesar's first return to Rome. Then, Caesar recounts the war in Spain and again returns to Rome. He probably had his scribe throw the narrative together for publication while he travelled from Spain back to Rome. Just as the *Gallic War* was for certain people so now the *Civil War* was for a select group of his supporters. Not to convince them of any position, Caesar wrote to them to confirm their trust in his abilities. He recounts his mistakes from a military point of view but however bad were his actions, his opponents were demonstrably worse. After all, Caesar was victorious.

The next section consists of reports sent to Caesar describing operations by two of his lieutenants. First, there are Trebonius' accounts of the siege of Massilia, including reports of Caesar's navy; second is an account of Curio's failed campaign in Africa, probably by Asinius Pollio. Caesar compiled these reports into a single narrative and entered them into his daybook. The third section runs from Caesar's landing in Epirus to his defeat of Pompey and then the pursuit to Egypt. The narrative ends there and is picked up in the Alexandrian war. The question of these texts' publication is hard to pinpoint. 'Book III' in an abbreviated form of the current editions of the *Civil War* may have reached the publishers when Caesar returned to Rome after his Asian campaign, right before his great triumph. Caesar wrote up the main narrative of 'Book III,' while he travelled on the Nile. After that, while he maintained his daybook, he had no time to write up the Alexandrian, African, and Spanish Wars because of his ongoing struggles to gain absolute power.

The Ides of March

Caesar's death came suddenly; upheaval followed. Caesar's heir became a force to consider. C. Octavius found allies, not only Caesar's military personnel but many of his business associates including Balbus, who managed Caesar's real estate interests in Rome. Octavius took the name Julius Caesar and contemporary documents refer to him by that name. He had a strong interest in polishing his newly minted father's reputation. Antony had taken custody of Caesar's papers, falsifying many statements in them, according to some commentators. But Antony had no interest in Caesar's personal papers except as they might reflect badly on himself, and that was fixable. He relinquished Caesar's personal records. Balbus and Octavius talked business; Caesar held extensive holdings and Octavius needed to know about them. Paying the largess as promised in Caesar's will required the movement of resources and liquidation of assets. They went through Caesar's private papers to find things that were not in Balbus' accounts. In this process, they came across Caesar's daybooks from his campaigns, including copies of his published works, probably seven books of the Gallic Wars, and what is now labelled Books I and III of the Civil War.

Caesar's vast wealth and extensive holding would keep the accountants busy for a long time. But Balbus also saw an opportunity for advancing the Great Caesar's image. Here was a mass of material, along with published works well received, and a vision of a narrative history of Caesar's campaigns by Caesar. Balbus chose the publisher and editor, the best in Rome, Titus Pomponius (Atticus). This work would present Caesar's material in a clear and objective way so those who supported Pompey and the senate might read it without feeling belittled by the narrative. Caesar, of course, was not objective and the editor was not interested in denying that fact. The important point of the book was that here, on papyrus, Caesar described his many campaigns, those against barbarians in Gaul, Egypt, and Asia, and those against Romans in Italy, Africa, and twice in Spain. He won all of his campaigns. How did he do it? Caesar explains it all in his book, Caesar's *Commentaries*.

Constructing the Commentaries

Constructing a book is different from authoring a book. Anyone can sit down and write but only a book editor can make it into other than a long sequence of words and organize the resources needed to take a single copy manuscript and turn it into a book that induces people to spend money. We can all agree that Caesar's *Commentaries* are a successful book. It is not without flaws, but it sells. The editor saw three different books joined into a trilogy. First, Caesar's history of his conquest of Gaul. All finished, with the exception of the last year, polished and capable of a little more polish, an exemplary example of fine Latin. Second, Caesar's rather hasty notes on his civil war campaign against Pompey, a work with rough edges but a powerful account. Third, Caesar's daybooks recount the later Civil War campaigns.

Titus Pomponius had the idea of publishing Caesar's *Commentaries* while Caesar was still alive. The seven books of the *Gallic War* and a version of the *Civil War* were in hand. To complete the book's architecture, the editor needed a connection between the Seventh Book of the *Gallic Wars* and the first book of the *Civil War*. He had Balbus invite Aulus Hirtius, a firm Caesarian and ally, to complete Caesar's *Commentaries*. Hirtius completed book VIII of the *Gallic War*, but political disagreements heated up and Hirtius became deeply involved. The ending of Book VIII and the start of the *Civil War* interlock. This concept was an editorial ploy to avoid actually discussing the causes of the Civil War. Roman politics at this time was volatile and Pomponius had long avoided joining any side. To strengthen the *Civil War*, the editor dropped the two reports, the siege of Massilia and Curio's defeat in Africa, between the first and second parts of the *Civil War*. Probably, he dressed these reports up, copying Caesar's style. That left the three campaigns in Alexandria, Africa, and Spain. Rather than extend the work to Caesar's death, which might tread on dangerous ground, the editor decided the *Commentaries* would end in Spain.

The editor took on the task of expanding Caesar's original *Gallic War* and *Civil War* narratives using the relevant daybooks. He was careful to retain Caesar's diction but smoothed over controversial issues. He kept the rough transitions and did not fill in episodes Caesar's notes missed. This gives the narrative a vital quality that a full and complete text would lose. The remaining daybooks held Caesar's notes concerning actions in Egypt, Asia, Africa, and Spain. The editor needed people familiar with military affairs and the details of military actions to compile narratives out of the notes. Only people who actually saw fighting as part of an army could breathe life into the daybooks' accounts. He chose three officers, probably either military tribunes or engineers of different legions.

The three compilers were each a soldier in Rome's army, but their experiences and perspectives were different. Their method of work was similar; they familiarized themselves with the notes, then told the scribe what they said happened and the scribe wrote it down, discussing with the narrator exactly what he meant. Caesar's words were used when possible. With the editor overseeing the process, the works produced interesting and coherent narratives.

The Alexandrian War

The compiler who put together the *Alexandrian War*, including the campaign against Pharnaces, was an engineer and officer who was familiar with the Alexandrian waterfront but had little knowledge of anywhere beyond the port area. He is particularly insightful regarding the city's water systems and construction methods. Unfortunately, he knew little about the general layout of Alexandria, hearing that Caesar's lines could only go so far because of a waterlogged area, which he calls a swamp. For generations, modern reconstructions of Alexandria show a swamp inside or near the city. More probably, following the reconstructions of Michael Bengtsson, the area was the Sema, the tombs of Alexander and the Ptolemies. When the

Alexandrians disrupted the water distribution system, the gardens flooded and that is what our compiler refers to as a swamp. As part of Caesar's engineering staff, the compiler followed Caesar north into Cappadocia and the war against Pharnaces. His narrative of Caesar's campaign, based of course on Caesar's notes, is particularly penetrating.

The African War

The soldier who compiled the *African War* was a cavalry officer. He has a good eye for ground but paid little attention to the wider issues of where certain villages were. He went where he was told and didn't worry about where he was; when he assembled Caesar's notes describing moves across the countryside, he got lost and it is probably impossible at this time to really straighten out the geography of many of Caesar's moves. Like Napoleon said of his soldiers, 'Don't ask my men about my campaigns, the only thing they saw was the pack on the back of the man in front of them.'

Another factor influencing the African campaign and its retelling is the fact the land on which the campaign took place is utterly flat. Long low undulations stretch as far as the eye can see until the land disappears into the murk at the foot of distant mountains. The sea on one side and far mountains on the other define east and west (or is it north and south?) depending on if you can see them, otherwise it is just the sun and at night the stars. A 'hill' might be a three-foot-high spot caused by shifting winds. The location of many of the little settlements that mark manoeuvres in the campaign is simply unknowable. One speculation is often as good as another. Further, modern research in the area has confused a number of the issues. Most historical atlases put Thapsus right at the tip of the broad peninsula on which the town was located. However, looking at the ground, I find it hard to agree that the existing site of Ras Dimass was the port of Thapsus. The islands on which sit El Jezira and Eddzira appear to form a navigational danger. I think it more likely that Tabulbah is the site of ancient Thapsus. This places Thapsus about four and a half miles northeast of Ras Dimass along the coast.

This compiler was not part of Caesar's inner circle and so was misinformed about some of Caesar's actual operations and objectives. Moreover, he was aware and sympathized with Cato's positions. Nevertheless, he was an eyewitness of the main battles and had sound military appreciation of battlefield strategy and tactics.

The Spanish War

The compiler of the *Spanish War* was more of a fighting soldier than the other two reporters. A literate officer, his knowledge and understandings appear to result from a career working up the chain of command from close to the bottom. He spoke to his scribe in a Roman-Spanish soldier's brogue, not using formal Latin but, at times, breaking down into ungrammatical idioms. In the text, the scribe understood the compiler and wrote down a close version of what he heard. Certainly, the book editor would not allow nonsense to appear on the pages of his book, but as the text travelled through the years in new editions, different editors tried to correct the improper Latin. This soldier knew the geography of the fields of combat and while he understood and supported Caesar's objectives, he had connections to Pompey's camp. He ends his narrative, following Caesar's notes, with Caesar's speech, delivered in the local Spanish brogue.

The Commentaries Travel into the Future

Pomponius now had his text; his first release was of a carriage-trade edition, on fine papyrus, beautifully scripted, for a goodly sum. Subsequently, he issued cheaper versions in larger numbers but, since copyright was unknown at that time, other, less distinguished booksellers produced cheaper copies still, not as carefully made but costing far fewer *denarii*. Within a half century, the work became standard issue in two editions: a schoolroom edition of the *Gallic Wars* for teachers and a complete collection for libraries and personal use. By the time of Hadrian, the Commentaries was a necessary item in any major book collection.

The wreckage of Classical literature began during the crisis of the third century. Pomponius and other book manufacturers used papyrus as the vehicle to carry the text. The rolls were made from sheets of Egyptian papyrus, treated, glued and worked into shape on which a scribe wrote the text. These rolls, as they age become more vulnerable to dampness, insects and fire. If just left alone in a proper environment, after a century or so, they will still disintegrate on their own. The very act of reading the old book will destroy it.

Normally the solution to this problem was to manufacture new copies. But during the third century crisis the flow of papyrus was interrupted by the political upheavals in the east which only added to the destruction by barbarian invasions of libraries and book collections in the Aegean area. The solution to the papyrus problem was the use of vellum in codices. Vellum codices were being issued when Pomponius was publishing but the product was considered cheap and substandard. Accounting ledgers, inventory books, and school texts were on vellum, which could be used and reused. While vellum scroll books were manufactured, most vellum books were formatted as codices. As the third century moved into the fourth century, vellum codices became the format of choice in the Mediterranean world. What survives of Classical literature was all transferred to vellum books.

There were two editions of Caesar's works: a school room text of the Gallic Wars and a complete collection of all his works either for secondary schools or private use. Many manuscript copies of the *Gallic Wars*, used as a text teaching Latin from the time of the Romans to the present, were located in the Renaissance. There were fewer manuscript texts of the *Civil Wars* and its three addenda. The first printed edition of the *Commentaries* is dated 1469 in Rome under Bishop Giovanni Bussi (Latin name Aleriensis), as part of Pope Pius II's efforts of putting ancient literature in print. This included the *Gallic War, Civil War*, and the addenda wars. At least ten different editions appeared in Italy before 1500. All the early printed editions rested on Italian manuscripts which held a fairly uniform text albeit with errors and mistakes. As the sixteenth merged into the seventeenth century, there were many editions of the commentaries printed throughout Europe. In England, Clement Edmonds produced a translation and commentary of Caesar's *Commentaries* in 1655.

The first critical edition of the *Commentaries* was by Franz Oudendorp in 1737. Collating some forty manuscripts, Oudendorp cleared up a number of textual problems. There the questions about textual problems remained until 1847, when Karl Nipperdey issued his critical edition of the *Commentaries*. His work resulted in his creation of a mechanical formula for readings of the manuscripts' archetype (work from which all subsequent manuscripts descended). He concluded that all texts of the *Commentaries* were descended from two main works: the *Gallic War* alone and a collection of all the commentaries. Further, he believed a certain five manuscripts of the complete commentaries were closest to the archetype from which all *Civil War* manuscripts descended.

Caesar's Commentaries: An Academic Study 1850-2020

There have been no major changes from Nipperdey's edition although new critical editions have clarified many fine points. Heinrich Meusel, in 1885, identified a new important manuscript followed by his finding of two other witness manuscripts in 1894. The 1894 Teubner edition followed these new discoveries. In 1898, Alfred Holder identified another witness manuscript, raising the number of significant manuscripts to seven, out of the many existing manuscripts. From these, Alfred Klotz constructed the 1926 Teubner text. In 1936, Pierre Fabre's Bude text included an eighth manuscript, and this remains the number of witness manuscripts. The whole problem of analysing Caesar's texts is well described by Virginia Brown, in her *The Textual Transmission of Caesar's Civil War*, (1972, Brill).

In the early 2000s new translations of Caesar's *Civil War* have appeared which are excellent. I find the following noteworthy.

Raaflaub, Kurt, translator and editor, *The Landmark Julius Caesar*, Pantheon Books, 2017. This is the best single collection of Caesar's works. The appendices are excellent; the chronology is the best ever done. Wonderful book!

Carter, John, translator, *Julius Caesar, The Civil War*, OUP, 1997.

Damon, Cynthia, translator, *Caesar Civil War*, Loeb, 2016.

Bibliographies

Some Important Older Works Narrating the History of the Roman Republic

North, Thomas, *The Lives of the Noble Grecian & Romans*, from the French Translations of James Amiot: London, 1580.
Lord North, 1535-c. 1604, held a number of military commands under Queen Elizabeth and translated a number of works into English. His vigorous style was widely appreciated at the time and has set standards for English prose. His translations of Plutarch brought Classical history to the English-speaking public.

Shakespeare, William, *The Tragedy of Julius Caesar*, first performed 1599, in First Folio, 1623
The Master's retelling of Lord North's 'Life of Caesar' and 'Life of Brutus'. A brilliant docudrama, as accurate as any dramatic production, the play presents the issues and themes of Caesar's rule.

Edmondes, Clement, *The Commentaries of C. Julius Caesar with Many excellent and Judicious Observations, together with the Life of Caesar and an Account of his Medalls*: R. Daniel London, 1655
Sir Clement Edmondes of Preston Deanery, 1566-1622, was clerk, then fellow in All Souls' college. In 1601 became French secretary to the Queen, remembrancer of the city of London, and master of the requests. He served the crown well and was knighted in 1617. He published his *Observations on the five first books of Caesar's Commentaries of the civil wars*, London 1600.

Howel, William, *An Institution of a General History from the Beginning of the World to the Monarchy of Constantine the Great*: Henry Herrington London, 1661
Howell, William 1638? -1683, was educated at Magdalene College, Cambridge. Receiving the BA 1651 and MA, 1655, he wrote the first detailed narrative of ancient history in the English tongue, published 1661. He later extended the history to the 'fall of Augustulus' published in 1683. Edward Gibbon thought highly of the work (Autobiography, ed. 1827 i. 33).

Echard, Laurence, *The Roman History from the Building of the City to the Perfect Settlement of the Empire by Augustus Caesar*: T. Hodgkins London, 1699
Laurence Echard, 1687-1730, was the son of a churchman and a churchman himself. He graduated with BA in 1692 and MA in 1695. Ordained and settled in a number of livings, he wrote many works, including translations and histories, including a

major history of England from the Romans to James I. The *Roman History* was one of his first historical works.

Vertot, Abbot de, (ET) *The History of the Revolutions that happened in the Government of the Roman Republic*: Ship in Pater-noster-row, 1721 2 vols
Rene-Aubert Vertot, 1655-1735, was a French clergyman who served several small parishes in Normandy. He wrote histories of revolutions in Portugal and Sweden before embarking on his Roman Revolutions. His last work was a multi volume history of the Knights Hospitallers of St, John.

Fr. Catrou and Fr. Rouille, (ET by Mr. Ozell) *The Roman History with Notes*: J. Bettenham London, 1727-8, 6 vols
Francois Catrou, 1659-1737, was son of a secretary to Louis XIV. His style of composition won him high marks in college; he joined the Society of Jesus (Jesuits) at the age of 18 and showed great promise as a preacher. For a decade, 1690-1700, he preached with success; beginning in 1701, Catrou worked on the staff of the new academic journal, the *Journal de Trevoux*, a monthly periodical publishing articles mostly by Jesuits. In this time, he began to write histories, first, a history of the Mogul dynasty, then a work on Protestant Fanaticism. He started his Roman history in 1725 and completed the work in 1737. He wrote the text and a companion, P. Rouille SJ wrote the notes. This is a large work: twenty-one quarto volumes in the original French edition, six massive volumes of over 600 tightly printed pages in the English translation. The text and notes still have their used today.

De Secondat, Baron de Montesquieu, (ET) *Reflections on the Causes of the Rise and Fall of the Roman Empire*: Glasgow, 1752
Montesquieu, an important French litterateur in the Age of Enlightenment, wrote about many subjects. His understandings of historical processes are illustrated in his Roman history in which he maintains general conditions shape events, not the actions of individual men. The Roman civil wars were not caused by the ambitions of either Caesar or Pompey but by the conditions of the time which would raise others to the same positions if either Caesar or Pompey were absent.

Rollin, M., finished by M. Crevier, (ET) *The Roman History from the foundation of Rome to the Battle of Actium; That is To the End of the Commonwealth*: London, 1754 16 vols
Charles Rollin, 1661-1741, at age 22 became a master in the College di Plessis and in 1694, he was rector in the University of Paris. In 1699, he received appointment as principal of the Collage de Beauvais. A Jansenist, he lost his official positions after the end of Philip Duke of Orleans' regency. Rollin began writing history after he was forbidden to teach. Using the new editions of Classical works made during Louis XIV's reign, he produced a massive work, the *Ancient History* (1730-38). Very popular into the mid nineteenth century, Rollins' *History* was an exhaustive compilation of what the ancient authors said rather than a reinterpretation of their materials. Continuing on, he began a *Roman History* but only completed a little better than half by the time he died.

Crevier, Jean Baptiste Louis, 1693-1765, was a pupil of Rollins and professor of rhetoric at the College de Beauvais for more than twenty years. He completed the *Roman History*, using the same sources as Rollins. His approach was better organized and more critical than Rollins but lacks the sense of style so well displayed by Rollins. Crevier wrote other works, a history of the Roman Empire to Constantine, a history of the University of Paris, along with translations of Pliny's Letters and Livy.

Ferguson, Adam, *The History of the Progress and Termination of the Roman Republic:* London, 1783 3 vols
Adam Ferguson, 1723-1816, was educated in Scotland, at the Universities of Edinburgh and St. Andrews. Speaking Gaelic allowed him to become the deputy chaplain of the Black Watch regiment in which he fought at the Battle of Fontenoy (1745). In 1754, he left the regiment because he had not received a living. He returned to Edinburgh and eventually became professor of natural philosophy at the University there, 1759. Interested in the moral conditions of Society, he wrote his *History of the Progress and Termination of the Roman Republic*, which illustrates his ideas. Released in 1783, the work was very popular and went through a series of printings. Friends with Adam Smith and David Hume, Ferguson worked on developing an understanding of society using a rational and empathetic approach.

Gillies, John, *The History of the World from the Reign of Alexander to that of Augustus*: Hopkins and Earle Philadelphia, 1809 3 vols
John Gillies, 1747-1836, went to the University of Glasgow; at age twenty, he substituted for a professor of Greek; he graduated MA in 1764. He spent some time in Germany but returned to Scotland by 1784. A noted litterateur, Gilles wrote a popular history of Greece, published in 1786 and often reprinted into the 1830s. His history from *Alexander to Augustus* is an early account of what was later called the Hellenistic Age.

Michelet, J., (ET by Willian Hazelitt) *History of the Roman Republic*: London, 1847
Jules Michelet, 1798 – 1874, was a famous and popular French historian. Rotary press and steel plate printing allowed the production of large numbers of cheaper books. Authors became celebrities and made a lot of money. Michelet in France, von Ranke in Prussia, and many others used railroads to visit libraries and archives and then transport their notes easily. Such authors developed a readable style and discussed interesting interpretations in their works. Michelet made his histories entertaining as well as informative. This is the first history of the Roman Republic for mass consumption.

Liddell, Henry, *A History of Rome from Earliest Times to the Establishment of the Empire*: John Murry, 1855.
Henry Liddell, 1811-1898, dean of Christ Church (1855-1891) and important educator was co-author of Liddell and Scott, *A Greek-English Lexicon*. His *History of Rome* brings to the fore questions of power and deliberative government; he

produced a beautifully illustrated *Students' Edition* in 1865. His friend, Lewis Carroll, wrote the *Wonderland* stories for Liddell's daughter, Alice.

Mommsen, Theodor, (ET by William Dickson) *The History of Rome*: London, 1862-6, 4 vols in 5
Theodor Mommsen, 1817-1903, was one of the most important classicists of the nineteenth century. He received the Nobel Prize in 1902, for being 'the greatest living master of the art of historical writing, with special reference to his monumental work, *A History of Rome*'. Mommsen wrote more than 1,500 works: he emphasized the use of Epigraphy as sources; published many important works on Roman Law; and used the new science of archaeology as an important adjunct to historical studies. His *History of Rome* ends with the Battle of Thapsus and is followed by a discussion of the problem of governing a free people and the evils of autocratic rule. As a politician, Mommsen supported nineteenth century Liberal Nationalism.

Long, George, *The Decline of The Roman Republic*: London, 1864, 5 vols
George Long, 1800-1879, after becoming a fellow of Trinity College, Cambridge, received the first professorship of Greek at the new University of Virginia at Charlottesville in 1825 where he stayed for four years. He moved to London and was first professor of Greek at the new University College in London. He held many prestigious posts; he was a founding member (1830) and for twenty years an officer of the Royal Geographic Society and his interests in education led to his membership in the Society for the Diffusion of Knowledge along with the Society for Central Education. He advocated modernizing textbooks and worked as an editor. For twelve years, he worked on the *Decline of the Roman Republic* (published 1864-74), a comprehensive narrative from the destruction of Carthage to Caesar's death.

Merivale, Charles, *The Fall of the Roman Republic*: London, 1st edition 1872, 2nd edition 1879
Charles Merivale, 1808-1893, after graduating from St. John's College, Cambridge, became a fellow of that college in 1833. Ordained a priest the next year, he spent many years as a college and university professor. Married in 1850, he became Chaplain to the Speaker of the House of Commons in 1863 and in 1869 received appointment as dean of Ely Cathedral. His main work, *A History of the Romans under the Empire* (1850-1862, 12 volumes) was his effort to fill the gap between the histories of Mommsen and Gibbon. Using this massive work as a resource, Merivale wrote a number of works including his *Fall of the Roman Republic*. An imaginative and colourful writer, Merivale's writing is entertaining.

Ferrero, Guglielmo, *The Greatness and Decline of Rome*: London, 1907, 5 volumes
Guglielmo Ferrero, 1871-1942, was an Italian litterateur who wrote works supporting classical liberalism. He opposed any kind of dictatorship. His history describes the Roman Republic's decline from a stable and functioning republic to an anarchy which resulted in a despotic government. Refusing to leave Italy under

the Fascists, he was kept under house arrest until he received an offer of a teaching post from the Institute of International Studies in 1929 in Geneva. He remained in Switzerland until he died.

Heitland, W. E., *The Roman Republic*: Cambridge, 1909, 3 vols
William Heitland, 1847-1935, educated at St. John's College, Cambridge and stayed at that institution as graduate and fellow until his death in 1935. His history is an excellent reference for facts but tends to be rather dry. However, his best work is *Agricola, a Study of Agriculture and the Rustic life in the Greco-Roman World from the Point of View of Labour* (1921), a compendium of information from many sources.

Holmes, T. Rice, *The Roman Republic and the Founder of the Empire*, Oxford, 1923, 3 vols
Thomas Rice Holmes (1855-1933) was educated at Merchant Taylor's School and Christ Church, Oxford. For many years he worked as an assistant Master at a number of preparatory schools. In 1888, he moved with his wife to Kensington where he stayed. He wrote exhaustive works on Roman history, including *The Roman Republic and The Founder of the Empire* (1923) in three volumes and *The Architect of the Roman Empire* (1928) in two volumes. Both works are excellent studies with an easy writing style that make them pleasures to read.

These works exemplify the dedicated scholarship and tireless efforts of Western scholarship's humanistic traditions to bring reason and understanding into the world.

Literary Sources
Appian (Et by John Carter) *The Civil Wars*: Penguin Books, 1996
Appian, (Et, Horace White) *Civil Wars*, Loeb, 1913, 2 vols.
Caesar, Julius (translated by Cynthis Damon), *Civil War*, Loeb, 2016
Caesar, Julius (translated by John Carter), *The Civil War*: OUP, 1997
Caesar, Julius, (Ed and translated by Kurt Raaflaub) *The Landmark Julius Caesar*: Pantheon Books, 2017
Caesar, Julius, (translated by A.G. Peskett, *Civil Wars*: Loeb, 1928
Caesar, Julius, (translated by A.G. Way, *Alexandrian, African, and Spanish War*: Loeb, 1955
Caesar, Julius, (translated by H.J. Edwards), *Gallic War*: Loeb, 1958
Caesar, Julius, *Complete Works*: Delphi Classics, 2013
Cicero, (translated by E. O. Winstedt) *Letters to Atticus*: Loeb, 1919, 3 vols.
Cicero, (translated by Evelyn Shuckburgh) *The Letters of Cicero the Whole Extent Correspondence in Chronological Order*: G. Bell and Sons London, 1920, 4 vols.
Cicero, (translated by W. Glynn Williams) *The Letters to his Friends*: Loeb, 1927, 3 vols.
Cicero, *Complete Works*, Delphi Classics Delphi 2014
Cornell, T.J., *The Fragments of the Roman Historians*: Oxford, 2013, 3 vols.
Dio Cassius (Et Earnest Cary) vols III, IV, *Roman History*: Loeb, 1914, 1916
Josephus, *Complete Works*: Delphi Classics 2014

Lucius Annaeus Florus, (translated by Edward Seymour Forster) *Epitome of Roman History:* Loeb, 1929
Plutarch, 'Caesar' in *Lives*: Loeb, 1925, volume VII
Plutarch, 'Pompey' in *Lives*, Loeb, 1925, volume V
Sallust, (vol 1, translated by J.C. Rolfe; vol 2, translated by John Ramset), *Works*: Loeb, 1921, 2015.
Suetonius (translated by J.C. Rolfe), *Lives of the Twelve Caesars*: Loeb 1924
Velleius Paterculus (translated by Frederick W. Shipley), *Compendium of Roman History*: Loeb 1924

Technical Bibliographies
Projector Machines
Athenaeus Mechanicus, (edited and translated by David Whitehead and P.H. Blyth, *On Machines*: Franz Steiner Verlag Stuttgartt, 2004
Campbell, Duncan, 'Ancient catapults, Some Hypotheses Re-examined' *Hisperia* (2011), pp 677-700
Campbell, Duncan, *Greek and Roman Artillery 399 BC–AD 363*: Osprey, 2003
DeVoto, James (Edited and translated), *Philon & Heron*: Ares Press, 1996
Keyser, Paul T., 'The Use of Artillery by Philip II and Alexander the Great' *The Ancient World*, 25.1 (1994)
Marsden, E. W., *Greek and Roman Artillery Historical Development*: Oxford 1969
Philo Mechanicus, (edited and translated by David Whitehead) *On Sieges*: Franz Steiner Verlag Stuttgartt, 2016
Schiefsky, Mark J., 'Technical Terminology in Greco-Roman Treatises on Artillery Construction' *Antike Fachtexte/Ancient Technical Texts*, ed. T. Fogen, 253-270. New York: Walter De Grutyter, 2005
Schramm, Erwin, (edited and translated by Willam Paul Dean) *The Ancient Artillery of Saalburg and Commentary on its Reconstruction*: Amazon, ND (1917) electronic edition

Caesar's Warships
Casson, Lionel, *Ships and Seamanship in the Ancient World*: Princeton, 1971
D'Amato, Raffaele, *Republican Roman Warships 509-27 BC*: Osprey, 2015
Davidson, J.A., 'The First Greek Triremes' *The Classical Quarterly*, Jan.-Apr. 1947, vol 41, No. 1/2.
Granger, John, *Hellenistic and Roman Naval Wars 336-31 BC*: Pen & Sword, 2011
Morrison, J.S., Coates, J.F. and Rankov, N.B., *The Athenian Trireme*: Cambridge, 2000
Morrison, J.S. and Coates, J.F., *Greek and Roman Oared Warships*: Oxbow Books, 2016
Murray, William, *The Age of the Titans*: Oxford, 2012
Wallinga, H.T., *Ships and Sea-Power Before the Great Persian War*: Brill, 1992

Alexandria and the Library
El-Abbadi, Mostafa, Omnia Mounir Fatgallah, *What Happened to the Library of Alexandria?* Brill, 2008
Fraser, P.M., *Ptolemaic Alexandria*: Oxford, 1972
Harris, W.V. and Giovanni Ruffini (Eds), *Ancient Alexandria Between Egypt and Greece*: Brill, 2004
MacLeod, Roy (Ed), *The Library of Alexandria, Center of Learning in the Ancient World*: I.B. Tauris, 2004
McKechnie, Paul and Philippe Guillaume (Eds.), *Ptolemy Philadelphus and his World*: Brill, 2008
Pollard, Justin and Howard Reid, *The Rise and Fall of Alexandria*: Penguin Books, 2006
Sousa, Rogerio, Maria Do Ceu Fiajho, Mona Haggag and Nuno Simoes Rodrigues (Eds), *Alexandria Ad Aegyptum, The Legacy of Multiculturalism in Antiquity*: CITCEM, 2012
Vrettos, Theodore, *Alexandria, City of the Western Mind*: The Free Press, 2001

General Bibliography
Andreau, Jean (Et Janet Lloyd), *Banking and Business in the Roman World*: Cambridge, 1999
Batstone, William, Cynthia Damon, *Caesar's Civil War*: Oxford, 2006
Billows, Richard A, *Julius Caesar, The Colossus of Rome*: Routledge 2009
Bonaparte, Napoleon, (Ed and translation by R.A. Maguite), *Napoleon's Commentaries on the Wars of Julius Caesar*: Pen & Sword, 2018
Bowman, Alan, Andrew Wilson (eds.) *The Roman Agricultural Economy, Organization, Investment, and Production*: Oxford, 2013
Brecht, Bertolt (Ed. By Anthony Phelan, Tom Kuhun, and Charlotte Ryland; ET by Charles Osborne) *The Business Affairs of Mr. Julius Caesar*: Bloomsbury, 2016
Brown, Virginia, *The Textual Transmission of Caesar's Civil War*: Brill 1972
Brunt, P.A., *Italian Manpower 225 BC–AD 14*: Oxford, 1971
Campbell, Duncan, 'Siegecraft in Caesar' in Eds. Jeremy Armstrong, Matthew Trundle, *Brill's Companion to Sieges in the Ancient Mediterranean*: Brill, 2019
Canfora, Luciano (ET by Marian Hill and Kevin Windle), *Julius Caesar, The People's Dictator*: Edinburgh University, 2007
Carter, J.M. *Julius Caesar, The Civil War Book III*, Aris & Philips, 1993
Carter, J.M., *Julius Caesar the Civil War, Books I & II*: Aris & Philips, 1991
Cook, J.A., Andrew Lintott, Elizabeth Rawson, *The Last Age of the Roman Republic, 146-43 B.C., CAH*, vol IX: Cambridge, 1992
Dando-Collins, Stephen, *Caesar's Legion*: John Wiley, 2002
Dodge, Theodore, Caesar: Riverside Press, 1900
Drogula, Fred, *Cato the Younger, Life and Death at the End of the Late Republic*: Oxford, 2019
Engels, Donald, *Alexander the Great and the Logistics of the Macedonian Army*: University of California, 1978
Erdkamp, Paul, (Ed), *A Companion to the Roman Army*, Blackwell, 2007

Erdkamp, Paul, *Hunger and the Sword warfare and Food Supply in Roman Republican wars (264-30 BC):* Amsterdam, 1998

Erdkamp, Paul, Koenraad Verboven, and Arjun Zuiderhoek, *Capital, Investment, and Innovation in the Roman World*: Oxford, 2020

Fields, Nic, *Julius Caesar, Leadership, Strategy*, Conflict: Osprey, 2010

Fields, Nic, *Warlords of the Roman Republic*: Pen & Sword, 2008

Finley, M. I., *The Ancient Economy*: University of California Press, 1985

Fletcher, Joann, *Cleopatra the Great, the Woman behind the Legend*: Harper Collins, 2011

Flower, Harriet, *The Companion to the Roman Republic*: Cambridge, 2014

Friedman, B.A., *On Tactics*, Naval Institute Press, 2017

Gabba, Emilio (ET P.J. Cliff), *Republican Rome, The Army and the Allies*: University of California, 1976

Gelzer, Matthias (ET Peter Needham), *Caesar Politician and Statesman*: Basil Blackwell, 1968

Gelzer, Matthias, (translated by Robin Seager) *The Roman Nobility*: Blackwell, 1969

Gilliver, Kate, Adrian Goldsworthy, Michael Whitby, *Rome at War, Caesar and His Legacy*: Osprey, 2005

Goldsworthy, Adrian, *Antony and Cleopatra*: Yale, 2010

Goldsworthy, Adrian, *Caesar Life of a Colossus*: Yale 2006

Goodman, Rob and Jimmy Soni, *Rome's Last Citizen, the Life and Legacy of Cato*: St Martin's Press, 2012

Greenhalgh, Peter, *Pompey*: Weidenfeld and Nicholson 1980-1, vol. 1, *The Roman Alexander*; vol 2, *The Republican Prince*

Griffin, Miriam, (Ed), *A Companion to Julius Caesar*: Wiley-Blackwell, 2000

Harris, Edward, "Finley's Studies in Land and Credit Sixty Years Later" *Dike* 16, pp. 223-46

Harris, W. V., *Moses Finley and Politics*: Brill, 2013

Harris, W. V., *The Monetary Systems of the Greeks and Romans*: Oxford, 2008

Head, Barclay V., *Historia Numorum a Manual of Greek Numismatics*: Oxford, 1911

Heitland, W.E. *Agricola, a Study of Agriculture and Rustic Life in the Greco-Roman World from the Point of View of Labour*: Cambridge, 1921

Hill, *a Handbook of Greek and Roman Coins*: Macmillan and Co., 1899

Holkeskamp, Karl-J (translated by Henry Heitmann-Gordon), *Reconstructing the Roman Republic*: Princeton, 2010

Holmes, T. Rice, "The Battle-Field of Old Pharsalus" *The Classical Quarterly*: Oct. 1908, pp 271-292

Hyarkness, Albert, *The Military System of the Romans*: D. Appleton and Company, 1887

Jones, Prudence, *Cleopatra a Sourcebook*: University of Oklahoma, 2006

Judson, Harry Pratt, *Caesar's Army: A Study of the Military Art of the Romans in the Last Days of the Republic*: Athenaeum Press, 1888

Kahn, Arthur, *The Education of Julius Caesar*: Shocken Books, 1986

Kamm, Antony, *Julius Caesar, A Life*: Routledge 2006

Kay, Philip, *Rome's Economic Revolution*: Oxford, 2014
Keaveney, Arthur, *The Army in the Roman Revolution*: Routledge, 2007
Keppie, Lawrence, *The Making of the Roman Army from the Republic to Empire*: Batsford, 1984
Leach, John, *Pompey the Great*: Croom Helm, 1978
Lintott, Andrew, *The Constitution of the Roman Republic*: Oxford, 1999
Marshall, B.A. *Crassus A Political Biography*: Amsterdam, 1976
Mattingly, Harold, *Roman Coins from the Earliest Times to the Fall of the Western Empire*: Methuen & Co, 1960
Meier, Christian (ET by David McLintock), *Caesar*: Basic Books 1982
Metcalf, William, *Oxford Handbook of Greek and Roman Coinage*: Oxford, 2012
Miller, Fergus, *The Roman Republic in Political Thought*: University Press of New England, 2002
Monsoon, Andrew, Walter Scheidel, *Fiscal Regimes and the Political Economy of Premodern States*: Cambridge, 2015
Morgan, John, 'Paraepharsalus – The Battle and the Town', *American Journal of Archaeology*: Jan. 1983, pp 23-54
Morrell, Kat, *Pompey, Cato, and the Governance of the Roman Empire*: Oxford, 2017
Morstein-Marx, Robert, *Julius Caesar and the Roman People*, CUP, 2021
Munzer, Frederick, (translated by Therese Ridley), *Roman Aristocratic Parties and Families*: John Hopkins University Press, (German text, 1920) 1999
Murrow, Alexander, Agostino von Haskell, and Gregory Starace, *Caesar's Great Success, Sustaining the Roman Army on Campaign:* Frontline Books, 2020
Osgood, Josiah, 'Julius Caesar and Spanish Triumph Hunting' in (Eds. Carsten Hjort Lange and Frederik Juliaan Vervaet) *The Roman Republican Triumph Beyond the Spectacle*: Edizioni Quasar Rome, MMIV
Osgood, Josiah, *Rome and the Making of a World State, 150 BCE–20 CE*:
Parenti, Michael, *The Assassination of Julius Caesar A People's History of Ancient Rome*: The New Press, 2003
Peer, Ayelet, *Julius Caesar's Bellum Civile and the Composition of a New Reality*: Ashgate, 2015
Reden, Sitta von, *Money in Classical Antiquity*: Cambridge, 2010
Remind, Peter, *The Roman Market Economy*, Princeton, 2013
Riggsby, Andrew, *Caesar in Gaul and Rome, War in Words*: University of Texas, 2006
Roller, Duane, *Cleopatra A biography*: Oxford, 2010
Rostovtzeff, M. *The Social & Economic History of the Hellenistic World*: Oxford, 1941, 3 vols.
Rostovtzeff, M. *The Social and Economic History of the Roman Empire:* Oxford, 1926, 2 vols.
Roth, Jonathan, *The Logistics of the Roman army at War (264 BC– AD 235):* Brill, 1999
Rowan, Clare, *From Caesar to Augustus (c. 49 BC–AD 14) Using Coins as Sources*: Cambridge 2019
Ruggiero, Paulo, *Mark Antony, a Plain Blunt Man*: Pen & Sword, 2013

Sage, Michael, *The Army of the Roman Republic*: Pen & Sword, 2018
Sampson, Gareth, *Rome, Blood & Politics, 133–70 BC*: Pen & Sword, 2017
Sampson, Gareth, *Rome, Blood, and Power 70–27 BC*: Pen & Sword, 2019
Sampson, Gareth, *Rome's Great Eastern War, 74–62 BC*: Pen & Sword 2021
Scheidel, Walter, Jan Morris, Richard Saller, *the Cambridge Economic History of the Greco-Roman World:* Cambridge, 2007
Scraps, David, *The Invention of Coinage and the Monetization of Ancient Greece*: University of Michigan, 2004
Sheppard, Si, *Pharsalus 48 BC Caesar and Pompey – Clash of the Titans*: Osprey, 2006
Sherwin-White, A.N., *Roman Foreign Policy in the East 168 B.C. To A.D. 1*: Duckworth, 1984
Silver, Morris, 'Finding the Roman Empire's Disappeared Deposit Bankers' *Historia: Zeitschrift fur Alte Geschichte*, Bd. 60 H. 3 (2011) pp. 301-327
Southern, Pat, *The Roman Army a Social and Institutional History*: ABC CLIO, 2006
Southern, Pat, *Antony and Cleopatra*: Tempus, 2007
Southern, Pat, *Julius Caesar*: Tempus 2001
Southern, Pat, *Pompey the Great*: Tempus, 2002
Steel, Catherine, *The End of the Roman Republic, 146 to 44 BC*: Edinburgh University Press, 2013
Stevenson, Tom, *Julius Caesar and the Transformation of the Roman Republic*: Routledge, 2015
Stoffel, Colonel, *Historire de Jules Cesar Guerre Civile*: Paris, 1887, 2 vols.
Syme, Ronald, *The Roman Revolution*: Oxford 1939
Tatum, W. Jeffrey, *Aways I Am Caesar*: Blackwell, 2008
Tempest, Kathryn, *Brutus, the Noble Conspirator*: Yale, 2017
Tempest, Kathryn, *Cicero Politics and Persuasion in Ancient Rome*: Continuum, 2011
Tyldesley, Joyce, *Cleopatra Last Queen of Egypt*: Profile Books, 2008
Ward, Allen Mason, *Marcus Crassus, and the Late Roman Republic*: University of Missouri Press, 1977
Westall, Richard, *Caesar's Civil War, Historical Realty and Fabrication*: Brill 2018
Wilson, Andrew, Alan Bowman (Eds.) *Trade, Commerce, and the State in the Roman World*: Oxford, 2018
Wiseman, T. P., *Julius Caesar*, History Press 2016
Wyke, Maria, *Julius Caesar in Western Culture*, Blackwell, 2006
Yarrow, Liv Mariah, *The Roman Republic to 49 BCE Using Coins as Sources*: Cambridge, 2021

Index

Achillas, 124, 147–9, 132, 207, 244
Adbucillus the Allobrogian, 101
Afranius, 33–5, 37–8, 40–8, 51–3, 63, 115, 192, 201, 217
Albinus, Aulus, 76
Alexandria, battles at, 131–42
Allobroges, 100–101, 103, 113
Antonius, Cato, 220
Antonius, Gaius, 31, 33, 77
Antony, Mark (Marcus Antonius), 6–7, 13, 19, 30–1, 85, 88–91, 94, 96, 104, 116, 158–60, 211, 234–5, 240, 244, 266
Aponius, 213
Ariarathes, 154
Ariobarzanes, King of Cappadocia, 159, 154
Arsinoe, 129, 131, 138, 142, 207
Ategua, Battle at, 216–22
Atia, 211

Balbus, L. Cornelius, 232, 288–91
Bibulus, M., 78, 81–3, 275–6
Bogud, King of Mauritania, 70, 146, 173–5
Brown, Virginia, 296
Brundisium, battles at, 21–34, 88–90
Brutus, Decimus, 34, 56–8, 71, 76

Caesar, Julius,
  start of civil war, 3–13
  campaign in Italy, 13–26
  Caesar's first stay in Rome, 29–31
  war in Spain, 32–53
  Caesar's second stay in Rome, 75–7
  Caesar in Eprius and Greece, 79–83, 89–119
  Caesar in Egypt, 124–42

Caesar in Asia Minor, 153–9
Caesar's third stay in Rome, 159–62
Caesar in Africa, 165–202
Caesar's fourth stay in Rome, 205–12
Caesar's second campaign in Spain, 213–29
Caesar's fifth stay in Rome, organizes management of Roman Empire, 230–5
Caesarion, 209, 211, 240
Calenus, Fabius, 81, 88, 99, 162
Calidius, Marcus, 17
Calvinus, Domitius, 108, 132–3, 165–9, 149–2, 235
Caninus, Acilius, 94
Cassius (Gaius Cassius Longinus), 78, 92
Cassius (Quintus Cassius Longinus), 13, 70, 91, 99, 145–7, 213
Cato, Marcus, 7–8, 13, 15, 32, 130, 144, 158, 174–6, 179, 200–201, 206
Cicero, Marcus, 9–11, 14–15, 17–20, 22, 29–30, 158–9, 234, 275–6, 279, 288
Cleopatra III, 126
Cleopatra VII, 124, 127–8, 138, 142, 207, 209, 238–40
Clodius, 87, 100, 209, 238, 276
Considius, 166–7, 177, 182, 195, 199, 201
Corduba, battles at, 214–18, 227–8
Corfinium, battles at, 13–24, 65
Cotta, M., 32, 59, 130
Cotys, King of Thrace, 92
Crassus, Licinius, 31
Crassus, Marcus, 5, 6, 9, 126–7, 211, 233, 237–8, 266, 273–6, 285, 288
Crassus, Otacilius, 90–1
Crassus, Publius, 84–5
Crastinus, G., 116–17, 119

Curio, G. Scribonius, 13, 30, 32, 63–9, 185, 290, 292

Deiotarus, King of Galatia, 149, 151, 154–5, 157, 159
Denarius, *denarii*, 4, 30, 44, 72, 76, 114, 160–1, 224, 279, 294, 299
Didius, 228–9
Dioscorides, 128
Dolabella, Publius Cornelius, 77, 158–60
Domitius Ahenobarbus, L., 8, 12, 18–24, 34, 52, 55–8, 65, 71, 118
Domitius, Calvisius, 91–3, 108–109, 115–16, 132, 149, 154, 156, 199, 235
Dyrrachium, battles at, 21, 24, 25, 32, 77, 80–3, 85, 89, 90–108, 116, 145, 255

Egus the Allobrogian, 101
Euphranor, 134–5, 138

Fabius, G., 34–8, 40, 42
Faustus, 22, 200–201
Favonius, M., 92
Friedman, B.A., 254

Gabinius, A., 78, 127–8, 130, 147, 238
Ganymedes, 131–3, 138
Gracchus, Gaius, 268
Gracchus, Tiberius, 267, 284
Gregory XIII, Pope, 210

Hegesaretos, 107

Ilerda, battles at, 35–40, 42–4, 46–7, 49, 57

Jesus of Nazareth, 278–9
Juba, King of Numidia, 64, 67–70, 144–6, 158, 165, 167, 170, 172–6, 179, 184, 187–9, 191–2, 194–5, 199, 200–201, 207

Labienus, 14, 18, 81, 86, 106, 114, 168–74, 177–8, 181, 184–5, 188–92, 196, 221, 226
Laelius, D., 78, 81, 94

Lentulus, L., 6–8, 18–19, 78, 103, 124
Lepidus, Marcus, 31, 71, 76, 146, 234–5, 266, 273
Libo, Lucius Scribonius, 77–8, 82–3, 88–9
Library of Alexandria, 242–5
Lupus, Rutiliius, 99
Lycomedes, 154

Marcellus, 3, 6–7, 14
Marius, 30, 205, 211, 231–2, 269–73
Massilia, siege of, 54–62
Milo, 75, 87, 158, 276
Mithridates, friend of Caesar, 139–40, 157
Mithridates VI, King of Pontus, 149, 152, 169, 238, 271–4
Money, business economy, 4–5, 75–6, 86, 126–7, 146, 206, 208–209, 229, 238, 241–2, 246, 274–5, 291
  Pompey's dealings, 8, 14, 19, 22, 78, 84–5, 88, 123–4
  Caesar's dealings, 12, 29–32, 35, 53, 71, 89, 102, 114, 158, 160–1, 232, 287
  Senatorial forces in Africa, 144–5, 200–201
  Army, 248, 253, 270
  In Classical economy, 278–85
Morgan, John, 112
Munda, Battle at, 225–7, 229
Muses, 241–2
Museum, the, 209–10, 240–5

Nasidius, Quintus Lucius, 57–8
Nile, Battle at the, 139–42

Octavius, Gaius (Thurinus), 211, 229–30, 234–5, 240, 285, 290
Octavius, Marcus, 267
Octavius, Marcus (Pompeian Commander), 77–8, 147–8, 182
Oudendorp, Franz, 295

Peisistratus the Athenian, 242, 280
Pharnaces, 149–53, 155–7, 207, 292–3

Pharsalus, Battle of, xvi, 112–19, 158
Philip II of Macedonia, 264, 281
Polybius, 101, 267, 287
Pompey the Great,
  start of war, 5–15
  war in Italy, 16–26
  Pompey's forces in Spain, 37–40
  Pompey faces Caesar, 81–3
  Pompey's new strategy, 84–94
  battles in Eprius, 94–110
  Battle of Pharsalus, 112–19
  death, 123–5
Pompey, Gnaeus the younger, 78, 95, 175, 213–16, 224, 227–8, 273
Pompey, Sextus, 213–14, 227, 229
Pomponius, Titus (Atticus), 10–11, 14–15, 17–22, 288, 291–2, 294–5
Pothinus, 128–9, 207
Projector machines,
  at Corfinium, 19
  at Brundisium, 25
  at Massilia, 55, 57–9, 62, 71
  at Epirus, 77, 94, 96, 99
  in Africa, 176, 187
  in Spain, 219
  on warships, 258, 261
  design and development, 263–5
Ptolemy II, 243–4, 261
Ptolemy IX, 126
Ptolemy X, 126
Ptolemy XI, 126–7
Ptolemy XII, 124
Ptolemy XIII, 127–9, 138, 143, 238–40
Ptolemy XIV, 142

Raucillus the Allobrogian, 101
Respina, Battles at, 167
Rufus, Caelius, 86–7, 158

Saburra, 68–9, 184
Sallust, 160, 179, 201
Scaeva, 99
Scipio (Quintus Caecilius, Metellus Scipio Nasica), 6–8, 22, 64, 66, 68, 78, 84–5, 91–3, 100, 108–11, 115, 144, 165, 167, 172–82, 184–5, 187–9, 191–8, 200–201, 205
Sittius, 175, 179, 184, 187, 201

Sosigenes, 210
Sulla the Dictator, 7, 126, 154, 205, 232, 234, 236, 266–74
Sulla, P., 98, 116
Supplies,
  Caesar in Italy and Spain, 11–13, 18, 22, 33, 38–42, 44, 46
  Pompey, 19, 24–5, 43, 47, 49–50, 52, 57, 82, 84, 96
  War in Eprius, 53–4, 80–1, 91, 95, 97, 100, 107–10, 112–13
  Curio in Africa, 63–4, 66–8
  Alexandria, supply problems, 129–30, 133
  Supplies in Illyricum, 147
  Northern Asia Minor, 150, 153
  Caesar's African campaign, 166–8, 195–6
  Scipio's campaign, 172–3, 177, 190–2, 194, 197
  Caesar in Spain, 213, 215, 217, 223–4
  Caesar on supplies, 247
  Structures of supply in Caesar's army, 247–56
  Naval strategy blocking supplies, 257
  Supply problems in the Late Republic, 269, 270

Thapsus, Battle at, 194–202
Trebellius, 158–9
Trebonius, G., 34, 54–5, 57–8, 60–2, 86–7, 146, 213, 217–18, 290
Tubero, 31–2

Utica, Battles of, 63–70

Varro, 33, 52, 53, 70
Varus, Attius, 16–17, 31–2, 63–8, 144–5, 185–7, 213, 224, 226
Varus, Quintilius, 65–7
Vatinius, 86, 147–8, 162, 168
Vergilius, 177, 196–7, 199, 201
Vitruvius, xvi, 236, 263

War at Sea,
  first battle at Brundisium, 24–6
  Massilia, 55–8, 71

Curio in Africa, 63, 69–70
Pompey in Eprius, 78, 80–2
second battle at Brundisium, 88, 90, 94
Caesar in Alexandria, 125, 129, 133–6
Caesar in Africa, 145, 165–6, 168, 173, 179, 186–7

Illyricum, 147–8
Caesar in Spain, 228
warships in Caesar's time, 257–62

Zela, Battle at, 156, 159